Hannah Lynch (1859–1904): Irish writer, cosmop

Hannah Lynch (1859–1904): Irish writer, cosmopolitan, New Woman

FAITH BINCKES

AND

KATHRYN LAING

CORK UNIVERSITY PRESS

First published in 2019 by
Cork University Press
Youngline Industrial Estate
Pouladuff Road, Togher
Cork
T12 HT6V
Ireland

British Library Cataloguing in Publication Data
A CIP record for this book is available from the British Library.

ISBN: 978-1-78205-333-0

Printed in Poland by Hussar Books.
Print origination & design by Carrigboy Typesetting Services, www.carrigboy.com

www.corkuniversitypress.com

For our parents
Marion Binckes, Barbara and Mike Laing
and for Alun, Mark, Gregory and Jamie

Contents

Acknowledgements

This book has had a long gestation period, beginning as a short biographical entry by Faith Binckes, which appeared in the *Oxford Dictionary of National Biography*. The details Faith traced proved tantalising enough to develop the material by joining forces with Kathryn Laing. An opportunity arose for testing out the possibilities of a more extended project at a conference held in NUI Galway. It was soon evident that conference papers would not be enough to do justice to a life and work glimpsed, but by no means discovered. Advances in digital technology changed the shape of the project further. As more and more newspapers, magazines and periodicals were digitised, it became apparent that Hannah Lynch was not principally an author of novels and short stories. Instead, her considerably larger body of work included several novellas, as well as dozens of pieces of travel and critical writing (and we are certain that there is more yet to be recovered). These excavations, alongside those of other scholars working on contemporaries of Lynch and in the broader field of the Irish *fin-de-siècle*, have triggered a necessary reimagining of this landscape.

In the process of mapping this territory, we have incurred many debts. We must acknowledge first Michael Counahan and his sisters, respectively grand-nephew and grand-nieces of Hannah Lynch. They have granted permission to quote extensively from Hannah Lynch's unpublished writings, shared biographical notes on their family and, at the eleventh hour, supplied our one and only image of the author. This is also reproduced here, with their permission.

Next, we have benefitted hugely from the enthusiasm, expertise and generous support of Maureen O'Connor and Tadhg Foley, who encouraged us from the first Galway conference, and who have provided valuable feedback on versions of chapters and articles.

Without generous financial backing from Research Seed Funding, Mary Immaculate College, much of the archival work carried out in Paris, Manchester, Oxford and Dublin would not have been possible. Financial support from Brasenose College and Worcester College, University of Oxford, and Bath Spa

University has also facilitated our peripatetic research. Maria O'Donovan of Cork University Press has been helpful, efficient and encouraging throughout.

In addition to this we are extremely grateful to numerous friends and colleagues who have helped us out with queries, conundrums and necessary tasks:

- Adrian Frazier generously sent us his considerable archive of notes on Mabel Robinson, providing an ideal head start for one section of the book.
- Marie Dumas helped us perfect our translation of several letters in French from Hannah Lynch and from Mary Robinson (Duclaux). Kyriaki Hadjiafxendi provided welcome detail on the translation of Lynch's novel *Daughters of Men* into Greek.
- Père Gifra Adroher has helped us explore Lynch's Spanish connections, translating letters and giving us an outline of a Spanish article written about Lynch and Pereda.
- Margaret Ward directed us towards useful sources and information about the Ladies' Land League.
- Jacqueline Bayard-Pierlot, great-granddaughter of Emile Duclaux, shared her memories of Mary Robinson, kindly looked out for material relating to Hannah Lynch while undertaking her own research, and sent us a photograph of Mabel Robinson. She also assisted us in our search for the Robinsons' literary estate. The biographical information and transcribed letters from Mary Robinson to her mother, made available on the le-petit-orme.com website, have proved invaluable, too.

We have also benefitted from the insights and knowledge of Clare Hutton, Alice Staveley, Michèle Mendelssohn, James H. Murphy, Mary Pierse, Michel Brunet, Jim Rogers, Sylvie Mikowski, Caoilfhionn Ní Bheacháin, Angus Mitchell and Judith Hill. Conor Montague provided information on Lynch, *Through Troubled Waters*, and the Clanrickard family. We are also grateful for suggestions from our anonymous readers at Cork University Press. Maria O'Donovan and Aonghus Meaney provided excellent editorial support.

Pere Gifra-Adroher and Jacqueline Hurtley helped us explore Lynch's Spanish connections, translating letters and giving us an outline of a Spanish article written about Lynch and Pereda. They also shared documents that provided further details about the date of Hannah Lynch's death and place of burial.

An array of librarians and archivists have aided us in our research. The Bodleian Library, University of Oxford, holds the widest range of first editions by Lynch that we have found in either the United Kingdom or Ireland, and its staff deserve our thanks. We must also acknowledge the New York Public

Library and the National Library of Ireland. Without archivists at the NLI, we would never have found the missing copies of *The Shamrock*, in which one of Lynch's most compelling early works appeared. Special thanks are also due to Norma O'Neill at the Mary Immaculate College library. Elsewhere, Fran Baker at the University of Manchester Library and Damien Burke at the Irish Jesuit Archive in Dublin deserve special mention. Dr David Sutton at Reading University assisted in our hunt for the literary estates of several 'orphan' sources. We would be very happy to hear from any copyright holders who we have not located, despite our searches.

We therefore thank these and the following archives for permission to quote from archival material:

- The Literary Estate of Katharine Tynan Hinkson for permission to publish excerpts from correspondence held in the Irish Jesuit Archives.
- Irish Jesuit Archives, Dublin for permission to publish material held with the Papers of Father Matthew Russell.
- National Library of Ireland, Dublin for permission to publish material from the Katharine Tynan Letters collection.
- Special Collections at the Brotherton Library, University of Leeds for permission to publish material from the Edmund Gosse Papers and the Father Thomas Dawson letters held in the Shorter Correspondence.
- The Royal Literary Fund for permission to publish material from its archives at the British Library.
- The Roman Catholic Archdiocese of Birmingham and the National Library of Scotland for permission to publish a letter held in the archives of William Blackwood & Sons.
- Manuscripts and Archives Division, New York Public Library Astor, Lenox and Tilden Foundations, New York City.
- Special Collections at the University of Manchester Library for permission to publish material held with the papers of Katharine Tynan Hinkson and Pamela Hinkson.
- Special Collections (Richelieu), Bibliothèque Nationale de France, Paris, which holds certain papers of A. Mary F. Robinson, F. Mabel Robinson, Louise-Cécile Vincens and Gaston Paris.

Last but definitely not least, we need to thank our families, who have also found themselves haunted by the ghost of Hannah Lynch. This visitation has taken the form of invasive piles of photocopies, holidays interrupted by library trips, and numberless computer-hogging Skype calls.

Earlier versions of some chapters have appeared elsewhere. A section of Chapter 1 was published as 'Hannah Lynch and Narratives of the Irish Literary Revival', *New Hibernia Review*, vol. 20, no. 1, 2016. Material in Chapter 2 has been addressed in K.S. Laing, 'Intellectual Lives and Literary Perspectives: female Irish writing at home and abroad', in Brendan Walsh (ed.), *Knowing Their Place: the intellectual life of women in the 19th century* (Dublin: The History Press, 2015), and 'On Women, on Art, on Life: George Moore (1852–1933) and Hannah Lynch (1859–1904)', in Maria Elana Jaime de Pablos and Mary Pierse (eds), *George Moore and the Quirks of Human Nature* (Bern: Peter Lang, 2014). Chapter 3 includes material addressed in 'A Forgotten Franco-Irish Network: Hannah Lynch, Arvède Barine, and the salon culture of fin-de-siècle Paris', *Études Irlandaises*, vol. 36, no. 2, automne–hiver 2011, pp. 157–71. Chapter 4 develops discussion of the New Woman begun in 'From "Wild Irish Girl" to "Parisianised Foreigner": Hannah Lynch and France', in Eamon Maher and Eugene O'Brien (eds), *War of the Words: literary rebellion in France and Ireland* (Rennes: Publication du CRBC Rennes-2, TIR, 2010). Chapter 5 builds on 'A Vagabond's Scrutiny: Hannah Lynch in Europe', in E. D'Hoker, R. Ingelbien and H. Schwall (eds), *Irish Women Writers: new critical perspectives* (Bern: Peter Lang, 2011). An earlier version of Chapter 6 was published as 'Irish Autobiographical Fiction and Hannah Lynch's *Autobiography of a Child*', *English Literature in Transition*, vol. 55, no. 2, 2012, pp. 195–218.

'A Name Writ in Water'?

She had no smug ideals... She wrote with a passion for perfection; wrote often day after day, night after night, without going out, neglecting her food, till her hand shook on the table in the preliminary stages of writer's cramp. Such a life was almost certain to end in bodily ill-health; but she was too wrapped up in things of the intellect to be greatly concerned with things of the body. She had a spirit courageous and adventurous. Where others with less great a spirit would have found it impossible to escape from the world in which they were born, she became a traveller, a citizen of the world, more at home in Greece and Rome and Seville and Paris than in Dublin, where everyone is clever, and no one is arduous or admiring. She became friends with some of the most distinguished of living people. She won, in fact, the prizes of life that are best worth the winning, although she died young and endured much ill-health; and, except for the few who value things literary, leaves a name writ in water.[1]

W ho was Hannah Lynch, and why should you want to learn more about her? Perhaps the best way to approach these related questions is by beginning at the end, and casting an eye over four accounts of her life produced shortly after her death in Paris, in January 1904. The first of these is printed above. Its author was Katharine Tynan, an early friend of Lynch and of her 'adventurous' literary family. Tynan noted the 'intellect' and 'spirit' that compelled Lynch to travel far from the Dublin of her childhood and early youth, and to become a cosmopolitan 'citizen of the world'. In return, she was rewarded not with material success but with friendship and artistic accomplishment. Like Virginia Woolf's Lily Briscoe a generation later, the perishability of reputation – particularly for single women – does nothing to undermine Lynch's achievement in pursuing her 'vision'. Tynan's account was generous, particularly as a complex relationship lay behind this apparently heartfelt tribute. Yet its subject could be mistaken for a medieval saint, physically drained by the rigours of dedication, neglecting society and the 'things of the body' in order to pursue her 'passion for perfection'.

A different picture of Hannah Lynch emerges from an obituary composed by Irish-American James Gibbs, published in the *Gaelic American* in February of the same year:

> She was the daughter of Mrs Cantwell, of the Star and Garter Hotel, in Dublin, being a posthumous child by a prior marriage, and she never knew [any] other father than James Cantwell, who was the partner, friend and host of the men engaged in the Nationalist cause. Her mother, too, was an ardent Nationalist, and carried the honors of her husband's hospitality. Her daughters were brought up in an atmosphere of rebellion, and Hannah's childhood was nurtured in patriotism.
>
> The drawing-room of the 'Star' was a *salon* in which nightly assembled a coterie of men and women who represented the talent and education of the Nationalists of Dublin, and the number and variety of the topics discussed aroused her inquiry and stimulated her 'gifts'.[2]

Gibbs paid tribute to Lynch's 'great literary ability', mentioning that as a girl she had contemplated a course at the Women's Medical College in Philadelphia, but instead had studied music in London. He also recorded a serious breakdown in her health in the early 1880s. Her talents as a writer were, he noted, nurtured in an environment in which art and politics intertwined, a '*salon*' of patriotic rebellion.

A third piece appeared in the London, Liberal review the *Speaker* in December 1906. Its author was Frances Low, a pioneering journalist and commentator on women's affairs, and its subject was 'luck'. Low compared Lynch to Pearl Craigie, another author who had died before her time but whose passing had prompted a shower of accolades. Low clearly intended to redress the imbalance:

> With the exception of a brief period in which she was contributing constantly to *Blackwood*, whose editor, with amazing lack of insight, treated her as any ordinary contributor, she suffered from extreme poverty. Her outspoken criticism upon Irish matters and especially upon Irish politicians, coupled with her scathing wit, made her enemies almost from her girlhood: and there was an article ... on some of the little literary gods of Dublin at that time which made for her undying enemies ... Her

life was full of colour and adventure and romance. She was little more than a girl – her portrait at that period shows her masses of yellow hair hanging over her shoulders – when she escaped to England, bringing with her the broken-up type of *United Ireland*. She went as a young girl to Greece and to Spain and her admirable articles in the old *St James's Gazette* and *The Fortnightly* and elsewhere ought to be collected into one volume, and once and forever settle the question of whether there is a woman who can write a melodious and graceful prose-style: she played the piano charmingly; she danced exquisitely; she was equally brilliant whether she was writing criticism, often of a sufficiently pungent nature, upon decadent French novelists or vivid descriptions of Spain and Greece and Southern France, or social or political articles, or – and here at least she has achieved distinction of the highest order – exquisite little stories for *Macmillan's Magazine* ... And towering above all other literary productions of the day is her Masterpiece that has never won the recognition it surely will, viz., *The Autobiography of a Child*. Yet the first of modern Irish writers does not figure at all in the 'Anthology of Irish Authors', edited by Miss Tynan; and the *Athenaeum* gave her half a dozen lines at her death, mentioning only her book on 'George Meredith', written when she was twenty-two, and Meredith unknown![3]

Low's hyperbolic account provided far more detail on Lynch's career, although not all of it was accurate. Low noted, as Tynan had done, Lynch's travels across continental Europe, and like Gibbs she described Lynch's engagement with the nationalist cause. In contrast to Tynan's depiction, Low's Lynch was no saint. She endured 'extreme poverty' rather than being driven by self-denial. Her name was 'writ on water' largely as a consequence of her 'pungent' observations and 'scathing wit', a talent for alienating powerful contemporaries having made her enemies 'almost from her girlhood'. If Gibbs' Lynch was an ardent patriot, Low's Lynch was far more ambivalent, outspoken in her criticism of her home nation despite her commitment to its independence.

The final of these perspectives was never published. It is a letter sent from the poet Mary Duclaux, best known in Britain by her maiden name A. Mary F. Robinson, to the French critic and editor Louise-Cécile Vincens, who used the pen name 'Arvède Barine'.[4] Both these women were part of Lynch's Parisian circle of 'distinguished' friends, to whom Tynan had alluded. It is the only account we have found that describes the cause of Hannah Lynch's death and the circumstances of her final days:

Chère Madame,

C'est une histoire bien triste. La pauvre fille, malade (nous disait-on) d'une coli-entérite souffrait depuis bien des mois d'horribles douleurs au ventre. Elle est venu nous voir cet été en Auvergne – je l'ai trouvée bien changée. Mais, tel était son entrain, son courage, qu'elle se remettait d'une crise atroce pour rire, pour causer, et même pour faire de longues promenades en montagnes. "C'est nerveux" disait elle – je la trouvais encore plus malade à notre rentrée à Paris en Novembre. Mais mon mari était gravement malade. Je n'ai pu le quitter que rarement pour aller soigner ma pauvre petite voisine. Heureusement la bonne Mme Clere lui a envoyé une excellente garde-malade.

Vers la fin de Décembre le docteur Lereboullet [?] qui la soignait avec un grand dévouement, insista sur un examen sérieux. De suite, il s'alarma, prononça même (mais pas devant la malade) le mot terrible que nous étions tous à redouter. C'était un cancer! Le 28 Déc, je l'accompagnais chez le Dr Tuffier, qui nous donna beaucoup d'espoir et qui généreusement offrait de faire l'opération qui serait suivie (disait-il) de longues années de santé. Chère Madame, c'était une boucherie inutile! Entourée d'amis dévoués, de ses sœurs, l'une venue d'Irlande et l'autre de Barcelone, qu'un règlement féroce ne laissant pénétrer auprès d'elle que quelques heures par jour – ayant tout ce qu'il fallait pour adoucir les derniers jours – pauvre Hannah. Elle est morte la nuit, toute seule, dans la chambre payante de Pavillon Dubbeau, à Beaujour. Tout cela est trop horrible, je ne peux pas en parler […] Elle a eu la fin la plus tragique du monde.[5]

It is a letter wrung with sadness and exhaustion, undated but presumably written after the death of Emile Duclaux in May 1904. Despite that, glimpses of Lynch's 'spirit', her 'courage' and 'enthusiasm' illuminate the account. The struggles of Lynch's life – and it is clear that there were many physical, financial and professional struggles – did not subdue her until the very last.

Any one of these memorials to Hannah Lynch would command attention, and when taken together they suggest a woman of unusual historical and literary interest. Why then was she so quickly forgotten, and why is she now so ripe for rediscovery? When Tynan described Lynch's name being 'writ in water' despite her talent and dedication, she might have had in mind the difficulty of achieving any sort of reputation in the rapidly expanding literary marketplace of the time. She might have been remembering Lynch's particular circumstances: her status as an unmarried woman, living abroad, writing for her life with the assistance of friends but without a husband, father or brother to supply a financial safety net. And if it seems unlikely that Lynch was the victim of the sort of cabal Low imagined – and in which she implicated Tynan – it is undeniable that the odds were stacked against any woman choosing such a path. Low's handbook to journalism *Press Work for Women* (1904), one of the earliest of its genre, did not pull its punches when describing the hurdles faced by any woman considering this career. The fact that this book singled out Lynch as an exception to the rule, a rare example of someone able to impress editors and to produce high-quality work while still meeting deadlines, is a testament not only to their friendship but also to Lynch's achievement.

As the decades passed, so Lynch became remembered more for being forgotten than for any of her writings, a bibliographical curiosity from the sharp end of the nineteenth century.[6] So, however, did the other women who had authored those early memorial pieces. The first wave of feminist recovery bypassed Mary Robinson, formerly considered one of the most famous literary women of her era. Low, a notable if less recognised figure on the journalistic scene, became even more obscure. Tynan, who had forged a position as senior literary stateswoman in Ireland and in London, featured as a person of interest in histories of the Irish Literary Revival, but little else. Only in the final decade of the twentieth century did the centrality and the diversity of women's involvement in the literature of a hundred years before begin to be recognised. This reappraisal is ongoing, and we hope that this book will form part of it.

The role of Irish women's writing and activism in the tumultuous closing years of the nineteenth century, and the early years of the twentieth, has become a distinctly twenty-first-century agenda, shedding new light on New Woman fiction, on Irish cosmopolitanism, and on a range of revivalist cultures. This 'lost archive' includes not only Lynch and Tynan, but contemporaries such as Jane Barlow, George Egerton, Fannie Gallaher, Rose Kavanagh, Rosa Mulholland, Emily Lawless, Somerville and Ross, and Alice Milligan.[7] The artistic-political milieu described by Gibbs has resurfaced in recent studies of Land War fiction, and increasing scholarly interest in the activities of the Ladies' Land League. It was as a member of this all-female nationalist group that Lynch came to smuggle *United Ireland* into print, a tale that we will explore in detail. Twenty-first-century scholarship has also returned to Mary Robinson, exploring the ethical aesthetics she evolved with Vernon Lee, and her status as a cosmopolitan *salonnière*. Low has recently been reintroduced into discussions of women's journalism, as part of the growing body of work on periodicals and their networks. Lynch's scattered obituary notices identify her as an agent in all these spheres. More important still, a study of Lynch's life and art reveals substantial interactions between these fields, the lost narrative of her life and writing intersecting and clashing with the established narratives of the period. Like a Jamesian *ficelle*, Lynch is at once an active participant in the story and a thread we can follow to reveal and to forge connections.

The type of convergence is best illustrated by an example drawn from the mid-point of Lynch's writing career. In June 1896 the *Freeman's Journal* published a brief account of a series of literary lectures delivered in Paris by 'Miss Hannah Lynch', followed by a transcription of one: 'The Irish Peasant: fact and fiction'. The paper supplied a prefatory warning, suggesting something of what was to come. 'One may not always agree with Miss Lynch's judgements', it observed, 'but her criticisms, free and at times perhaps extravagant, are always brilliantly and pointedly delivered.'[8] The reason for the caveat soon becomes clear. As expected, in this lecture Lynch addressed Irish literature and national character, but with an important departure from the norm. She did not, she announced, intend to expound on 'the development in folk-lore or in the historical romance', or to discuss male writers such as Douglas Hyde or Standish O'Grady:

> Instead we will examine the value of Irish local atmosphere and characters revealed in Miss Jane Barlow's really charming and masterly 'Irish Idylls' and in the Honourable Emily Lawless's highly polished literary stories, 'Grania' and 'Hurrish'. These are undoubtedly the best stories the young school of Irish Celts has produced.[9]

This insistence on the superiority of female authors was unusual enough, proposing as it did a canon of female revivalists against that being established by W.B. Yeats. But Lynch followed it with a far more daring statement. Her analysis and critical appreciation, especially of Lawless' *Grania*, became the occasion of a full-throttle assault on the condition of Irish women:

> As girls they think it natural they should be sacrificed to their brothers, natural they should be tyrannized over by their fathers, and ordered to marry for the convenience of families. And when they in turn have children they train them in the same dreary and unjust traditions, and make the girls wait upon the boys and give up everything for them.[10]

This uncompromising lecture offers a nexus of literary and feminist critique, presented in a cosmopolitan setting and reflecting Lynch's own negotiation of her identity as a modern, female, Irish author. Speaking to a French audience, and published in an Irish paper, Lynch diagnoses and praises the female 'Irish Celts', but avoids associating herself with them. The authority she possesses when discussing the position of Irish women, on the other hand, is apparently rooted in first-hand experience. This position, as both insider and outsider in Irish writing and culture, was in itself a sort of tradition, one that would go on to play an acknowledged role in the shaping of twentieth-century literature in English.

So, who was Hannah Lynch? By now the reader will have a clearer idea, and consequently a few more unanswered questions. Who were the nationalist figures in her family? How did she come to 'rescue' the type of *United Ireland* during its banning in the early 1880s? What was her association with Katharine Tynan, and with Mabel and Mary Robinson?[11] Why and where did she travel? Most importantly of all, what and how did she write? These are all questions that this book will address and in some cases answer. It is intended primarily as a study of Lynch's literary output. This comprises ten novels, including her early, novel-length text 'Defeated', early short stories and novellas serialised in nationalist papers such as the *Shamrock* and the *Weekly Freeman*, one collection of short fiction, *Dr Vermont's Fantasy and Other Stories* (1896), and a series of uncollected shorter tales. Her final novel, *Autobiography of a Child* (1899), was first serialised in *Blackwood's Magazine*, and was later translated into French.[12] Her diverse travel writings encompassed numerous articles and two full-length studies: *Toledo: the story of an old Spanish capital* (1898) and *French Life in Town and Country* (1901). These were supplemented by a series of translations from French and Spanish. In addition to this Lynch was an active literary critic throughout her career. Her book-length *George Meredith: a study* was published by Methuen in 1891, and she wrote extensively and comparatively on French literature while working as Paris correspondent of the London literary review the *Academy* between 1896 and 1903. In between times her witty and exacting critiques – as well as her passionate and generous endorsements – of figures in Irish, British and Continental literature appeared in periodicals and newspapers including the *Freeman's Journal*, the *Fortnightly Review*, the *Contemporary Review* and the *Westminster Review*.

As we have been researching Lynch, so it has become increasingly obvious that life and art were intertwined, although existing gaps in her biographical record, combined with the quality and quantity of her writing, have meant that we have not written a fully developed 'literary biography'. We have also tried to resist drawing conclusions about her personal life from her fiction. As *Autobiography of a Child* (1899) makes clear, Lynch was well aware that 'biography' and 'history' are genres open to subversion, deformation and play, and that women's lives are particularly susceptible to misinterpretation. Nonetheless, as we have followed the thread of Lynch's career, we have been drawn into intersecting webs of interest and association. Many of these are rooted in her early life in Ireland and her experiences as an Irish woman, whether at home or abroad. Consequently, some elements of her biographical history are worth outlining from the beginning.

Lynch's stepfather, James Cantwell (1818–75), was a Young Irelander. Like his friend John Mitchel, Cantwell's involvement in the 1848 rebellion led to his flight to Pennsylvania, settling in Philadelphia and becoming involved in the Fenian movement there. Thomas G. Connors records that Cantwell operated as a Fenian agent in Paris in 1860, and Cantwell's correspondence records his travels between Paris and various cities in England and Ireland.[13] In a letter sent in November of that year, Cantwell describes his decision to settle in Dublin, a move which had at first seemed impossible until he 'was met with a proposition of a business partnership and a matrimonial one'.[14] This matrimonial proposal must have been made by Lynch's mother, Anna (née Calderwood) – a formidable woman of Scottish Presbyterian stock whom he had known and courted before his political activities intervened.[15] As the first child of this union was born in 1861, Gibbs was correct in thinking that Cantwell was the only father figure Hannah Lynch would have known.[16] Cantwell's contacts attempted to arrange for his appointment as American consul to Dublin in the early 1860s, although the appointment was greeted with hostility in some quarters, especially after his acquisition of The Star and Garter.[17] This might have contributed to the fact that Lynch's early novellas are particularly sharp on the snobbery faced by those 'in trade'.[18] Nonetheless, Cantwell seems to have remained a high-profile Dublin figure. His name appears regularly in the *Irish Times* throughout this period, as a member of the Home Government Association, the Home Rule League and the Amnesty Association. He also worked to shape the political landscape in other ways. A couple of letters to the *Irish Times*, sent in the 1860s, record Cantwell's involvement in the erection of monuments to famous Irish cultural and political figures, such as Edmund Burke and fellow Young Irelander William Smith O'Brien. When Cantwell died in November 1875, a matter of months after Mitchel, he was buried in Prospect Cemetery, Glasnevin. Cantwell's associations with figures such as Mitchel, Stephens and O'Mahony place him close to the centre of the Young Ireland and the early Fenian movements.[19] There is also evidence to suggest that he knew Jeremiah O'Donovan Rossa, leader of the 'dynamite campaign' of the 1880s and one of the British government's most wanted men.[20] In other words, Cantwell's nationalist commitments continued, albeit in a different form, from his altered position as a prominent and well-to-do citizen and family man. The Star and Garter, as well as being a local landmark, became a convenient meeting point for those sympathetic to the cause.[21]

This brief history of James Cantwell's nationalist commitments is a characteristically male affair, yet his was a household full of women. Lynch's sisters, Mary, Nannie and Virginia, were joined by four stepsisters, Teresa, Brigid, Patricia and Anna Josephine Cantwell. This was the environment that Katharine Tynan encountered in the early 1880s, or slightly before. Her image of the Lynch-Cantwell household resembled Gibbs' to a striking degree:

> In their house I really entered the literary atmosphere. One of them was Hannah Lynch, whose novels appealed to the discriminating. She was one of the few people I have known who eat, drink, and dream books ... They were all literary in so far as devotion to literature goes; and the well-packed bookcases of the house filled with the great things were a wonder-world to me after my miscellaneous and very odd reading.
>
> These sisters, with their mother, were quite at home amid the alarums and excursions of the Land League. Their father had been a Fenian, one of the useful ones who stood a little outside the danger zone, so to speak... These girls grew up among the writers, thinkers, orators, politicians, conspirators of their day. The names that dropped from their tongues with an easy intimacy opened the doors of a wonder-world for me.[22]

As Cantwell had died in 1875, this was not a case of a male figure introducing his family to the 'alarums and excursions of the Land League'. Instead, the Lynch-Cantwell sisters and their mother played an active and independent role. As we know, the Lynch sisters – Nannie, Virginia and Hannah (and some of the younger Cantwells) – like Tynan herself, were involved in the Ladies' Land League between 1881 and its dissolution in 1882. It is very likely that it was the Ladies' Land League, or another of Lynch's early nationalist connections, that introduced her to F. Mabel Robinson and her more famous sister.

Unsurprisingly perhaps, given her own interests and position at the time, Tynan did not dwell long on the political dimension of her friendship with the Lynch-Cantwell sisters in her retrospective accounts.[23] Instead, she outlined in some detail how the family introduced her to a Dublin bohemia with Parisian overtones, thus broadening her own narrow perspectives:

> My new friends had a catholic taste in reading. They were musicians, and they had languages. They had seen, and were seeing a world far beyond my ken, for they had all gone to convent schools abroad, and after their school days they had gone to Spain and Austria and France and Italy as English governesses to the children of noble families.[24]

And while Tynan had already begun publishing poems in the late 1870s in magazines such as the *Graphic* and 'Dublin Penny Papers', she credits the family with providing her with the literary education she lacked.[25] They introduced her to authors and texts such as Michelet, George Sand, Burton's *The Anatomy of Melancholy*, and Brown's *Religio Medici* and, perhaps most importantly, gave her the opportunity to read poets such as Swinburne through the access the sisters had to the Royal Dublin Society's library in Leinster House:

> In the ordinary course of things I should never have found my way there alone. The Royal Dublin Society was at the time very much the appanage of the Ascendancy in Dublin. The bookish family, being travelled and adventurous, had no hesitation in entering there and taking me with them. Oh indeed, I thank them with all my heart. What subtle processes of education went on in my mind and heart in that lost paradise I cannot say.[26]

Thus, Tynan made it clear that this 'bookish family' had a powerful impact on the shaping of her early ideas and literary tastes before she went on to forge her own influential networks in Dublin and London.[27]

Tynan's description of the Lynch-Cantwell sisters as seasoned Continental travellers by their early youth suggests a pattern of life associated with an Irish Catholic elite, whose children were often educated in convent schools abroad.[28] Lynch gave a glimpse of her educational history in a letter to the editor published in the *Speaker*: 'I have spent the years from seven to seventeen in different convents, and the only one I have no deplorable remembrances of is the French convent.'[29] Other aspects of their early lives fit this class profile less well. Later in life the Lynch-Cantwell sisters travelled partly to work as governesses – governesses to aristocratic families, perhaps, but governesses all the same. Mabel Robinson put it rather more bluntly when presenting Lynch's case to the Royal Literary Fund in 1895: 'When first I saw these girls there were eleven of them, all earning their bread as governesses, secretaries or [?] now some are dead, others have entered convents, but none are in a position to give their sister the help that she requires.'[30] The paradigm novel of the governess, *Jane Eyre*, certainly made its mark on Lynch's *Autobiography of a Child*, which also catalogues the abuse suffered by its young Irish heroine while at an English convent school. Our knowledge of Lynch's governessing career is slight, but evidence suggests that she spent some time working for the Handcocks, a landowning family of Carantrila (sometimes Carrowntryla) Park, County Mayo.[31] Lynch might not have encountered a madwoman in the attic at

Carantrila, but she did find out about a scandal in the family's past. This scandal, which was rumoured to have involved the murder of sisters in order to make way for their brother, formed the backbone of her first novel, *Through Troubled Waters* (1885). Its point about the sacrifice of young Irish women anticipated Lynch's argument in her Paris lecture of 1896, and this was combined with criticism of the Church and of the rural inhabitants of the west of Ireland. The two families concerned apparently bought up copies of the book and destroyed them.[32] For once, *United Ireland* found itself in agreement with the landowners, albeit for different reasons. In a lengthy review of the novel, Lynch was accused of playing up to English stereotypes of Irish priests and peasantry, although the reviewer conceded that this was an inevitable consequence of the dominance of London publishers.[33] In a reply to the editor, Lynch batted this observation aside, insisting that the book had been written for an Irish audience. She went on to invoke several figures from English and French literature who had criticised their home nations, authors whose work, like hers at that point, trod a line between realism and naturalism:

> Thackeray and Dickens exposed frightful phases of English life, and no Englishman assumes that they were enemies of their country. Daudet, himself a Southerner, paints the South of France in fierce and vivid colours. I have not heard that he is on that account regarded in France as sympathetically German. George Sand was no less a Frenchwoman because she wrote 'Mauprat'; neither am I anti-Irish, or less sincerely patriotic than my indignant critic, or any other lover of Ireland, because I acknowledge that Irish men and women are not perfect and free from blame.[34]

This robust response shows her placing her early writings about Ireland in a determinedly European context. The focus on women's lives that drove *Through Troubled Waters* was also represented in her list of authors, as she was careful to include her early heroine George Sand. Her reply to *United Ireland* is just one example of the pugnacity Low described, which we have already witnessed in the Lynch of the mid-1890s. This remained a characteristic of her work until the last. She could be an excoriating critic, fiercest on topics that might have inspired the greatest caution in others, and she was more than happy to defend herself in print.

'Did you see this dreadful *United Ireland* review of Hannah Lynch's book?', Tynan wrote to her literary mentor, Father Matthew Russell, soon after the piece appeared. 'It will sell the book but if such things were written of me I would call on the earth to swallow me.'[35] The ever-canny Tynan recognised that controversy could pay, but it does not seem likely that this was Lynch's primary motivation. In fact, she almost always replied to published criticism, and when men attempted to undermine her authority in print, made sure that she responded in kind. In 1901, 'F.Y.E.', a reviewer in the *Speaker*, questioned her ability, as a woman, to provide an accurate impression of French society in *French Life in Town and Country*.[36] Lynch wrote to Vincens from Henley in April 1901, fuming at the article and at an accompanying letter, but reassuring Vincens that she had 'cravaché' – 'horsewhipped' – its male author in her response: 'Je me suis vengé du noble seigneur. Il m'envoyé un article avec une longue lettre bête et impertinente. J'ai reponds [?] une autre beaucoup plus longue mille fois plus impertinente.'[37] After a different critical scuffle in the *Academy* in the same year, once again over French culture, Arnold Bennett defended her, but felt obliged to note that she seemed 'perfectly able to take care of herself'.[38] Bennett was right, but Lynch's private correspondence also reveals the anxieties that lay beneath the provocative persona. If taken too far, her criticisms and her vigorous self-defence could weaken the formal and informal networks upon which her career depended.

One of the few incidences of Lynch not answering back came in an encounter with Oscar Wilde in 1884. At this point Lynch and Tynan, both former members of the disbanded Ladies' Land League, were in the business of breaking into the London literary scene.[39] This was Tynan's recollection of a meeting between Lynch and Wilde that took place that year at Lady Wilde's London home:

> I remember that Hannah Lynch's introduction to him was in this way. Lady Wilde said: 'This is Miss Hannah Lynch, Oscar: a young Irish genius.' Oscar: 'Are not young Irish geniuses as plentiful as blackberries?'[40]

Rather than seeking redress in print, Lynch seems to have steered clear of Wilde in almost all her critical writings, from the height of his fame to the depths of his disgrace, when both of them were living in Paris.[41] The one substantial comment on his work that we have found – a review of *Lady Windermere's Fan* – was both pointed and ambivalent. Lynch compared the play unfavourably to Pinero's *The Second Mrs Tanqueray* and the work of Ibsen. She argued that the current fascination with 'artificial brilliance', 'limelight, and social glitter' was a symptom of declining standards of 'sincerity and taste' to be found even in Dublin, where critics and audiences used to know better.[42] This did not, however, mean that she was immune to their attraction herself:

...we hail as a second Sheridan the first man who is clever enough to string a rosary of reminiscent epigrams, and, with the aid of a scene or two of real strength, persuades us of a strikingly original talent. I willingly number myself among the vicious, as I have to admit that I enjoyed 'Lady Windermere's Fan' almost as much as if it had been a first-rate work.[43]

This acerbic, witty voice was far from the only one she developed. As Low noted, Lynch wrote one of the earliest critical works on Meredith: *George Meredith: a study* (1891). When *Punch* noticed the book, it punned on its author's name, suggesting that the encounter might prove fatal for its subject: Meredith had been 'LYNCH'd'.[44] Quite the opposite was true. Lynch noted that Meredith's work divided opinion, suggesting that 'this proves the texture and quality of his influence', but wondered how anyone could fail to appreciate his achievement:

He has introduced a new element into English literature – a healthy and purely philosophic realism, which differs as widely from the realism of Fielding as it does from the realism of Zola. To French wit, he brings German profundity of thought, the whole wrought into a thoroughly Saxon setting. Vividness of conception, intensity of vision, and strength of diction – combine these qualities, and you have an English such as no other writer has given us. It is beautiful, with a beauty of its own, and there seems to be no feat of which it is not capable. He has ransacked our language until he has wrought it, through a process of bewildering originality, into a flexibility, a forcible simplicity, a majesty and a rhythm that, in his prose, surpass poetry. Never before have we received such a lesson in the unimaginable resources of language. Never before did we so understand how written words may be made to seize us, fell us, captivate us ... He does not describe or paint: he simply vitalizes inanimate objects. And if he had not made us his debtor in any other way, we must thank him for his great and perfect disciple, Mr. Robert Louis Stevenson.[45]

This text was to be Lynch's only sustained critical study, although, as we have started to see, common points of reference emerge throughout her substantial body of articles and reviews. As such, *George Meredith: a study* offers a rare opportunity to see Lynch the critic in full flight. Most notable is the way in which Lynch's tribute to Meredith's unique style opens up the 'resources' of her own prose. The claims she makes for his 'English' – its peculiar beauty and generic fluidity, its linguistic iconoclasm, its 'forcible simplicity', its ability to animate rather than 'describe' – look forward to critics such as Arthur Symons, and, after him, modernists such as T.S. Eliot. Thus, while this statement reflects Lynch's continued commitment to literary realism, it also indicates her awareness of the vast potential for stylistic innovation within its parameters. This is a path we can see her own work treading, as in her later writing she deployed elements of literary impressionism, and experimented with multiple narrative perspectives. Lynch's focus on Meredith's technique was, as ever, paired with an emphasis on the politics of nation and of gender. Writing explicitly 'as an Irish woman', she praised the 'big Saxon giant' for his representation of female characters in general, and Irish women in particular.[46] She drew attention to an interrogation of masculine foibles and misplaced ideals that matched, and no doubt influenced, her own:

> Can a young gentleman with a proper respect for himself feel romantically disposed towards a young woman, even if she is divinely beautiful, when she owns a capacity to dine off potatoes? or ascend to heaven on an aria when the prima-donna refreshes herself with bottled stout?[47]

George Meredith: a study might have been close to what Richard Le Gallienne called the 'Meredithyramb', but it demonstrates Lynch's critical credentials while reflecting the themes that dominated her fiction. Appropriately enough, Meredith had seen manuscripts of several of Lynch's novels while working as a reader for the publisher Chapman & Hall.[48] He recognised her abilities – 'By all means encourage the lady. She has real powers.' – but his admiration for her intelligence and writing style competed with concerns over her plotting and subject matter.[49] *The Prince of the Glades* explored the political condition of Ireland overtly, which seemed to him an unpromising topic:

> The writer's ability does not seem to me to show so well in this instance. But the task of creating interest in Fenianism would try the cleverest pen: and the hero has Fenian fever. It pains me to say that, though she always writes readably, the subject and cast of the story are not likely to win public attention. Impress upon her that you speak as publishers who have to look to remuneration for their ventures.

Meredith's dismissal of Fenianism as a subject of interest illustrates *United Ireland*'s point about the effect of English publishing on Irish writing – although *The Prince of the Glades* did find an English publisher in Methuen, the firm that also brought out Lynch's study of Meredith himself. These reports, with their interest in marketability as well as style, offer a snapshot of the publishing terrain that Lynch, in common with most writers, had to navigate. Willingly or not, she did adopt many of the measures necessary to maintain her position as a marketable woman author. That is, she wrote 'romances', stories about childhood such as 'The Little Marquis' and 'A Village Sovereign', and published in outlets such as the *Girl's Realm*, *Good Words* and *Hearth and Home*. As we will see, however, even cosy themes were frequently shot through with irony and ambivalence.

Lynch's choice of genres and of publishing venues reflected her negotiation of an emerging and complex professional field. In addition to the women-centred publications mentioned above, she maintained a longstanding publishing relationship with the *Freeman's Journal* in Dublin, and produced pieces for *United Ireland* and Father Matthew Russell's *Irish Monthly* early in her career. Her work appeared in London in established reviews, such as *Murray's Magazine* and *Macmillan's Magazine*. Her most enduring association with a London periodical was with the *Academy*. And while some journals – such as the *Academy*, the *Speaker* and the *Contemporary Review* – were liberal in outlook, others cause us to consider the rather unexpected alliances that literary networks could promote, and the heterogeneity of periodicals as texts. In her obituary piece, Frances Low mentioned Lynch's work for the *St James's Gazette*, which was edited by her brother Sidney Low from 1888. This was a relatively conservative paper, which leant its support to the imperialism of figures such as Cecil Rhodes. Its former editor, the veteran of literary reviews Frederick Greenwood, had been even more conspicuously Tory, openly opposing Gladstone and greater autonomy for Ireland not that many years before. And yet Lynch dedicated her collection *Dr Vermont's Fantasy and Other Stories* (1896) to Greenwood. Was this a case of paying her dues to a senior figure, a friend of George Meredith, whose politics she was prepared to ignore, or something else? Related questions are raised by her presence in *Blackwood's Magazine*, generally considered another pro-imperial Tory organ. *Autobiography of a Child* not only provides a graphic account of the humiliations meted out to an Irish girl in an English school, it describes the anguish endured by an Irish woman whose sweetheart is hanged for unspecified Fenian activity. As it was serialised almost simultaneously with Joseph Conrad's *The Heart of Darkness*, it allows similar questions to be posed. Did the fact that this was a story about a child allow Lynch to smuggle an anti-imperial text into a pro-imperial journal? Or does the appearance of both suggest that *Blackwood's* approach to imperialism was more nuanced than it might seem? This balance – or tension – between the radical and the conservative, the idealistic and the pragmatic, marked Lynch's feminist politics, too, and characterised her approach to the category of New Woman fiction.

Her relationship with religion is equally central, but even less clear. Thus far, we have no evidence of Lynch defining herself along specific religious lines. Her mother might have been Protestant, but Lynch was educated in convent schools. This experience was certainly formative, even if she remembered it with loathing. In *French Life in Town and Country*, she expressed her dislike for such institutions so strongly that an American reviewer in the *Catholic World* assumed that she was an overzealous English Protestant.[50] And, living in Paris among a mostly Protestant-Jewish literary group, it seems she did identify with Protestantism to an extent. One of her letters to Louise-Cécile Vincens, who was definitely Protestant, anticipates meeting her in church. Yet in *French Life*, she also aligned herself with Victor Charbonnel, a radical priest excommunicated by the archbishop of Paris. In the *Academy*, she voiced her support for Ernest Renan, another Catholic renegade, with whom her Parisian circle was also connected. One of her other longstanding correspondents was Father Thomas Dawson OMI, who was close to A.M. Sullivan and to the American reformer Henry George during the period of the Land Wars.[51] Dawson was also a close friend of Katharine Tynan (he was godfather to one of her children) and continued a correspondence with her after Lynch's death.

Lynch's friendship with Father Dawson was clearly an important one, suggesting shared networks within which the political, the literary and the spiritual overlapped, and to which Lynch still felt connected even when she had deliberately distanced herself from them. Though they were far from frequent, her letters to him cover the period from October 1885 to February 1895, representing the fullest record of her travels between England and Ireland prior to her more permanent move to Paris. At present, Lynch's movements can only be reconstructed from letters that survive in the collections of others, or from the travel writing which we will explore in more detail in Chapter 5. Nonetheless, even these reasonably limited resources give an impression of a mobile and highly independent woman. It is in her correspondence with Dawson that we learn about one of her early European trips, an extended visit to Greece. Although she described herself mischievously as an 'infidel' in one piece, her stay on the Greek island of Tenos (now more commonly known as Tinos) was facilitated by Dawson's connections with the convent that hosted her. The first few letters were sent from Tenos in late 1885 and early 1886, the final from Athens in September 1887. In them, she writes as a largely solo female traveller, reporting on the comfort and hospitality of the convent where she is staying, her fascination with Greek philosophy, and her expeditions into the countryside. Her pleasure can be summed up by a single comment: 'I enjoy perfect freedom.'[52] These letters also demonstrate that her sense of personal liberation did not blunt her political sensibilities. For example, in November 1889 she asked Dawson for his opinion on Parnell, who had been the subject of a 'Special Commission' earlier in the year. She went on to lament the 'interior quarrels' going on in Ireland, highlighted by the recent 'scenes' at the Thurles Convention, noting that 'the Greeks fight now between themselves, but they all united splendidly against the Turks. The [impression?] is that all the Greeks regarded the Turks as their enemies & only some of the Irish think so of the English.'[53]

As well as benefitting from Dawson's contacts in Tenos, it appears Lynch was keen to exploit his contacts in Athens: 'About your friend's letter. In the spring I shall go to Athens. The Superiors here will give me an introduction to the Archbishop, but if your friend would furnish me with one to [Schlie??] or any other Athens Celebrity it would be of great [help?] to me, as I shall write letters for *Freeman*.'[54] Her other contacts in Greece included the wealthy, cosmopolitan Demetrios Bikélas – to whom she dedicated the Greek-set novel *Daughters of Men*, which he subsequently translated – and Lynch was in Greece again in March and April of 1902. She travelled regularly to Spain, where her sister Nannie worked for one of the 'noble families' Tynan mentioned in her memoirs.[55] She was in Madrid in April 1895, and in Barcelona in May 1901, and her travel writing describes a series of locations in addition to this: the Canaries, Venice, Lucerne, Verona, Monserrat and Fontainebleau, to name a few. As we will see, Lynch's identity as a traveller – her 'travelling identity', even – informed much of her writing.

These extensive Continental travels were interspersed with return visits to Ireland and by periods of time spent in various London locations. We know from Tynan's correspondence that Lynch was in London, working in the British Museum, in March 1885, before she went to Tenos. This was the result of a contact Tynan had provided, and Lynch's progress was reported to Tynan as follows: 'She is learning the Reading Room fast, & I expect that she will soon not only know it well but become a highly popular institution. She seems very clever & industrious & likely to make her way. She is certainly very bright & intelligent & pleasing & she is an ornament to the Museum.'[56] This letter confirms Lynch's presence in one of Victorian London's pre-eminent sites for female intellectual labour. It also confirms the gendered nature of that space, with the young woman reader deemed 'an ornament to the Museum'. Lynch wrote to Dawson from Bloomsbury in March 1888, from Hampton Court in November 1893 and early 1894, and from an address near Portman Square just before Christmas of that year. Immediately after this period and until early 1895 she was seriously ill. This was caused by a thyroid condition but also, it seems, by exhaustion and stress.[57] In addition to Mabel Robinson, her successful application to the Royal Literary Fund was supported by Walter Besant (Lynch was a member of the Society of Authors) and by Meredith.[58] It is unclear whether or not she entirely recovered from this episode, although she certainly soldiered on. She published her novel *Denys D'Auvrillac: a story of French life* (1896) and her short-story collection *Dr Vermont's Fantasy and Other Stories* (1896) in the following year. The former included one of Lynch's putative New Woman figures, an independent female artist named Mary Sumers, who was teamed with a sympathetic young Frenchman. The dedication was to 'A. Mary F. Robinson' this time, and it laid out Lynch's intention to counter the caricatures of French life found too frequently, she observed, in popular English novels.[59] She was equally productive in 1897, which saw the publication of *Jinny Blake: a tale* and *An Odd Experiment*. Here, Lynch's engagement with New Woman fiction was even more overt, although, in her 'Paris Letter' columns in the *Academy*, she continued to question the genre.

The increasingly visible association between Lynch and France in these years suggests that she might well have made a semi-permanent move to the country around this time. Certainly, by the period of her appointment as the *Academy*'s Paris correspondent she was relied upon to produce regular columns. In the later 1890s her work began to appear in better-known London magazines. This was the era of contributions to *Blackwood's Magazine*, *Macmillan's Magazine* and later still to the *Contemporary Review*. The backlash that followed the serial publication of *Autobiography of a Child*, which included legal threats from the Church and debate surrounding the generic status of the book, disturbed Lynch, but helped to build her profile. The French translation, *Très Véridique Histoire d'une Petite Fille* (1902), was supportively reviewed by her French circle. By this point Lynch was working as a translator herself, publishing English texts of dramas by the Spanish playwright José Echegaray, the novelist José Maria de Pereda, and works by French historians. But by April 1903, she was once again too ill to write. Her second Royal Literary Fund application was also successful – her supporters this time included William Blackwood and C. Lewis Hind – and relatively generous, being made up of two payments of £100 and £50. By the time of the second payment, in December 1903, Lynch was aware of how serious her condition had become. She wrote to the fund on 22 December to thank it for its generosity, but was unable to give any positive news. She was being cared for by a nurse, she wrote, adding that 'I despair of ever being well.'[60] Sadly, as we know, she was right, and she died shortly after New Year, on 11 January 1904.[61] For a while, it seems the Robinson sisters had some of her literary effects, including the manuscript of a final novel, set in Paris. This novel, along with the bulk of her correspondence, remains lost – a tantalising final gap in the archive.

This brief outline of Lynch's life, like so much else about her, challenges simple categorisation. She was successful, but often lacked professional security. She needed her friends, but valued solitude and independence equally highly. She often wrote warmly of the traditions of female decorum in life and in literature, but appears to have revelled in breaking them – evading the authorities in her Land League days, scrambling on board steam boats to Greece unaccompanied, putting her male critics in their place in no uncertain terms. She loved Ireland and Irish literature but, like Moore, Joyce and many others, was also compelled to write from a position of self-imposed exile. As we have already suggested, her work is also valuable for the way it challenges central assumptions about gender, genre and nation in this period. In the following chapters, we will undertake this exploration in the proper depth.

In the first chapter, we focus principally on the 1880s, tracing the intersections of Lynch's political and literary life that expose the imbrications of the feminist and activist Ladies' Land League and the earliest formations of the Celtic renaissance. Such an approach enriches recent reappraisals of the revivalist period, outlining an alternative narrative and broader understanding of this time. We explore first Lynch's engagement with the Ladies' Land League and its implications for her life and career. This includes her writing that directly addressed the Land Wars, and the questions of power and gender that lay beneath their surface. We start to explore the interaction between the political, literary and publishing circles within which Lynch moved in these early years, sometimes comparing her trajectory to that of other literary Ladies' Land League figures such as Katharine Tynan. This leads us to address Lynch's satirical portrayals of her encounters with the emerging revivalist cultures of the decade, and to assess what her work has to tell us about the diverse literary ecology of a period before the dominance of Yeats' Irish Literary Revival.

The second chapter retains the period focus of the first. It expands the discussion of Lynch's Land War fiction to consider more specifically her feminist, proto-New Woman fiction about the Ladies' Land League and the writings of female contemporaries Fannie Gallaher and Mabel Robinson, the latter an English novelist and ardent supporter of Irish nationalism. It also considers the wider feminist political networks emerging from the Ladies' Land League. Lynch's early, Ireland-set fiction will also be compared with that of another, far better-known contemporary, George Moore. Despite shared literary networks in London and Paris, Moore and Lynch do not appear to have ever met, but their 1880s fictions intersect in crucial ways. A comparative discussion of *A Drama in Muslin* and *Through Troubled Waters* addresses their mutual preoccupations (female education and identity, for example) explored via Big House and west-of-Ireland settings, and their diverging narrative treatments, inflected by both gender and class differences. Such an approach also contributes to recent scholarship that has identified a distinctive mode of *fin-de-siècle* Irish realism in texts of this period, a counter-narrative to the revivalist aesthetics promoted by the Dublin coterie cultures Lynch satirised later in the decade.

In the third chapter, we turn our attention to the 1890s, following Lynch from the salons of Dublin and London to those of Paris. Lynch's movements through these three capitals, negotiated by way of friendships and female-orientated societies and networks, provide a map of interconnecting political and literary spheres comprising various mixed interests. This 'real Mesopotamia' – to borrow a phrase of Mabel Robinson's – shares many of the characteristics of the cosmopolitan scene articulated by Ana Parejo Vadillo and Stefano Evangelista. However, we argue that an examination of Lynch's career suggests not a model of seamless, hospitable plurality but a less tidy heterodoxy, reflecting a variety of unstable and sometimes competing views. In the second section of the chapter, we explore in detail how Lynch responded to this environment in her critical writing about, and from, Paris. We focus on her weekly 'Paris Letter' for the *Academy* in which she discussed literary representations of Ireland and imperialism and anti-Semitism (via her coverage of the Dreyfus Affair). We close with an appraisal of her often ambivalent critical reviews in this weekly letter of women's writing on desire and female sexuality.

The fourth chapter uses Lynch's 'Mesopotamian' perspective of the mid- to late 1890s to investigate her various engagements with the problematic category of the New Woman, a topic that exercised her a good deal in the 'Paris Letters', explored in the previous chapter. We situate Lynch's interest in 'sympathy', touched upon previously via relations between nations, within critical readings of New Woman fiction, looking at points of association between both discourses in her novel *An Odd Experiment*. We then pursue this focus on the New Woman figure, who often happens to be Irish, through readings of unsettled and hybrid identities in her other novels of the period and their explicit cosmopolitan contexts. We conclude by paying special attention to recurring motifs of escape, representations of modern modes of travel and transnational boundary crossings, and the trope of *vagabondage* in Lynch's portraits of these mobile, modern women.

In the fifth chapter, we examine a broad cross-section of Lynch's substantial body of travel writing, in which this mobile, independent figure appears as the author herself. We position Lynch's work within the context of Victorian women's travel writing but argue that her outsider and anti-imperialist stance complicates and also raises questions about the practices and perspectives of the Victorian woman traveller. This section tracks through her work from her earliest publications in the genre – depictions of Ireland published in Ireland and in North America – and addresses a range of topics. These include: Lynch's engagement with ongoing debates about the traveller and the tourist; her affinities with, and differences from, Robert Louis Stevenson and Pierre Loti; and her concern with the lives of women in the countries she traverses. We then move on to explore in detail her various strategies for defining a style. At different times this 'vagabond's scrutiny' balanced political commentary with experiments in impressionism, literary and cultural commentary with comic anecdote, satirical observation with lyrical description.

The sixth and final chapter is devoted to Lynch's best-known and most debated book: *Autobiography of a Child*. This sustained experiment in life-writing and penultimate novel of her career brings together many of the prevailing concerns of her *oeuvre* and in particular the impact of gender and nation on identity formation. It also offers a fully fledged prequel to the rebel girl and New Woman fiction published earlier in her career. In this chapter, we try to answer a series of questions this novel raises – how to read a book that contains such a plethora of generic signatures and intertextual reference, that is self-consciously engaged with the difficulties of writing a memoir of childhood and is, equally self-consciously and explicitly, not straightforwardly autobiographical, a text that creates such powerful impressions and yet constantly questions its own validity, exploring its own conditions as a narrative and the impact of narratives as a way of structuring experience. We explore its textual hybridity, reading it in multiple generic contexts and also in its first publishing venue, *Blackwood's Magazine*.

The Ladies' Land League, Political and Literary Networks, and Narratives of the Irish Literary Revival

In this and the following chapter, we focus on the 1880s. During these years, Lynch found publishers in Ireland, London and America, producing travel pieces as well as short fiction and novels mainly set in Ireland. The decade began and ended with key experiences that further shaped Lynch's literary career and her views on Irish nationalism and gender. These included her involvement in the Ladies' Land League from 1881 to 1882, and her invitation to Katharine Tynan's literary salon in 1887, where she met, among other nascent revivalists, W.B. Yeats. These provide a focus and framework for this chapter, which first examines Lynch's political and literary networks during this decade. This focus illuminates forgotten links between the Ladies' Land League and the earliest formations of the Irish cultural and, more specifically, Literary Revival. Definitions of revivalism of this period are complex, often contested and require rethinking, as Gregory Castle and other scholars working in the field have suggested: 'The myriad ways in which revivalist aesthetics and ideologies were expressed makes it impossible to regard Revivalism in monolithic terms and to restrict it to the literary revival of W.B. Yeats, J.M. Synge and Lady Augusta Gregory.'[1] Attention to Lynch's earliest publishing contexts and literary contemporaries contributes to a body of scholarship that has begun to foreground a much more complex narrative.[2] We conclude then by addressing Lynch's satirical portrayals of emerging revivalist coteries of the decade. The first of these was a spoof published in the *Dublin Evening Telegraph* in January 1888, based on her observations of Katharine Tynan's literary salon, which she had attended along with W.B. Yeats, Douglas Hyde and George Russell (Æ) in December 1887. The second, 'My Friend Arcanieva', published in

Macmillan's Magazine in 1895, was modelled on other Dublin coteries, one that centred around Charles Oldham and the Contemporary Club and gatherings at the home of John O'Leary and his sister Ellen. Both satires are markers of Lynch's self-distancing from the political and the newly emerging literary scene in Ireland and serve to complicate further the narratives surrounding the Irish cultural renaissance.

As Tina O'Toole has observed, 'the Ladies' Land League in 1881 may be seen as a paradigm shift: the moment when "New" possibilities for Irish women begin to emerge', and Lynch's writing needs to be considered in relation to these.[3] The often female-centred literary, political and publishing networks that were cultivated by its members provide a significant context for the consideration of a cross-section of Lynch's writing during this period, including the newly emergent subgenres of Land War fiction of the 1880s and proto-New Woman fiction.[4] A novella, *Marjory Maurice* (serialised in the *Shamrock*, 1884–85) and two novel-length works – 'Defeated' (in *Beeton's Christmas Annual*, 1885) and *The Prince of the Glades* (1891) – featured characteristics of both. Lynch offered the most direct and striking account and defence of her Ladies' Land League activities in *Marjory Maurice* and a short story for girls, 'A Girl Revolutionist', published later in the *Girl's Realm* in 1899. These texts will be considered in the context of other Land War fiction in Chapter 2.

Countering the neglect of the Ladies' Land League both in the immediate aftermath of its demise and subsequent histories of the period, recent studies agree that it was an extraordinary and highly significant organisation.[5] It has been described as 'a crucial first link in a chain of female political agency which stretches forward into the early twentieth century to connect with other feminist nationalist and suffragist organizations such as *Inghinidhe na hÉireann* and *Cumann na mBan*'.[6] As well as providing 'tangible role models for first-wave feminists', these 1880s activists can also be connected with 'emerging New Woman writers alike in the period'.[7] The Ladies' Land League was established at the very end of January 1881 and fully disbanded by August 1882, having been set up by Charles Stewart Parnell's sisters, Fanny and Anna. Initially, its activities were framed in order to fit an image of appropriately womanly behaviour: it was principally a relief fund, designed to alleviate the suffering of families either evicted, left financially desperate by the imprisonment of male breadwinners, or both. Although such support was a political act in itself, as hostilities between the land movement and the British government intensified, so the remit of the Ladies' Land League developed in response. These efforts were largely coordinated by Anna Parnell, who rapidly outstripped even Davitt's expectations to become an inspiring, energetic and highly organised leader. More controversially, Parnell not only addressed many of her politically charged speeches to women specifically, but had her own vision of the way in which the campaign should be pursued.[8]

Just as James Cantwell had been close to the heart of the Young Ireland movement, so Hannah, Nannie and Virginia were at the centre of the Ladies' Land League. As Jane McL. Côté notes, since many newspaper reports of the time provide only the surname and title of individuals, it can be difficult to tell which is the 'Miss Lynch' in question, but some details are certain.[9] Around 1881 Nannie and Virginia were still based in Dublin, and they both became assistant secretaries to Anna Parnell. Nannie's name appears as one of the signatories to the first manifesto, presented by Anna Parnell in Dublin on the last day of January 1881. Margaret Ward records that Hannah was secretary of the Ladies' Land League, and put her name to the league's first address, on 4 February of the same year.[10] However, it is possible that this is another instance of confusion between the two sisters, as newspaper reports confirm that around the same time Hannah became honorary secretary of the London branch, which held its first meeting towards the end of February.[11] This London branch included Helen Taylor, feminist and stepdaughter of John Stuart Mill, a Miss Spender of the Women's Suffrage League, and Frances (Mrs A.M.) Sullivan, who was president. Her husband, Alexander Martin Sullivan, was at that point the MP for Meath and a friend of Thomas Dawson.[12] Significantly, A.M. Sullivan was also the editor of Dublin journal the *Nation*, one of the most influential nationalist papers, with links to the Young Ireland movement of the 1840s.[13]

The manifesto of the London branch of the Ladies' Land League illustrates the care with which its authors framed their actions. Emphasis was placed on the feminine, humanitarian aspect of the organisation, with worrying nationalist overtones diluted by its appeal to 'sympathetic Englishwomen':

> We appeal to every woman in England who has a heart to feel for victims of affliction and oppression, to aid us in alleviating the sorrow and misery which thus threaten so many of our sex. Naturally, we appeal especially to the women of Irish birth or blood, whom God has blest with secure and happy homes, but we have good assurance that many a kindly Englishwoman's heart and hand will be with us in our work. It is essentially woman's mission, and no more pure and noble duty could engage them than this of lightening the anguish of the prison, or dispelling the darkness of the desolate home.[14]

The manifesto demonstrates that, far from women simply becoming objects of sympathetic outrage, the language of the Ladies' Land League made the notion of 'sympathy', and women's supposed predisposition to it, a plank in its oppositional rhetoric. Sympathy allowed the league to present a highly political venture in a manner that placed it above narrow political concerns, emphasising and even essentialising the feminine nature of its enterprise at the precise moment when its critics were decrying it as unnatural and unwomanly. In an already incendiary atmosphere, the Ladies' Land League strengthened its case further by presenting itself as an organisation composed of 'ladies'. Katharine Tynan recalled being told that she was 'too democratic' when at one early meeting she wondered aloud why 'ladies' rather than 'women' had been chosen for the name of the organisation.[15] In one sense this response supports a reading of the league as essentially class-bound, composed of ideologically motivated, middle-class young women who nonetheless possessed the social prejudices of their era. However, by including all its members under this heading, the league also made an adroit pre-emptive move against the accusations of unladylike behaviour that were likely to proceed from active political engagement. After all, the work undertaken by the Ladies' Land League was, to borrow Margaret Ward's phrase, 'in complete defiance of every expectation regarding the traditional role of Victorian women'.[16] The performance of femininity, and the power relationships it concealed or manipulated, would recur as a topic in Lynch's writing for many years. She would also explore the question of 'sympathy' as a mode of engagement between individuals or nations, in early overtly political texts such as *The Prince of the Glades* (1891) as well as in more intrapersonal studies such as *An Odd Experiment* (1897). This language connects with Lynch's respect for George Eliot, her knowledge of Sydney Owenson's work, and with the ethical aestheticism of her friend Mary Robinson, yet the early context of the Ladies' Land League is equally important.[17]

The interwoven politics of gender and nation textured every aspect of the Ladies' Land League's activities. Even those men who were supportive of the organisation struggled to free themselves of the expectations of their time. One of the most well-known incidents in its history is its responsibility for maintaining publication of *United Ireland*, a Land League paper in which the 'No Rent Manifesto' had appeared. Copies of the publication had first been seized, but, thanks to the ingenuity of the Ladies' Land League, not only did *United Ireland* continue to be produced, but the police found it almost impossible to keep out of circulation.[18] This is the sort of verbal activism that would have appealed to Lynch, and in the memoirs of Henry George she is identified as one of the editors during this key period:

Miss Hannah Lynch, sister of Miss Nannie Lynch, the efficient assistant secretary of the Ladies' Land League, and Miss Cavanaugh [*sic*] were installed as editors, and Miss Nannie Lynch and Mrs Moloney (treasurer of the Ladies' League whose husband was recently sent to Dundalk [prison] on reasonable suspicion) took charge of the business department.[19]

This high-profile and risky work, which involved intellectual as much as physical daring, also illuminated the more subtle gender prejudices in operation. William O'Brien, editor of *United Ireland* and imprisoned during this period, offered this retrospective account of the drafting of

> … a body of sweet girl graduates into *United Ireland* office[s] to take the place of the outlawed men; and most unselfishly and valiantly, for several months, they kept its accounts and supplied some of its most piquant writings, and foiled the police raiders by a thousand ingenious feminine devices for circulating the paper.[20]

Anna Parnell had encouraged young women to become involved largely because of the 'physical strain' involved in the work.[21] Here, that youth translates into the stock figure of the 'sweet girl graduate'. For Edmund Leamy, whose poem 'The Frothy Executive' paid comical homage to the young women of the Ladies' Land League, these were still 'soft-eyed maids escaped from their mamas' for all their devotion to the 'noble cause'.[22] *The Tale of a Great Sham*, Anna Parnell's long-suppressed and highly critical account of the gender politics at work within the Land League movement, gave the following account of a conversation between one of the Lynch sisters and another leading male editor of the time:

> After having circulated her first 30,000 copies of *United Ireland* around the country, in spite of a cordon of detectives drawn round the office, Miss Lynch had occasion to interview Mr Gallagher [*sic*], the editor of *The Freeman's Journal*, about some part of our business; after this was settled a conversation ensued, in the course of which he remarked: 'I hear that the Ladies' Land League are going to take over *United Ireland*, but it is absurd to think a handful of girls can defy the government.' She might have asked him, when there was no question of defiance being conducted by physical force, why couldn't girls defy as well as anybody else? But the circumstances made it more prudent not to give him any grounds for supposing that she did not agree with him.[23]

Anna Parnell's emphasis on the word 'defiance' in the above account is telling. In their involvement with this group, the Lynch sisters were defying three levels of authority simultaneously: breaking the law, flouting the conventions of the Church, and failing to observe norms of female behaviour that seem to have been endorsed in varying degrees by conservatives and radicals alike.

Katharine Tynan credited Hannah Lynch with carrying *United Ireland* over to Paris, as well as with a similar act of clandestine distribution. Police records documented in Myles Dungan's study of *United Ireland* certainly testify to her involvement:

> One of the most prominent, enterprising and tenacious members of the Ladies' Land League, Hannah Lynch, seems to have made the survival of *United Ireland* a personal project. When James O'Connor was arrested under the Protection of Person and Property Act on 8 December 1881, according to Mallon [Superintendent John Mallon] 'he was instructing Miss Hannah Lynch in the duties of being a sub-editor'. The following week Mallon recorded that the main business of *United Ireland* was being performed by, among others, Hannah Lynch and her two sisters, Nannie and Virginia. Lynch was present on 15 December for the most significant DMP raid on the Abbey Street premises.[24]

The only version of these experiences Hannah Lynch offered (as far as we know) was published many years later in the short story 'A Girl Revolutionist', which we discuss in Chapter 2. Here, the young heroine, Moya O'Connell, not only attempts to start up a no-rent campaign but ends up becoming a fiery and revolutionary editor of the proscribed paper *Erin*. She smuggles the 'stereo plates' out the back door of the paper's offices and into a taxi, down to the port and over to England.[25] It is still unclear whether this is Lynch writing directly of her own experience, or giving an account of Nannie's and Virginia's, or some mixture of the two. Either way, the fictional *Erin* and the historical *United Ireland* episodes showed that evidence of women's abilities was not enough to disrupt the status quo. The ultimate demonstration of this came in August 1882, when the Ladies' Land League was disbanded, principally as a consequence of the agreement Charles Parnell had struck with Gladstone in May. Already mourning her sister Fanny, who had died suddenly in July, and feeling deeply betrayed by the male executive, Anna Parnell withdrew from public life. *The Tale of a Great Sham*, which she wrote in the early twentieth century, remained unpublished for nearly eighty years.

The story of the Ladies' Land League confirms the difficulties women encountered when trying to impose themselves upon a dominant political culture or historical record. This holds true, in this instance at least, even when that political culture or historical record is alert to suppression and resistance in other areas. Lynch's writing provided a direct riposte to this silencing of women by certain forms of masculine discourse. The events of 1881–82 also suggest an intriguing connection between Lynch's feminism and her later distrust for certain forms of nationalism – most clearly apparent in her writing on the Dreyfus Affair in the later 1890s – and to the hierarchies of the Church. Throughout her life, Lynch would remain a staunch anti-imperialist, and would frequently criticise the arrogance bred by British power. But this did not, for Lynch as for many other Irish writers, lead to an unquestioning relationship with her home nation.

By her early twenties, Lynch had learned some hard lessons about the structures of power and gender, and about both the achievements and limitations of idealism and self-determination. But there were other ways in which the brief existence of the Ladies' Land League had enduring consequences for her and for her writing career. Her active participation in this group provided material and insights for her writing on Ireland and in particular Irish female identity, but also the experience of editing and running (albeit briefly) a proscribed publication. Through the organisation, whose membership included several women with literary as well as political aspirations, she also made numerous connections, laying the groundwork for the more extensive literary networks in Dublin and London. The first set of contacts we will explore here were linked to specific periodicals. Second, we discuss Lynch's publishing networks established alongside members of the Ladies' Land League and aspiring writers Rose Kavanagh, Katharine Tynan and Mabel Robinson (who will be discussed in more depth in Chapter 3). Finally, we consider how Lynch's publishing networks forged through Ladies' Land League connections illuminate the forgotten cultural significance of that feminist and nationalist organisation to the foundations of the nascent cultural revival, channelled by Yeats and other emerging revivalists into what became known as the Irish Literary Revival.[26]

Anna Parnell's wry account of the interview between John Gallaher and one of the Lynch sisters cited earlier, and the connection between A.M. Sullivan and the London branch of the Ladies' Land League, demonstrate the importance of publications such as *United Ireland*, the *Freeman's Journal* and the *Nation* to the nationalist cause. Marie-Louise Legg has anatomised the 'central and essential' role periodicals played in 'the spread of Land League activity' in the 1880s.[27] She cites John Pope-Hennessy's article 'What Do the Irish Read?' of June 1884, which paid particular attention to the three papers named above:

An English Member of Parliament, who has little or nothing in the shape of such a popular national literature of his own to speculate about, may ask, Do the Irish read no newspapers? No doubt they do; and the proprietors of *The Freeman's Journal*, *The Nation*, *United Ireland*, and other popular newspapers, have very substantial reasons for knowing that the Irish reading public is a large and increasing one.[28]

Pope-Hennessy, formerly a Conservative MP but of a Catholic family from Cork, had good reason for his pointed comparison between the 'popular national literature' of England and of Ireland. English 'literary men', and English politicians, would be foolish to ignore the reality of a literate population both 'large and increasing', especially as its tastes were being shaped by a lively nationalist periodical culture. This was the culture that effectively launched the career of W.B. Yeats between late 1887 and early 1888, when he was given 'the most important break of his career' by *United Ireland*.[29] It is important not to construct a homogeneous category of 'nationalist' periodicals at this point – equally so to bear in mind that 'What Do the Irish Read?' and Yeats' publications of 1887–88 were separated by several eventful years. Nonetheless, this was the environment in which Lynch cut her literary teeth, too. It is a bibliographical irony that a form which was designed to be accessible to large numbers of readers should have ended up being one of the least accessible to later scholars of the period, as newspapers and magazines have enjoyed mixed fortunes within library collections and digitisation projects. Nationalist newspapers and periodicals and their female networks were certainly central to the development of Lynch's early career, as they were to other literary-minded members of the Ladies' Land League. Buried with these publications are, we might imagine, many other significant works by women authors.

The *Shamrock*, a weekly illustrated penny paper that had its roots in William Smith O'Brien's Young Ireland movement, was one such publication, in which Lynch appeared from at least 1882.[30] It had been purchased, along with the other struggling Dublin papers *Flag of Ireland* and the *Irishman*, by the Land League in 1881.[31] The *Shamrock* and its varied stories were enthusiastically promoted in the equally nationalist *Irishman*.[32] The tenor of both publications is made clear in a pitch for the *Shamrock* in the 24 June 1882 edition:

The Proprietors of *The Shamrock* have the pleasure to announce that this week's issue commences an entirely new and improved series of that favourite National Magazine. Its pages will contain a plentiful supply of first-class fiction by the most famous Irish writers. Special attention will be paid to rendering the Illustrations as numerous and highly finished as possible, and two Irish Artists of eminence have been specially engaged with that object. It is printed on IRISH-MADE PAPER, and no pains or expense will be spared to equip *The Shamrock* for the work of driving pernicious English literature by fair competition from the favour of our Irish youth.[33]

Included in the pitch is a promotion of a new story – 'The Massingers' by 'Miss Hannah Lynch, a young lady who has made a triumphant entry into the gallery of Irish writers, [and who] will establish the reputation of the authoress for subtle insight into character, and a descriptive power remarkable for wealth of colour and delicacy of shading'.[34] Stephanie Rains explains that the *Shamrock*, like other 'Irish story papers' popular at the time, was:

> …able to exploit the powerful alliance of national and religious agendas within the 'social purity' movement's condemnation of imported British papers. Where the British papers were accused of sensationalism and immorality as well as undermining Irish culture and identity, their Irish rivals were keen to present themselves as wholesome and patriotic alternatives.[35]

In 'A Glimpse of South Ireland in Winter' published in the *Shamrock* in March 1883, Lynch seemed as keen to establish her literary credentials as to assert her patriotism. She opened her impressionistic passage on Waterford and its surrounds with a reference to *Daniel Deronda*, the conventions of travel writing, and her experiences of travel since childhood. 'The Massingers' serial, which ran from 24 June 1882 until 25 November 1882, also established a narrative slightly at odds with the stated aims of the new *Shamrock* announced in 1882: 'Everything in *The Shamrock* shall be Irish and racy of the soil – its writers, its humour, its illustrations, its drollery, and we fear not to say, its morality'.[36] Literary allusions preface each chapter of a tale beginning in Rome where the wealthy but aimless Englishman Arthur Massinger falls for the talented daughter of a famous Italian artist. Most striking for us, however, is Lynch's novella 'Marjory Maurice'. As the most extended depiction of the Ladies' Land League that Lynch produced, it offers a rare opportunity to study her awareness of how the women in the league were represented and perceived both within and without the movement. The story ran from December 1884 until the end of March 1885, appearing alongside a run of strikingly feminist articles. This feminism can be explained by the fact that Lynch was not the only former Ladies' Land League member on board.

Rose Kavanagh, the 'Miss Cavanaugh [*sic*]' whom Henry George remembered taking over the editorship of the proscribed *United Ireland* with Lynch, had experience in editing other nationalist papers, too. Tynan recalled that 'I first met Rose in the days when Richard Pigott was editing the *Irishman* and Rose *The Shamrock*, a little weekly paper, in the same office in Middle Abbey Street.'[37] Not only was Rose Kavanagh involved in editing the *Shamrock*, she, Lynch and Tynan were contributors. Lynch had contributed to a 'Christmas on the Hills' collection of fiction in the Christmas 1883 issue alongside them. She continued to be active in William O'Brien's *United Ireland* and in 1884, the year of Pope-Hennessy's article, Lynch and Katharine Tynan contributed political skits to a collection, 'A Castle Christmas-Eve; the tales the portraits told', in the *United Ireland* Christmas supplement.[38] Given these contributions, the surprised and critical response Lynch later received in nationalist reviews seems even more explicable.

In the same year a paper of slightly different political cast, the *Freeman's Journal*, at that point owned by Edmund Dwyer Gray, began its longstanding support for Lynch, announcing the publication of 'A Backward Glance at the City of the Pale' in Boston's *Donahoe's Magazine*.[39] The *Freeman's Journal* carried adverts for her work throughout 1885 and 1886 and published two Irish stories, the longer 'Laogaire: a story of the days of Grattan', which was serialised in the *Weekly Freeman* from March to November 1888, and 'The Last of the O'Moores' in the *Weekly Freeman's Christmas Sketch Book* for 1889.[40] In a letter she wrote to Thomas Dawson in 1888, Lynch not only revealed the value of the editor's backing, but also her disappointment that promised connections to the London literary scene had failed to materialise:

> Mr O'Connor is trying to give me work on his new paper 'The Star'. The worst of radical papers is that they never go in for anything literary or elevated and I am tired of the rights [?] of the people. The *Evening Telegraph* will also take a short London letter from me once a week. E. Dwyer Gray promised to do the world and all for me when I came to London, but he has not kept his word so far.[41]

In fact, Dwyer Gray, proprietor both of the *Freeman's Journal* and the *Dublin Evening Telegraph*, had died following a short illness a few days after Lynch had sent her letter to Dawson.[42]

The *Freeman's* value as a publishing outlet for Lynch extended to other women from her Ladies' Land League network. In June 1883, the *Weekly Freeman* had established another publication: the *Irish Fireside*. It was the brainchild of Caroline Gray, Edmund Dwyer Gray's wife, who 'sought to foster native talent in the "Irish Fireside" and to attract readers from all sections of society, irrespective of class, gender, age and location'.[43] It began as a weekly literary magazine, 'circulated as a supplement to the *Weekly Freeman*, and which later developed into the Irish Fireside Club'.[44] The magazine tends to be referenced most in relation to W.B. Yeats, who published 'his first surviving piece of prose' there.[45] However, the paper is equally important for its provision of literary and editorial opportunities for former members of the Ladies' Land League, including Jennie Wyse Power, Katharine Tynan, Rose Kavanagh and Lynch herself.[46] Rose Kavanagh was appointed editor of the *Irish Fireside* in 1887 and she established, under the pseudonym 'Uncle Remus', what became an immensely popular column – the 'Irish Fireside Club for boys and girls'. Like many members of the group, she was 'an avid supporter of equality for women', and her column enabled her to include and encourage contributions from children of both sexes.[47] Indeed, her relationship with the *Freeman's Journal* also proved enduring, despite Dwyer Gray's early death.

Lynch, like numerous other aspiring writers of the period, also contributed to the *Irish Monthly*. Founded in 1873 by Father Matthew Russell SJ, this literary magazine had, as Murphy outlines, a distinctly Catholic focus, the first issue describing itself as an 'Irish monthly magazine of religious literature'.[48] This publication was significant for its practice of promoting women writers (Katharine Tynan, Rose Kavanagh and Rosa Mulholland, for example, appeared regularly in its pages).[49] It also attracted contributors who later became synonymous with Yeats' Irish Literary Revival movement, as 'Yeats encouraged his peers to publish there, and gave the *Monthly* cultural status during the Literary Revival'.[50] Lynch's final piece was published in the same number as Yeats' first contributions to the paper, two poems, 'Remembrance' and 'The Stolen Child'. Her first contribution, 'Nature's Constancy in Variety', a celebration of Irish landscape, was published in August 1883, followed by 'The Ursulines of Tenos' and 'November in a Greek Island', in May and July 1886.[51] This was a fairly fleeting engagement with such an important literary outlet, a fact Lynch attributed to her failure to toe the correct theological line. In February 1886 she wrote, wryly, to Thomas Dawson: 'You need not watch <u>The Irish Monthly</u>. As Father Russell is convinced that I am bent on demoralising a credulous public he fights shy now of associating my name with his religious newspaper.'[52] Whether it was Lynch's habit of spending Sundays 'wandering about on foot' or on muleback, freely expressing herself to her guide about the state of the roads, or purchasing antiquities from a Greek priest on a Sunday that caused offence, there is no record of any later publications by Lynch in this magazine.[53] As we know, this was not the first example of her rejecting the protocols of the Irish newspaper and periodical press.[54] Her loss of an outlet in the *Irish Monthly* was probably more damaging than her spat with *United Ireland* as far as earning a living by writing was concerned, but it is also indicative of the independence and difference which she continued to assert. Low's picture of Lynch as an unwelcome irritant in certain circles might have been exaggerated, but it was not entirely untrue.

The points of connection between Yeats' early ventures in the Irish periodical press and those of Lynch illuminate the centrality of nationalist (and, unexpectedly, religious) publications, and the interpenetration of the literary and political spheres. They also illustrate the necessity of playing the field in order to find the right outlet, and of establishing a viable voice in a contained yet relatively diverse marketplace. But the apparent consonance between the positions of these two very different writers is explained partly by the presence of Katharine Tynan, who constituted one of Lynch's most important contacts from the Ladies' Land League.[55] Lynch's studies in London, and her role as London secretary of the organisation, would have given her a preliminary entrée into the literary and cultural scene in the city. Katharine Tynan's correspondence during this period offers an insight not only into her own energetic cultivation of important literary London networks, but also her efforts on Lynch's behalf. While Lynch's early association with the *Irish Monthly* was fairly inconsequential, Tynan's played a pivotal role in her career.[56] Most significantly, Russell's friendship with Alice and Wilfred Meynell, who 'existed at the hub of London's literary life', introduced Tynan to Charles Kegan Paul, who published her first volume of poetry, and 'to Henry Cust, editor of the *Pall Mall Gazette*, the newspaper that was to become the most important outlet for her work'.[57] Meynell certainly frequented some of the gatherings Lynch might have attended (Mary Robinson moved near to the Meynells in Kensington in the early 1880s), but there is no evidence that Lynch became intimate with, or benefitted from being in, the Meynells' orbit. Nonetheless, by 1885 Lynch, like Tynan, had also found publishers in London. Her first novel, *Through Troubled Waters*, was brought out by Ward, Lock & Co. in that year. Her second full-length work – 'Defeated', advertised as 'By the Author of *Through Troubled Waters*' – appeared in *Beeton's Christmas Annual* at the end of 1885. Tynan and Lynch both attended the first Literary Ladies' dinner in London, in 1889. Both belonged to the Irish Literary Society in London established in 1892. These and other London activities will be explored in more detail in Chapter 3.

The parallels between them – their Dublin Catholic middle-class back-grounds, convent educations, and their literary and publishing histories during the 1880s – were partially rooted in familial connections and political affiliations.[58] As we have seen, Tynan acknowledged that it was the Lynch-Cantwell household that refined her literary aspirations, noting of the Ladies' Land League: 'I found there my first real touch with literature.'[59] Tynan's emphasis on the literary aspect of this feminist political movement is striking for the wider history of Irish women's writing in the early to mid-1880s, but for our exploration of Lynch and Tynan, one particular question stands out.[60] Given the relationship between nascent revivalist movements and nationalist networks and publications at that point, how significant were the alliances forged during the short life of the Ladies' Land League? Recent scholarship on the founding of the Southwark Junior Irish Literary Club, 'in the autumn of 1881 by members of the Ladies' and Men's Land Leagues based in South London', is starting to illuminate exactly this connection.[61] Francis Fahy, who was credited with founding the club in 1882, wrote to the editor of the *Nation* correcting the facts of an article about the Junior Club, stating that: 'The merit of founding the Junior Irish Literary Club belongs not to me, but to the three patriotic ladies – Miss Thompson, Mrs Rae, and Mrs A.M. Sullivan, who founded it as a protest against the arrest of Mr. Parnell in 1881.'[62] Scholars revisiting histories and differing narratives of the cultural renaissance of this period have argued that the Southwark Irish Literary Club was in fact 'one of the most important early institutions for the development of the Irish cultural revival'.[63] This adds further weight to the argument that the Ladies' Land League should be viewed as a group who shaped the literary, as well as the political and social, history of Ireland.

On this point, Lynch and Tynan were once again on related, yet very different, paths. Lynch's active involvement in the London branch of the league placed her at the heart of the earliest stirrings of the Irish cultural renaissance in that location as well as in Dublin. But her departure from Ireland to various European destinations – including her extended stay in Greece – was also indicative of an increasing sense of alienation from the nationalist culture the Ladies' Land League had initially supported. As we know, Lynch did return to London and Dublin intermittently, but showed a growing affiliation with more cosmopolitan cultures she encountered elsewhere. In contrast, Tynan, whose literary and political aspirations and networks sprang from very similar sources, remained in Dublin, attracting a gathering of writers, poets and artists to her salon in her childhood home, 'Whitehall' at Clondalkin. The history of this salon has become part of the history of W.B. Yeats and his early development as a poet, as well as the history of the Irish Literary Revival, or more specifically the Anglo-Irish Literary Revival.[64] Tynan's centrality to the foundations of this movement was recognised by Yeats himself. He 'acknowledged the importance both to the direction his poetry would take and to Irish literature more generally when in 1908 he publicly credited her with being one of the triumvirate who embarked on a venture to "to reform Irish poetry" and thereby kindled the Irish Literary Revival'.[65] Ironically, in later years after she moved to London, Tynan found herself excluded from that inner circle, an exclusion Lynch ensured for herself much sooner and in dramatic fashion.[66]

In December 1887, Lynch, recently returned to Dublin, accepted an invitation to attend one of these Clondalkin gatherings. Douglas Hyde noted the event in his diary:

> After Chapel I brought Sheehan with me and we walked to Katharine Tynan's. We arrived there about 3.30 and found Yeats and a friend of his, Russell, an art-student, there before us. There were also two sisters, Misses Lynch, from Dun Laoghaire, one of whom spoke intelligently enough. She had lived in the Aegean and in Greece for a long time, and spoke modern Greek. She had written a novel.[67]

It is uncertain whether the other 'Miss Lynch' was Nannie or Virginia, but the identity of the Greek-speaking novelist sister is clear. It is curious to see Lynch, whose life had been so obviously interesting, summed up and dispatched in a couple of bland sentences. Perhaps the sense of patronising faint praise was not lost on her at the time as, in sharp contrast to her reported encounter with Oscar Wilde, she did not let it pass unrebuked. When she provided her version of the event, it was highly satirical and very public, appearing in the *Dublin Evening Telegraph* under the title 'A Dublin Literary Coterie Sketched by a Non-pretentious Observer'.[68] Lynch begins by contrasting 'happy Goths, Vandals, and philistines' with 'the Representatives of the arts and culture' – the aesthetes – before drawing specific attention to some of the characters:

> O'Reilly, an artist, allegorical and mystic, so very earnest and so preternaturally clever as to be enveloped in pretty pathos…Augustus Fitzgibbon, considered by himself and his friends to be a poet of Titanic power, who may accomplish great things, and who may not, but whose boyish head is in the meantime being turned in the most delightful and most deplorable fashion by the circle which is fortunate to revolve round this elsewhere unappreciated star…
>
> This is something like the conversation that will take place if it is Fitzgibbon who has read.
>
> 'D-doesn't F-Fitzgibbon r-read b-beautifully!' O'Reilly will stammer.[69]

Having begun with observations about the general derivativeness of Dublin society and its aesthetic pretensions, Lynch concludes with a comment on good manners:

> It would be well if the men would condescend to bend their ethereal and Titanic minds to the acquirement of small attentions and small courtesies justly expected by ladies from men. Perhaps this is treading on Gothish ground, as it may be Goths only who are expected to be polite and deferential to women – for these young aesthetes, whatever may be their private opinion, would not grace a Parisian salon. A man loses nothing intellectually by studying to be gracious and well-bred; and Irish Corinnes and Sapphos will not be less fascinating for being cordial, sweet-mannered, and unpretentious.[70]

It is easy to read an element of personal indignation in Lynch's critique, perhaps prompted by the sense of being the target of a barely disguised snobbery that may have sprung from assumptions about her class, gender, religious and aesthetic differences. But this was more than simply an opportunity for revenge. It was also an act of literary and feminist self-assertion, where she actively and dangerously defined herself against or away from a literary movement that was to become dominant by the end of the nineteenth century. As Foster has pointed out: 'The talents of the revival supplanted extant Irish novelists as representers of significant Irish feeling and opinion. They did not dam the flow of native fiction; by forming an artistic mainstream themselves, they merely caused it to appear by comparison as a middlebrow tributary.'[71] Humorously siding with 'the Goths' in her piece, Lynch also anticipates this divide opening up between 'high' and 'middlebrow' literature and culture during this period and perhaps betrays a sense of anxiety about her own place as a writer:

> The Goths[72] may be dispatched in a sentence. Harmless young men of the ordinary type; fond of cards and horses, perhaps politically tinctured, indisposed towards speech in the drawingroom or cultured sense, and left mildly amazed and inquiring by the talk going on around them. Gothish young ladies are only less hopelessly unsatisfactory by the charm of youth, of sex, of pretty hair, and pretty frocks, and our unconquerable belief in their greater adaptability and susceptibility to the influence of aestheticism. They always love Strauss, Miss Jessie Fothergill, and Rhoda Broughton, sometimes Miss Braddon, and sorrowful to relate, frequently Ouida. They care little for poetry, but they are deliriously grateful to all

purveyors of light literature, and, being Irish, are full of innocent fun, and high spirits, and unconscious wit.[73]

Her satire gives a glimpse from another perspective of the rapidly shifting world of letters in late nineteenth-century Ireland and a comic slant on an emergent group who were already mythologising themselves. Her satire on the aesthetes and their 'determined self-promotion'[74] is heightened by a nod to an earlier literary model – neoclassical satire and the eighteenth-century salon full of bluestockings and dandies – so Sappho and Alcaeus read poetry to each other and Raphael and Angelica Kauffman compare sketches while Fitzgibbon reads and O'Reilly admires. The satire is significant in the context of Lynch's own *oeuvre*, anticipating aspects of her later short stories and of a particular mode of comic writing that came to the fore in 1890s Irish fiction.[75] As well as making a point about literary and social snobbery, Lynch's sketch observes and critiques gender inequalities already latent in the gathering:

> Things may move a little less harmoniously if the editors and reviewers prove more kindly and more appreciative to Sappho than to Alcaeus, and in defiance of the public, Alcaeus will persist in privately thinking himself the greater poet. But for comfort he will fall back on his friend O'Reilly, or his fervent admirer Mr Horatio Blennerhauset, who coquettes impartially with Prose and the Muses and is remarkable in his set for an unfathomable profundity of mind …[76]

Lynch aimed her comments on gender and poetic popularity with precision: 'Sappho' must be based on Tynan, whose poetry had already proved a great publishing success. She teamed this with an interrogation of the reinventions in progress of an Irish literary and national identity that she also observed during her salon visit. This identity, she suggests, is derivative and inauthentic:

> Aestheticism, read by happy Goths, and Vandals, and philistines as an inconvenient and extravagant pressure of enthusiasm, ventilated by curious adjectives, gowns out of fashion, and generally contorted tastes, may be fainting away in England, like the dying and much-exhausted century. But let us be thankful that such is not its condition on this side of the channel. It may not be exactly flourishing, and, in the present state of trade, it is hard to expect that anything should flourish here or elsewhere.[77]

This was, without doubt, Lynch's skit 'on some of the little literary gods of Dublin at that time which made for her undying enemies'.[78] It is worth pointing out that not everyone who was spoofed took offence. Æ (George Russell), the model for O'Reilly, at first 'found it hard to laugh at the portrait of his own stammering admiration of WBY until "when I thought of what poor Willie Yeats would think, I began to scream with laughter and enjoyed it immensely".[79]

The person most upset by Lynch's mockery was, Low claimed, Tynan herself, despite Lynch's care in demonstrating her friend's artistic parity with Yeats.[80] This claim is complex, as all accounts of broken friendships must be, and is made doubly tricky by the fact that we are missing Lynch's perspective. Our main resources are Tynan's letters to Russell, which fall suspiciously silent in the months immediately after the article. When Lynch was mentioned after this hiatus, Tynan gave the impression that she had risen above the breach. She noted that she had run into Lynch at the *Irish Fireside* office in October 1888, 'and behaved to her with perfect friendliness. She was quite surprised, I think, but life is too short for quarrelling.'[81] Having received a letter from 'H. Lynch' – hardly the warmest form of address – after this meeting, Tynan declared to Russell: 'We are excellent friends again.'[82] But when in 1892 Tynan wrote a piece for the *Speaker* on recent Irish fiction, Lynch's name was not mentioned. This, rather than *The Cabinet of Irish Literature* (1902–03), might have been the exclusion that Lynch had mentioned to Low.[83] There is another particle of evidence in a letter Jane Barlow sent to Tynan in 1894. Barlow mentioned a recent publication by E.M. Lynch, adding that 'I hope that Mrs E.M. Lynch is no connection of your enemy.'[84] This letter does not help us to understand whether Tynan had ever really forgiven Lynch, whether she did not consider her writing to fit the 'Irish' canon she had assembled, or whether it was Lynch who treated Tynan as an 'enemy' in the wake of the 1892 article. Either way, the word 'enemy' echoes around varying accounts of their relationship. It even recurs a decade on, and a little more than a month after Lynch's death, when Tynan sent Russell the obituary piece we cited at the opening of this study:

> The cutting I enclose contains, I think, all I said about poor H.L. in the PMG [*Pall Mall Gazette*]. I knew so little of her for ten years past that I had very little to say. I did not do it till I saw that no-one else was going to do it, for, you know, she didn't like me & I didn't feel it to be exactly my place. However I felt that someone ought to commemorate her ... Her dislike for me had no foundation at all in fact. It was only that her [?] sisters, when she worried them used me as a retaliation, exaggerating my successes & friendships so as to vex her. I never had anything but kind feelings towards her. I remember that once I accidentally missed her name

in a causerie on Irish novelists in *The Speaker* but that was long before I was married & she had done very little work. I doubt if she had published a book & the omission was only because I forgot her. I would have always done anything I possibly could for her. And when I found that she was dead I was really grieved that I had not tried while she yet lived to win her to a reconciliation. Not that there was [ever?] any quarrel but she somehow took it for granted that we were enemies.[85]

This is such an intriguing letter, its regret tinged with self-justification. Perhaps sibling rivalry really did conspire with professional rivalry to make a continuing friendship between these two women impossible? Tynan's letters reveal her generosity and her affection for her female peers, but the tension between supportiveness and competition is in evidence, too. This is exemplified by a comment Tynan made on learning that Rose Kavanagh had been appointed editor of the *Irish Fireside*: 'And of course she needs it far more than I do. But I need it too.'[86]

In 1895, the question of where Lynch figured in the salon cultures of late nineteenth-century Dublin, and how she represented their aesthetic and gender politics, recurred, when she produced a second satirical piece on the subject. Unlike 'A Dublin Coterie', 'My Friend Arcanieva' was published at a safe distance, appearing pseudonymously in the London *Macmillan's Magazine*.[87] The story also seems to combine elements of two Dublin groups: the 'Contemporary Club' established by Charles Oldham, and the 'At Homes' presided over by Ellen O'Leary and her brother John, the latter recently returned from political exile. We know that Lynch attended the O'Learys' as she appears in recollections of these gatherings, some of which confirm that she was not always the desired feminine combination of 'brilliant' and 'pleasing'. In Hester Sigerson Piatt's nostalgic memorial essay on 'John O'Leary as a Guide of Youth', she describes Hannah Lynch as 'a more sombre personality' than Katharine Tynan, with a 'wit … of a more mordant kind. But that she too could be more genial and kindly to a very young unknown girl the writer knows from experience.'[88] In another portrait of John O'Leary and his circle, D.J. O'Donohue describes Lynch as 'one of the most brilliant of the women writers of the time' but 'who seems to have got on the nerves of the group. She certainly possessed a vein of sarcasm and not a little wit, and she was not disinclined to indulge them.'[89] Such was the established reputation of her 'powers of satire' that Ellen O'Leary's reaction, following her first encounter with Lynch, was one of disappointment:

Hannah Lynch was so wonderfully quiet, so little aggressive, and so disappointing in looks that I found her neither interesting, exciting nor aggravating. She would be handsome, or, at least, have the remains of beauty only for her eyes – they have no feeling in them. The last sentiment, I suppose, she'd wish to excite is pity, yet that is exactly what I felt towards her ... However, she seems one who is never occupied with herself, and, perhaps, found some pleasure in listening and looking around her.[90]

Ellen O'Leary's 'pity' might have been tempered had she suspected that Lynch was not quiet and watchful because she was a diminished figure 'never occupied with herself', but because she was a writer mentally gathering material for a tale.

'My Friend Arcanieva' is narrated by a character named 'Paddy' who is liked but patronised by other members of his literary club, 'The Athenaeum'. Particularly condescending is a character named Oldberry, probably based on Charles Oldham. The story also features a Russian imposter, Arcanieva, and Paddy's sister Bridget. The model for Arcanieva was one Ronan Lippmann, who infiltrated Dublin literary society (London and Boston literary society, too) including the Contemporary Club.[91] Arcanieva's fraudulence operates on several levels in the story, highlighting the inauthenticity of this particular coterie culture, its snobbery and parochialism: 'We in Dublin are insufficiently accustomed to foreign influences, and hence our awe of the foreigner ... We grew proud and ostentatious, and spoke with frantic volubility of Tolstoi and Lermontoff and Ivan Tourgenieff.'[92]

Lynch also employs Arcanieva's deceptions to expose the attitudes to women that circulated even in such supposedly enlightened company. The homosocial Athenaeum Club, where matters of cultural and national identity provide a major topic for discussion, is depicted as another encounter with misogyny, especially through the way in which Bridget features in the story. It is Bridget, of course, who is the ultimate victim, not only of Arcanieva's fraud, but of the intellectual pretensions and vanity of the club members, including her brother. Paddy describes Bridget as his 'second self', whose literary opinions and insights he values highly, and Oldberry asserts that 'we all worship the ground she treads on', but she is not part of the club.[93] However, it is she who speaks up to correct Arcanieva's pronouncements on the childlike quality of the Irish: 'Yet Bridget found voice to make a spirited protest for the honour of her beloved land.'[94] In fact, Bridget's passionate defence echoes portrayals of Ellen O'Leary: 'Faithful and true to her lofty ideals of religion and patriotism, she was one who would have died cheerful for either.'[95] To an extent she, Bridget, and Lynch occupy a similar place – on the margins of the 'Club', representing the relegation of women's role in the political and cultural transformations of Irish identity to another footnote in the history of the Irish Literary Revival.[96]

In the light of Lynch's collision course with these coteries established in the mid-1880s, it is tempting to situate her in Foster's category of writers who wrote, from the 1880s onward, '*in conscious reaction against*' the Irish Literary Revival.[97] As scholars working in this field more recently remind us, however, terms and definitions relating to cultural shifts during this period are complex and require revisiting. In her study of Alice Milligan, for example, Catherine Morris demonstrates how 'Milligan represented an alternative to the dominant currents that fed and defined the Irish Renaissance', thus bringing back to the surface one of the many 'artists, activists, and initiatives [buried] beneath the sediment of accreted myths'.[98] Lynch's focus in both her satires is on the earliest manifestations of that myth-making, one of these being the deification of woman at the cost of her reality.[99] Lynch's experience of a female-centred political movement, and, arguably, a female-driven cultural revival, at least at its earliest stages through literary and editorial contributions to nationalist periodicals in Ireland and the formation of the Southwark Irish Children's Club in London, would have led her to expect a different direction for the reinvention of Irish culture and identity. That direction is the one she applauds Lawless and Barlow for taking in her 1896 Paris lecture on 'The Irish Peasant: fact and fiction', suggesting that they represent the best of the 'young school of Irish Celts'. They are worth reading, according to Lynch, for their introduction to 'a world made up of quaint prejudices, beliefs, recollections, fears, and traditions – the legendary elemental world of the primitive Celt, peopled with fragments of dreams, where ghosts are one of the rooted facts of existence …', a feature that aligns their work, ironically, with the aesthetic interests of Yeats' Irish Literary Revivalists, who nonetheless found them wanting.[100]

Lynch's own literary alignments differed from those of Lawless and Barlow. A closer examination of her 1880s fiction in its diverse generic contexts and alongside more of her Land League and literary contemporaries follows in the next chapter, demonstrating further her dissenting engagement with the reshaping and reinventing of Irish identity and culture at this juncture.

CHAPTER 2

A 'Vortex of the Genres': Literary connections and intersections

James H. Murphy coined the phrase a 'vortex of the genres' to describe the aesthetic field in which Irish women writers worked in the closing decades of the nineteenth century.[1] This analogy captures the way these authors vigorously stirred up existing forms, hybridising them according to the demands of an equally mobile literary, political and publishing scene. Lynch, from her earliest publications, was close to the heart of this vortex, and her writing expressed its stresses as well as its energy. In order to balance her political, artistic and financial requirements, she produced fiction that drew upon a series of existing templates – romance, Gothic, the detective story, the historical novel. Like many of her compatriots, she cross-pollinated, contributing to emerging forms and adding to a growing body of work written by women, about women.

In this chapter, we extend our preliminary examination of the fiction she published during the 1880s, developing our analysis in the light of new scholarship on one of the most prominent of those emerging forms: Land War fiction.[2] Initially, we will briefly return to the texts mentioned in the previous chapter – 'Defeated' and *The Prince of the Glades* – and touch upon Lynch's later story 'A Girl Revolutionist', with its depiction of daring and disillusionment. But the focus of this section will be Lynch's earlier novella 'Marjory Maurice: a tale of Irish life in recent years', published in the *Shamrock* in 1884–85. 'Marjory Maurice' appeared at a point when the magazine often featured stories of female courage or endurance, possibly due to Rose Kavanagh's editorial influence. As we will see, Lynch developed this genre in a clearly feminist direction, responding with her usual verve to criticisms of the Ladies' Land League, and in the process producing a dramatic and surprising portrait of Dublin life in the early 1880s. We will read these writings in the context of two neglected Land War novels that share a direct connection to Lynch: Fannie Gallaher's *Thy Name*

Is Truth: a social novel (1883), and Mabel Robinson's *The Plan of Campaign: a story of the fortune of war* (1888).[3] As we know, Mabel Robinson and Lynch were friendly, and their writing shares an interest in the role played by journalism in national and gender politics. Fannie Gallaher, daughter of the *Freeman's* editor John Gallaher, was brought up in a similar sphere to Lynch but with a different view on the project of the Land Leagues and in particular the membership of the Ladies' Land League. So different was the latter, we argue that 'Marjory Maurice' contains moments of direct reproof to *Thy Name Is Truth* and the satirical clichés it contained.

Next we turn our attention to Lynch's first published book, *Through Troubled Waters*, and read it alongside George Moore's *A Drama in Muslin* (1886), not as Land War fiction (although Moore's novel does belong to this genre) but as further examples of that 'vortex' of genres, specifically in relation to their engagements with naturalism, realism and the themes of marriage and female development. While there is no evidence yet of Lynch and Moore having met, they shared a personal and literary network as well as overlapping themes and concerns in these west-of-Ireland-set works. Lynch's novel, read in dialogue with Moore's, exposes features of a distinctive mode of *fin-de-siècle* Irish realism, as well as 'a *form* of what we might call Irish aestheticism'.[4] We argue that this distinctive realist aesthetic was already at odds with the views of the Dublin literary coteries Lynch went on to satirise, and supplies further evidence of the female-dominated revivalist aesthetic Lynch was still promoting in her 1896 Paris lecture.

Irish Land War novels of the 1880s and 1890s are summed up by Margaret Kelleher thus:

> Like many other novels of the period, they employ standard plots from sentimental fiction – social and economic obstacles to lovers' relationships, love triangles, etc. – but in their depiction of contemporary politics they also take on a substantial burden of representation involving political tensions, contemporary class antagonisms and debates regarding gender roles.[5]

This hybrid of romance and politics often included the murder of a landlord, a court case, resolution – sometimes in the form of marriage – and heroines verging on New Womanhood. Lynch's fiction adds to this mix disillusionment with the patriarchal attitudes embedded in Victorian ideologies generally, and in the nationalism of the period more specifically. Her critical portrayal of the ways in which ideals of masculinity and the heroic shaped Irish nationalist identity is sharpened by the portrayal of proto-feminist heroines.

If Anna Parnell used one of the Lynch sisters as an illustration of the tangled roots of sexual and radical politics in *The Tale of a Great Sham*, Lynch returned the gesture in 'Marjory Maurice' as well as in *The Prince of the Glades*.[6] Georgina Templeton, 'a very slender young lady, in black, writing' who presides over the Ladies' Land League office in 'Marjory Maurice' and who is described later in the narrative as 'Pretty and fragile-looking, with a proud, cold little face so unlike that of an agitator's', is clearly modelled on Anna Parnell.[7] *The Prince of the Glades* was dedicated to Anna Parnell and had grown out of a short story Lynch published in the 1889 *Weekly Freeman's Xmas Sketchbook*, 'The Last of the O'Moores'. Set in the period of the 1867 Fenian Rising, the story in brief, and the novel in three volumes, trace the fortunes of Godfrey O'Moore. A young man of ancient and noble Irish lineage, Godfrey is abandoned on an estate in Ireland while his family pursue leisure and pleasure in Paris. Godfrey has Fenian sympathies and the novel opens with an illicit meeting of rebels and news that a formidable foe of the O'Moores has returned to his family seat with his daughter, Camilla Knoys. The stage is set for a convoluted plot of romance, rebellion and fratricide through which conventions of masculine and feminine behaviour and the nature of heroism are scrutinised. For example, Camilla, the rebellious heroine, is fully prepared to fall in love with Hugh O'Neill, the leader of the rebellion – until they actually meet:

> Bear in mind that the lady's soul had nourished itself, rather as a stimulant than wholesome food, exclusively for the past month on the thought of O'Neill; that all her life she had yearned avidly for personal knowledge of a truly heroic man; that her ears had drunk in eagerly a pleasurable sort of gossip of the one in question, and that where others would be disposed to rejoice at the sight of an eagle, her hypercritical and fastidious nature would only meet inquiringly an archangel in the flesh. This to explain her acute disappointment.[8]

Hugh O'Neill has misconceptions of his own. In a Meredithian manoeuvre, Lynch gives him a dash of masculine egoism:

> He believed in her patriotism but he had enough of the vanity of his sex to share the masculine faith that woman's patriotism generally starts from the particular man – the man in this case upon strong evidence being Mr. Hugh O'Neill.[9]

The novel did not depict O'Neill as cowardly and chauvinistic, nor did it portray Camilla as deluded in her commitment to the cause. But it did reflect on some of the male – and perhaps the female – attitudes that had coloured the experiences of the 'sweet girl graduates' of the Ladies' Land League. As Tina O'Toole has pointed out, Lynch pushed back against gendered discourse in her narration as well, describing her heroine 'in masculinised terms'.[10] Such interrogation of gendered notions of the heroic was equally evident in her fiction about the Land Wars of the early 1880s. 'Defeated' is narrated by the initially priggish lawyer Richard Sheridan.[11] The heroine Minna Davis, with whom Sheridan falls in love, is far from masculine, but does not embody conventional femininity either:

> Presently I was conscious of being introduced to a girl in every respect different from my previous ideal. I had always admired the fragile, helpless build, fair colouring, and sweet appealing eyes. Now, no indication of timidity or appeal was apparent in Miss Davis. She was amazingly tall – I should say nearly five feet eleven – slight, with charmingly supple movements, and a figure that curved down to a girlish waist ... Another stone from the arch of my feminine ideal removed![12]

The cigarette-smoking Lady Riversdale delivers yet another blow to Sheridan's 'feminine ideal', observing that if he is like most Irishmen he will 'bore Minna to death in a month with your theory on her duties, and tirades in the I-object-to-my-wife style'.[13] Sheridan is also forced to confront challenges to his masculinity, provided by other men. The plot pits him against the swarthy, more manly and attractive Laurence Garnet, as well as an English viscount whose courtly and polite behaviour is equally threatening:

> From the slight glimpses I had had of my latest rival, I saw that he was as unlike Garnet as possible, and as strikingly unlike me. Handsome after the conventional type – blonde hair and pale bronze face; the eyes, as I learned later, were deep clear grey; physique splendid; manners finished.[14]

It could also be argued that in these fictions of Fenian rebellion or the Land Wars, Lynch confronts not only ideals of masculine behaviour typical of the late Victorian period, but the Parnell myth itself. 'The "Irish fetishism" of their "Chief"', as Valente describes it, is evident in contemporary discourses, memoirs and subsequent biographies.[15] Romantic Parnellite figures are a feature of several nationalist and more specifically Land War novels of the 1880s and early 1890s, so Lynch's often unheroic male characters might be read as a deliberate inversion of the convention and a direct challenge to the shabby treatment of the women of the Ladies' Land League.[16]

Lynch's invocation of romance – a genre she both deployed and deflated – remained a signature of her work. But particularly in the case of *The Prince of the Glades*, with its strong connection to Anna Parnell, it is difficult not to hear an echo of the latter's profound disillusionment with the male Land Leaguers in whose hands the fate of the Ladies' Land League had ultimately rested.[17] Sharp criticism from the nationalist press was perhaps to be expected, especially in papers that had been supportive of Lynch's career. Yet other readers also struggled to place her, politically, as we can see from this response to *The Prince of the Glades* by the *Dublin Review*:

> Although the dedication of these volumes to Miss Anna Parnell implies nationalist proclivities on the part of their author, the course of the narrative does not seem appreciably coloured by political sympathy. The story of an abortive conspiracy, in which the peasantry, after careful drilling and discipline, desert their leaders on first contact with the dreaded police, gives no exalted idea of Irish patriotism, and seems rather to point the moral of the hopelessness of such attempts.[18]

The ending of the novel was certainly pessimistic – its central characters either die or go into exile – but not unrealistically so. Fanny Parnell had died suddenly. Anna Parnell had left the political scene, and Nannie had quickly returned to governessing abroad. The *Irish World* reported in late 1882 that 'Miss Lynch, late secretary of the Ladies' Land League has gone to Spain. Dr Kenny and other friends presented her with a watch and chain.'[19] Gibbs records that Hannah Lynch required an 'extended stay' on the Isle of Wight in order to recuperate from her involvement, although it seems that this took place in 1881.[20] But the *Dublin Review*'s sense that Lynch's attack upon an 'exalted idea of Irish patriotism' necessarily implied a lack of 'political sympathy' would seem to be wide of the mark. For her these acts of truth-telling were gestures of fidelity in a wider sense. Lynch's defence of *Through Troubled Waters* in *United Ireland* made sexual politics part of this project: 'Whatever my reviewer's experiences may have been, mine certainly have not been such as to justify a serene belief in the universal prevalence of masculine chivalry and morality, and of womanly gentleness, in Ireland, and it is scarcely fair to expect me to prove my patriotism at the expense of truth.'[21]

The importance of presenting even unpalatable 'truth' clearly resonated with Lynch, not least because there had been so many glaring examples of misrepresentation of the Land Leagues. This was another topic that she addressed head on. In 'Defeated', Lynch temporarily stalled the narrative to allow Sheridan to deliver the following cutting assessment of the British and Irish press, when it is revealed that Lord Riversdale's killer was not politically motivated after all:

> The discovery of Lord Riversdale's murderer and his mistake cannot have delighted the heart of the Tory and Saxon Press, disturbed as the eloquent leader-writers were in the midst of their denunciations of that monster of iniquity – the unfortunate Irish tenant-farmer ...
>
> There never was a country so admirably secure as ours in pens ready to cry out on every possible occasion that the honour of Ireland has been outraged, and that her people should put on the mourning and aspect of deep disgrace. If two noble lords, neither English nor owning an acre of land in the country, were to amuse themselves by shooting each other somewhere between Donegal and Cork, there should surely appear leading articles next morning holding Ireland responsible for the deed.
>
> It was certainly humiliating to have to acknowledge that this last beautiful example of suffering landlordism was only a case of mistaken identity, which had its origins in personal passion. But most of the writers did their work with that grace for which they are remarkable in all emergencies, hinting that if Barney Kellet had not murdered Lord Riversdale, it was simply because opportunity was missing ...[22]

The intersections between gender and nationalism, between the discourses of heroism and those of disillusionment and even demonisation, were even more pertinent to Lynch's writing directly about the Ladies' Land League. Fictional depictions of the group seem to have been rare, although there were a considerable number of satirical cartoons parodying and stereotyping the movement and its members, mainly in the British papers. The fact that it took considerable persistence (and more than a little good luck) to find the pieces we discuss below suggests that further archival work might reveal a different picture.

'A Girl Revolutionist' (1899) offers a striking fictional portrayal of Lynch's early radical politics (not without a touch of self-mockery and humour). Published in the same year as *Autobiography of a Child*, the girl revolutionist Moya O'Connell is, in many ways, a matured 'rebel Angela', the child heroine of Lynch's autobiographical novel. Couched in the relative safety of 'girl's fiction' and published well after the events it portrays, it exploits the specific editorial aims of the *Girl's Realm* to focus on initiative, courage and the heroic.[23] The portrait of Moya O'Connell's revolutionary activism and involvement in the

Ladies' Land League also echoes features of Camilla Knoys, a young woman with a gentry background, rallying the rebels before their apparent enthusiastic support melts away. It was, the narrator recalls, 'an exciting time', and under Moya as acting editor, 'Never was *Erin* so virulent, so venomous, so spirited an organ.'[24] But once again the short text ends with an anticipation of defeat for the idealistic young revolutionary. Moya is saved by Lord Fitzling, who vouches for her and her contraband-filled trunk when she arrives in England (he assumes it is full of no-rent manifestos and pots of paste), but he advises caution: 'It's your first batch of illusions, child. Would you believe it, when I left Cambridge twenty years ago I dreamed of freeing Ireland. We all go through it and recover.'[25]

The sense of defeat and disillusionment that infuses both later texts is a feature of Lynch's earliest attention to the subject in 'Marjory Maurice', too. Written and published in the more immediate aftermath of the dissolution of the Ladies' Land League, this story is fascinating for multiple reasons: the ways in which it tackles issues of misrepresentation and misidentification by characters in the story and by the press, its direct and impassioned defence of the league itself, its unabashed presentation of these figures as modern and yet highly feminine, and its sharp critique of marriage. As we know, this was a serial novella published in an Irish periodical that aimed to be both political and popular, and which shared an interest in female bravery with the *Girl's Realm*. The story bore two key signatures of periodical writing. First, it was topical. As a tale of 'recent years' it described events that were making their passage from an immediate, into a more historical, past. In the later *Autobiography of a Child*, Lynch would mix identifiable historical figures and events with semi-fictional counterparts, and with aspects that appear to be pure fiction. 'Marjory Maurice' walked the same boundary, but far closer to the event, and in a publication whose readers shared that history to a greater extent. The sense of a shared context was central to the second strategy this tale used. That is, the story referred to other contemporary texts readers might have known. The characters in 'Marjory Maurice' are readers themselves – not only of literary works, but of the sort of periodical publications Lynch knew well, whether these were friendly to the Ladies' Land League, hostile to it, or something in between. The general criticism presented in 'Defeated' was, in the case of 'Marjory Maurice', far more specific.

The cast of characters Lynch assembled suggests that not only was this period host to a 'vortex of the genres', it also witnessed a parallel social vortex. The scene is set early: 'Towards the end of February, 1882, a young lieutenant in the navy was sent from Portsmouth to replace a brother officer in the H.M.S. *Adversary*, stationed then at Roiville, a very favourite port of navy men, and a well-known Dublin sea-side resort.'[26] Officers stationed here rapidly become a source of fascination for the local young women, particularly the frivolous and flirtatious socialite Evelyn Handcock. Handsome, intellectual hero Denzil Dalrymple – from an Irish family, proud to have attended Cambridge University (like Parnell and anticipating Lord Fitzling in 'A Girl Revolutionist'), but wary of the Land Leagues – is unimpressed by open flirtation. He is equally sure that the last place he will find a woman of grace and substance is among the members of the Ladies' Land League:

> But bad as meeting with a popular Land Leaguer would be, he remembered that there was something infinitely more objectionable to come in contact with in this eccentric island, and that assuredly was a lady Land Leaguer. If the girls were not vulgar or aggressively political, there was really no reason to assume that they would turn out much worse than the ordinary English woman's-righter, except that there would be a stronger amount of excitement in watching how this hybrid creation of agitation would conduct herself in society.[27]

An encounter between Dalrymple, a fellow officer and members of the Ladies' Land League is initiated by Evelyn. She invites them to five-o'clock tea at Eden Park on the following evening, 'announcing for the occasion the greatest novelty of the times – two Lady Land Leaguers, who had promised to come, old schoolfellows, she explained, and rather nice girls'.[28] The social and political mix, naval officers, Land Leaguers and Ladies' Land Leaguers, journalists and foreign correspondents who frequent the Handcocks', 'noted for having all kinds at their house', is a striking feature of this story.[29] Combinations of these divergent social strata appear in diverse and surely incompatible spaces – not only the home of the Maurice sisters' uncle, but 'At Homes' aboard 'The Adversary', the offices of the Ladies' Land League, and even Kilmainham Gaol.

Through Dalrymple's repeated encounters with the Maurice sisters in these various contexts, Lynch launches her critique of contemporary hostilities towards the 'modern woman', and the especially negative representations of politically engaged women in the press. Like Richard Sheridan in 'Defeated', Dalrymple's conventional expectations of femininity and feminine behaviour are satirised. In a fit of jealousy Evelyn Handcock describes Morna as a 'fast woman' who 'drives home every night at twelve o'clock from some kind of an office – often after that – on a fast car'.[30] Dalrymple is doubly shocked by this information, briefly becoming a comic figure in need of re-education: 'I thought ladies did not drive on cars even with an escort'.[31] Morna's involvement with the Ladies' Land League is portrayed as particularly disturbing to Dalrymple because his impressions of the movement have been supplied by the press. Diane Urquhart has traced how the 'mainstream British press underwent a distinct change, moving from printing verbatim speeches without passing judgement, to front page opinion pieces castigating the female land movement'.[32] Dalrymple's first meeting with Marjory is indicative. Described as 'a furious red-cap' prior to his introduction, he finds his expectations thwarted:

> Dalrymple stared at her in blank astonishment. He had been building hopes on a woman of the Louise Michel type, with vibrating voice and full assertive gaze; a woman merged into a kind of hybrid hysterical manhood, whose chief accomplishment would lie in her power of talking people down.[33]

The mention of 'Louise Michel' and the 'red-cap' drew upon various mocking or threatening images of revolutionary women in circulation. The woman of Dalrymple's imagining may have been triggered by a cartoon in the English comic *Funny Folks*, depicting Anna Parnell 'In Bad Company'.[34] As Urquhart observes, the Louise Michel associations with the figure 'Wearing a Phrygian liberty cap, with a sinister Charles Parnell whispering from the sidelines', are clearly identifiable.[35] Lynch's challenge to this stereotype is also channelled through Marjory's more serious sister Morna, although it is hard to think that Michel – an anarchist feminist who had fought for the Paris Commune – would have been a wholly negative figure for Lynch, even if the Maurice girls are held up as a counter-example.[36] This point is driven home when Dalrymple reflects on his changed perspective:

> I remember somebody telling me over the other side that these Land League women dressed nearly like men or the Nihilists, in double-breasted coats and ulsters and jerry hats, some of them carrying pistols in their pockets, and meeting in a place they called an office where they smoked cigars and cigarettes and drank brandy and water. Then again, I was fully persuaded that they were not ladies, or even women of average intelligence or education, certainly neither womanly nor pleasant. By Jove! What remarkable mistakes we do make.[37]

The source of this image is identified later in the story, when the same negative representation is returned to in Morna Maurice's conversation with her admirer, Herbert Mercer Hamilton. Hamilton is a 'learned Irish scholar' similarly involved in the Land League, who takes its misrepresentation to heart. Morna admonishes him using this example:

> Read the things that are been [*sic*] constantly written of us in the Conservative papers, and by the English Press, too. And yet we only laugh at them. Didn't some English comic paper show us up drinking brandy, smoking cigars with our feet on tables, and pistols sticking out of our jackets. Could anything be worse than that? And yet we didn't worry ourselves.[38]

Another cartoon from *Funny Folks* shows just such a meeting.[39] While the statement in 'Marjory Maurice' suggests that these women were being portrayed as dangerously undisciplined, *Funny Folks* misrepresents them in a different sense, giving the impression that guns and alcohol have replaced tea and cakes as social props, as the women play at being radical.

The conversation that the text held with contemporary periodical media was enabled by the fact that the social circle Marjory and Morna move in is populated by journalists – as Lynch's family circle was in Dublin, and as her later London networks would be, too. Personal indignation erupts in the story through the narrator's direct intervention, bemoaning the fact that the London press had linked the Ladies' Land League directly to the Phoenix Park assassinations:

> We know the Conservative Press rushed frantically at the Land Leaguers – some going the length even of accusing the Ladies' Land League of having participated in the outrage. Delicate and fragile women, with clear consciences and sweet natures – some of them young and light-hearted girls – were represented by the most rabid of their enemies as actual murderers, while others were content with the milder accusation of conspiracy. It is laughable now; it was laughable then to those who were acquainted with the members of that most energetic, earnest-working, and enthusiastic organisation.[40]

We know this happened to Lynch. In 1886, *John Bull* pointed the finger at her (probably mistaking her for Nannie) and other members of the Ladies' Land League, although the mention in 'Marjory Maurice' suggests that a similar rumour was fairly established.[41] Lynch's novella was not only a riposte to satire in the British press but to negative portraits much closer to home. The impassioned intervention by the narrator already cited is worth quoting in full:

I write of the LLL as a mere spectator, as one who, a member, was entirely dissociated from such genuine and hard work as the most insignificant member of it accomplished in Sackville Street. A recent effort in literature has branded them with a cruel injustice – as frivolous, notoriety-hunting, and unwomanly. The formation of that body – though a deeply regrettable fact for its own sake – served, if nothing else, to prove to those who were just enough to recognise it – not many those! – that a woman may work as hard as any man, with a conscientiousness every true woman brings into work once chosen, however distasteful it may be, disinterestedly, since they, unlike their fellow-workers, can never hope to achieve fame by labours of that nature, and keep within her, warm, the sweetest fibres of womanliness and tenderness. I do not think I personally knew a lady Land Leaguer who was not kinder to her sex, more upright, and more earnest – a little excitable, if you will, in some cases, where youth and high, fresh spirits justified excitement – more generous and true-hearted, than most I have met with under more usual circumstances. I like to record the pleasant fact as a tribute to much natural goodness, that has been so falsely coloured.[42]

The 'recent effort in literature' is more than likely Fannie Gallaher's *Thy Name Is Truth: a social novel* published in 1883, a year before Lynch's novella began serialisation.

Fannie Gallaher had immediate insight into the world of contemporary journalism and its engagement with Land War issues – her father was the 'Mr Gallagher [*sic*]' whose conversation with one of the Lynch sisters we learned of in the previous chapter. Margaret Kelleher's account of John Gallaher suggests that it was not only the Ladies' Land League's editorship of *United Ireland* that he found dubious:

Gallaher's father, John Blake Gallaher, was … editor of *The Freeman's Journal* for twenty-six years and the influence of the *Journal* appears not only in the novel's accounts of political speeches and political rallies (many of which read like journalistic treatments) but also in the author's ambivalence towards the methods employed by the land league.[43]

Early on in the narrative, Fannie Gallaher gives a detailed account of the inner workings of a nationalist newspaper, the *Eastern News*, and the plot revolves partially around the activities of the paper and its journalists. Gallaher, like Lynch in 'Marjory Maurice' and 'Defeated', notes with irony the press frenzy triggered by Land War events and issues. She also features characters based on thinly disguised political figures. The novel's depiction of the Ladies' Land League, however, could not be more different from Lynch's. 'Boy' McDonnell, son of the editor of the *Eastern News*, having attended a Ladies' Land League protest, relays in scathing terms the event to his father: 'they talked such consummate twaddle. I never heard anything like them', and the satire is extended through the names of members – Miss Peckant who presides, for example, and Miss Versatile and Miss Looney (treasurers) and Miss Blab and Miss Booley (honorary secretaries).[44] The editor is equally hostile to this women's movement and concedes a column only in his paper 'of their palaver, of their confounded tomfoolery'.[45] The hostility aimed at the movement is particularly interesting given the characterisation of the central female character, Aileen Parthe, who is educated and independent, like many of the heroines of the Land War genre. In a conversation with a literary-minded landlord, Mr Mitford, Aileen, who also has literary aspirations, reveals her position. She declares that she cannot tolerate 'the women's rights women of the day', but concludes:

> We women are only now beginning to receive the attention which, as part of the human race, was always our right. We have been hampered, hedged in, held back, trammelled, so that it really came to be a fact that whenever we happened to develop as much vigour as enabled us to express ourselves strongly on current affairs we were there and then pronounced to be unnatural or masculine. Now, however, the fetters are being taken off, and I am hoping that a clever woman will soon cease to be an abnormity in society.[46]

Aileen's proto-feminist sentiments but lack of sympathy for the Lady Land Leaguers offers a sharper insight into that movement that clearly split opinion not only in relation to nationalist politics, but feminist politics, too.[47]

If 'Marjory Maurice' is a direct response to *Thy Name Is Truth*, it responds on two separate fronts. While making its ardent plea for understanding and insight into the motivations and practices of the Ladies' Land League, it is also a scathing indictment of men, marriage and the romance plot – a plot which *Thy Name Is Truth* utilised, marrying Aileen to 'Boy' O'Donnell. As we know, Lynch seemed to enjoy writing unheroic heroes. But 'Marjory Maurice' features at least two seriously attractive men: the scholarly and committed Herbert Mercer Hamilton and the idealised heroic, literary and musical Dalrymple, both of whom vie for the hand of Morna Maurice. Their desirability is important, throwing Morna's commitment to a single life into sharp relief. Early on in the novella, she makes it plain that her rejection of marriage is based on powerful personal experience: 'I have seen a great deal of how men persecute women in domestic life and crush out their individuality and moral strength.'[48] In conversation with Hamilton Morna makes further disheartening observations to her would-be suitor: 'I have no disbelief in the beauty of perfect marriage. But when I look round I think it must be an ideal only, for I see nothing to justify our hope in it'; 'I don't think marriage broadens the sympathies; it restricts them to the home circle ... I think I could be more useful in the world unmarried'.[49] Instead, she proposes an alternative role model for herself – 'It has always been my ideal to fashion my life on lines as clear as those of Hypatia' – single, scholarly, a modern woman of her time.[50] Morna's ideals chime to some extent with those of Georgiana Templeton, who discusses the pros and cons of men and marriage with Marjory in the offices of the Ladies' Land League: 'I never saw or read of any man worth falling in love with except perhaps Leonardo da Vinci.'[51] It is a striking scene where the public and supposedly masculine sphere of 'the office' now occupied by women is fused with the private sphere of female conversation. Here, interspersed with instructions issued relating to letters about evictions and other league matters, there is a witty repartee about desirable men in literary fiction and history, Georgiana's sharp criticism of Marjory's fiancé, and a declaration of her own preferences: 'I've taken great stock of men in public assemblies, at parties, in churches and at meetings and I find them all a dead level of monotony and coarseness. There is more variety in ten women's faces than in a hundred men's.'[52]

While the narrative tracks Morna's attempts to resist the attractions of both her suitors, her younger and prettier sister Marjory is already engaged to the thoroughly unheroic and mercenary Frank Harston, who abandons her in favour of an heiress. The narrator's intervention at this point asserts literary precedence and the opportunity to satirise male and female behaviour:

> I am obliged to paint my little heroine, with whom I am as much in love as ever was Trollope with his favourite heroines – as sorrowing and suffering for a worthless, effete specimen of manhood, simply because she suffered and sorrowed; but I would infinitely prefer to picture her philosophically indifferent and sensibly engaged to that harmless fellow on sea. But girls are rarely philosophers, especially if they have once had the misfortune to fall in love; then they become absolute idiots, though men, either possibly to look picturesque and complaisant, somewhat falsely assume that privilege.[53]

Marjory's drastic response to Harston's rejection – 'She visited the Exhibition frequently, attended parties and concerts, laughed and chatted most brilliantly, and wished herself at rest in Glasnevin all the time' – swiftly followed by her wasting away and dying, anticipates the ending of many a New Woman novel.[54] Morna's retreat to a convent following the sudden death of her sister, refusing Dalrymple's final proposal, also seems to repeat the limited possibilities for feminist heroines, characteristic of this yet-to-be-labelled genre, or a failure of vision attributed to their authors.[55]

The conclusion to this novella seems hasty and disappointing then, the consequences perhaps of constraints laid on serialised fiction in 'story papers' such as the *Shamrock*. While it refuses the conventional conclusion of romance ending in marriage of both Gallaher's and her own novel, 'Defeated', its narrative of possibilities and potential for these energetic, modern and indeed feminist characters is suddenly cut off with no alternatives. This conclusion does, however, replicate the impact of the sudden dissolution and disbanding of the Ladies' Land League and the disillusionment and displacement that followed. Mabel Robinson in *The Plan of Campaign: a story of the fortune of war* (1888) offers a glimpse of the 'afterlife' of some of these women and an insight into political and social Dublin life of the late 1880s that crosses and intersects with both Gallaher's and Lynch's novels in significant ways.[56]

Mabel Robinson (1858–1954), artist, novelist, journalist, translator and lesser-known sister of the English poet and essayist Mary Robinson, was among the most important and enduring connections Lynch made early in her career.[57] Lynch's link with the sisters lasted until the end of her life, and laid the foundations for one of the most significant networks of her years in Paris. This network and the London and Paris salons of Mary Robinson will be discussed further in the next chapter. The precise contours of Mabel Robinson's friendship with Lynch are uncertain, but it is more than likely that they first met through the Ladies' Land League either in London or Dublin.[58] Robinson, who studied at the Slade School of Art in London, was also concerned with social and political issues, and she was especially engaged with the dramatic events playing out in Ireland.[59] While she was described in an obituary as a 'devoted English supporter of the Parnell movement, a friend of many Irishmen and women', the sources of Robinson's intense interest are not absolutely clear.[60] It may have been sparked by her meeting with George Moore at her home in 1877, or, more likely, through female art-school networks. Anna Parnell (1852–1911) had also been an art student in London (Heatherley School of Art, 1875), and it is possible that it was at her instigation that Robinson had attended 'the heated debates in the House of Commons over the introduction of home rule in Ireland'.[61]

Additionally, her interest may have been heightened by her friendship with Charlotte McCarthy. McCarthy, an artist who may have attended the Slade or Heatherley Art School, was treasurer of the London Ladies' Land League and daughter of the Irish MP Justin McCarthy.[62] Mabel Robinson's fascination with Ireland was certainly fired further in 1882 when she spent time travelling around the country with the McCarthys, attending political meetings, listening to Dillon and Parnell speak, and observing Land War-related events.[63] Robinson was caught up directly with the subversive activities of the Ladies' Land League, acting as one of the conduits of information between London and Dublin.[64] She also prided herself on her likeness to Anna Parnell, noting in a letter dated August 1882 that 'I am so like the fair Anna that when I went down to the cabin on the steam boat Mrs A.M. Sullivan thought I was she. Evidently mind and face have something to do with each other.'[65] These experiences and her active involvement with the league had an impact on her writing career and her non-fiction and fiction. For example, the final chapters on home rule and Land League issues of Robinson's *Irish History for English Readers: from the earliest times to the close of the year 1885* (1886) document the key debates and events of the period.[66] *The Plan of Campaign: a story of the fortune of war* (1888) is similarly detailed in its description of political events, offering eyewitness accounts of political meetings and evictions.[67] Published in the aftermath of the dissolution of the Ladies' Land League and based on the period later in the 1880s when Land Leaguers set in action what was known as the 'Plan of Campaign',[68] the novel is of particular interest for several reasons.[69] It gives posthumous life to some of the key participants in the organisation, illustrating Robinson's own experience and involvement, voicing the sense of disillusionment that many in the organisation felt after its dissolution, and offering another perspective on the political network that was to prove so important for Lynch's literary life.

Like other Land War novels of the period, *The Plan of Campaign* mixes into what can be described as a naturalist narrative, conventions of the *roman à clef*, political commentary, romance and the murder of a hated landlord.[70] In a similar way to Moore's *A Drama in Muslin*, the romance and political plots are run in parallel, and it soon becomes clear that 'plan of campaign' refers not only to tenants and rents but to male and female relations. The novel opens in the political and literary salon of the Anglo-Irish Pamela Molyneux, a former Ladies' Land Leaguer. This character was more than likely modelled on Anna Parnell (although her short-sightedness also suggests Katharine Tynan):[71]

> In her younger days she had played a leading part among the Lady Land Leaguers, speaking on platforms, defying the police at evictions,

constantly hoping for the glorious martyrdom of imprisonment. The worry and excitement, the anxiety and responsibility of that time had worn out her youth; thought did not brace and rejuvenate her as it does persons of great vigour ...

Her enforced retirement from politics – (a retirement resulting only from the ungrateful attitude of the men who, on their restoration to liberty, had dismissed the lady volunteers with scant gratitude or courtesy) – her retirement from politics had left her at a loss for a hobby; nothing excited her after the thrilling game of nationality. The woman's question did not rouse her interest; she believed that the Parliamentary Franchise would do little to lessen a political disability that was the effect of the illiberal, prejudiced and, as she believed, envious mental attitude of men, and when Woman's Suffrage was included in the Conservative programme she abandoned a cause for which she had never felt much enthusiasm.[72]

Robinson's portrait of Pamela Molyneux provides an explanation of the division between the Ladies' Land League and contemporary, mainly British suffrage societies, whose conservatism, including hostility to home rule, alienated them from Irish-nationalist aims.[73] Her outspoken critique of the treatment of the members of the Ladies' Land League echoes the disgust Anna Parnell voiced in The Tale of the Great Sham. It could be argued that the progression of the narrative also registers a kind of defeat in that the lively debate in the novel's opening pages – 'Every lady in the room, except Miss Considine, was repeating her stock of arguments in favour of woman's place in politics, and the men either in support or protest were making no less noise' – is resolved into marriages.[74] Even Miss Molyneux, who 'had a profound contempt for men thinking them a poor, weak, erring set of creatures; endurable in the close relationship and daily intercourse of marriage only to women endowed with great tolerance, malleability, and denseness', succumbs to the romance plot.[75] Her salon, however, does not only facilitate romance, for those who gather there not only diverge in opinions over women but over Ireland, too. So the landlord Robert Gough argues with the Land Leaguer Kinsella, and the enthusiastic nationalists and former Ladies' Land Leaguers, sisters Miss Lynch and Mrs O'Regan, glare disapprovingly at the frivolous and tantalisingly beautiful Miss Featherstone who also attends the political soirée. The press features in this novel, too. Titus Orr, who insists on seeing events from both sides, as the Freeman's reporter, attends political meetings and discourses on rent boycotts, but dines with landlords. The unlikely gathering of such characters in Miss Molyneux's salon as well as at the Orrs' house – which was 'a real Mesopotamia, for the young men, though interested in politics, could not ally themselves with either party, and respectable people of all shades of opinion met on this neutral ground' – serves, like Lynch's 'Marjory Maurice', to offer more nuanced perspectives on the dynamics of Irish society.[76] This includes a sympathetic portrait of the impoverishment suffered by some of the gentry. Miss Dromore notes wistfully: 'I fear ill-educated daughters of distressed Irish landlords are not at a premium just now. To be quite candid; I've tried for one or two places and I haven't got them.'[77]

Aileen Parthe in *Thy Name Is Truth*, Miss Molyneux in *The Plan of Campaign*, Minna Davis and Lady Riversdale in 'Defeated', Camilla Knoys in *The Prince of the Glades*, and the Maurice sisters in 'Marjory Maurice' typify the independent heroines of contemporary Irish Land War fiction.[78] Alice Barton in George Moore's *A Drama in Muslin* is perhaps one of the most successful (and certainly best known) of these figures in the broader canon of this subgenre in that she is able to choose who to marry *and* become a writer after renouncing her privileged status, and Ireland, in order to escape the confines of class, gender and nation. Shared interests in emancipated Irish women are not the only parallels between the work of Lynch and Moore during this decade, however.

In the context of literary connections and intersections foregrounded in this chapter, the most immediate link between Lynch and Moore are Mary and Mabel Robinson, whom Moore met in 1877 in London.[79] The friendship with the sisters was lifelong for Moore as it was for Lynch, and both writers benefitted from the literary connections Mary Robinson's London and Paris salons generated. Lynch's position as a governess at Carantrila Park, not far from Moore's estate, Moore Hall in County Mayo, establishes another intriguing intersection.[80] A convent-educated heroine, the big house and provincial surrounds form the subject and setting of their novels published within a year of each other, *Through Troubled Waters* and *A Drama in Muslin*, serialised and then published in book form in 1886. Further convergences, despite class and gender differences, include a Catholic upbringing, traumatic schooling abroad and engagement in land league issues – as landowner (Moore) and as member of the Ladies' Land League (Lynch). Both writers lived in intermittent, self-imposed exile from Ireland in London and Paris. They shared, to some extent, intersecting literary networks and nationalist and feminist leanings, as well as experiments in New Woman fiction, autobiographical fiction and literary impressionism.[81]

Moore's novel has received considerable critical attention now as both a Land War novel and as an important example of the growing body of the New Woman fiction published during this period. In the context of Moore's own *oeuvre*, the novel marks an important nexus of his own aesthetic interests – Naturalism, realism and an anticipation of a more modernist art form.[82] *Through Troubled Waters*, Lynch's first published novel, is not a Land War novel, although it includes many of the features that became typical of this short-lived genre. As such, it deserves further attention in the context of social and political concerns of that period.[83] It also offers a glimpse into a little-known aspect of Lynch's life – her own, unhappy experiences as a governess – as well as insight into dominant interests, concerns and modus operandi as a novelist. Significantly, this first full-length novel by a financially unsupported young woman was neither ingratiating nor cautious. The stir *Autobiography of a Child* would cause in 1899 seems relatively mild compared with the provocative content of, and the furious response to, this earlier book. *Through Troubled Waters* often presents a bare-knuckle assault on received ideas about male and female roles, the nature of motherhood and marriage, priestly behaviour, and aristocratic dignity. In the guise of a romance, the novel offers an interrogation of social expectations, especially in relation to the lives of women in Ireland. Education for women and distorted relations between daughters and mothers who are either monstrous or pathetically diminished are also features of this novel and Lynch's later fiction. The novel, like Moore's, is plotted around interclass romance (Nora, daughter of a farmer, marries the heir to the big house), albeit a more conventional one than *Drama*, where the heroine leaves the big house and marries beneath her.[84] The striking parallels in their satirical portraits of society in the rural west of Ireland and Lynch's depictions of provincial life and the inadequate education, prospects and lives of Galway girls provide a unique perspective that both intersects with, and differs from, Moore's depictions in his *Drama in Muslin*. In their depictions of the 'muslin martyrs', as Moore describes them, Lynch's novel provides a nuanced account from a different gender and class perspective, offering the insights of an insider which should be read alongside Moore's sympathetic, objective but inevitably distanced depictions of these experiences.[85]

Thus, Lynch offered positive female characters and empowering represent-ations of Irish women in her early fiction. But she was also interested in debunking both the pejorative and the idealised templates in circulation. *Through Troubled Waters* prefigures this interest, interrogating not only idealised images of Irish men and women, but religious practices and, in this novel, the west of Ireland, with a particular focus on Connacht. Lynch's provocative description of Father Nolan as being 'typical of the worst type of Connaught peasant: coarse-featured, heavy-jawed, devoid of a spark of wit or geniality' was not the only aspect of the novel to stir up anger in the nationalist circles with which she was so familiar.[86] In the 'dreadful' review published in *United Ireland*, the reviewer complained that 'this typical priest of the novels is a fitting complement of the libellous pictures in which *Punch* so often endeavoured to convey the same notions of what the average P.P is like in Ireland'.[87] The review concluded:

> If the painful acquaintance it is compelled to make with immorality and crime and brutal coarseness were likely to be helpful in ameliorating actually existing evils or curable defects in our social condition, we could pardon the glass which the author holds up to nature, distorted and unnatural though the reflection which she presents to our censure be.[88]

Causing offence and making enemies was a Lynchian characteristic and one established early on in her career. George Moore, who had already established himself as a controversial writer, provoked a similar stir with the publication of *Drama in Muslin*, offending ascendency family and friends as well as a broader readership with his critical depictions of Irish life. 'As soon as the novel began its serialisation in January 1886, Moore allowed himself to be drawn aside into a dispute with one signing himself "An Amazed Parent" of a child at the Convent of the Holy Child, the scene of the opening chapter of the novel.'[89] Its similarly satirical portrait of the parish priest Father Shannon, 'a large fat man, whose new, thick-soled boots creaked terribly as he ascended the steps of the altar', generated ire akin to Lynch's portrait of Father Nolan in *Through Troubled Waters*.[90]

No social class is left unscathed in either of these novels. For example, the cultured and sensitive hero of *Through Troubled Waters* is the disinherited heir and illegitimate son of a decadent earl and a mother who, according to rumour, had poisoned her daughters. The nouveau-riche Dillons, family of the heroine Norah Dillon, did not fare much better than the corrupt aristocratic parents of Huntly St Ledger, as Lynch unleashed some gleeful sarcasm:

> The Dillons lived five miles beyond one of the Galway towns, in a square, ugly house, situated in a centre of desolate fields, the monotony of which was occasionally broken by stone walls for hedges, and by magnificent specimens of bovine excellence. The house was as remarkable for its disagreeable aspect as the family was for its exceeding unattractiveness.[91]

The Dillons (whose ancestors had been 'lucky in commerce') share many of the same characteristics as Moore's newly gentrified family the Goulds, who also inhabit one of those 'box-like mansions' and whose family money derives from ventures in India.[92] The pedigree is enough in provincial Galway where 'three generations of landlordism are considered sufficient repentance of shopkeeping in Gort, not to speak of Calcutta', and in Lynch's equally biting satire, the Dillons have cultivated 'ultra-aristocratic views and aspirations'.[93] Wat Clarke, whose 'cunning and servility' are 'too characteristic of the wretchedly-used peasant' and who has a 'reputation of being mysteriously leagued with the fairies', does not have a counterpart in Moore's novel.[94] But his daughter Kitty, 'with that singularly beautiful complexion which belongs to the Western type', like Moore's more upper-class May Gould, falls victim to seduction and abandonment.[95]

The depiction of the ignorant and clumsy parish priest in *Through Troubled Waters* – who denounces from the altar the innocent Kitty Clarke as corrupted by St Ledger – would have been as startling to Irish readers as Moore's ungainly Father Shannon, who mumbles Latin Mass for a congregation described as more animal than human.[96] Moore's naturalistic depiction of the congregation – 'The peasants came, coughing and grunting with monotonous, animal-like voices; and the sour odour of cabin-smoke frieze arose ... and whiffs of unclean leather, mingled with a smell of a sick child' – is anticipated by Lynch's equally detailed and unsparing attention to the interior of the chapel: 'Those who know much about country congregations in poor localities will recognize the odour.'[97] Such observations in Lynch's novel doubtless contributed to the anger of the antagonistic reviewer in *United Ireland* who suggested that, 'from the key in which it is pitched ... it will have a large sale at least in England'.[98] Lynch's retort in her letter to the editor, William O'Brien, is significant: 'The story was not written for an English market as the critic must well know. He cannot be ignorant that I first wrote it for an Irish paper, through which it would more easily reach those so greatly in need of correction.'[99] If Lynch's tale of 'bucolic indignation and morality in the west of Ireland' was meant as a social corrective, it anticipates James Joyce's defence of *Dubliners* as 'a moral history' and 'a nicely polished looking glass'.[100] The opening pages also register a bitter note on the impossible position of the governess. Lynch's outburst vividly illustrates the notoriously uncomfortable condition of the governess during the Victorian period, apparently unchanged nearly forty years after the publication of *Jane Eyre* and *Agnes Grey*.[101] The behaviour of the Dillon family towards their governess is indicative of this:

> Even Lizzie could toss her little nose up at the unfortunate governess who had lately left, owing to Charlie's courteous language when he addressed

her as a 'd-- fool' … This happy individual had also heard herself described by Lizzie as 'one of mamma's servants, and a bothersome servant too'.

Such pleasant trifles as these furnish us with an explanation of the brief stay of finished young ladies from remote parts, prepared to instruct the youthful mind in every needful department. Original as it may be to inspect semi-barbarians from a close point of view, the unoriginal and simple-minded are apt to find the process slightly inconvenient and unpleasant in a short time; even the magnificent remuneration of twenty pounds a year failed to open an avenue of endurance for the governess after the first three months.[102]

It also anticipates her later and equally angry reference to the plight of the governess in *Autobiography of a Child* where the narrator laments the conditions for Irish daughters in a country that is 'the very wretchedest land on earth for woman'.[103] The prospects for these women are grim, bred only to become an 'army of inefficient Irish governesses and starving illiterate Irish teachers cast upon the Continent'.[104]

While *Through Troubled Waters* is not a classic governess novel, Lynch provides a glimpse into the unequal and awkward conditions of that life before focusing on the plight of Irish women through her sharp observations of the Dillon family. She examines, in particular, mother–daughter relations and the lack of education for women. The maternal figures in this novel, Nora's cowed and helpless mother Mrs Dillon and her 'rich and unlovable grandmother' Mrs Blake, provide thoroughly negative models of female relations, motherhood and, to some extent, marriage that recur throughout her later fiction.[105] Nora is trapped by her tyrannical grandmother, who 'had promised to endow Nora with a fortune of ten thousand pounds on the condition that the girl lived with her', the fortune being the bait, as Nora observes, 'which was supposed to lure her successfully into the matrimonial market!'[106] Moore's Mrs Barton in *Drama in Muslin*, who goes into 'the matrimonial market armed to the teeth', and Lynch's Mrs Blake are clearly cut from the same cloth, sharing their domineering and cruel behaviour with other mothers in late nineteenth-century Irish, especially Anglo-Irish, fiction.[107] According to Vera Kreilkamp, during this period 'ruthless gentry chatelaines begin to mimic the roles abdicated by defeated and increasingly impotent landlords. Without an adequate social and political arena for their ambitions, these women prey not on a dwindling tenant or servant class, but on their own children.'[108]

Nora's options are further limited, as the narrator outlines in the novel:

What did she see before her but to live in this sort of existence, dull, lonely, and uneventful, unless she married? And that seemed a worse alternative; for her closest acquaintance with married life for a woman was her mother's, and she shuddered when she pictured herself like her sad little mother, tied for life to a man whose love expended itself in brutal oaths and curses, who spent his days looking after his land and cattle, and returned at night to yawn and snore over his paper, and retired to rest without one tender word, one loving glance or caress; all vitality lost in the worries and cares of a large family; reaping no joy or peace or comfort from maternity; and helpless in the chaos of her noisy children, with their ceaseless quarrels torturing her tired head, and brief-staying governesses and tutors, only able to moan piteously to her grown daughters, 'Oh, never marry! never marry! It is a terrible burden.'[109]

Nora's limitations also include an inadequate education – a subject dear to emerging New Woman fiction of the period and central to both Moore's and Lynch's novels.[110] *Through Troubled Waters* is prefaced with a dedication to George Meredith 'as a slight token of a very sincere admiration', and the story traces, among a multitude of complex strands, the education of the heroine, Nora Dillon, who 'cared nothing about reading' and whose convent training has left her ignorant and foolishly innocent.[111] Likewise, *A Drama in Muslin* opens with a depiction of the convent of the Holy Child, where the Galway girls in white dresses are shown to be ill-prepared for their return to Ireland and the intertwined battlefields of political conflict and the marriage market. Nora's education is shown to begin when she meets Huntly St Leger, the newly returned son and disinherited heir to the disputed house and estate, Cardune. He has lived in France and, like Lynch, is more worldly than the inhabitants of the small County Galway village, their lack of culture and sophistication made evident through the embarrassed reaction of the Dillon siblings to St Leger's nude artwork he proudly shows them. Nora realises that 'had they been cultured and refined, they could have enjoyed openly the beauty of that torso without finding its nudity obtrusive'.[112] As an antidote to her inadequate upbringing, St Leger starts Nora off on a reading list of Meredith, Shelley, George Eliot, Charles Dickens and Bret Harte. The list for self-improvement through reading, a list that particularly helps to shape Nora's knowledge about the place of women in society, is characteristic of the 'female *Bildungsroman*' novel that, in 1894, following Sarah Grand's coining of the term, became known as New Woman fiction. Nora, whose initial reading skills and instincts towards

New Womanhood are revealed to be limited, is particularly alarmed by the heroine of Meredith's *Tragic Comedians*:

> How could any girl who respected herself have strong opinions on politics and side with democracy, willing to throw over caste and order to marry a man of the people who was held in abhorrence by all distinguished circles? It was inconceivable and distressing. And a girl, brought up in the restraint and instinctive timidity of womanhood, to give expression to such a bold terrible thought! 'Barriers are made for those who cannot fly'. Surely that meant something wrong and unwomanly![113]

Nora's reservations were not Lynch's, who prescribed reading Meredith's portraits of women as 'a healthy antidote against the nauseous and abominable travesties of themselves and their species circulated by the libraries' in her literary study of his work.[114] By exposing to gentle satire Nora's limitations and Meredith's virtues as a portraitist of 'young militant womanhood', Lynch achieves a double effect: a critique of the cultivation of ignorance and innocence in young Irish women and a model for new kinds of womanhood.[115]

The list of texts included for Nora's education, calculated to disturb and influence, anticipates the one recorded in her last novel, *Autobiography of a Child*, as an aspect of the shaping of the protagonist Angela, and her rebel identity. It also forms a significant parallel with the reading undertaken by Alice Barton in *A Drama in Muslin*. Alice, whose interest in literature is more advanced than Nora's, is also encouraged to read more selectively and to start writing by a male mentor, John Harding. Harding, who writes novels that 'are not supposed to be fit reading for young ladies', encourages Alice to embark on a literary career which, as he predicts, will take her to London.[116] Alice's departure with her husband from Ireland for London has been interpreted in various ways, mirroring Moore's frequent exiles from his own class and country and his frustrations with the Irish situation.

Through Troubled Waters ends with a significant departure, too. The happy couple, Nora Dillon and Huntley St Leger, are reunited after various travails, not in Connacht but in Killiney. This landscape is celebrated and dwelt on at some length: 'Killiney at all hours, in all seasons, is indescribably lovely ... Foam-fringed blue waves rush to kiss the grey and golden sands, over which rise indented and irregular hillsides, the lovelier far for their very irregularity, weird in the oneness of their effect, with dark woody masses, wide meadows, and scattered seats'.[117] Lynch's obvious preference for this Dublin landscape in contrast with the west of Ireland was a shared one with Katharine Tynan and anticipates one of several disconnections between her and the members of the emergent Literary Revival she was to meet at Tynan's salon in December 1887.[118] Her refusal to mystify or mythologise the west or indeed its inhabitants aligns her much more closely not only with Moore's naturalist aesthetic but with several contemporary Irish women writers, too.[119] Further, in her recent analysis of a dialogic between realism and aestheticism in selected fiction by Lynch's contemporaries Emily Lawless, Somerville and Ross and Katherine Cecil Thurston, Alison Harvey identifies how their writing works 'In contradistinction to th[e] revivalist aesthetic and its dependence on nation– woman allegories, Irish legends, and (typically male) national heroes'.[120] Instead, their works suggest how

> ... the realist novel is the literary genre that has the greatest power to rethink sex, class, and national identity in Ireland. Their prose fictions of modern Irish life center on the lived realities of Irish women and interrogate both colonial feminizations of the nation and the ways in which nationalist politics and discourses reduce peasants to 'authentic Celts' and women to what Eavan Boland calls 'fictive queens and national sibyls'.[121]

Lynch's admiration for Lawless' treatment of the plight of women in Irish society, articulated in her 1896 Paris lecture on the 'Irish Peasant', reinforced her position against this mythologising of women and against the emergent aesthetics of the Yeats-directed Literary Revival. In this defining lecture, outlined already in our Introduction, Lynch dwells the most on their representations of the reality of peasant women's lives in Ireland, although her analysis, particularly of *Grania*, suggests the plight she outlines extends across classes:

> This cold ideal of life probably conduces to the loveless martyrdom of Irish women. Certain it is that their role is a dull and inferior one compared with that women play elsewhere. They are held as cheap, are as little considered, and dwell as persistently in the shadow of insignificance as in Eastern lands where chastity is not understood. An Irish wife is the sorriest object under the heavens ...
>
> Women's business on earth is just to suffer. This figure of Honor, consumptive, ascetic, beautified in the refining process of pain and by the ennobling influence of an unselfish devotion, has the charm, the clear-cut, pallid profile of some saint of an Italian master. Her patience is not inarticulate or animal, but a chosen endurance that washes human nature of all stain and lifts it above our common life.[122]

Significantly, Lynch's commentary on *Grania* in this lecture draws attention to the aesthetics of the narrative through an impressionistic and painterly evocation of the way in which the realism of the novel, its focus on the hardship of women's lives, its capture of the heroine's essence, is achieved: 'that fascinating tale of Galway life, a picture in grey or purple tones, with just a splash of scarlet in the flame-like inarticulate soul of Grania'.[123] Lynch's appreciation of the aesthetics and subject of the works of Barlow and particularly Lawless clearly resonates with her first novel, set on the west coast of Ireland and exploring similar themes. So rather than writing against the nascent cultural revival during the 1880s and early 1890s, which also saw the earliest formations of the Irish Literary Revival, Lynch was writing for a different kind of renaissance, one that was woman-centred and required an awakening to certain realities in Ireland before cultural transformation could take place. Such a position aligns her with Lawless and Barlow as well as with writers like Joyce and Moore, who, like Lynch, were ambivalent about the direction taken by those who came to dominate the revival narrative, but whose writing contributed to and embodied that revival.[124]

By the end of the 1880s, matching Lynch's own peripatetic lifestyle, her often Irish and almost always feminist heroines are figured as travellers and wanderers not in Ireland but across Europe. Apart from her 1891 tribute to Anna Parnell in *The Prince of the Glades*, most of Lynch's novels and short fiction are marked by a cosmopolitan and transnational turn that reflected her own experiences of education, travel and residence outside Ireland. Instead, London and Paris, with their many women-centred literary salons and growing opportunities for publishing, offered more to a writer like Lynch. This allowed her to continue examining, from a Europeanised perspective, the shaping of gender and national identity both generally and more specifically in relation to *fin-de-siècle* Ireland.

CHAPTER 3

'A Real Mesopotamia': London coteries and Paris letters

This chapter will address Lynch's engagements with, and responses to, the groups with which she associated from the mid-1880s to the 1890s and onwards in London and in Paris. As we will show, the patterns established within these networks mirrored those of her familial 'salon', and of the co-operative *esprit de corps* of the Ladies' Land League. Additionally, they provided the sociable, semi-professional atmosphere so vital for women making their way as independent agents in a male-dominated world. These circles were overlapping and interconnected, with figures such as Mabel Robinson running as lines of continuity from her early years in Dublin right through to her final months in Paris. Tracing the path of Lynch's career amplifies our understanding of the transnational fabric of Irish women's writing at this point in terms of its content and its aesthetic concerns, but also the social contexts through which it was produced and circulated. It illuminates the enduring influence of Lynch's early political contacts, despite her own later critiques of nationalism.

These networks of continuity and of interconnection stretched across nations and decades, and were as dynamic as they were resilient. Their female members, who were increasingly conspicuous in the periodical press, responded to events and addressed specific discourses as they emerged. The visibility of women as writers frequently played a dual role, as their participation in cultural production became part of the wider issues under discussion. High-profile female journalists such as Emily Crawford not only reported on international current affairs, but acted as advocates for women writers generally, for women in journalism, and sometimes for journalism itself. In 1889, the Women's Suffrage Bill generated intense debate, between 1893 and 1894 the label 'New Woman' crystallised existing discussion on modern female identity, and the Wilde trial of 1895 generated a backlash against so-called 'Decadent' authors.[1]

The first phase of the Dreyfus Affair took place in Paris during the same period, erupting more fully from 1897. In the coming years, *'l'affaire'* catalysed extensive and violent public debates on questions of national and religious identity in France, and was widely discussed in Britain and in Ireland. All these events took place against the backdrop of frustrated attempts to achieve home rule, and of ongoing colonial competition between Britain and France.

Crawford was nearly twenty years older than Lynch, but the parallels that exist between their lives and careers reflect some of the elements that will form the focus of this chapter. Crawford was an Irish Protestant from County Longford, educated largely by her mother, who moved to Paris in 1863 after her father's death. Her first professional earnings came from a regular 'Paris Letter' she wrote for an American newspaper. After her marriage to an older and more established journalist, the couple became a writing team, and her reputation continued to grow after his death. While she lacked the matrimonial contacts, Lynch also found herself drawn to an older generation of men and women who made their careers in journalism, often in combination with other political and artistic interests. Many of these figures were Irish themselves – if 'Marjory Maurice' is semi-autobiographical, they might have been connected to Lynch's family circle in Dublin – or had Irish or Franco-Irish affiliations. Some time after her move to Paris, Lynch, like Crawford before her, became a Paris correspondent. Writing in the London *Academy* from late 1896, Lynch used her 'Paris Letters' to make her own statements on the Dreyfus Affair, and to comment on Decadent literature, women's writing, imperialism and nationalism. Her response to these issues was textured by her position as a professional critic, by her networks of friends and associates, and by the ambivalences and allegiances visible in her fictional prose. Thus, the volatile compound that made up Lynch's particular set of circumstances mirrored the volatility of both the historical moment and the animating concepts listed above. As we will see, Lynch's critical writing from the period reflects not so much a seamless cosmopolitan hybridity as the 'real Mesopotamia' Mabel Robinson described in her depiction of Dublin society in *The Plan of Campaign*, and which was featured in 'Marjory Maurice'. This heterogenous mix was linked by old allegiances and common causes but seldom, if ever, spoke an agreed language in a single voice.

Lynch's London affiliations illustrate her active engagement in the groups, debates and discourses through which ideas of new Irish identities were being forged at the *fin de siècle*. Lynch was thus at the heart of a 'crucial shift in the London-Irish literary world', due to the role played by the London Ladies' Land League in the establishment of the Southwark Junior Irish Literary Club, the later Southwark Irish Literary Society and then the Irish Literary Society.[2] This was a shift in outlook, 'a division between two generations of Irish literary emigrants: one, long resident in London and becoming increasingly entrenched in British life, the other, recently arrived and soon to reject the cultural compromises of their elders'.[3] The Southwark Junior Irish Literary Club and its reincarnations were a marker of this shift, and signalled the emergence of a nascent Irish revivalist culture, led by figures such as W.P. Ryan and D.P. Moran. While there is no archival evidence of Lynch belonging to the earlier clubs, it is unlikely, with the close connections between the Ladies' Land League and the Junior Irish Literary Club, that she was unaware of them. She is listed as a member of the Irish Literary Society, reinvented by Yeats in 1891, giving a well-attended lecture on the subject of 'Irishmen in the Service of Spain' in London in 1895.[4]

The revivalist culture that was important for Lynch in the 1880s shaped her 1890s networks in unexpected ways, connecting her with a more cosmopolitan community of writers in London and across Europe. She had made clear her ambivalence about certain elements of that culture in her *Dublin Evening Telegraph* spoof, and would do so again in her sceptical tale 'My Friend Arcanieva'. Instead, it was the older home-rule generation, represented by figures such as T.P. O'Connor and Justin McCarthy, who featured more in her London literary landscape and intersected with the networks that grew out of her Ladies' Land League affiliations.[5] If assimilation indicated 'compromise' for some, to others – Lynch among them – it offered opportunity.

As we know from Lynch's 1888 letter to Thomas Dawson, she was familiar with O'Connor, who it seems offered her work writing for the *Star*. Her rejection of this offer illustrates her awareness of the perceived divide between literary writing and political journalism, a divide she could successfully bridge in other outlets. At first sight, the links between Justin McCarthy and Lynch seem less direct, although they had both appeared in the *United Ireland* 'Castle Christmas' edition in 1884. On closer inspection, their shared literary and political networks come into focus, and once again are woman-centred. Charlotte McCarthy's friendship with Mabel Robinson has already been noted, and it is possible that Justin McCarthy's proximity to the Pre-Raphaelite 'literary and artistic Bohemia' around Fitzroy Square in the 1870s led him into contact with the Robinsons senior.[6] By the mid- to late 1880s this 'Bohemia' was an established part of the cultural landscape, and McCarthy had clearly become a part of it.[7] Ella Hepworth Dixon recalled that 'The first time Oscar Wilde loomed on my horizon I was painting, together with Charlotte McCarthy and my sister, a portrait of Justin McCarthy the younger, in their hospitable house in Bloomsbury'.[8] McCarthy features as a host and frequenter of several London literary salons that overlap with Lynch's established and more passing literary connections. For instance, it was McCarthy who gave the novelist and journalist Richard Whiteing his first break on the *Evening Star* in the 1860s.[9] Whiteing would later become the long-term partner of Alice Corkran, another of Lynch's London contacts whose life and writing crossed nations, genres and generations.

Corkran is best known now as the author of children's fiction, but this limited profile belies a more far-reaching and wide-ranging set of interests, and a far greater prominence at the time. She produced works of art criticism and acted as editor of the magazine the *Girl's Realm* from 1898. In addition to publishing several stories by Lynch, as well as Tynan, Jane Barlow and Mary Robinson, the *Girl's Realm* was a forum for writing on the expanding opportunities for young women. Lynch acknowledged Corkran publicly in return, via a dedication in her collection *Dr Vermont's Fantasy and Other Stories*. More recent research into the Corkran family by Michèle Milan confirms that they, like the Robinsons and the Lynch-Cantwells, were also moving in Franco-Irish circles in the late nineteenth century, appearing on occasion in Wilde's correspondence.[10] In fact, Milan concludes, the 'entire family were dedicated cross-cultural mediators, acting as ambassadors for French culture in the English-speaking world'.[11] The 'entire family' included Alice's caustic and witty sister Henriette, another former Slade student, whose autobiography recounts (in not entirely glowing terms) a meeting with Mary Robinson at the home of Justin McCarthy.[12] The most complete account of the Corkran-Whiteing household in the 1890s comes from the equally caustic 1932 memoir by American novelist Gertrude Atherton, who had met Whiteing at one of the soirées thrown regularly by Elizabeth O'Connor.[13] Through him, she and her sister-in-law were invited to the Corkrans' Thursday 'salon' at their house on Mecklenberg Square, which Atherton attended regularly afterwards. Atherton evidently saw Corkran as slightly old-fashioned, describing her as 'one of the last outposts of the old order' whose status rested on her family's connections with the Brownings. Whether this was true or not, it is clear that these Thursday salons were intergenerational affairs at which women writers were welcome. Atherton recalled conversations with women whose careers stretched from mid-Victorian to the early modernist, on one occasion spotting Mary Elizabeth Braddon, and on another chatting with May Sinclair.[14] It was there that she also encountered Lynch. Thus, it is not entirely clear whether the *Girl's Realm*'s inclusion of Irish women writers such as Lynch, Tynan and Barlow arose from London networks of female authorship or from existing affiliations in the London Irish literary and political diaspora. It might be a mistake to try to distinguish between the two, given the way that such networks intersected. The categories that are vital when trying to determine or to construct distinctive elements of a complex field – differences between literary authors and journalists, journalists and politicians, artists and writers, New Women and other feminists, older and younger generations, even between writers of different nationalities – are less stable in the sort of 'Mesopotamia' under discussion.

This intermixing was echoed in the relationship between the female-centred salon culture that Lynch shared with the Robinsons, Tynan and Corkran and the clubs and societies for women that were also being established at this point. The overlap between these two spaces – one still rooted in the home, the other moving out into traditionally male territory beyond it – indicates a parallel motion with, rather than a break from, the position occupied by women writers of previous eras. It also gives an indication of the range of different positions available to women when negotiating their place in the professional sphere. Such spaces would have been especially important for Lynch. On the whole, the fact that in-house salons blurred the boundaries between the 'professional' and the 'personal' was advantageous to women like her, still marginalised in the cultural marketplace. Nonetheless, as she remained single, and when in London never lived the sort of existence that led to a home suitable for a regular 'at home', she probably remained in orbit, more guest than host. Conversely, clubs and societies, with their emphasis upon non-domestic spaces, elided differences in social status between women who shared similar professional aims.

This emerging female club culture was exemplified by an annual event that attracted significant, and sometimes satirical, attention from the London press in 1889 and throughout the 1890s: the Literary Ladies' dinner.[15] As its name suggests, this was a high-profile gathering of women writers, whose first meeting took place at the Criterion restaurant in London on 31 May 1889. Lynch attended the inaugural event, along with Meynell, Tynan and figures such as Mona Caird, Amy Levy, Mathilde Blind, Clementina Black and Graham R. Tomson (Olive Schreiner had had to excuse herself).[16] The women ate, drank, smoked, read from their work, made toasts and gave speeches. In short, they enjoyed the sort of homosocial conviviality previously reserved for male-only clubs and societies. Linda Hughes notes that:

> … the founding of the Literary Ladies was on one hand a claim to equal status and privileges enjoyed by male authors, and on the other part of the larger entrance of women into the public spaces of London … The club not only represented significant innovation in *fin-de-siècle* authorship but also, more crucially, precipitated in the press the 'props' (bloomers excepted) that would typify – and target – the New Woman from 1894 onward.[17]

Bearing Hughes' statement in mind, a closer examination of one specific account of the 1889 dinner demonstrates and extends O'Toole's contention that the Ladies' Land League was intimately connected to the rise of the 'Irish New Woman'. The female correspondent from the *Pall Mall Gazette* copied down a waiter's plan of the seating arrangements. Here, we find 'Miss Lynch' sitting next to 'Miss Taylor', who is placed next to 'Miss Tynan', who in turn sits next to 'Miss Cochran' (very likely Alice Corkran).[18] Assuming that Miss Taylor is Harriet Taylor, a London Ladies' Land League contact for Lynch and Tynan, representatives of this short-lived Irish feminist and political group were a substantial presence at this foundational literary event for women writers.[19] Mabel Robinson, listed in the *Pall Mall Gazette* report as among those invited yet not able to attend, suggests another point of crossover between Irish political activity and literary London. The activism promoted by the Ladies' Land League left traces not only on early revivalist cultures, but on emerging feminist institutions that, on the face of it, had no connection with Irish affairs.

Yet it is important to note, as Hughes does, that the emerging tropes of the New Woman were far from fixed, and that not every woman present could be aligned with them. Equally, Lynch would adopt a range of positions towards her Irish identity and towards the New Woman in her work, while still embodying many key New Woman attributes in her life. It is here that we can draw a parallel with the second of Lynch's important London contacts, her later champion, Frances Low. Like Corkran, Low was involved with the world of magazines and journalism – her obituary described her as 'a pioneer figure among women journalists' – and the two are likely to have known of one another.[20] Unlike Corkran and Robinson, it was Low's generation, rather than that of her parents, that established itself on the intellectual scene.[21] There's no evidence that Frances married, and throughout her career she personified, and promoted, the figure of the independent, resilient woman. This seems to set her apart from the more 'feminine' professional sphere discussed earlier, but, as Alexis Easley has discussed, the distinction is not straightforward.[22] Low promoted female independence, but she was what might be called a 'conservative' feminist, throwing her support behind the anti-suffrage campaign in 1907. Her writing promoted professionalism but also supported the centrality of women to domesticity and to the home. It was through Low that Lynch contributed to the domestic magazine *Hearth and Home*, which routinely publicised Lynch's work and which would publish a series of her articles on the Paris Exhibition in 1900.[23]

When we place Lynch in these several, intersecting circles, a composite picture emerges, shaped by the contrary forces acting on it. Lynch appears here both as a supremely modern figure – mobile, unattached yet well-connected, publishing widely and earning her own money – and as a loser in the quasi-Darwinian literary marketplace – a rootless spinster, lacking financial security, with reputation enough to survive but not to flourish. Like Low, she was a journalist, part of a tradition of Irish journalists working between London and the Continent that included some of her valuable London contacts.[24] But the negativity directed towards journalism as a profession – negativity directed at women and at Irish journalists in particular – could well have contributed to her disavowal of the profession in print, and to her privately expressed preference for 'literary' writing.[25] Lynch was a 'New Woman' *avant la lettre*, present at a high-profile public gathering of such, and yet she criticised New Women writers particularly harshly in her non-fiction texts.

The 'powers of distance' Lynch had at her disposal were various then, and should be considered as intellectual (through her generally contrarian perspective) as well as geographical.[26] Her voyages to Greece and to Spain evidently involved networks both familial and professional, and would allow her to reflect at length on questions of affiliation in her travel writing and in novels such as *Rosni Harvey* and *Daughters of Men*. Evidence of the interpersonal connections underpinning Lynch's Greek and Spanish writings is slight at present, however, although we know something of the significance of Dawson's religious networks, and of the role played by Bikélas in promoting and translating her work.[27] Conversely, there is plenty of material to attest to the significance of France to her career and to her sense of self.[28] In 1903, she stated that she had first come to Paris, 'with the intention of settling', fifteen years earlier – that is, around 1888. If this is the case, she certainly did not settle, although she might have visited regularly.[29] Our outline of her movements in the early 1890s is sketchy, but by the end of 1893 she was back living in London, and seems to have stayed there for the course of that year.[30] Just before Christmas 1894 she wrote to Dawson from an address near Portman Square, noting dejectedly the 'wretched' state of her health.[31] The situation deteriorated further, and when she wrote again in February 1895 it was from Margate, where she had been 'an invalid for six weeks'.[32] After a brief return to Portman Square in March, she headed off to Madrid in April, presumably to stay with Nannie. Here, she wrote briefly on the subject of translation of a novel from Russian to French about Sophia Kovalevsky – a pioneering mathematician who had sparred (intellectually) with Herbert Spencer – the manuscript of which she had sent to Alice Corkran.[33] Back in London by September, she was installed in literary Kensington, giving her address to Gaston Paris as 19 St Mary Abbots Terrace, just a few doors from number 14, an address Corkran had used in 1891.[34] These brief snatches of correspondence do not provide evidence of any very close friendship between Lynch and Corkran, but the two women certainly remained in touch and clearly shared interests in women's rights and in French literature. *Hearth and Home* and the *Freeman's Journal* record Lynch's presence in Paris in order to give lectures in the early to mid-1890s: on Robert Louis Stevenson in May 1891, and on 'The Irish Peasant' in 1896.[35] The *Hearth and Home* piece mentions an earlier lecture on George Meredith – the origin of her critical study of 1891 – although no date for this has come to light.[36] By the later 1890s, Lynch was in Paris more frequently, writing to Egan Mew from there in August 1898, and sending a letter from 15 Avenue de Breteuil in early 1899. From 1900, she had settled at 60 Avenue de Breteuil, which was to remain a semi-permanent address. This was reasonably close to Mary Robinson's home at number 39.

The Robinsons, then, run almost seamlessly from Lynch's London life to her career in Paris. *Hearth and Home*'s brief description of the 'brilliant assemblage' who attended Lynch's 1891 Meredith lecture suggests a Robinson connection. The audience included the critic Hippolyte Taine, who Havelock Ellis recalled meeting at the home of Mary Darmesteter.[37] Taine along with Bourget and Barrès were all early members of the Robinson-Darmesteter salon, as was the medievalist, critic and scholar Gaston Paris, another of Lynch's Parisian friends whose *Medieval French Literature* she translated into English.[38] It was in a column following Paris' death in 1903 that Lynch wrote about her visits to the French capital fifteen years previously. How much poetic licence there was in this column it is impossible to say, but the picture she drew was a transposition of the intellectual-domestic culture of London salons. 'I constantly met him at intimate little dinners', she recalled, 'where he charmed us all by lamp-shade with his witty and suggestive talk. I never heard anyone tell a tale so supremely well as he.'[39] These 'intimate little dinners' could have been hosted by Paris himself – in 1903, Lynch mentioned having heard the poet Anna de Noailles read at Gaston Paris' home – by the Darmesteters, or by other mutual friends.[40] One such mutual friend was James Darmesteter's fellow historian Gabriel Monod.[41] Monod would go on to become a prominent Dreyfusard, whose campaigning would leave its mark on Lynch's Dreyfusard stance in her 'Paris Letters'. Henry Ferrari, editor of *La Revue Bleue*, was another of Monod's pro-Dreyfus contacts, and it was in this magazine that Lynch published her lengthy article on Rudyard Kipling, in the number for 31 October 1896.[42] In 'Oxford', which Lynch described in a *Freeman's* piece in October 1895, she alludes to Frederick Conybeare.[43] A Fellow of University College, Conybeare was another orientalist, whose pro-Dreyfus stance was evident in his account *The Dreyfus Case* (1898).

The stellar intellectual company into which James Darmesteter, then Emile Duclaux, inducted Mary Robinson, and into which either she, Mabel or both must have introduced Lynch, was therefore composed of influential academics as much as it was literary figures.[44] The insights we have into her life in Paris are equally intriguing. Lynch's letters to Vincens and to Gaston Paris allow us to see her in the role of host, for once. Not only was Alice Corkran invited to stay, but Lynch invited Vincens to take tea with them both. She discussed meeting Charles Legras at her apartment – the purpose of his visit was to receive a copy of *Autobiography of a Child* to review in the *Journal des Débats* – and mentioned that Marcel Prévost attended a private violin performance she held there.[45] This image, carefully framed though it might have been, chimes with an account published in *Harper's Bazaar* in 1902:

> Still running over the remarkable people in Paris of whose intimate life I know something, I think of Miss Hannah Lynch, who is said to be the most gifted woman Ireland ever produced … She writes regularly the Paris literary letter for the *London Academy*, a month or two ago had articles in the current number of three of the great English reviews, while at the same time her famous 'Autobiography of a Child' was appearing in a French translation in *La Revue de Paris*. But, going over to take tea with her one afternoon in her little apartment in the Avenue de Breteuil where she lives with 'That proud being Pasht, my cat', she showed me with delight the work of her odd moments in the re-upholstering and re-curtaining of her whole *salon*.[46]

Lynch's performance of feminine delicacy mixed with professional excellence fitted well with the model of salon culture presented by Robinson, Meynell and to an extent Vincens. But this is not the only description available. After Atherton's meeting with Lynch at Corkran's salon, it seems she and her sister-in-law arranged to stay with Lynch as 'paying guests', and Atherton recorded her memories in *Adventures of a Novelist*. They were not so flattering, although to a modern reader Lynch comes off far better than her snooty visitors. Atherton's sister-in-law Aleece diagnosed Lynch as 'one of those Bohemians'. Sure enough, during their visit Lynch forgot to pre-order lunch, failed to stick to an itinerary, and, to Atherton's dismay, appeared 'at the breakfast table in her nightgown with face unwashed and tousled hair'.[47] For all her talent she was a 'tragic figure', Atherton stated, although she 'got something out of life, for she lived in the Paris she loved, and had distinguished and devoted friends'.[48]

The picture of Lynch that emerges from this evidence is incomplete and contradictory, but gives a good indication of the networking and social labour that went on behind the more public face of her writing. This was a woman whose 'distinguished and devoted friends' played a vital role in her attempts to establish a literary life in Paris. Like the Robinson circle with which she was so closely aligned, Lynch was embedded in the 'affective networks created by a cosmopolitan world: networks of intellectual friendships and networks of love'.[49] As we will see in the next chapter, these cosmopolitan 'affective networks' were explored at length in her fiction from this period. But, as ever, Lynch was as drawn to tension and confrontation as she was to sympathy and fellow-feeling, and was as likely to confound expectations of feminine tact and good behaviour as she was to endorse them. In addition to the 'horse-whipping' she handed out in the *Speaker*, after Bourget changed sides during the Dreyfus Affair and aligned himself with Catholic conservatism, Lynch mocked him at length in the *Contemporary Review*. She took aim at his snobbery, as well as the chauvinism that lingered despite his new-found piety: '*Regimes* may pass and Republics may go, but woman remains ever for the eminent M. Bourget a creature of vaporous underwear and man the eternal explorer of her charms'.[50] She reported Gaston Paris' amusement to Vincens: 'On le trouve d'une férocité excessivement drôle – M. Gaston Paris a écrit que c'est "brilliante et fulgurante".'[51] As she had discovered in 1888, such spiky and opinionated criticism did not always marry successfully with the decorous femininity that was expected of her, and which she herself projected elsewhere.

The non-fiction writing that emerged from Lynch's Parisian residence shows this oscillating balance – between well-regulated femininity and edgy outspokenness – at work. When required, Lynch could push decorum to the fore, although not entirely at the expense of her own opinions. Her *Hearth and Home* articles on the spectacular 1900 Paris Exhibition were in this vein, the first instalments listing appropriate places to stay for visitors and denouncing the 'Moulin Rouge and other resorts of Montmartre' in scandalised tones.[52] As she started to focus on the build-up to, and the opening of, the exhibition, so a more familiar writing voice asserted itself. She instructed readers that they must use 'Monsieur' and 'Madame', even when addressing servants, 'or you will pass for an uncouth and vulgar foreigner'.[53] This comment on republican etiquette was made in the context of her less than ladylike tramping through muddy building sites around Les Invalides, urged on by amused and kindly workmen:

> An afternoon means a pair of boots to be given away, for nobody on earth could be expected to clean them. The Parisian workmen are, however, a pleasant and good-humoured class. They cheer you along your painful path by encouraging cries, 'Not an agreeable way for elegant boots,' 'A rough path for an afternoon promenade,' 'It's good for the health, a bath of mud, so they say.'[54]

This playful acknowledgement of the politics of class and gender was later matched by a poignant comment on empire. Her descriptions of the exhibition itself were vivid and detailed, but she acknowledged that this spectacle was also an advertisement for France's imperial power. She paused for a moment to contemplate a panorama celebrating the recent colonial conquest of Madagascar, noting:

> It is to be hoped that among the crowned and uncrowned Sovereigns who may be expected, the unfortunate Ranavolono [sic] will not be tempted to visit Paris for the Exhibition. The panorama of Antananarivo would assuredly not be calculated to delight her.[55]

Lynch did not elaborate on the identity of 'the unfortunate Ranavolono', but she was referring to Ranavalona III, the Malagasy queen whom the French had first deposed, then permanently exiled, in the late 1890s. This image of the dispossessed monarch, gazing upon a celebratory depiction of the fall of her capital city, was fleeting but tragic, another example of Lynch's commitment to writing about the experience of women and of the colonised.[56] Her 1896 *Revue Bleue* article on Kipling, which praised Kipling's depiction of the Irish soldier Mulvaney, had pointed out his limitations when it came to such female characters, and therefore female readers:

> Une chose pourtant est inquiétant pour sa renommée: c'est qu'en général il n'a pas pour lui le public féminin, cette partie la plus fidèle, la moins oublieuse du monde qui lit, la seule peut-être qui sache se passionner pour un auteur. Cette froideur, pour ne pas dire cette antipathie, s'explique aisément: Kipling ignore les secrets du coeur féminin ... Ses nouvelles, ses contes, ses ballades sont essentiellement composés en vue d'un auditoire masculin.[57]

No large claims can be made here for Lynch's opinion on the masculinism of the literature of empire, although the article makes it clear that this is how Kipling's writing generally works, with notable exceptions such as 'Without Benefit of Clergy'. But it is worth recalling that Lynch's 1891 study of Meredith pinned his reputation on precisely his ability to write compelling female characters, and Irish ones at that.

The fact that Lynch was in a position to build a life for herself in Paris, and to write with authority about French literature and culture from the mid- to late 1890s, suggests a confluence of personal and professional factors. She might have been a tousled 'Bohemian' in some respects, making her own curtains and upholstering her 'salon' without the aid of a decorator, but she was clearly financially stable enough to undertake such a project. It is tempting to connect this stability to her tenure as Paris correspondent for the *Academy*, and to the regular income it provided. Her first column appeared on 21 November 1896, around the time that Charles Lewis Hind became editor of the paper. Hind knew the Meynells and their circle, and he was also a friend of Pearl Craigie, daughter of the *Academy*'s new owner.[58] It was Craigie with whom Frances Low would compare Lynch in 1906 as evidence of the transforming power of wealth and contacts in women's literary careers. But it is also possible that Craigie, who had become president of the newly formed Society of Women Journalists in 1895, might have had a hand to play in the decision to appoint a female correspondent. There were also potential connections within the Robinson–Darmesteter circle. Gabriel Monod operated in the same role during the 1870s and into the 1880s, with Paul Bourget also contributing a handful of pieces. However Lynch landed the job, she wrote well over one hundred columns, stopping only in September 1903.[59] The 'Paris Letters' were essentially review pieces that also kept readers abreast of developments in the wider French artistic and cultural scene. Occasionally, Lynch branched out further, producing titled articles that covered territory closely related to the columns. For instance, when one of Lynch's characters in her short story 'Brases' praises the French poet Sully Prudhomme, we can look to her December 1901 *Academy* column on Prudhomme to compare his assessment with her own.[60] These titled pieces were sometimes (though not always) signed with Lynch's full name, while all her 'Paris Letters' merely carried the initials H.L. One of the features of Lynch's tenure at the *Academy* was the coverage she gave to female authors. The fact that her full name was published elsewhere in the journal, when added to her comments on women and women's writing, also made it clear to some that she was female herself.

Lynch's gender, then, was a sort of open secret, deducible from her choice of material as well as her signature. But what about her Irishness? Occasionally, the two issues overlapped, allowing her different approaches to be compared. This statement, from 5 March 1898, is a good example:

> When I open a book and find men much given to much sitting in twilight and talking of their souls, with a certain imprecise and unintelligent eloquence, I know the writer to be young, and suspect him of a strain of Celtic blood ... What, in Heaven's name, does it all mean? we are answered by the inscrutable, fathomless, picturesque Celtic *vague*. *Les*

> *Pierres qui Pleurent*, by Henry Bourgerel, has all the defects, without in
> any considerable degree the qualities, of Celtic literature. There is too
> much talk of the soul; too much abuse of woman, whom he qualifies as an
> animal without a soul, a statue coarse, heavy, without physical grace. Mr.
> Meredith has said that a woman may be judged by her estimate of her sex.
> I judge the moral and intellectual fibre of a male writer by his estimate of
> women.[61]

Her respect for Meredith, and her feminism, were evident here. But her criticism
of Yeatsian revivalism was more oblique, made principally by way of her swipe at
young men 'given to much sitting in twilight'.[62] This interest in 'Celtic literature'
might hint at her national identity, but it certainly did not do so very strongly.
In the previous year, she made an even subtler statement on the same theme,
when reviewing Bourget's story 'Neptunevale'.[63] This tale concerned Ireland
more specifically. It was set in the west, and had been inspired by a trip Bourget
had taken with Yeats:[64]

> There is even a fresh and graceful note in the Irish sketch, 'Neptunevale',
> which would have been completely charming if M. Bourget could, for
> a moment, have forgotten his vexed theory of psychology. He places
> before this quaint and touching little romance – if one may dare to call
> by so simple a name the work of so tortured a master – the mournful
> Irish proverb, 'There is hope from the sea, but no hope from the grave'. M.
> Bourget has not escaped the indescribable fascination of that melancholy
> and humorous race, which seems chiefly to exist for the pleasure of being
> misunderstood and wondered at. He, too, wonders, and admires in that
> sentimental, amazed temper most intellectual sympathisers fall into on
> this debatable ground. He writes regretfully of the 'beautiful island so
> little visited by his compatriots, and so worthy of being much visited'. He
> returns to Ireland, drawn thither again by its depth of green, its clear dark
> width of water, its isle-spotted lakes and veiled skies: 'in a word, by the
> inexplicable charm of its matchless melancholy', of the tender and fatal
> pathos that ever enfolds it, as a kind of mist upon judgement.[65]

As before, there was nothing in this piece to suggest that Lynch is Irish
herself. On closer inspection, however, some hints emerge. The review probes
the way in which Ireland and its people are represented in the story. While
Lynch supported Bourget in his 'indescribable fascination' with Ireland and
the 'melancholy and humour' of its people, she was also careful to note that

'Neptunevale' could not be read as an accurate or objective assessment. The nature of Ireland and the Irish remains elusive, concealed by the 'sentimental, amazed temper' that descends upon even 'intellectual sympathisers' like a mist. Her observation that the Irish 'seem to exist chiefly for the pleasure of being misunderstood and wondered at' seems to be aimed at the 'picturesque Celtic *vague*' outlined above. Its light irony could lead a reader to question what it feels like to be on the receiving end of misunderstanding and wonder – a question she could address more extensively in her fiction from the same period. In other words, Lynch's review emphasises Ireland's status as 'debatable ground'. When writing again on the subject of French engagement with Ireland in February 1899, she was more generous to Bourget, but her position on the Irish 'character' lost this element of nuance. Her column of 11 February 1899 compared 'Neptunevale' favourably with two non-fiction studies, Charles Legras' *Terre d'Irlande* and Baron E. de Mandat-Grancey's *Chez Paddy*:

> [*Terre d'Irlande*] is conspicuously deficient in the hasty and absurd generalisations and judgements that made the reading of *Chez Paddy* an exasperation. M. Legros [*sic*] is an intelligent and fair-minded traveller, and produces the views of the landlord and of Mr William O'Brien with impartial accuracy. Personally, I would have preferred a little less politics, and more of scenery, incident, and traveller's impressions. He pays tribute to the beauty and mournfulness of the Irish landscape, but his pen has not seized it for our captivation. In this has M. Bourget alone succeeded in that delicate, wistful, and lovely little masterpiece, 'Neptunevale'. Here, in a few exquisite pages, has he compressed all the quaintness, the sadness, the tenderness, the unfathomable deeps of romance, faith, superstition, terror, and devotion of the most inconsistent of national characters, the most changeful, attractive, and inexplicable of lands. The best book on Ireland has yet to be written. I doubt if it could be written by an Irishman, and am certain no Englishman could write it. The ideal author would either be a sympathetic Scotchman, with something of Stevenson's temperament, or a Catholic Frenchman, with some of the intellectual loftiness and liberality of a Montalembert.[66]

Although Lynch praised Legras' balanced account of the current political condition of Ireland, contrasting it with the 'hasty and absurd generalisations' of *Chez Paddy*, she made some generalisations of her own, suggesting on this occasion that Bourget's depiction of the Irish 'character' was fairly true to life. Lynch's professed preference for descriptive, topographical writing about Ireland once again hints at her awkward position as an Irish author writing for a London periodical, but also suggests her own sense of the conflict between political and 'literary' writing.[67] But her choice of Robert Louis Stevenson and Charles de Montalembert suggests that this conflict could, and should, be bridged. Stevenson was a brilliant stylist who had also commented on the hypocrisy that lay behind English empire-building, at home and abroad. Charles de Montalembert, a contemporary of Sand, was not only a liberal Catholic, he had written sympathetically about Irish independence in his study *L'Avenir Politique en Angleterre* (1856). Thus, Lynch's direct discussion of Irish cultural and national politics was refracted through the defining lens of the column: its aim to present French affairs to a predominantly liberal, English readership. She was certainly never as outspoken on Irish affairs in her 'Paris Letters' as she would be in her fiction or in her travel writing. This interplay of forces, both subtle and direct, is clearly visible in her treatment of the Dreyfus Affair from 1897.

Lynch's first mention of Alfred Dreyfus came in her column of 5 June 1897, which followed the usual format and reviewed two or three books in succession. The first of these was a French study of British global dominance, Edmond Desmolin's *A Quoi Vient la Supériorité des Anglo-Saxons*.[68] Lynch described the book as a 'searching study of English superiority over the unhappy Gauls', and she clearly found it hard to take seriously. It held 'in fierce contempt all the things the French, with lamentable levity, have hitherto been content to shine in: the elegant arts, cookery, the vaudeville, and the genius of dressmaking'.[69] In the meantime, 'the enterprising English are marching across the face of the world, atrociously strong and flourishing and successful'.[70] Desmolin planned to combat this situation through extensive social reform but even then, Lynch observed, he 'plaintively asks, would all that suffice to transform a poor devil of a Latin or a Celt into a fine Anglo-Saxon ogre?' Not for the last time, she compared the book to the didactic series of children's stories *Sandford and Merton*, or a tale 'of the idle apprentice and the good boy' – noting that, as usual, one's sympathies remained with the 'bad subject' rather than with the 'good subject', who 'quotes the Bible and seizes the goldmines of Golconda'. Lynch's commentary on Desmolin's critique of French failings explicitly connected the 'Latin' with the 'Celt', using the author's national typology to subvert, rather than support, his book's central argument. Her reference to the twin pillars of Britain's imperial project – capitalism and missionary work – undermined the supposedly superior position of the 'fine Anglo-Saxon ogre' by denying him the reader's 'sympathies'. It was to this notion of colonial enterprise and its failures of sympathy that Lynch turned next, reviewing former prison governor Paul Mimande's study of the penal colonies of French Guyana: *Forçats et Proscrits*:

> Whatever may befall one, there is some alleviation of the worst
> prospective misery in the knowledge that one is never likely to be sent
> to Cayenne. It is amazing that even in this cravatted and civilised period
> of humanity any portion of the inhabited globe should be able to gather
> such an accumulation of horrors about it as French Guiana ... One
> dreams of tropical splendours below the equator, but M. Mimande very
> lucidly and ruthlessly dispels all such naive illusions. Filthy little towns,
> abominable prisons, the home of every foul disease, abject populations,
> burning and desert isles, miserable officials, leprosy, malaria ... The book
> would be a just and kindly one were it not for the spiteful and needlessly
> cruel pages about Dreyfus, who reached Cayenne for deportation to the
> Isle of Salvation, one of the worst of the group in Guiana waters, while M.
> Mimande was making his tour of the settlement. That unfortunate man
> has surely been cruelly enough punished. A compatriot might pass that
> dark and silent figure condemned to such solitude at least in silence.[71]

At this point Lynch was not professing Dreyfus' innocence, but her
observations leave little doubt as to her opinion of his punishment or
Mimande's presentation of him. Its specific cruelty mingles with the more
general horror of the penal colony, in which prisoner, warder and native
population all endure a bleak parody of 'tropical splendours below the equator'.
The focus of this critique emerges in the 'dark and silent' figure of Dreyfus, an
image which conflates the shadows to which he has been 'condemned' with a
standard depiction of dehumanising racial otherness. And yet, Lynch points
out, Dreyfus is not only human but a 'compatriot' of the author, who, as he has
been denied the right of speech, should not be insulted further by being made
an object of discussion.

Therefore, in this column Lynch reflects on the colonial power of both
the British and the French, and upon related systems of imprisonment and
deportation. She left the resonances between Dreyfus' experience and the
experiences of Irish prisoners and exiles entirely unspoken, although she
would not do so forever. As the months rolled on, so the extraordinary events
of the affair began to gather momentum, and Lynch's Parisian circle placed her
in the advance guard of the Dreyfusard cause. Monod was one of the first to
publicly call for a retrial in November 1897, around the time that Zola began
his campaign in *Le Figaro*. By the time Lynch reflected on the Dreyfus case in
her 'Paris Letter' for 19 February 1898 she could safely observe that it 'has at
last landed us in full hysterics'.[72] She opened the column questioning whether
there was any point even trying to discuss recent literature, when the topic on

everybody's lips, dividing opinion 'from palace to basement' was the case – including, of course, Zola's interventions:

> It has become positively dangerous to speak of anything but the weather to your dearest friend. And even the weather is sure, sooner or later, to bring us back to the dangerous latitude below the Equator, by the explosive mention of a certain island, and the eternal, inevitable, question of Dreyfus's innocence or culpability.[73]

Lynch condemned the 'despotic traditions' and 'inquisitorial pride' of the army, as opposed to Zola's 'noble demand for justice to the individual'.[74] But the focus of her ire was a leading article in *Le Figaro*, in which its military specialist, using the name 'Saint-Genest', had announced his conviction that Dreyfus was guilty because, as a Jew, '*he was antipathetic to all his brother officers*, Christians!'[75] If in her previous piece she had commented on an absence of 'sympathy', here she focused on the presence of its counterpart: 'antipathy'. In doing so, it should be noted, Lynch both played to, and punctured, feelings of superiority on the part of her English readers:

> Whatever the faults of the English – and they are not more perfect than the French – at least they do not publicly advocate the dispatching of a British subject to distant penal settlements for life on the ground that he is generally anti-pathetic. Indeed, the amiable Saint-Genest went a step further. With a candour we can never sufficiently commend, however much it may shock us, he admits, because of this antipathy, that if it had rested with him he would gladly have 'suppressed' Dreyfus instead of sending him to the Île du Diable. This is refreshing. One asks oneself in dismay, can it really be possible that we are at the end of the nineteenth century? What is the measure of the progress of civilisation, after all, if it leaves Paris to-day not considerably removed from the fifteenth [century]? 'Death to the Jews!' 'To the river with Zola!'[76]

She closed this article with another colonial comparison, reviewing Jean Hess' *L'Ame Negre*, a series of high-coloured, pseudo-anthropological tales about the Yoruba of Nigeria. Lynch turned the notion of racialised superiority on its head, citing a section in which a tribal leader exercises excellent judgement. 'Why not import him to Paris to preside over the *affaire Zola* where, alas! such a chief is in terrible need,' Lynch interjected.[77] 'Decidedly, the Whites have gone further than the Blacks, and have fared worse, as this subtlety and cleverness are not ours.'[78]

Lynch's early defence of Dreyfus and Zola in the *Academy* is compelling not only for its passion but for her decision to position it in the context of reviews addressing militarism, empire and race. While her *Academy* readers were unlikely to be hardline imperialists, Lynch made sure that they understood that the English were 'not more perfect' than their neighbours across the Channel. The fact that the competing national interests of these two global powers produced similar examples of oppression was especially important for Lynch, as an Irish Dreyfusard, to note. The British press and public, like her, generally supported Dreyfus, although, unlike her, this stance was at least partly motivated by anti-French sentiment. Unsurprisingly, British assertions of moral superiority had been greeted with extreme scepticism in Ireland.[79] For some, aware as Lynch was of the British justice system's dealings with Irish prisoners, it was enough to draw attention to the hypocrisy. Others felt that a more public statement of support for their old ally, France, was needed, which necessarily involved an attack on the Dreyfusard cause. In January 1899, Lynch tackled this issue, not in the pages of the *Academy*, but in the correspondence columns of the far more conservative *St James's Gazette*.[80] Her letter, written in response to an anti-Dreyfusard statement made by Michael Davitt in *Le Figaro*, is the only occasion we have found when Lynch confronted the position adopted by several prominent Irish nationalists vis-à-vis '*l'affaire*'.[81] The veil she drew over her Irishness in the *Academy* was entirely absent. She was, she noted, writing explicitly 'as an Irishwoman':

> As a professional Irish patriot it is fitting that Mr. Davitt should side with France in her conflicts with England. But, as an Irishman who has suffered with the weak in strife against the strong, who has thundered repeatedly against injustice and iniquity, I find no words, as an Irishwoman, to express my indignation and surprise on finding this victim of oppression to-day on the side of injustice and iniquity in another land …
>
> Perhaps Mr. Davitt is an admirer of the late lamented Colonel Henry, one of the heroes of modern France, and believes that the 'Affaire' is supported by the gold of England and Israel.[82]

As Lynch's response makes plain, Davitt had put his support behind the official French line, attacking the British press for its 'vile calumnies' against the French officers in question, and alluding to the Dreyfusard cause as a 'miserable plot'.[83] The figure who Lynch described, with grim sarcasm, as the 'late lamented Colonel Henry, one of the heroes of modern France', had accused Dreyfus during his court martial and later forged several important documents in an attempt to confirm Dreyfus' guilt. After Henry's disgrace and death in prison in 1898, he had become something of a martyr figure for the most anti-Semitic elements of the anti-Dreyfus side. Her reply drew attention to the sort of ethical contradiction that Irish papers had pinpointed in the British response. Davitt was effectively standing against a man for whose cause he would have fought vigorously in a different context. Lynch's 'indignation and surprise' might have originated from her knowledge of Davitt's radical position at the time of the Land Leagues. But it might also have been an effect of the anti-imperialist position that she and Davitt also shared. In fact, Davitt had only mentioned Dreyfus in the closing paragraphs of an article that denounced British imperialism in terms very similar to Lynch's herself. In a letter to Vincens written after a two-month stay in Ireland in early 1900, Lynch would make a surprising statement about England, which she followed up with a condemnation of imperialism in the press:

> Je suis attristée pour la civilisation, moi qui admirais tant l'Angleterre comme une grande race et une grande nation, eh bien, les impérialistes m'en ont dégoûté. Ce que la Presse parlait là-bas comme chez nous, est devenu néfaste, mensongère et infâme! [sic] Les seuls gens logiques, sensés, et francs sont les Boxeurs de Chine.[84]

Lynch's support for the Boxer Rebellion, which had aimed to drive foreign interests out of China by force, might have been rhetorical. Yet her comparison between the lies circulating in both the English and the French pro-imperial press at the time identifies imperialism itself as a problem, amplifying the already oppressive force of national self-interest that she would see on display at the Paris Exhibition. It is interesting to consider how Lynch's various experiences of nationalism, from her youth in the Ladies' Land League to the nationalism of the Dreyfus years, might have led her to consider it as a concept. She confirmed her anti-nationalist convictions to Vincens, too: 'Tous mes amis savent que je suis carrément anti-catholique, anti-militariste, anti-nationaliste – que je suis très républicaine,' she wrote in 1901 ... [J]e déteste franchement les aristocrates modernes, les snobs et les [???] de la Patrie Française.'[85] Given the context, we can assume that she had the predominantly Catholic, royalist, anti-Dreyfus French nationalists in mind. But her jab at Davitt's position as a 'professional Irish patriot', whose national allegiances had led him into a moral blind spot, suggests a more general scepticism on her part. The most obvious antidote to this position, a form of cosmopolitanism, was not something Lynch wholly subscribed to either, as we will see in the following chapter.

Throughout the Dreyfus Affair the influence of Lynch's Parisian circle was evident, through her solidarity with Jewish intellectuals and her hostility to royalist conservatives. It connected with a point she made in her 1901 letter to Vincens: 'Je n'aime que les faibles, les humbles, les déclassés, les malheureuses, les infortunés de la terre et du destin – et de ce côte-là, c'est plutôt les femmes qui s'y trouvent ...'[86] On one hand, this identification with the 'humble' and marginalised sounds more than a little pious. On the other, it returns us to Lynch's drive to represent female experience, and in particular the experience of women on the frontiers of socially accepted roles and relationships. The final aspect of Lynch's 'Paris Letters' that this chapter will address is the question of how she discussed women's writing in her columns. This was an issue that united many of the elements already considered – the influence of Vincens, the impact of social status on women's behaviour, the question of how female identity and female sexuality should be expressed and represented – although it did little to resolve the internal conflicts these generated.

The first of these concerns Vincens herself, an accomplished figure who, like Low, could be characterised as a conservative feminist. She was pro female education and women's rights, but vigorously opposed to the Anglo-American New Woman. Her article 'Les Gauches Féministes et le Mariage', published in 1896, castigated a roster of New Woman novelists for what she considered to be their innocence in thinking that 'free love' could liberate women.[87] Lynch's column of 17 July 1897 shows that she knew of Vincens (who she mentions using her pen name) and approved of her writing: 'In a serious line, the single notable woman-writer is Arvède Barine.'[88] Lynch's letters to Vincens began after the publication of *Autobiography of a Child* in 1899. Soon after this, she was writing to express her horror at two New Woman novels she had been sent: Grant Allen's *The Woman Who Did* and Arabella Kenneally's *Dr Janet of Harley Street*:

> Dieu de Dieux, quels livres terribles! Je viens de lire 'The Woman Who Did' comment est-ce qu'un public [en-]dehors d'une maison de santé tolère de pareil imbécilités? Et cet autre, 'Dr Janet of Harley Street'. Mais pour quel espèce de gens sont-ils écrits?[89]

Like all correspondents keen to make a good impression, Lynch laid it on a bit thick, and it is likely that some of her anti-New Woman vigour in the 'Paris Letters' can be attributed to the presence of her influential friend. But Lynch clearly had her own misgivings, which she had already expressed in very similar terms. In her 'Paris Letter' for 26 November 1898 – a reading of Strindberg's *Inferno* – she attacked George Egerton for endorsing the view of women propounded by Strindberg and Nietzsche: 'I believe it was George Egerton who informed us that only Strindberg and Nietzsche, neither of them sane, understood and measured the inherent badness of woman.'[90]

Thus, Lynch's position seems reasonably clear. She, too, was a 'conservative feminist', critical of the New Woman project, or perhaps a 'social purity' feminist, rejecting the continued sexualisation of women in modern literature. And yet the more of the 'Paris Letters' you read, the harder it is to maintain this interpretation. One reason for this difficulty is the fact that Lynch was writing from France. French feminism and Anglo-American feminism were not cut to exactly the same pattern, although they shared numerous common traits and an equal number of internal disagreements. For example, the influential suffragist Marguerite Durand, a former actress and journalist, famously capitalised upon conventional notions of femininity while advancing the cause of women's rights. 'Feminism owes a great deal to my blonde hair', Durand quipped, 'I know it thinks the contrary, but it is wrong.'[91] Not all feminists were convinced by Durand's approach, clearly, but this strategic, even political, use of the desirable and desiring female body was equally visible in literature. 'Gyp', a popular novelist whose books landed on Lynch's reviewing table with alarming regularity, has been described by Alison Finch as the inventor of a 'quintessential "new woman" character, "Paulette".'[92] Slangy and cheeky, frank about her sexuality and the fact of women's relationships before marriage, you might imagine that Lynch would disapprove of such a character. But this was not the case. Largely as a consequence of Gyp's fervent anti-Dreyfusism, Lynch's columns of the late 1890s did indeed denounce her, charting her descent into 'gross attacks upon foreigners and Jews'.[93] Yet in March 1898 Lynch recalled a time when Gyp, despite a tendency to 'cheerless twitter', had embodied a distinctive French tradition with regard to her writing about women and sex: 'Her object may be to shock us, but she wishes us all the same to cry out disapproval in the same breath "What a delicious little sinner!"'[94]

This expression of simultaneous 'disapproval' and delight was not unique to these columns. It reminds us of Lynch's ambivalence towards *Lady Windermere's Fan*, which she confessed to thoroughly enjoying in spite of herself. The subversive power of pleasure is also visible in her travel writing, as we will see in her accounts of Greece and Venice in Chapter 5. Given her own commitment to writing about women's experiences, and her own obvious awareness of sexual double standards, the role of desire and sexual pleasure could not be excluded from Lynch's developing notions of a modern female identity. The significance of the issue is indicated by the fact that it was the topic of her very first 'Paris Letter', appearing in the figure of one of her early literary heroines, George Sand. Katharine Tynan had recalled Lynch and her sisters reading Sand while at home in Dublin, and it was a review of Sand's correspondence with Sainte-Beuve that Lynch chose as her principal subject. She opened by meditating on the ethics of publishing private correspondence, before turning to an example of one of its positive consequences:

> It is of considerable documentary value to discover that [Alfred de] Musset was not above an audacious appropriation of George Sand's ideas, not even re-clothed in his own language. The most famous and admired passage in that charming comedy 'On ne Badine pas avec l'Amour' is copied textually, without the alteration of a single word, from one of the letters of advice to him after the rupture.[95]

Most obviously, in drawing attention to Sand as the originator of a 'famous and admired passage' by a male author, Lynch struck a feminist blow, reversing the stereotype of women as muses to, or imitators of, men. But the publication of Sand's correspondence also drew Lynch to consider issues of female sexual etiquette, as it left little doubt that 'this woman of genius divided her time between literature and *liaisons*'.[96] Ultimately, she decided that the triangle of Sand, de Musset and Chopin was forgivable, less so the fact that, to quote Liszt, Sand's heart was 'an omnibus, adapted for public claim and the carriage of many'.[97]

Lynch's decision to openly address Sand's love life is striking, more so her decision to excuse the 'triangle' model of sexual relationships. As we will see in the following chapter, this sort of triangulation would figure prominently in her own fiction, aligning her with some of the New Woman authors she purported to dislike. When discussing the poet Anna de Noailles, whose first volume *Le Cœur Innombrable* had recently appeared, Lynch warned against the 'omnibus' model. And yet, once again, in doing so she sounded simultaneously admiring and ironic. Critiquing the volume's current popularity, she picked up on de Noailles' self-conscious exoticism, the eroticism of her writing, and the privileges of her class:

> She is an Eastern princess mislaid in France in the twentieth century and has married a French nobleman, consequently in these democratic days she may tranquilly drive a coach and four through the walls of conventionality, over the carcass of expiring respectability. And when she tells young girls in verse ... that the evening is warm and they should go forth into the woods and take the first lover handy, that being the sole lesson of life, well, we explain it to ourselves as the sort of thing an Eastern princess might be expected to say.[98]

In one of her final columns, published on 25 July 1903, Lynch reviewed de Noailles once again, reiterating many of her original points. Lynch repeated that her vision of female sexual liberation was profoundly affected by her social status: 'protected by fortune and rank from the pitiable consequences of frailty, one of the privileged few who can impose their follies and caprices on society and not suffer for their sins'.[99] This language – of 'frailty', 'folly' and 'sin' – was judgemental and retrograde, but Lynch combined it with an insistence that a 'woman has as much right to produce an immoral book as a man, and when we read her book our only consideration should be its value or its worthlessness'.[100] In the same piece she discussed Renée Vivien's poetry, seemingly unsure how to prioritise the various issues raised by the content of the verse, by Vivien's use of classical traditions, by her provocative queer persona, and by responses to it. Lynch declared – perhaps tongue in cheek – that 'I am one of those impervious to the claims of Sapho [sic]', citing numerous fragments before claiming that they were at once 'insignificant' and 'lofty and luminous'.[101] As she had done for de Noailles, she praised Vivien's style, but questioned her content:

> The French renderings are in form impeccable. There is a sobriety, a classic chiselling of expression in the verse of Renée Vivien which are remarkable. One regrets the subject, and feels that a woman's talent in our days might be more worthily employed than in incensing the memory of Sappho.[102]

Lynch ended on a bizarre and melodramatic note, linking this brand of neo-Decadent literature to the arrest of the eccentric provocateur and hedonist Baron Fersen.

Perhaps it is a mistake to place too much weight on these very late columns, written when we know Lynch was in declining health and struggling to work. But the tension they exhibit is instructive, even if her expression of it was heavy-handed. Lynch's reviews of French women writers helped to establish her own position by implication. Her admiration for the 'chiselled' formalism of Vivien, which in some ways echoed Mary Robinson's poetic style, suggests that she was sympathetic to modern developments in literary techniques, while remaining dubious about their subject matter. But her writing on Sand, and her praise of de Noailles' conquest over 'expiring respectability' hints at Lynch's own attempts to find a form through which to address female intellectual and sexual experiences, issues that she explored throughout her fiction. It is this subject that will form the focus of our next chapter.

CHAPTER 4

Odd New Women: Sympathy, cosmopolitan modernity and *vagabondage*

The 'Paris Letters', with their reflections on Ireland, French nationalism, Decadent literature and women's writing, are valuable in assessing how Lynch's authorial identity was shaped from the middle of the 1890s onwards. These columns offer an index to her preoccupations, and demonstrate the pressures generated by her position as an unsupported female emigré, reliant on bonds of friendship for more than just emotional support. But the columns also privilege a particular voice: decisive, witty, acerbic or outraged. They were not a suitable venue in which to explore the ambivalence that they also registered, particularly on questions of identity and sexual politics. Lynch's fiction from 1896 provided exactly such a venue. While it still includes plenty of fiery polemic, it also contains some of her most exploratory writing. In these texts Lynch not only utilised modern forms but addressed provocative modern subject matter. The plot of *An Odd Experiment* (1897), which centres on a wife's decision to take her husband's young lover into the family home, could have been one of Grant Allen's 'livres terribles'. Novels such as *Denys d'Auvrillac* (1896) and *Jinny Blake* (1897) and certain tales collected in *Dr Vermont's Fantasy and Other Stories* (1896) were interventions in the New Woman debate, building on earlier works such as *Daughters of Men* (1892) and *Rosni Harvey* (1892). Lynch's engagements with this combustible category show clear lines of affiliation with other New Woman authors, and can certainly be seen as contributions to the emerging category of Irish New Woman fiction. In the first section of this chapter dedicated to Lynch's fiction of the 1890s, we will explore this terrain in detail.

As Regenia Gagnier suggests, New Woman fiction explored 'the scope and limits of autonomy and independence, solubility and separation, within relationship', often emphasising the emotional conflicts involved in these negotiations.[1] In her writing from this period, Lynch's experience of intractable, unequal power relationships tangles with a more optimistic modernity rooted in a 'worldly and broad-minded sympathy for a common humanity' that traversed national as well as sexual boundaries.[2] Her ongoing exploration of authority and gender was also refracted through her involvement with the international networks outlined in the previous chapter.[3] Thus, the final section of the chapter begins with a discussion of Lynch's explicitly cosmopolitan New Woman narratives. *Rosni Harvey, Jinny Blake, Denys d'Auvrillac* and *Daughters of Men* are striking for their transnational contexts. Drawing on her own travel experiences, Lynch gave readers a flavour of other cultures operating in cosmopolitan, polyglot capitals such as Athens and Paris.[4] In these books the heroine (often Irish), in revolt against marriage and other markers of the conventional destinies of woman, traverses foreign countrysides or crosses seas and nations in search of different possibilities. Gagnier's analysis of New Woman fiction as 'acute self-consciousness and the reckoning of relationship' and the 'networks of friendships and networks of love' identified by Vadillo as foundational to the cosmopolitan ethics of Robinson and her circle, are particularly pertinent for reading Lynch here, an author so aware of international, as well as inter-personal, relations.[5] These networks extend beyond the texts to epigraphs and dedications, where Lynch acknowledges some of her cosmopolitan connections.[6] We conclude by paying special attention to the transnational boundary crossings of these New Women or 'vagabonding daughters' and the motif of escape through international and modern modes of travel, central to many of these texts.[7] The nature of travel itself, of being in transit, enables the heroines to reinvent themselves and allows Lynch, a writer described by one of her reviewers as '*déracinée*', to take a mobile, shifting position on a number of subjects.[8] The narrative of modern travel, on trains and steamers to foreign destinations, allowed Lynch to expand on her preoccupation with gender and national identity, on misreadings and misunderstandings across gender, class and nation. Thus, while 'cosmopolitan' seems an appropriate term to use for Lynch's enduring engagement with the literature and culture of other nations, her writing was never utopian or entirely hospitable.

In 1902, Lynch offered the following description of Mary Robinson to the readers of the *Fortnightly Review*:

It is one thing to adopt a country, and quite another to be adopted by that country. In the case of a woman, marriage with a native is not sufficient. She may live for ever in her husband's land a foreigner, unsympathetic and unrecognised … Madame Darmesteter (now Madame Duclaux, but we prefer to call her by her familiar name) began her married life by a complete conquest of the Paris of letters, and then that portion of fashionable Paris interested in letters. For a time her conquest was purely personal, a conquest based upon feminine charm and grace, and a large and exquisite sympathy.

Before she wrote in French, the translation of her poems, with a preface by James Darmesteter, had made her known to French readers as a poet. Writing of this volume, M. Gaston Paris says: 'Never was the originality of a poet, always so difficult to render, seized with greater force and subtlety, wedded with a keener sympathy, expressed with greater fidelity; never, perhaps, was a soul more intimately penetrated by another soul.'[9]

This review was bound to be fairly glowing, but what is striking is the term that Lynch repeatedly used. Robinson's work, and indeed her entire aesthetic and personal existence, exemplified the notion of 'sympathy'. It is this quality that guaranteed the mutuality of Robinson's adoption of France, and its adoption of her. Likewise, Lynch imported Gaston Paris' use of the term to describe the sympathetic penetration of James Darmesteter's translation and Robinson's verse, a level of communion that was presumably intended to mirror their married love.

Lynch's evocation of 'sympathy' to address both the interpersonal and the transnational tied her into a series of related contexts. First, the word was resonant for Mary Robinson personally. In the 1880s, Robinson and Vernon Lee had begun to develop what Emily Harrington calls an 'ethical aesthetics' in their respective poetry and prose.[10] Harrington suggests that 'In their intellectual and affectionate exchange, Robinson and Lee considered how art could generate sympathetic compassion and understanding in the reader.'[11] This 'intellectual and affectionate exchange', which might also be classified as 'love', was famously terminated by Robinson's marriage to Darmesteter, although Lynch's review suggests that her association with the term survived this rupture. This survival was presumably due, at least in part, to the far wider circulation of 'sympathy' as a concept. Within Robinson's circle, her sister Mabel also explored the same term in several of her novels published during the same period.[12] *Disenchantment* (1886), for example, urges in an exchange between the two central female characters, Augusta Desborough and Delia Mayne, about Augusta's alcoholic and dying husband, not simply sympathetic understanding but an embodied and empathic engagement with his suffering.[13] '"Put yourself in his place ... Realise ... No; that's not enough. Realise. For a moment be him!"'[14] The possibility of developing an ethical aesthetics is touched on as a subject in exchanges between the two women who, during an exercise in sketching a landscape together, discuss sympathy and the limits of language: '"Poor words! they're like women – undervalued; and yet they make quite as much difference to our happiness as deeds ... But sympathy! Oh, well, that shows itself by instinct; words make no difference one way or the other".'[15] Ana Parejo Vadillo has suggested that the prominence of the term was a consequence not only of the Robinson–Lee relationship but also of Robinson's status as a cosmopolitan figure well versed in French and other literatures. Naturally, this was a context shared by Mabel, but also, as we know, by Lynch herself.

Beyond these contexts stands a longer, and profoundly complex, history, repeatedly caught up with questions of gender and politics.[16] For Jil Larson, sympathy was a key category for late-Victorian authors such as Schreiner and Hardy, and was central to the New Woman project.[17] For Larson, 'New Woman writing was an emotional literature that afforded its audience a fresh way of thinking about emotion', redeeming its 'cognitive power' and destabilising a doctrine of differently gendered 'spheres' of response.[18] Rachel Ablow suggests that Victorian 'sympathy' itself was 'a mode of relating to others and of defining a self', thus marking a transition from eighteenth-century conventions of sensibility towards a twentieth-century interest in otherness.[19] The distinctive cultural aspects of this 'otherness' have been discussed at length when considering the role of sympathy in the early nineteenth-century writings of Sydney Owenson (Lady Morgan), and her 'national tale' *The Wild Irish Girl* (1806). Julia Wright observes that 'Ireland's colonial condition was ... [often] foremost in Sydney Owenson's writing' and that she used 'conventions of literary sensibility to add emotional force to her political points'.[20] But, as Katerina Bartoszynska points out, the tensions inherent in the concept survived in the text. *The Wild Irish Girl* does not simply advocate a theory of sympathetic understanding – between nations, and between women and men – but explores its limitations and failures.[21] Lynch clearly knew the book. The eponymous heroine of *Jinny Blake* merges elements of Lynch's biography, particularly her European travels, with aspects of Owenson's.[22] Jinny describes herself as 'your wild Irish girl' who 'must bolt in revolt' from a series of prospective suitors and society's requirement that she marry.[23] This reading of *The Wild Irish Girl* as a book about the problem of sympathy resonates strongly with Lynch's text, contrasting with her later depiction of Robinson as the personification of achieved integration and union. The novel explores the emotional implications of the more heterodox environment that Larson describes, which 'constructs a contextual ethics of particularity'.[24] This heterodox particularity is complemented by Lynch's depictions of a cosmopolitan modernity in which national identities are not erased, but hybridised and recombined. One of Jinny's suitors is Don Fernan O'Neill, a Spaniard of Irish descent, who bursts into tears when Jinny sings him 'one of the melodies'.[25] The reserved American Mr Trowbridge reminds her of a 'Yankee Charles Grandison'.[26] The texts that we will analyse in the following section do not describe an accomplished merging or 'interpenetration', but a messy series of adjustments, often ambiguous and generally still in process. To return to the terminology of a previous chapter, this was a 'Mesopotamian' model of the world.

This uncertain territory, and a range of sympathetic emotional attachments that exist between nations, friends and lovers, was addressed in several of the short texts that made up *Dr Vermont's Fantasy and Other Stories*. The characters were an international collection that would recur in her novels – Irish, French, Russian, Spanish, English – and third-person, omniscient narration gave way to a more mixed economy that included framed narration and a combination of multiple first-person narrators. Most tales included stark reminders of the restrictions placed on women's lives, while also reflecting on masculine perspectives on women. 'Brases' is narrated in the first person by 'Gontron', a Frenchman who falls in love with an aristocratic Irish woman while he and his English friend Trueberry are touring the country. His romanticised vision of her as an embodiment of Erin is only dislodged by a different image of the perfect woman, drawn from the idealistic poet Sully Prudhomme. It is a fantasy that his equally infatuated English friend shares, although his chosen poet is Robert Browning.[27] Despite claiming kinship with a local Irish 'peasant' – a 'brother Celt' – the narrator can neither stomach the *Poitín* nor the information that the man offers him on the impossibility of divorce, as it is clear that Brases is living separately from her womanising husband.[28] Imagining her suffering, Gontron experiences the sort of sympathetic identification attempted in Robinson's *Disenchantment*:

> Every nerve thrilled with a sympathy so complete as to make her retrospective pain most personally mine, to thrust my own individuality from its old bright environment out for ever into her desperate loneliness.[29]

This moment of supreme engagement coincides exactly with Gontron's realisation that any relationship between the two of them is impossible, blocking a simple romantic solution. It is worth noting that the possibility of a simple political allegory, the alliance between Ireland and France, is blocked at the same time. But Lynch took things a step further. Although Gontron controls the narrative, he is not in control of Brases' feelings, as it is made clear that she is extremely attracted to his friend. The Frenchman battles chronic jealousy, as political allegory is replaced by a series of highly charged emotional set pieces. Gontron assumes that his friend has 'won', as it is clear that he returns Brases' affection. In fact, the Englishman is also dismissed. The tale closes with both the English and the French suitors leaving the country separately, despite the fact that Trueberry is 'full of sympathy' for Gontron's distress.[30] In the closing sentences the narrator withdraws, viewing his beloved, and Ireland, through a haze of distorting tears: 'She was dim to my sight, a mere blurred grey figure, with light about her head, and the landscape looked watery and broken, as if seen through bits of bobbing glass.'[31] The story used the same tropes of romance that Lynch had consistently punctured in her earlier writing, but here the first-person narration makes the effect harder to define. The narrator's criticism of Catholic attitudes towards divorce, 'the illimitable price exacted for limitable error', and of sexual double standards seems to echo Lynch's own opinions.[32] Gontron's sympathy, like the feeling Trueberry bears on his account, is genuine, and this sentiment does overwhelm the considerable forces of desire and envy. But the story also drew attention to the misty-eyed Celticism Lynch had discussed in the *Academy*. Its noble yet distorted view of women does nothing to alter the status quo. Ultimately, as the men ride away, Brases and her children must be left behind. She has exerted choice and shown superior emotional control, but her options are still woefully limited.

Male reflections upon love, and the lives of women and children, were the main topic of 'A Page of Philosophy'. In it, a collection of café-haunting aesthetes are touched in a 'perceptible start of emotion' by the story of the death of a little girl, and the fate of her mother, a Spanish poet who relocates to a freezing northern town after her marriage to a Russian philosopher.[33] The story allowed Lynch to channel her role as a critic: it contained some sharp commentary on Decadence, Naturalism ('romance upside down') and Symbolism, on Spanish culture, and on the institution of marriage.[34] But its main preoccupation is with the sentimental education of the Russian Krowtosky – 'whose name diverted the channel of murmurous, half-abstracted discourse to which we had lent an attentive ear' – a misogynist pessimist who dismisses women as either 'dolls' or 'animals', until he meets the unpretentiously intellectual Pilar.[35] Krowtosky's love for his wife and his grief at the loss of his baby daughter mark his arrival at intellectual and emotional maturity, but the central narrator points out that this is only a partial account. He only has Krowtosky's perspective on his wife, retailed to him via letters – 'Her I only know on report that cannot exactly be described as impartial' – and her side of the story is told through the words of these two principal male figures.[36] For example, Krowtosky's observation that 'The real Pessimists are women ... Man occasionally rises up and takes his oppressor by the throat, but woman never', can be read as a symptom of his emotional naiveté at this point in the story, or as a legitimate reflection on social norms.[37] This narrative technique allowed the text to promote the idea of familial love and the importance of children, but also to tell a parallel story of cultural dispossession, the reality of poverty, and the silencing of women as wives and mothers.

The collection's title story 'Dr Vermont's Fantasy' looked at similar terrain, but from a very different narrative angle. The 'fantasy' in question is the cynical nihilism of Dr Vermont, a man cauterised to emotion since the death of his young wife. On one level the tale could be seen as a dark reworking of Stevenson's 'The Suicide Club', as Vermont plans to lead a group of his associates from the Parisian Café Lander in an act of collective suicide to mark the end of the nineteenth century. In the course of the story the emotional appeals of his wife's sister, Mlle Lenormant (who is secretly in love with him), of his neglected daughter, and of one of the men in his group pull him back from the brink. As the clock moves through its midnight chimes and the men stand with pistols in hand, something mysterious happens:

> ... had there been a ray of light above or around, Dr Vermont's face would have been seen to undergo a wonderful and beautiful change. Honest affection that makes no attempt at concealment, humanised it ... The worst of us, you see, have our heroic moments, only it often happens that, like Dr Vermont's, they pass unnoticed in the dark.[38]

Again, the story emphasised the vital importance of emotional engagement, which turns a gesture of despair into a celebration of the possibilities of the new century. It is a turning point that Vermont conceals. Instead, he pretends that the arrangement has been an 'excellent joke', instructing them 'we fire heavenward – a good omen – then we shake hands again'.[39]

There was another important deviation from the tragedy that concludes 'A Page of Philosophy', or the return to the status quo that ends 'Brases'. Rather than the male figures telling this story, much of the text is seen through the eyes of a female first-person narrator, a lone female Irish traveller. The first four sections of the story appear to divide the characters into particularly gendered spheres, as all the women are assembled on the semi-deserted island, and all the men are in the Café Lander, but these environments are not quite as they seem. The 'domestic sphere' is a rambling Gothic manor with a huge disorganised library, in which Mlle Lenormant is engaged in writing a biography of Julian the Apostate. The traveller-narrator also toys with the expectations of the other characters within the frame of the story itself. As she and her French friend get to know one another, the Irish woman teases her about her perceptions of Ireland and its people:

> I assured her that the Irishman was not born who could not change his opinion at a moment's notice for the fun of the thing, and in the midst of comedy fall foul upon tragedy for pure diversion's sake. She shook her head despondently, and decided at once that there could be no earnest scholars, no born leaders of men, in a band of amiable buffoons.[40]

The cliché of the Irishman as 'amiable buffoon' offers a lesson in the importance of not being earnest here, as Mlle Lenormant's serious single-mindedness leaves her unable to recognise the working of the narrator's own playful wit. These 'feeble jokes', as the Irish narrator describes them, are not identical to the 'excellent joke' that Dr Vermont uses to conceal his own revelation.[41] All the same, they contribute to the sense that emotional engagement, while vital, is seldom straightforward. Not only does it take place in a specific context, but, like a joke, it can be ambiguous and transgressive. David Marshall's description of sympathy as a 'polyvalent sense of elective affinities' understood in 'ambivalent and often contradictory' ways seems to sum this up perfectly.[42] Theories of sympathy could be wedded to a rational framework and made functional – to a certain extent this is what happened to Adam Smith's 'fellow feeling' when it was adapted to fit theories of sympathy between individuals and within nations.[43] Nonetheless, while 'Brases', 'A Page of Philosophy' and 'Dr Vermont's Fantasy' all argue for the value of emotional connection, Lynch was equally interested in its paradoxical and subversive potential.

It is exactly such a subversive dynamic that drives *An Odd Experiment*, a book that engages overtly with the figure of the New Woman, and with the genre's interest in relationality, sexuality and emotion.[44] Reviewers expressed mixed feelings. The *Saturday Review* noted that, despite being rather over-written, it had 'an originality and significance of its own', and that 'one expects anything rather than the commonplace from Miss Lynch'.[45] The *Academy* found it 'remarkably clever', but while noting a resemblance to a Kipling story, overlooked a more obvious resonance between the novel and Sarah Grand's *A Domestic Experiment* (1891). Grand's text features the unlikely alliance of two women, Dolly and Agatha, across class lines. They subvert the plans of Agatha's husband – who has almost certainly had an affair with Dolly – and of several other unsympathetic characters before yielding to 'the form of the marriage plot' in one way or another.[46] Grand's novel was more complex than Lynch's stripped-down narrative, but at its heart lay similar, potent questions about relations between women, and the importance of the inconsistencies and surprises of sympathy in mapping a new social order.[47]

An Odd Experiment is set in a well-heeled suburban Surrey, and revolves around the decision, made by the super-rational and 'inscrutable' Mrs Raymond, to take her husband's beautiful young mistress Blanche into their home.[48] It is made explicit that Henry Raymond and Blanche have been lovers, and that Mrs Raymond's decision is not that of a 'complaisant wife – a kind of legitimate Madame de Pompadour'.[49] Instead, she intends to expose both Blanche and her husband to exactly what their infidelity means by keeping herself in the equation. 'You are both entirely free to act as you choose, but you must expect to be judged by your conduct in the test.'[50] This test is to be carried out in as disinterested a fashion as possible, without recourse to conventional platitudes or moral hierarchies, and with a mind to the fact that women's relationships to one another should not be seen to fall into the reductive categories propounded by men. As Kate Raymond states: 'we women are not all cast in one vulgar mould. In spite of the poets, the novelists, the essayists, jealousy is not the essential, the universal note of our character.'[51]

An Odd Experiment is also a book in which the shifting power relations between husband and wife are used to explore gendered tropes: Mrs Raymond is highly unsentimental (like many New Women), while her husband is 'broken upon the wheels of emotion', stating at one point, 'I only crave sympathy.'[52] National identity is drawn into this, too, as Henry Raymond is Irish. But easy paradigms and didactic conclusions are complicated by the narrative structure of the novel, which refracts descriptions through the perspectives of each of the characters in turn. For Mrs Raymond, her husband's nationality explains a lot about his passionate nature, for Henry Raymond it does not enter the picture. This wandering focalisation means it is uncertain whether it is Henry Raymond or the narrator who makes the following observation on the way British women smile at men:

... half-surrender to his sex's superiority, half-impetuous claimant of as much of his heart as was free, – the peculiar irritating smile of the Anglo-Saxon woman for man, the creature of her scarcely delicate worship, that one sees on the face of no other woman of Europe.[53]

The novel repeatedly returns to such ideas of power. 'Do you accept my control of the situation?' Kate Raymond asks Blanche, during their first encounter.[54] As it lacks any form of emotional connection, Mrs Raymond's experiment treads an uncertain line between statesmanship and oppression. She appears 'commanding', 'imperious', 'regal', and although Blanche – like Jinny Blake – frequently considers 'revolt', she also feels grateful and affectionate towards her.[55] Readers are invited to share Blanche's ambivalence. Mrs Raymond is genuinely admirable, 'above shabby sentiment' or gossip.[56] But her unassailable position has its limitations, as we also learn that 'her tact, discretion, and judgement were qualities she had never learnt to distrust'.[57] The 'harmony of Mrs. Raymond's rule extended even to her offspring, whose obedience she secured by implied rather than overt exaction', and Blanche finds herself being drawn into this family.[58] She is passed off as a 'cousin' whenever anyone calls to the house, and the children start to regard her as such, much to Henry Raymond's discomfort.[59] This idea of family (a paradigm with political overtones) offers the promise of inclusion, but control is always at work. When alluding to the subject of a possible pregnancy, Mrs Raymond offers her assistance in the following terms: 'For once think of your own advantage, and acknowledge your fealty to a generous enemy', after which the narrator notes, 'She did not command; she persuaded. This was the secret of her power, and only intelligent servitude to her unobtrusive supremacy could divine the secret imperiousness of that persuasion.'[60]

If Mrs Raymond is imperial, then Blanche is colonised, on the cusp of an era of 'intelligent servitude' in which she exists not as an individual, but as part of a neatly organised system entirely devoid of Larson's 'contextual ethics of particularity'. As Blanche notes of her 'generous enemy', 'She kept her conversation above the personal note, and, indeed, only trafficked in personalities as illustrative and typical. They helped her to classify or point a moral.'[61] Since this 'broad understanding' exists without sympathetic understanding, it dispenses with any real sense of how a subject might exist outside its parameters.[62] The questions Blanche puts to herself when considering her 'ordeal' revolve around the social embarrassment, emotional pain and sexual frustration she knows she will experience, but these pale into insignificance once the situation is actually in play. When finally left alone with her lover after his wife has retired to bed for the evening, Blanche breaks down under the pressure. She holds 'her palms over her face and rock[s] in uncontrollable emotion' before running out of the room and up the stairs 'like a mad thing'.[63] As Foucault would point out, Blanche's madness seems to spring from Mrs Raymond's logical system. By the latter part of the book, Blanche is numb and exhausted, taking consolation in the prospect of suicide.

The turning point comes during a long sleepless night, in which Mrs Raymond, like Isabel Archer in *The Portrait of a Lady*, wrestles with the complexities of the situation.

> Could she so grievously have miscalculated her resources, so egregiously have misunderstood herself? To have started so fortified against the lesser emotions, secure in the tranquillity of the spectator, and all at once, without premonition, find herself so surprisingly engaged in the conflict as one of the sufferers! Even as a momentary weakness, the position shocked and disconcerted her.[64]

It is in this state that she encounters and talks to Blanche: 'Mrs Raymond spoke with warmth, a sincerity of emotion that surprised herself even more than her listener. Blanche understood it was no longer the woman of the world, throned above suffering, who addressed her, but an equal, a sister.'[65] Mrs Raymond concludes with the announcement that 'What I have now to decide, is my duty as a wife, as a sentient fellow-creature toward another. I am striving to discover what is best for us three wounded mortals.'[66] When Blanche questions the word 'three', Mrs Raymond gives the following answer: 'The bolt shot at you, dear, has hit me through my husband.'[67]

This properly sympathetic connection, in which Mrs Raymond not only identifies with Blanche but also recognises herself, is preceded by a moment of physical and verbal intimacy between the two women.[68] Blanche is invited to kiss Kate Raymond, who then, to Blanche's bewilderment, embraces her and looks her straight in the eyes; 'her look was a second caress', the narrator informs us.[69] In this context, Blanche's questioning of the relationship between the 'three wounded mortals' takes on additional resonance, as does Mrs Raymond's reply. Mrs Raymond's wound is caused by love, but is this simply a question of a woman suffering through her husband's infidelity or – as the scene strongly suggests – a woman who has come to feel a form of love for her 'sister' in the triangle? Lynch pushed the issue further in the final section of the novel. The most radical solution to the 'odd experiment' – a three-cornered relationship of some configuration – is ultimately prevented by Blanche's bustling and dominant young stepmother-to-be, Miss Baruna, who intervenes to whisk

Blanche away on a world tour. In one sense a convenient *deus ex machina*, the effusive Miss Baruna openly declares her 'love' for Blanche, an object she dreams about more than she does her prospective husband:

> You poor sweet dear! I'm prepared to worship you. You're the poetry to my prose – the flower on the table of life, while I'm the pot-au-feu. I fell in love with you at once, and dreamed of you instead of the Colonel.[70]

For her part, Kate Raymond treats Miss Baruna as an upstart rival, asking Blanche if she is really prepared to let the other woman 'carry you off'.[71] The moment of sympathetic intimacy is replaced by another form of power struggle, this time between two women for the affections of a third.

The language of the closing section of *An Odd Experiment* echoes a fleeting moment in 'Dr Vermont's Fantasy'. In it, the female traveller is trying to get to the bottom of her interest in the reclusive Mlle Lenormant. She admits to finding her 'a character of unusual fascination – not in the sense of sexual attraction, but from the point of view of study'.[72] This phrase is striking, introducing the idea of desire between women while simultaneously distancing the narrator from it. Perhaps the narrator's failure to find a term that adequately describes her 'fascination' is a reflection of a problem she is observing, recognising the uncertain terrain upon which we encounter others, in which emotions cannot be placed in convenient categories, even very subversive ones. In *An Odd Experiment*, however, the 'reckoning of relationship' goes deeper into this territory. Its title hints not only at Grand's *A Domestic Experiment*, but also the 'experiment' in sexual chemistry conducted in Goethe's *Elective Affinities*, the text that informs David Marshall's definition of 'sympathy'. For Grand and for Goethe, this was a heterosexual affair. However, Richard Dellamora's 1990 analysis of an erotics of 'sympathy' in the writings of Winckelmann and Pater established that a different, queer reading of the term was in circulation at the time when Lynch was writing.[73] Lynch had a paradigm of same-sex erotic sympathy within her immediate circle, in the example of Mary Robinson's earlier relationship with Vernon Lee. Yet in 1902 Lynch would use the word 'sympathy' only to describe the marriage between Mary Robinson and James Darmesteter, and at the moment it is impossible to know whether or not she was aware of Robinson's previous love. As we have seen, when Lynch wrote about Renée Vivien in the *Academy*, she was far from approving. But this criticism was underpinned by her impatience with what she perceived as the indulgence of wealthy 'cosmopolitans', figures out of sympathy with their host nation, in contrast to Robinson. The iconic figure of sexual dissidence in this era was, of course, Oscar Wilde. And yet, to date, we have not found a text by Lynch that either satirised or defended him during the period of his trial, imprisonment or his residence in Paris. Was she sympathetic? Did she feel some continued affiliation with the Wilde family, whose salons she had attended years before? Was her position affected by the fact that the *Academy* – the most obvious place for such a piece by Lynch to have appeared – was reserved on the topic of the Wilde trial in general? Or is it simply that such a piece is waiting to be discovered? As with everything about Lynch's own romantic life, her stance on love between men, or love between women, is currently obscure.

Therefore, Lynch's contradictory feminist sentiments regarding the New Woman, and the kinds of boundaries that sympathy might transgress, are left in suspension at the close of *An Odd Experiment*, as in her writing more generally. Neither the old order nor the new emerge on top, as Blanche quits the Raymond household for semi-voluntary exile. The closing words 'Who knows?', offered by Blanche in response to Miss Baruna's assertion that she will never need 'that woman's friendship', leaves open the possibility of a genuine relationship between the two characters, but also between the two very different modes of being.[74] Lynch's position as a cosmopolitan Irish author makes the text alert not only to the positive political possibilities of sympathy – as Mary Robinson and Sydney Owenson had been – but also to the pervasive discourses of dominance, which could be most devastating when enacted by those accustomed to invulnerability. The inconsistencies and surprises of sympathy survive the *fin de siècle* in Lynch's writing, but have to exist in concert with ongoing questions of power.

An Odd Experiment is one of the few novels Lynch published in the 1890s where national borders are not crossed, international travel is only anticipated, and the cosmopolitan mix of characters is confined to English, Irish and 'South American' in an English suburban setting. Instead, in this novel the domestic thresholds that are repeatedly traversed represent alternative boundary crossings that are not explored to the same extent again in her other 1890s fictions. These other novels also share more features with her earlier Ireland-set fiction: the fearless New Woman type like Morna Maurice or Camilla Knoys who prefer politics to marriage, for example, and the recurring preoccupation with the question of education for women as well as fraught mother–daughter relations.[75] In addition, as outlined earlier, novels including *Rosni Harvey, Jinny Blake, Denys d'Auvrillac, Daughters of Men* and *Clare Monro* are particularly striking for their cosmopolitan and transnational settings. *Rosni Harvey* and, in particular, *Jinny Blake* offer the most concentrated focus and vivid illustration of

Lynch's cosmopolitan portraits and transnational New Woman figures through which issues of national identity and gender roles are debated.[76] Rosni Harvey is the most cerebral of Lynch's heroines, her 'exquisitely sympathetic' manner perhaps embodying most fully the ideals of Robinson's cosmopolitan set.[77] Rosni's New Woman credentials include self-education through reading, a loss of faith, and an interrogation of the uses of marriage.

> A more absolutely lonely girl could not well be conceived, and her one great pleasure lay in study. Her studies were all sombre and serious. She read Spinoza's *Ethica* and Kant's *Kritic* in the original; she was profoundly versed in German literature and held her own views on German metaphysics; secretly inclined to Positivism, but was not very clear upon the matter. Her attitude towards Rousseau was that of disciple to master; poetry ranked with her lighter studies, where she showed herself original … Browning and Wordsworth she admired; Tennyson she did not greatly care about. Even in her choice of fiction she had no sympathy, no chance of developing her impressions by conversation. Her mother was an immoderate consumer of the lightest of intellectual nourishment, and her father never read anything.[78]

The unsympathetic environment in which she grows up – 'There were no points of sympathy between her and her parents' – is altered briefly when she falls in love with her brother's tutor, Randal Lismore.[79] It is his faithlessness that sets Rosni on a different course, her subsequent international travel and cross-cultural encounters introducing her to various possibilities for sympathetic relations between men, women and other nations. After the death of her parents and only sibling, and the failure of her romantic hopes, Rosni develops ambitions beyond that of matrimony: 'Instead of marriage, she wanted a private purse to carry out vast plans for the improvement of the race.' Her desire to escape includes further education and an aspiration to study medicine, which sets her travelling. She was going to 'an alien land, in pursuit – not, O ye gods! of a husband, but, sad to tell, of a diploma'.[80] Travel, in this novel, becomes an alternative to marriage and sets Rosni on a course far from Ireland to Athens, the Greek island of Tenos, Smyrna and Constantinople and back to Ireland and marriage after all.[81]

In *Jinny Blake*, the protagonist is a modern woman who exhibits many of the characteristics of the contemporary New Woman figure. But Jinny's awareness of the instability of identity – 'We are all, you as well as I and others, made up of a heap of inconsistencies' – gestures towards a latent modernist sense of self.[82]

Jinny's rebellious attempt to escape the confines of her gender – 'One is born a woman, and I hate it' – and marriage – "Unstable as water", you know. I may go unmated for life. Why not?' – is carried out through a series of cosmopolitan encounters.[83] These exchanges take place between characters with different national identities (Irish, Spanish, French, English, American) and who, like Jinny herself, are as likely to express themselves in French as in English.

Like Rosni Harvey, Jinny Blake has naive ambitions for social reform rather than marriage: 'Women were to be rescued by other women, the poor and trodden by the wealthy and honoured.'[84] For Jinny, 'Escape had become almost a permanent instinct in her life' – an escape from the condition of femaleness itself – and her quest for an alternative takes her from London through France, Spain and, like Rosni, on to Constantinople.[85] Other alternatives to marriage include the pursuit of artistic careers. For example, in *Denys d'Auvrillac* the English artist Mary Sumers lives a bohemian life in Paris and shocks French provincial society with her unconventional behaviour during her sojourn in the countryside. For the French provincial ladies she is alarmingly androgynous, smoking cigarettes, painting 'en plein air' and 'persistently in revolt against the exactions of the marriage market.'[86] *Daughters of Men* opens with a description of an illustrious and highly cosmopolitan gathering at the Austrian embassy in Athens. It is here, among the Russian princes, English politicians and French, German and Irish scholars as well as German and Greek aristocrats that the celebrated but controversial Athenian pianist Photini Natzelhuber makes her appearance. Although she is not, in the end, the focus of this narrative, the challenges of this incongruous figure with her masculine looks, defiantly unfeminine behaviour and musical brilliance are heightened by the glamorous international setting in which she is first glimpsed, and the shock and distress of the perceiver, the young Austrian Rudolphe Ehrenstein. Genteel, slightly feminine and in love with his expectations of woman as muse, his first encounter with Photini is traumatic:

> He found her, and the discovery sent a shock of horror through him that almost stopped the beating of his heart. She was in the centre of a noisy laughing group of men, smoking a cigarette and holding an empty liqueur glass in her hand into which the Baron von Hohenfels was pouring some brandy, laughing boisterously and joking hideously. Every nerve within him thrilled in an agony of shame, this the glorious interpreter of heavenly sound! this the artist he so passionately desired to reverence as a woman, while worshipping her genius![87]

Like the misty-eyed Frenchman in 'Brases', Ehrenstein's idealised views of femininity distort his perceptions, in a novel that repeatedly probes attitudes towards gender and nation both in the patriarchal and conservative Greek society as well as in the cosmopolitan world that exists alongside it.[88]

Most of Lynch's 1890s fiction, then, deployed an anti-marriage or at least interrogation of marriage plot, typical of emergent New Woman fiction. Quests for alternatives often ended in failure, death or were in the end resolved by marriage. The latter resolution, characteristic of most of Lynch's 1890s fiction, lies partially in market and economic demands – Lynch needed to sell her novels – but these marriages also constitute aspects of her 'cosmopolitan modernity', discussed earlier, the establishment of 'affective communities', and a gesture towards the possibility of sympathy between men and women and among nations.[89] Rosni Harvey, whose Irish admirer, like Jinny Blake's, turns out to be fickle, marries the ultimate cosmopolitan, Ulysses Parthenopolous, who 'had been brought up between England and France, and could scarcely escape the mixed influences of both nationalities'.[90] The star-crossed lovers, Greek Inarime Selaka and Turkish archaeologist Daoud Bey (working in Greece under the alias 'Gustav Reineke'), overcome her father's horror – 'the Turk was the symbol of all that is most hateful in his country's past' – to become an exemplary couple in *Daughters of Men*.[91] In *Jinny Blake* the marriage plots, through which the possibility of sympathy across nations is explored, are more complex. Jinny's childhood friend, the very English Nanny Brown, makes a romantic marriage to an impecunious Spanish aristocrat and they settle in London to make their living as artist and writer respectively. There is no Englishman in contention for Jinny's hand, and unlike her forebear, the wild Irish girl of Sydney Owenson's influential novel, there is no allegorical union suggested between divided England and Ireland. She has plenty of suitors, however, but rejects Pepe, the young, passionate and highly eligible Spanish marquis, and the Irishman Charles Nugent, both of whom compromise her respectability in subplots that suggest resonances with Henry James' *Daisy Miller*. These Jamesian echoes continue in the conclusion of the novel when Jinny agrees to marry the quiet and steady American John Trowbridge, who is as dogged and devoted as Caspar Goodwood in *The Portrait of a Lady*.[92] Out of sympathy with the national cultures and gender politics of the marquis and Nugent, Jinny's acceptance of Trowbridge is significant for its lack of idealism and romance: 'You can woo me after marriage. But I want to get away from myself, from England, from all I fear to remember. You will help me, John, and I will try to be good to you.'[93]

As the significant body of scholarship dedicated to women and public spaces (that is, mainly urban spaces) in the late-nineteenth century has revealed, the *flâneuse* is a complex and contradictory figure.[94] Lynch's version of the *flâneuse*, the Irish female vagabond, is not only urban and nor is she confined to the contours of Ireland.[95] Nor was the concept of the female vagabond unique to Lynch. Dúnlaith Bird, in her study of European women's Oriental travelogues from the 1850s, identifies the 'central concept of *vagabondage*', defining it:

> ... as a search for identity through motion, a physical and textual
> elaboration ... It emerges as a totemic concept in European women's
> writing from the 1850s, inciting a reformulation of what it means to be a
> woman by pushing out the physical, geographical, and textual parameters
> by which 'women' are defined.[96]

While, in true fashion, Lynch's writing does not fit neatly into this paradigm, the recurring allusions to solitary female wanderers as vagabond figures suggest a deliberate use and understanding of the trope.[97] As Bird elaborates, the idea of *vagabondage* 'offers an alternative model of mobility and gender scrutiny', a model traceable throughout Lynch's *oeuvre*.[98] In her non-fiction she tramps through forests and up mountains, travels by ship and train, often unaccompanied, and, as a solitary figure exploring on foot remote Spanish and French rural villages, is at times tantamount to a spectacle.[99] The vagabond heroines in her fiction create similar sensations, often in dramatic circumstances and using modern modes of transport.[100]

A striking example of this kind of heroine, setting off abroad and flouting expectations of their sex, can be found in another short story Lynch wrote for the *Girl's Realm*, 'A Girl's Ride on an Engine', which features the sixteen-year-old Ella Morgan setting off alone on a desperate journey by train and steamer from Sussex to Jersey in a bid to see her dying mother. Ella, an example of the 'New Girl' and subject of an array of recent critical work, misses the last train to Southampton but arrives there in time for her steamer by agreeing to travel on an engine – 'You'll have to stand with the stokers, and keep your nerve.'[101] As Kristine Moruzi has pointed out, Ella's 'unique experience of riding the engine highlights her modernity, since she is not safely contained within one of the travelling carriages'.[102] It also marks a further invasion of male spaces, highlighted by the stationmaster's wry observation that although young ladies have 'taken to the bicycle ... they've wisely left us the engine', while the journey itself, aboard 'The red-eyed beast', marks a terrifying sense of a loss of self amid disordered and distorted perceptions.[103]

> She ceased to be a thinking creature, and became merely a bag of nerves
> in that thunder of unfamiliar sound. Sensation and sight were so acutely

merged into one, and indivisible, that she could make no distinction between what she was seeing and what she was feeling ... Of the landscape, even as a shadowed mass, nothing was visible. It, like her own personality, had crumbled out of existence upon waves of horrid smoke. The universe had resolved itself into velocity and howl, into red flames and vapour, and sharp pricking pain of visage and blighted vision.[104]

The story offers a tale of transformation and initiation into a new sense of being, a passage from girlhood to womanhood not only through the experience of solitary travel but through raw contact with modern technology that alters her sense of time and space: 'she would have been puzzled to say if she had been a century or a minute on the wings of steam'.[105] As in the New Woman fiction by writers such as George Egerton and Charlotte Mew, 'urban mobility becomes a motor for the articulation of a gendered, modern consciousness' in this story.[106] In addition, Ella's close encounters with friendly male rail workers who ensure the success of her journey further demonstrate Kate Krueger Henderson's point that public transport tended to further complicate the 'Victorian ideological segregation of class and gender'.[107]

In other narratives where these vagabond heroines cross geographical and sometimes class borders and boundaries, they also cross boundaries of acceptable female behaviour and allow Lynch, cultural observer and critical commentator, to voice a range of opinions about Ireland and Irishness, Britain and imperialism, Spain and the Spanish, Greece, France and more.[108] For example, in *Rosni Harvey*, published six years earlier than her *Girl's Realm* story, Lynch depicted another dramatic journey of a lone woman, this time the eponymous heroine in desperate pursuit of a steamer she has missed. Believing that the cousin with whom she is travelling to Constantinople is aboard, Rosni risks her life taking a small boat across the choppy Mersey to catch up with the steamer as it leaves Liverpool.[109]

> At the starting-point, a large concourse of spectators was eagerly gathered. The waves dashed up against the wharf, and every one admired the extraordinary courage of the slight girl who was going to brave that angry tide in a mere cockleshell.[110]

Rosni steers the boat as 'the men made violent and futile efforts to save the drenched girl from the spray dashing over her' and 'When the boat drew alongside the steamer, Rosni seriously began to speculate on the probability of her succeeding in scaling the perpendicular, wave-washed and impossible stairs thrown down for her use'.[111] She manages to board the ship safely but in a bedraggled and less than ladylike state. It soon becomes clear that Rosni's actions have provoked both admiration, as a 'heroine of a romance', and condemnation among the cosmopolitan passengers: 'It is perfectly astonishing how young girls travel nowadays, and especially in this country; I confess I don't care for the custom.'[112] This disapproval is double; Rosni is aboard unchaperoned, as it turns out, and her dramatic arrival thoroughly unfeminine. Potential accusations of Rosni's occupying a morally dubious position on board the steamer are averted, however, because of its accidental nature. The trope of unplanned or spontaneous travel as a way of sanctioning the solitary woman traveller is another shared with narrative modes of *vagabondage*.[113] As in 'A Girl's Ride on an Engine', modern modes of travel offer another occasion for multinational groupings and exchanges about national and gender identities. On board ship, a space that is potentially neutral in terms of national borders and social conventions, Rosni encounters gender and racial prejudice in the figure of the obnoxious Mr Lee (a forebear of Virginia Woolf's Richard Dalloway in *The Voyage Out*), the very antithesis of the sympathetic outlook she embodies.

Rosni also meets and converses with multilingual Ulysses, who is as exasperated as she is by Mr Lee's attitude towards every nation other than England: '"Those people who go about raving on the subject of their country, and insulting all others, should really be locked up."'[114] In the widely travelled and highly educated Ulysses, Rosni finds the sympathetic company she lacked at home in Ireland, sharing views on books and politics and in particular a sharp critique of empire and particularly colonialism in Africa and the action of missionaries worrying 'the poor barbarians into Christianity'.[115] Rosni's observation, 'The absurdity of the thing is, that while these English missionaries go off to bring civilization and religion into other countries, they leave in their own land a far greater depth of ignorance, savagery, and heathenism', offers a counterpoint to Mr Lee's earlier claim as English shores recede from view that it is '"the last glimpse of civilization we shall have until we see it again"'.[116] It also anticipates a similar setting and conversation between Conrad's Marlow and his fellow sailors as they await the turn of the tide aboard the *Nellie*, contemplating the nature of civilization and the dark places of the world. Away from home and in this cosmopolitan space, Rosni Harvey is forced to recognise the precariousness of her own national identity, realising that 'Ireland has no real nationality in foreign lands, except for the enlightened few, who recognise it dimly as an English province subject to periodical rebellions and famines'.[117] Ulysses outstrips even this 'enlightened few', spelling out the tensions between Ireland and England to his cousin Sappho: 'Perhaps you are not aware that there is an eternal enmity between the races, and that the deepest insult you could inflict on either is to mistake one for the other.'[118] His observation, and his later refusal to play 'God Save the Queen', highlights the sympathetic nature of this character and confirms him as an ideal match for Lynch's Irish heroine. It also lays out the possibility of rapprochement through sensitivity and respect for difference, as well as through mobility and 'interpenetration'.

While gender, national identity and relations between nations is the focus of Rosni Harvey's journey on the *Thessaly*, it is specifically gender differences that surface in another steamer journey in *Jinny Blake*. Here Lynch describes a similar scenario where the heroine boards a ship in flight, this time from her ardent aristocratic Spanish admirer and his enraged father, who disapproves of Jinny's national and class differences. On this ship bound for Constantinople, the revelation for the solitary, cigarette-smoking Jinny is not the condition of her Irishness, but the condition of femaleness. She is forced to recognise on that journey that 'A sole lady, and she young and fair, on board a boat constructed for males had the natural effect of turning a sentimental captain and all his men into a circle of ecstatic servitude.'[119] *Jinny Blake* is as focused, however, as *Rosni Harvey* on the issue of Irishness. The action of this novel is staged across a range of European countries, revealing and examining a cosmopolitan Irishness through which Lynch voices her double criticism of the fact that 'the Saxons [are] still ruling over in Erin' and that women can only move 'from vexed liberty to servitude'.[120] Schooled at a French convent along with a Spanish princess and the English 'Miss Brown' who she meets again in Spain, Jinny's education, like Ulysses' in *Rosni Harvey*, epitomises the experience of transnational contact and cultural transfer. She recalls teaching her foreign friends about Ireland as they celebrated a St Patrick's feast: '"We all wore shamrocks", she continued, "and we sang a rebel song, just as heartily as if we were all conspiring against England."'[121] But Jinny's rebel Irish self is consistently hybridised, like Don Fernand O'Neill already noted, or the little Spanish duke, Diego, who speaks English with an Irish brogue because he has an Irish nurse. Jinny, described at one point in the narrative as 'Jinny Blake of Normandy', is based in London but, on agreeing to marry John Trowbridge, requests that she be taken to Italy away from England and from herself.[122] The ending of this novel is more muted than that of *Rosni Harvey*, where Rosni is finally happily paired with Ulysses and restored to her beloved Ireland. Jinny, despite her attempt to assert independence by fleeing both society and relationships, capitulates to marriage. Her acceptance, made on her own terms, 'That you take me as I am', and on the understanding that she is yet to fall in love with her future husband, is illustrative once again of Gagnier's definition of the New Woman fiction which assesses 'the scope and limits of autonomy and independence, solubility and separation, within relationship'.[123]

It is also indicative of Lynch's testing of the possibilities and limits of sympathy, and of the cosmopolitan aesthetics that shaped these novels. For Jinny's reticent acceptance of marriage should be understood in relation to her earlier observation of disconnections not only between men and women, but between classes and nations, disconnections Lynch sought in these fictions to understand and possibly overcome. Midway through the novel, Nannie and Jinny compare the treatment they have received (often at the hands of other women) in various countries and in different class contexts. In summary, Jinny declares:

> Races as well as classes and sexes have their own tram-lines, of which they have the air of bolting for accident and disaster. Boys are simply asked not to be cowards, and women are simply recommended to be chaste. Yet the pure woman may be the meanest and biggest liar unthrashed, she may have a taste for brandy, and knock all the other commandments into smithereens. And your man of courage may be a bestial ruffian and drive a dozen women to the grave. It isn't only the Spaniards who are topsy-turvy. I'm afraid, Nannie, we're all wrong, and so besotted with our different conventionalities that there is no getting hold of a clean and reasonable aspect of virtue that will do for all weathers, all nations, all sexes, and equally for public and private use.[124]

In this passage, modern transport becomes a metaphor for disconnection and unbridgeable distance, in contrast with the liberating forces of engines and steamers in Lynch's other fiction, where either a raw and dynamic sense of self is realised or boundaries of self and nation can potentially be breached.

However, prior to this conversation with Nannie, Jinny does have a fleeting experience of occupying a different space, inhabiting an alternative identity and travelling in a different skin, to adapt Bird's phrase.[125] Seeking to escape the claustrophobia of Spanish aristocratic society and the pressure to marry, Jinny fantasises about being someone other than a young woman confined by class and gender definitions. She imagines herself as Don Quixote, scouring 'some empty plain on a fleet horse'[126] and discusses with her young stepmother, Lady Jewsbury, the possibilities and limitations of cross-dressing, with reference to Shakespeare's Rosalind and the forest of Ardennes. Proposing a walk, in disguise, through the bustling streets of Madrid, Jinny is thrilled by the prospect of *vagabondage*: 'I want a taste of street life. Let us go out like a party of foreign vagabonds, and see what the common people are doing.'[127] This brief adventure allowed Lynch to revel in observation, while drawing attention to the various gendered performances for which this 'street life' is the stage. The passage is worth quoting at length:

Hooded and cloaked, the ladies went out into the noisy, bright streets ... It was all delightfully foreign, rich in colour, with a loud urgence of strange speech in the air against the still half melancholy thinness of Spanish dance music. The freed servant-maids were abroad, flirting paper fans beneath the heaven thick sewn with large soft stars. Their males-in-waiting made amorous sentinels along the side walks, and sent the bowboy's shafts through the night air upon a whizz of southern hyperbole. Here and there a lady shot past on the arm of a cavalier, showing an opaque white cheek under a cloud of mantilla, her high heels striking a resonant flap along the pavement. Sometimes an ostentatious fellow stood in a full glare of light, and let it be seen that he wore an embroidered jacket and a red silk sash. He at least was in no doubt of his own effectiveness, and posed admirably for the stars when there was no woman by. Or a graceful shade in cap and sombrero travelled romantically down a narrow cleft of gas-lit silence, like the tail-end of a mediaeval history worked by snatches into our trousered and hatted century.

Women and girls in variously-hued skirts, some with carnations in their hair or fastened into the joining of the handkerchiefs across their bosoms, danced with men in short jackets and sashes or in European coats, according to their business and situation in life. They danced not only with grace but with a consummate art and gravity born of a conviction that dancing is the great affair of life. They were not boisterous nor merry; they were simply artists exercising a noble and neglected art. When the musicians burst into a modern waltz, Jinny could not stand out against an overmastering temptation.[128]

Intoxicated by this carnival of colliding historical, topographical and sensual effects, Jinny seizes Lady Jewsbury and the two women whirl 'around among the servants and loafers of Madrid on a delirious spin'[129] before their disguises slip and they feel obliged to leave. This short interlude is fascinating for two reasons. First, it aligns Lynch most closely, albeit briefly, with contemporary cross-dressing female figures associated with *vagabondage*, who transgressed social, gender and indeed sexual codes. We can remember Lynch's early affection for the writings of George Sand here, although her sharp observation of the 'art' of masculine self-construction (the sash, the embroidered jacket) is also of note. Second, it provides a flavour of Lynch's powers of description as a traveller and observer, traceable throughout her fiction and travel writing. Her distinctive style and perspective is the subject of the next chapter.

CHAPTER 5

'The Vagabond's Scrutiny': Hannah Lynch in Europe

B y now it will be apparent that Lynch's taste for travel was absolutely central to her writing. Her examination of the relationship between 'national character' and the 'character of nations' acted as the frame for many of the discussions of interpersonal relationships, agency and liberty which dominated her novels, criticism and short fiction.[1] In this chapter we will look in detail at Lynch's non-fictional travel writing, exploring its generic range, as well as its ambivalence, astuteness and considerable wit. Even discounting her 'Paris Letters', there is an impressive amount of such material, and the potential that even more will be discovered as interest in her work develops. Presenting a generous cross-section, we aim to address some of the central issues in play. These include Lynch's engagement with ongoing debates about the traveller and the tourist, her affinities with, and differences from, male travel writers such as Pierre Loti, and her pervasive concern with the lives of women in the countries she traverses. All these concerns helped to shape her own topographical style, which might be described using her phrase 'the vagabond's scrutiny'.[2] As we have seen, the figure of the vagabond, used so negatively in depictions of the Irish abroad, was one that Lynch appropriated and positively glossed.[3] Therefore, this chapter will also examine Lynch's sometimes concealed, sometimes overt references to Ireland and its political condition. Her cosmopolitan range of allusion asserted her position within the international literary field, but also offered a different way of writing the politics of 'home'.

The condition of liberty had been a preoccupation of Lynch's fiction from the start, and in her travel writing it found a literal transcription. Many of her pieces presented Lynch as the object of confusion, scrutiny, misperception and comical outrage. But, as she was in control of the narrative, in doing so they also permitted her to perform acts of scrutiny, to defy convention, to make assumptions, and to assert her authority as a subject. Like her Anglo-Irish counterpart Beatrice Grimshaw, a self-declared 'Revolting Daughter' who 'bought a bicycle, with difficulty [and] rode it unchaperoned, miles and miles beyond the limits possible to the soberly trotting horses', or like Somerville and Ross, or Emily Lawless, Lynch appropriated and reinvented the practices and perspectives of the Victorian woman traveller.[4] Dúnlaith Bird's study of Francophone *vagabondage* addresses the balance Lynch needed to strike when presenting her often solo voyages: 'Travelling is trouble: motion connotes upheaval and change. How then do certain women travellers write their way out of trouble, constructing vagabonding gender identities at once unsettling and appealing to their European readers?'[5] Her writing identity, already refracted through a variety of lenses, was further complicated by the outlets in which she appeared. These enabled or necessitated a different voice according to their market, as well as reflecting the point in Lynch's career when they were published. When she was writing for the *Freeman's Journal* or for an Irish-American publication such as *Donahoe's Magazine*, Lynch's travel pieces often praised the beauty of the Irish landscape and poured scorn on English arrogance and ignorance. When she was writing for *Hearth and Home* or *Good Words*, the inflection was understandably very different, reflecting what her English audience would find acceptable. Her travel pieces on the Canary Islands, Catalonia and the Acropolis demonstrate the range of approaches she took to this issue, even seemingly neutral pieces carrying traces of her commitments.

Having become an observer of foreign places in childhood, her early training and experience are evident in the acute observation of detail in her early article 'A Backward Glance at the City of the Pale', published for an Irish-American readership in Boston's *Donahoe's Magazine* in 1884. Tracing the history of Ireland through the transformations of Dublin's architecture and landmarks, Lynch introduced the piece with two quotations from Victor Hugo's *Notre Dame de Paris*, beginning a longstanding practice of refracting readings of Ireland through European travels and texts. The first of the quotations she chose was a famous section from Chapter 2, 'Paris à Vol d'Oiseau':

> Mais une ville comme Paris est une crue perpétuelle. Il n'y a que ces villes-là qui deviennent capitales. Ce sont des entonnoirs où viennent aboutir tous les versantes géographiques, politiques, moraux, intellectuels d'un pays, toutes les pentes naturelles d'un peuple; des puits de civilisation pour ainsi dire, et aussi des égouts, où commerce, industrie, intelligence, population, tout ce qui est sève, tout ce qui est vie, tout ce qui est âme d'une nation, filtre et s'amasse sans cesse, goutte à goutte, siècle à siècle.[6]

Hugo viewed the city as an expression of both historical time and the particular history of a people. Lynch emphasised the latter in her second quotation: 'Le temps est l'architecte, le peuple est le maçon.'[7] Her account of Dublin from the era of the Danes until the present day aimed for a similar effect, offering a detailed description of the evolution of the city until 1782. This tracked across Dublin street by street, finally lingering on the old Parliament House on College Green:

> At what hour, in what light, is it not beautiful? Victor Hugo calls *Notre Dame* a vast symphony in stone: might we not call this house a vast and sublime ode to liberty in imperishable writing, round which all the best hopes, the eternal passion and aspiration of a suppressed nation are centered irrevocably.[8]

Architectural and cultural history merge, just as they do in Hugo's Paris, although in Lynch's account of Dublin this is a painful graft. She replaced a religious edifice with a political one, and observed that the Parliament House offered a sense of continuation alongside a parallel feeling of loss. Vanished buildings evoked present memories, as she imagined a visitor standing on the ground formerly occupied by the Corn Market: 'but the spectator of to-day would have no room for other memories than the loved memory of Robert Emmet and his tragic death'.[9] The disjunction continued throughout the latter part of the article, which dwelled on the developments that had taken place in Dublin over the previous century – the majority of which was, of course, after the Act of Union. Here the 'imperishable writing' of the older cityscape was juxtaposed with reminders of colonial intervention – such as the 'meaningless ugliness of Nelson's Pillar' – and ongoing resistance – the 'gilt vulgarity of King William remains in sublime unconsciousness of its double unattractiveness, happily relieved of its fatal prominence by the really admirable statue of Grattan near it'.[10] She continued:

> But some of us, perhaps, picture to ourselves regretfully the grim towers, the irregular streets, the labyrinthine lanes, and vaguer plans of old Dublin, with its strongly marked individuality, its thousand quaintness and incongruities, over which the sunshine and shadow fell so unequally long, long before it became the City of the Pale.[11]

Thus, her conclusion highlighted loss and retrospect, her choice of title not only referring to Ireland's lost heritage, but also to the 'backward glances' of a potentially homesick emigrant readership.

Hugo's Paris provided Lynch with a lens through which to anatomise her own native city. What emerged through this exploration was not only nostalgia, but rebellion. This was a rebellion against the English presence, certainly, but also a more subtle rebellion against the template of the epigram. Despite their shared aims, Lynch rejected the swooping overview of Hugo's text, preferring the wandering, street-level, vagabond perspective, in accord with 'irregular streets, the labyrinthine lanes, and vaguer plans of old Dublin, with its strongly marked individuality'. Lynch frequently aligned the actual winding, 'irregular' topography of particular cities with their aesthetic and cultural potential. Her preference for this viewpoint can be read as a feminist strategy, in keeping with some of her contemporaries. As Heidi Hansson points out in her study of Lawless: 'When women writers describe the landscape, an important question is therefore whether they continue the male tradition of the eighteenth and nineteenth centuries or whether they create new models that express a feminine, or perhaps feminist, understanding of the land.'[12]

The strategy Hansson pinpoints can be glimpsed in an even earlier piece. This was Lynch's debut for Father Matthew Russell's *Irish Monthly*: 'Nature's Constancy in Variety'.[13] Published in 1883, it was a melancholy meditation on the solace to be found in nature. While this piece, with its evocation of mood, landscape and description, could not be more different from the detailed, factual and densely packed history of Dublin in 'A Backward Glance', the preferred perspective is once again that of the vagabond. 'Only those who have rambled aimlessly among green wild hills and delicately sloping valleys', she wrote, 'can know how colour and perfume may penetrate.'[14] Lynch prescribed sheer immersion, where 'an immense depth of personal acquaintance with colour, tint, leaf, and shape' should gradually be established, in opposition to the more superficial reactions to landscape by 'the shallow insipidity of the effusive tourist', the 'admirer of the gushing or aesthetic school' and the 'bearish' Dr Johnson who finds 'one green field is precisely like another green field'.[15] By distinguishing herself from these various readings of landscape, Lynch, in one of the earliest examples we have of her published travel writing, asserted a particular position and writing identity that she continued to develop in her later work.[16]

'Nature's Constancy' provided a template for the many interests and preoccupations that are evident in her later writing. After laying out the different methods of engaging with nature, Lynch narrowed her focus to Irish landscape in particular: 'And here in Ireland we have no need to turn abroad in search of the beautiful or the picturesque.'[17] But the perspective was an international one, as the Irish landscape was filtered through the lens of the European, and refracted back again in all its dazzling beauty:

> When I first saw the dark blue of the Pyrenees lying under its translucent veil of brilliant sparkling snow, resting high up against a sky of lighter blue, I looked in speechless wonder and delight; but when, years later, I caught a glimpse of the Commeragh [*sic*] Mountains, one clear February day, I saw no difference in the beauty, notwithstanding the immensity and impressiveness of the Spanish range (I was young then and an indifferent traveller).[18]

This lambent language flickers on and off in descriptive passages across her prose fiction, and is heard briefly in the description of Ireland embedded in her reading of 'Neptunevale'. The skewering of Ireland's 'romance' that takes place in so much of her writing can sometimes be suspended in her topographical texts.

The intensity and power of her evocation of place became associated with a form of literary impressionism, although these early Irish pieces predate the currency of the term. This approach was not restricted to her writing on Ireland, as we can see from a brief exploration of one of her most popular full-length travel books, *Toledo: the story of an old Spanish capital*, published by Dent in 1898. Dent was a reputable and popular publisher and, as such, the book was both excerpted and widely reviewed.[19] The *Daily News* announced that 'Tourists on the Continent will find that Dent volumes are excellent guide books', and endorsed Lynch for her 'well known' translations and 'studies from the Spanish'.[20] The *Leeds Mercury* described Lynch as 'favourably known by an ambitious critical estimate of George Meredith, as well as by a group of clever, refined novels of her own', and designated the book a 'picturesque monograph'.[21] The *New York Times* concluded that: 'The author has handled her subject in such a fascinating manner that we are sure all readers will close the volume with a longing to see the home of so much former grandeur … so vividly and faithfully described.'[22] On 10 May 1899, a reviewer in the *Freeman's Journal* proclaimed *Toledo* a 'Brilliant Book By an Irish Authoress'. It was described as a 'tour de force', Lynch as 'the ideal traveller and the ideal narrator of travel', and particular praise was accorded to her description of Toledo's cathedral: 'it combines every quality of the guide, without one single defect of the guide-book; but only those who have essayed descriptive writing of this kind can estimate the triumph over literary difficulties and the skill with which she tells everything without a hint of pedantry or lecturing dulness'.[23] The *Academy* for 2 September 1899 contained an equally approving review, but with an important distinction. The anonymous author went further than the writer in the *Freeman's Journal*, not only praising *Toledo* for its particular qualities, but using it as evidence that a 'new literature of topography is springing up – a literature which is more concerned with the spirit of a place than with its form':

> The new topographer is different. The first thing he does on arriving in a place is to throw himself onto his back and dream. He postpones all minor inquiry until he has caught the spirit of his surroundings. He thinks less of the place than of the human spirit which has passed into it; he is solicitous to find not a description, but a metaphor … This method lifts topography to a higher notch on the literary scale.[24]

This author noted that Lynch was 'sealed in this new school', citing the 'intensely modern' Maurice Barrès on her opening page.[25] Two years later, in 1901, a further article appeared. Entitled 'A Plea for "A Man in the Street" Topography', and quite possibly by the same author, it gave a less affirmative presentation of this 'new school'. It asserted that 'now impressionism is your only wear, and real topography is starved into moods and frittered into epithet'. Lynch was included in the list of notable exceptions:

> With what is called 'the spirit of place' we have full sympathy. The literature which gives it expression fascinates us. Beautiful writing in this kind has been done by Mrs Meynell, 'Vernon Lee', Miss Hannah Lynch, Mr Henry James, Mr Arthur Symonds [*sic*], and many other writers whose names will occur to our readers.[26]

This selection of reviews provides a useful index when considering how to situate Lynch's travel writing within its contemporary field. The *Freeman's* careful distinction between the 'quality of the guide' and the defects of the 'guide book' touched on the most delicate issue. By the 1880s, the word 'tourist' had carried negative implications for some time, against which the more adventurous and independent 'traveller' could define themselves. The 'guide book' was, of course, increasingly synonymous with the former. Lynch was aware of this distinction, but she was also aware of the pretension that could underpin it. She mocked this specifically in an 1897 *Freeman's Journal* piece on her visit to Montserrat.[27] Explaining how she came to find herself toiling along the edge of a precipice in dizzying heat – 'no image but that of the grave, dug particularly deep, seemed cool and dark enough for broiled skin and aching eyes' – she concluded:

> I made the mistake of listening to Spaniards before going to Montserrat, instead of consulting Murray or Baedecker. I pride myself, foolishly enough, on having travelled over most of Europe, to the confines of Turkey, without a red-covered guide book. This is my weakness and my folly. It saves me from looking like a tourist, object of my horror and unjust contempt, since there is nothing on earth more respectable, more worthy of our admiration, than a tourist.[28]

Lynch's wit was as mordant as ever, but her revelation of the 'folly' of rejecting the 'red-covered guide book' is telling if we take the widespread praise of *Toledo* into account. For, despite its status as 'picturesque monograph' by an author of 'clever and refined novels', *Toledo* was a species of guidebook, part of a series aimed precisely at 'Tourists on the Continent', which would run on into the late 1920s. Lynch's other full-length travel text, *French Life in Town and Country* (1901), fell into a similar category. It was part of the series 'Our European Neighbours', published in London by George Newnes, and by Putnam & Sons in New York. Including volumes on Spain, Italy and Germany, these books were advertised as practical and informative, rather than in any way literary.[29] Such publishing contexts might have exposed a far wider readership to her work, but in doing so they once again threatened Lynch's status as a high-brow, literary author who could be compared with more established writers of the 'new school' as renowned as James, Symons, Meynell and Lee.

Lynch was forced to confront this issue head on in March 1901 when the *Speaker* published 'F.Y.E.'s hostile review to *French Life in Town and Country*, which we noted in the Introduction, and which led her to 'horsewhipping' its author in the correspondence columns. Having established Lynch's 'credentials', and noted her 'Irish origin', the reviewer went on to take issue with several aspects of her account.[30] Her apparent lack of 'a vigilant distrust of personal experience as the one sufficient basis on which to found moral judgements affecting vast human groups' was one of these failings, and this became a 'serious limitation' in large part due to her position as 'a foreign journalist in Paris'. Journalists, the author stated, were 'by professional instinct' liable to misrepresentation, they were 'wont to herd together', and were 'readily affected by superficial enthusiasms'. Lynch's response was predictably swift and robust:

> He calls me a journalist, which I am not. I write about new French books from time to time and sketches or essays of travel when I have seen anything worth writing about. Many of these little papers appeared in *THE SPEAKER* years ago, but they do not pretend to be journalism. I do not herd with journalists, for I know none.[31]

Lynch's desire to avoid the label 'journalist' was hardly surprising given the general prejudice underpinning the *Speaker*'s review.[32] In response, Lynch placed her travel writing more firmly within a literary tradition. Her magazine columns were 'essays or sketches', or 'little papers', disconnected from the implication that she was only writing them for the money as she only produced them when there was something 'worth writing about'. Authors whom Lynch admired – Stevenson in particular – had already combined the roles of novelist, literary critic and contributor of travel articles. Much the same could be said of Lynch's immediate contemporary Vernon Lee, and of the other exceptions listed in the 1901 *Academy* article. If the review made an implicitly gendered criticism in its reference to journalism, it was totally open on the subject only a few lines later. When the *vie de café* was so central to French culture, and yet was 'almost a closed book' for 'women who respect themselves', what authority did Lynch have to comment upon it?[33] The same argument applied for boys' schools, and for the army, both of which *French Life in Town and Country* roundly criticised. Again, Lynch did not bother to hide her irritation, driving her point home with reference to the nationality of the reviewer:

> As a specimen of masculine superiority it is droll ... A woman is as competent to give an opinion on conscription and the French Army as an English reviewer, for the limitations of her sex are not greater than are those of his nationality ...
>
> The Bal Bullier and the Moulin Rouge are much frequented pilgrimages of pleasure I may be supposed to know enough about on hearsay. But such arguments are idiotic and prove again that that mysterious thing British prudery perpetually strains at gnats and swallows camels. Should we say that M. Brieux, being a man, had no business to write a play about wet nurses ... ? For women have served in the army before and since the days of Joan of Arc, and women may frequent public halls and cafés and other such resorts; but no man can ever have any practical experiences as a wet-nurse, which does not prevent M. Brieux from telling the world how mothers should act.[34]

Lynch's frustration at such attitudes, not only typical of the British, was voiced across the breadth of her work. Critique and satire of gender stereotypes and prejudice are a feature of her travel writing, something she shared with many women travel writers of the period.[35] The position of the Victorian woman traveller, in relation to other genres, to male writers, and to the 'new' space they occupy in this field, was already complex, and numerous critics have highlighted 'the range of tones and discourses in women's travel writing of the late Victorian era'.[36] Maria Frawley, for instance, outlines a number of motivations and consequences for women of travelling and writing during this period: it offered an escape from the confines of the private sphere, a possibility for exploring and expressing independence, a means of intellectual survival, and a way of asserting and connecting with cultural authority. Travelling also became a potential mode of social criticism, in which 'writing about other societies enabled women to critique their own'.[37] However, the majority of scholarship is focused on women writers whose identity and perspective is shaped by their connection with England as home and as a colonial power against which, or along with which, they write. For such authors, distance could be enabling, giving leeway to criticise, but also providing a space in which to solidify their own sense of identity relationally to that 'home'. This focus has been valuable in establishing the field and in opening up a critique of colonial agendas – and particularly in noting that feminist principles and anti-imperial sentiments did not necessarily go hand in hand. However, it can generate the sense that the only women authors of any significance were, to all intents and purposes, looking through 'British' eyes. This inevitably marginalises the narratives of those such as Lynch and her Anglo-Irish contemporaries, whose national identities complicate established parameters for reading travel writing of this period.[38] As Lynch made clear in most of her travel writing intended for English or American readers, 'home', and the identity of the writing self, was elsewhere.

The idea of the 'double-voiced discourse', so typical of women writing in the nineteenth century, is particularly apposite in relation to Lynch's work in this genre.[39] It enabled a balance to be struck between the unsettling and the appealing aspects of *vagabondage*, earlier noted by Bird. Taking *French Life in Town and Country* as an example, we can see that one element of this balance was tonal. As the horsewhipped reviewer 'F.Y.E.' observed, Lynch wrote with 'volcanic severity' on Catholic convents and on the army, while praising many other aspects of French cultural life, openly offsetting the negative against the positive.[40] But elsewhere she used a different tactic. For instance, she framed her comparative reading of the English and the French in veiled terms familiar from her 'Paris Letters': 'I, who am neither French nor English, can testify to the magnanimous recognition of national virtues of both to each other'.[41] The second chapter of the book turned on a comparison between Paris and London. Here, Lynch displayed an in-depth knowledge of both capital cities and, having highlighted her insider/outsider status as a 'Parisianised foreigner', she once again claimed the freedom and authority to comment on both. Her criticism of British imperialism, 'the British virtuous youth, [who desires] to mould all humanity upon his own stiff and starched effigy', is made slightly, inserted into a comic narrative of the characteristic types of both nations.[42] Lynch's 'impartial' commentary and satire became more witty and cutting when she considered gender issues. Recounting an incident in the French countryside where her impulsive departure from a group to pick blackberries prompted comments about improper behaviour, she commented: 'I suggested writing, with their aid, the things a man and a woman (especially a woman) cannot do in France, but on consideration found it would make too large a volume.'[43] Earlier in the text, she pointed out the role women played in the rural economy, and the resistance they encountered upon trying to enter the professions, using the word 'feminism' explicitly:

> It would be difficult to find a people to whom modern feminism is more repugnant than the French, and hard to name one that owes more to the intelligence, goodwill, and incessant labour of women. Frenchmen object to women in the liberal professions, and make a desperate hue and cry the day a talented lady seeks leave to wear the lawyer's toque and gown. Yet the fields are tended by women; flags are waved at railway-gates by them; in the lower ranks they bravely do all the rougher work of men, and nobody lifts a voice in protest.[44]

Lynch's desire to restore the deeds of such women to historical record was matched by her insistence in pointing out the distortions to be found in male-authored literature. Her 'eyewitness' accounts in *French Life* were pitted against the notion of women one might build up from reading modern French novels. Here, Lynch revisited ideas of cultural misrepresentation she also explored in *Denys d'Auvrillac* and in her 'Paris Letters':

> The foreigner who only judges that role from the novels he reads ... will be all at sea as regards the part woman plays in French life. He will conceive her first playing the hypocrite up to the doors of marriage, and then playing the devil ever afterwards ...[45]

This gives us a sense of why the *Speaker* reviewer made her as angry as he did. All the issues of national, narratorial and gendered identity that Lynch had carefully laid out were reduced to a single, crude question about her sex.

The exploration of such stereotypes continued in Lynch's writing on Spain. Lynch's familiarity with Spain is evident in her many articles on its landscape, cultural practices and language, presumably assisted by Nannie's long association with the country.[46] Lynch also worked as a translator, translating a play by Spanish dramatist José Echegaray in addition to working with the novelist José Maria de Pereda.[47] One of her most trenchant critiques of the gender inequalities of the nineteenth century is voiced through her impressions of life for Spanish women in 'The Senora of To-day', published in the *Freeman's Journal* in 1894:

> ... within what mean and intolerable limits of action, thought and education she is confined by tradition ... She is furthest from being happy from any woman I know of, and I have listened to her confidences, married and maiden ... All over Spain the life of the street and that of the house is fashioned exclusively for the convenience of men. It is merely modified Orientalism, with, I imagine, a flavour of grossness foreign to the meditative Eastern. Women's tastes and exactions and varied daintinesses of mind and body are of no account.[48]

Asserting an intimacy with the lives of Spanish women – 'I have listened to their confidences' – an intimacy enabled through her understanding of the language, she writes with the authority of an insider but with the international perspective of an outsider. The fact that she invokes 'Orientalism' and thus contemporary discourses and perceptions about the constrained lives of Oriental women reinforces her critique.[49] But Lynch did not always highlight her ability to pass easily from the 'outside' to the 'inside' of Spanish culture. In an amusing 1895 article in the *Speaker*, 'A Spanish "Master" at Home', she described an impromptu meeting with José Maria de Pereda, 'the modern Cervantes', that almost unravelled before it began.[50] Arriving unaccompanied and unannounced, Lynch is first interrogated in a dark hallway by this 'singularly handsome Spaniard', before being taken into a study where she sits 'trembling and stupefied on the sofa, he standing with folded arms before me, breathing menace from crown to heel: "Explain this intrusion to my satisfaction, madam, else I shall not hesitate to fling you out of the window". Such the unspoken phrase, and I felt the cocked pistol before me. What might be the effect of my incorrect Spanish?'[51] On finding out who Lynch is, Pereda's demeanour alters entirely, and the rest of the article is taken up with Lynch's transcription of her interview with him. In fact, Lynch's engagements with Pereda would go on to become even more fractious and complicated. As Salvador García Castañeda has shown, in 1897 Lynch took serious offence when Pereda sent two friends to meet her on a subsequent visit, mistaking a mark of courtesy towards a woman for its opposite.[52]

Lynch's depiction of herself in 'A Spanish "Master" at Home', and the extent of her later affront, points to one of the most significant features of her travel writing: her frequent reminders to the reader that she, like many of her fictional heroines, was travelling alone. This self-presentation as a kind of energetic, solitary *flâneuse* is as evident in Lynch's travel writing as it was in her fiction, despite her vocal dislike of 'decadence'. It was combined with a variety of other concerns. In 'Montserrat', for instance, she noted the attention she received as a lone female traveller, but was quick to point out that this only provoked extra consideration from local people. In the first pieces she published in *Good Words* in January 1896, 'Impressions of the Canary Isles', she used her isolation as a pretext for exercising her evocative impressionism to the full:

> You have the place to yourself. A new moon curls like a shred of silver upon the shadowy blue, and the warm and lucent stars shed a twilight above the town lights. Forms and profiles are oddly revealed … So warm is the air, so subtle the scent of brine, so illusive the quiver of the stars and the white shaving of a moon swimming in indigo, that if you happen to be neither blighted nor bored, you are ready enough to count yourself on the rim at least of the garden of the Hesperides.[53]

But even here, social commentary sneaked in. Lynch stated that the reason why she could enjoy this spectacle so exclusively was because this was one of the 'forsaken nights' in Santa Cruz, when anyone who could afford to went to the theatre, and anyone who could not 'shut themselves up in their houses, prisoners of pride and their neighbours' opinion'.[54] Earlier in the same passage, Lynch made a telling observation about the military, emphasising their swaggering dominance over the local women: 'the manoeuvres of the conquering officers pacing up and down, with their eye upon some form of subjugated womanhood, flirting their canes or trailing their swords and gossiping between drinks at the café'.[55] As an English, Christian, domestic magazine, *Good Words* had a different audience to either the *Academy* or the *Freeman's Journal* or even the overtly 'Liberal' *Speaker*, but nonetheless Lynch positioned herself as a highly literary, independent and feminist writer, marginalised by choice from the imprisoning norms of social expectation.

This combination of differing emphases demonstrates how astutely Lynch bridged the supposed gap between literary and more popular travel writing. It also shows how her range of reference helped not only to underline her intellectual status – as in the casual mention of the Hesperides – but could also embed a political point within an apparently apolitical, picturesque piece. Alec

Hargreaves has discussed this refracted ideological perspective in Pierre Loti's impressionism, too, a particularly salient point as Lynch, like Loti, had expressed a desire not to subordinate aesthetics to politics within her work.[56] For instance, in the 1899 *Academy* article mentioned in the previous chapter, she criticised Legras' study of Ireland for its focus on politics at the expense of descriptions of landscape.[57] And yet it seems rather too coincidental that both Loti and Lynch's other preferred travel writer Stevenson were overtly hostile to British imperialism.[58] Lynch's other *Good Words* piece, 'A Tramp Through the Forest of Fontainebleau', was haunted by Stevenson, and it is through this dialogue that the piece emerges as an example of the way in which Lynch positioned herself simultaneously as an author as sensitive to political connotations as to literary ones.[59]

Perhaps the best example of this combination of interests was another of her 'little papers' from the *Speaker*, published in October 1894, with Loti as its focus. Entitled 'A Day in Pierre Loti's Town', it showed Lynch utilising the balance of literary reference, impressionism and topographical exactitude for which she would later be praised in the *Freeman's Journal* and the *Academy*. The piece also allowed her to align herself with a contemporary French author, one equally renowned as a traveller and a stylist. A sailor by profession, Loti's work was highly regarded in Paris at this point, and his writing would go on to influence later authors, notably Conrad.[60] Lynch's narrative recounts her pilgrimage to Loti's home in Rochefort, a barracks town which is also the unlikely location for his 'queer little semi-Japanese cottage'.[61] Lynch emphasised Loti's outsider status, using Rochefort's architecture and layout to express his distinctiveness by comparison:

> It runs in lines so straight between the Hospital and the Arsenal, that it would be physically impossible for the most absent-minded person to lose his way in a first walk across and around it. Stiff and vulgar, it rises out of a flat and marshy land; while a dull rampart upon the edge of the fields encircles the half-dozen parallel and horizontal buildings that are called streets. There is no break in uniform monotony, except the curious curve of Pierre Loti's street, which doubles its course, and in reality forms two distinct streets.[62]

The 'curious curve' of Loti's street, its doubled course, and the 'queer' little house at which he hosted extravagant costume parties are evidently emblematic of Loti himself, a figure regarded with deep suspicion by Rochefort's inhabitants. The masculine, militaristic monotony of the architecture, with its undivided line between arsenal and hospital, seems at first to forbid the wandering perspective for which Loti was renowned, and with which Lynch herself experimented. The gendered implications of this division of space are further brought home when Lynch, attempting to play the *flâneuse* despite the unpromising territory, finds herself the object of constant scrutiny. Tired by her trip, she stops outside the naval hospital, and instantly attracts a crowd of recuperating marines:

> Incommoded by this attention I moved away: they marched down in a shrill-voiced body to the verge of the grounds to see the very last of me, gesticulating and commenting. I was beginning myself to regard a woman as a rare and strange-looking animal in this stagnant town of uniformed males. Soldiers and sailors, sailors and soldiers. I found it at last monotonous. Even at dinner … I was flanked and fronted with every possible variation of French officer, each one in uniform.[63]

Again, Lynch's position as an unaccompanied woman in a town full of 'soldiers and sailors' seems ripe with threat or excitement. However, rather than emphasising this, she presented the men as a harmless if annoying herd, providing her with the opportunity to observe 'the childish curiosity of the naval and military mind'.[64] Lynch reversed gender stereotype by suggesting that these men en masse were neither virile nor dangerous, but tedious, infantile and even slightly hysterical. It is not only the men of Rochefort who demonstrate this odd fascination with her. On the walk back to the station, Lynch described a gaggle of townspeople of both sexes and all ages, who follow her, one step behind, along the way:

> The consciousness of so many eyes fixed relentlessly upon your back startles and unnerves, and I was glad to find shelter from all this eyeshot in the station, outside which they patiently stood until the train bore the solitary stranger away.[65]

Lynch leaves the reader uncertain as to whether she has been chased or escorted out of town. Either way, her own position as a 'solitary stranger', an alien element as was Loti himself, is emphasised.

This practice of reading location through a kaleidoscope of different filters – earlier representations, gender, politics, language, impression – came to define Lynch's 'vagabond's scrutiny' of self and other. Lynch explored the way in which travel, by its nature, provoked 'curious' sensations in the traveller, as well as exposing them to the curiosity of others. She examined this condition most acutely when writing about one of the world's most famous tourist destinations: Venice. In contrast to many authors of the period, Lynch wrote far less about Italy than she did about France, Spain or Greece. She published a piece about a journey between Lucerne and Verona in the *Freeman's Journal* in August 1899, in addition to her 1892 translation of Francois Perrens' *The History of Florence, 1434–1531*.[66] Venice appears as a location in her novel *Clare Monro*, and is also mentioned in a 'Paris Letter' of 8 July 1899, in which she discussed its impact on another of her favourite authors, George Sand.[67] Most stylistically striking are the two short pieces, published in the *Freeman's Journal* on the 29 and 30 December 1899. These framed the city as a vortex of overwhelming, and often conflicting, impressions, an effect also noted by Vernon Lee.[68] The prose was as compressed as Venice itself, as Lynch abandoned sequential narrative in trying to capture how the sensation of being in the city connected with its dizzying collocation of architecture, culture and history. She opened by recommending that one should visit Venice when young, since, as an older person, it is impossible to escape the depictions of others: you 'too insistently remember Canaletto and Ruskin'.[69] But this assertion was immediately overwritten by her own rapturous exclamation – 'But oh! the surpassing loveliness of it at every hour' – a rapture that resists being captured in writing: 'I know, for I tried to read Mr Grant Allen's interminable description of St. Mark's.'[70] Throughout the pieces, Lynch sketched a map of literary and artistic markers – not only Ruskin and Canaletto, but William Dean Howells' *Venetian Life*, Titian's *Assumption*, Goldoni's theatre, Tamayo's *Un Drama Nuevo*, Bellini, Tintoretto, Palma Vecchio – only to avoid the anticipated description and to dwell instead upon 'a brief, flashing recognition of delight – each traveller's individual homage'.[71] The most sustained example of this delight is enunciated in the following passage, in which Lynch elaborated upon an analogy of the city as a 'triumphant courtesan, half-Pagan, half-Byzantine Christian', too 'superbly sensuous' to be subsumed by abstraction or logic. She described the view of the Grand Canal from her room, which was worth the extortionate rent since 'if you can subsist on that and an orange you are in Paradise for a moderate sum':

> It is a sight one never tires of, just as the luxurious sensation of the unique movement (rather the negation of movement) of the gondola, as you repose on low, soft, broad cushions, and sink slantingly into the very heaven of exquisite rest, is one you can never, I believe, come to enjoy unperceived. Nothing so irrational, nothing so unlifelike, could ever come to be taken for granted. 'Tis a taste surely of Mohammed's paradise, too sensual, too physical, too demoralising to be associated with a heaven more ideal.[72]

This passage stands out in Lynch's work for its emphasis on sensuality, female sensuality in particular, and for its curious obliqueness. In an evocation of pleasure that could have been drawn from one of the 'Decadent' authors Lynch criticised so harshly, she examined an odd, suspended moment that drew together the joy of looking, of feeling, and of being looked at, conflating subject and object in a 'unique movement'. Her fleeting slip into the language of psychology – 'nothing so irrational' – combined with the more ambiguous phrase 'nothing so unlifelike', suggests simultaneously the otherworldly, the unnatural and the aesthetic. On this point Lynch corrected other *fin-de-siècle* authors, insisting on her joy in place of the anxiety or melancholy that pervaded many other accounts.[73] For all the 'interminable' architectural accounts of the way in which Venice combines Eastern and Western influences, it is in this sense-impression that the confluence of cultures can be really understood, as Lynch's 'demoralising' bliss caused her to dwell upon non-Christian notions of paradise.

Lynch's discussion of Venice also allowed her to combine impressionism's focus on individual experience with the historical, literary and cultural palimpsest explored in many of her other travel pieces. As in her account of Santa Cruz, there was a brief instance of overtly political comment – she noted the relaxed demeanour of the Venetian workmen, contrasting their 'seemliness and unconscious refinement' with the 'brutalised victims of harsh Anglo-Saxon progress'.[74] However, there was another kind of resistance in evidence, as Lynch drew attention to the religious outrages committed by Christians upon the Venetian Jewish community.[75] While some elements of her experience of Venice suggest an effective merging of cultures, and of religions, as an Irish author Lynch was equally interested in the way in which cultures survived, or emerged from, conflict. The *Freeman's* Venice articles were not the first time she had reflected on such issues from outside Ireland, as they visibly impinged not only on her account of the expulsion of Jews and Muslims from Toledo, but on the writing she produced while in another country placed liminally between East and West: Greece.[76]

In recent years, scholars have explored the significance of Greece as a destination for female travellers during the nineteenth and twentieth centuries. Evgenia Sifaki has countered the focus on English women writers with a reading of Sydney Owenson's 1809 'Greek' novel *Woman: or Ida of Athens*. Sifaki acknowledges the role Owenson played in the development of the 'national tale' and points out her 'rather unique position as both woman writer and feminist, and Irish national and nationalist'.[77] Lynch both appropriated and readdressed the idea of the 'national tale' in her own Greek novel *Daughters of Men*, sharing

Owenson's 'rather unique position' in more ways than one. Unlike Owenson, Lynch could actually travel to Greece herself. As we noted in the Introduction, she made her first trip in 1885, three years after the collapse of the Ladies' Land League. During this period, she stayed in an Ursuline convent on Tenos – courtesy of connections provided by her friend Father Thomas Dawson – and published a further two articles in the *Irish Monthly*, the outlet for her earlier piece on Irish landscape. Lynch's essays 'The Ursulines of Tenos' and 'November in a Greek Island', both published in 1886, were largely personal and picturesque. If anything, they resembled an informal dialogue between Lynch abroad and 'my readers' at home, rather than deploying the voice of the sharp-witted and feminist outsider of many of her later travel pieces.[78] But even then Lynch seems not to have purged her work of all its radical elements, as already outlined in Chapter 2.

The idea that 'pagan' Hellenism was in some respects superior to present-day Christianity was not addressed in Lynch's *Irish Monthly* articles. More central to her correspondence with Dawson was her reading of the politics of modern Greece in relation to Ireland, a topic that would also appear in her *Academy* article 'On the Acropolis', which we will discuss below. As we have seen, in an 1889 letter she commented on the way in which local differences had been overcome in the cause of a wider liberation: 'The Greeks fight wars between themselves, but they all united splendidly against the Turks. The [impression?] is that all the Greeks regarded the Turks as their enemies & only some of the Irish think so of the English.'[79] While this reinforced the tropes with which she had framed her Venetian epiphany, constructing Eastern 'otherness' by aligning her own culture with Greece, it also shifted this classic orientalist strategy. While the Irish would find themselves othered – even orientalised – in certain discourses, for Lynch it is the British Empire and the Ottoman Empire that are directly comparable, preparing the ground for a corrective analysis of the relationships between the Turks, the British, the Irish and the French. Her position also undermined the notion of the 'Celt' embedded in Arnoldian classicism, a tactic Yeats had also deployed when trying to reinscribe notions of Irish national character.[80]

Lynch opened up this territory in a lengthy review essay she published in the *Westminster Review* in January 1893, soon after the publication of *Daughters of Men*. Entitled 'Greece of To-day', it was a reading of two modern French studies of Greece, interspersed with her own recollections. She opened sardonically: 'Modern Greece, I am assured upon the indisputable authority of the newspaper critic, is a subject that does not engage the sympathies or the interest of the British public.'[81] Given this supposed lack of interest, she continued, Greece 'consoles herself with the admiration and affection of France, by which she feels herself in a measure adopted'.[82] Lynch's appreciation of the pared-down, liberated life of the Greeks – 'this race loves freedom above all, even freedom from its own laws' – opened into a contrast between their living conditions and those of even middle-class Irish families, who are also worse off than 'people of narrow means in England':[83]

> I have eaten at modest Greek tables better soup than would be eaten at the same tables in France ... Roast beef may not abound, nor are cutlets an indispensable addition to the midday meal; but except in Lent they live much better and have more varieties at table than the middle and lower classes in Ireland. Indeed, if we except meat, I should not hesitate to put their diet above that ordinarily consumed by people of narrow means in England.[84]

This specific Irish analogy was not pursued, but neither was it entirely dismissed. The Greeks loathed conscription and deplored state-sanctioned executions, she stated, in stark contrast to the way in which an English hangman might make a living 'lecturing upon his ghastly trade in the provinces or writing upon his experiences for the benefit of an unhealthy curiosity'.[85] Lynch was probably thinking about William Marwood, the English public executioner responsible for the hanging of 'the Invincibles'. Marwood enjoyed a certain celebrity in Britain at the time, and gave some public lectures.[86] In closing the piece, she reflected upon the two characteristics that had made Greece 'indomitable in servitude: patience and subtlety', concluding that with these 'great weapons at command ... Greece is not far off a strong and dignified development'.[87] Although Greece did not stand in for Ireland here – Lynch never simply superimposed one culture onto another – the image of a modern, united, free and 'dignified' nation was an important one.

This semi-submerged correlation between Ireland and Greece was more clearly visible in 'On the Acropolis', published in the *Academy* for 14 June 1902, and later reprinted in the *Living Age* in the same year. It took as its subject a return visit to perhaps the most iconic of all Greek monuments. In doing so, Lynch made reference to a recently commissioned painting of Ernest Renan 'saying his famous prayer on the Acropolis' – a cosmopolitan paean to Hellenism which had also attacked Christianity.[88] Lynch played down Renan a little, emphasising the difficulty of the subject – 'Nobody on earth is of any significance on the Acropolis' – and commenting on the way it embodied principles unknown to Gothic or medieval art, or even to other famous Greek sites – 'the immortal dream of perfection neither national nor provincial, unmarred by the traces of superstition, of prejudice, of violence, exaggeration or meanness'.[89] Renan's influence resurfaced as she shifted her attention to other monuments and artefacts: a stele recently shown to her by an 'American excavator at Corinth', and Alexandre Falguière's memorial to Byron.[90] Perhaps remembering her experiences writing for the *Irish Monthly*, Lynch turned first to the stele,

> ... on which were carved three figures, two nobly draped and seated, the third in shabby clinging garment, knotted at the waist, and standing. 'I judge that fellow must have been a Christian,' said the professor of archaeology contemptuously, 'from the mean and humble look of him.' And my companion, herself a devout Christian, had become so far demoralized by admiration of all left of a dead faith, as to add, in reluctant acquiescence: 'They were so fond of playing the martyr, those Christians.'[91]

While not overtly critical of contemporary Christianity, Lynch the 'infidel' is apparent here, the 'Pagan' atmosphere of Greece completing the 'demoralising' project she thought Russell had detected in her work in 1886, and which would appear again when she wrote about Venice in 1899. Further transgressions were to follow as she contemplated Byron. She observed that the 'statue is where it should be, for where should Byron be if not on Grecian soil', and that the 'Greeks are grateful, lastingly grateful to Byron'.[92] As she examined the topic of nationalism more closely, so her tone changed:

> ... watching a group of British tourists arrested in front of this commemorative statue in honour of an Englishman's disinterested death in an alien cause, I marvelled as we ever must at every turn of life, at the glaring inconsistencies of nations and individuals, remembering the tone of some Imperialist papers of London upon the action and death of Villebois Mareuil who, like Byron, adopted a quarrel not his own and died for a people who were not his. But after all it is possible the Turks found for Byron a contemptuous term the equivalent of 'foreign mercenary' with which the sacrifice of the French officer was gracelessly tossed off in England.[93]

While paying tribute to a famous Englishman, Lynch slipped in a slice of anti-imperialist critique. Villebois-Mareuil was a French colonel who had taken up arms against the English in the Boer War, dying in April 1900 after a last stand at the Battle of Boshof. The fact that she was writing as a 'Parisianised foreigner' championing a Frenchman, rather than as an Irish woman championing a fellow countryman, might have given her greater licence, but the point against not only 'Imperialist papers' but imperialism itself was decisively made. Her earlier comment on the restrictions, or even the prejudice and the violence, of 'national or provincial' monuments and architectural styles also came into a different and sharper focus.[94] While attacking narrow interests it looked forward to a time when a spirit of participation might enable countries to see beyond their individual horizons. This final point was vital for Lynch, who, like Renan, drew parallels between nations and individuals, but, unlike him, used it to draw attention to their shared foibles, the 'glaring inconsistencies' that prevented the British from seeing why someone like Villebois-Mareuil might resemble one of their own national heroes. Even cultural nationalism did not address such issues, and, although Lynch dearly wanted self-government for Ireland, she refused to ignore the fact that designating individuals according to their nationality, or their sex, or indeed both, could be as divisive as it was uniting.

Lynch explored this problem throughout her career. The author who had argued against large families on the grounds that they tended to generate scapegoats found plenty to object to in reductive nationalism, particularly when combined with political conservatism.[95] Some of her most passionate denunciations of this tendency have already been discussed with reference to her coverage of the Dreyfus Affair. But Lynch picked up on more mundane manifestations of national pride and prejudice, too, once again using her own experience as a template.[96] In 'The Senora of To-day', she took a light-hearted approach to this sort of relativism:

> 'The Catalan is the worst bred man in Christendom,' I have heard a Spanish nobleman assert. A soft-mannered and high-bred Spaniard may be permitted to make so comprehensive a statement if he has not travelled in other lands to discover how universal, how cosmopolitan, is 'the worst bred man in Christendom'. We decide to-day in a fit of anger that it is the Englishman, and to-morrow a ruffian Frenchman ... Or just as we have given the apple to a bearded German, a gentleman of Castille staggers our judgement.[97]

At first it appears that Lynch is discussing regional and class divisions in Spain – a situation she would use in a later piece to reflect on the relations between the English and the Irish. But the humour lies in her observation on the truly 'cosmopolitan' figure of the 'worst bred man', who appears 'universal', yet distinctively national at the same time. She invites her readers to enjoy this paradox in her inclusive address to them. As an observer of numerous cultural conflicts, her 'cosmopolitan' perspective enabled her not only to consider the generalisations and intolerances of others, but to observe her own responses in a variety of situations. This was the approach she adopted in her 1892 travel piece 'On Board a Spanish Steamer', also published in the *Freeman's Journal*, which contained several pointed comments on the subject of men and their manners. She noted just how frequently the Spanish passengers spit – there is 'not a clean spot as large as a penny on the whole vessel' – but even worse offence is caused by her encounter with another 'appalling young man', who is 'holding forth on glorious Britain and Spanish savages':

> However, I was able to assure myself on landing at Las Palmas that the expectorating Spaniard is not by any means the worst thing in male humanity. At the worst, he is only a dirty gentleman, but the clean, well-washed English cad who swaggers about a foreign hotel, informs the foreign waiter who understands English that there is nothing decent or civilised, no honesty (save the mark!) out of England, is so greatly his inferior ... that I am almost reconciled to the spitting.[98]

'On Board a Spanish Steamer', then, in common with *French Life in Town and Country*, incorporated a direct attack on masculine, imperial arrogance into its discussion of cultural difference. However, as in 'On the Acropolis', there was another aspect in play. The piece then went on to relate a conversation with 'an amusing Scotch engineer':

> He had travelled the world over and found no place like Scotland, no race like the Scotch race, and no liquor like Scotch whiskey. But for Scotland, he asserted, England would be nowhere, as all her men of genius were Scotch. He was convinced that there was Scotch blood in Shakespeare's veins ... In fact, the refrain of the national lyric was that the Scotch is the finest race in the world (pronounced with rolling r's), has made the greatest mark, is the most successful, and has never been beaten by England. This is a sore point to insist upon to an Irishwoman; but tenderness has never been a feature of the Scotch character. As a balm, he was kind enough to say that he preferred the Irish to the English, and that in Scotland our men of genius are more appreciated than those of our mighty enemy.[99]

Lynch's outline of her conversation with the Scottish engineer certainly addressed the idea of England as a shared 'enemy', and did not depict his 'race-conceit' as being quite as obnoxious as that of the young Englishman's.

But simultaneously, the desire to claim national ascendancy and indulge in supremacist discourses, particularly when in conversation with a person of another nation, and of another sex, is held up to scrutiny. One 'sore point' is the exclusionary nature of his diatribe, which demonstrates a lack of 'tenderness', of fellow-feeling or identification, with his interlocutor.[100] In other words, he lacks the sympathy she valued so highly. Lynch noted the dangers inherent in being guided by a nationalist fervour that takes on the attributes of the imperialism from which it seeks to liberate itself.

Lynch's humour is clearly visible in 'On Board a Spanish Steamer', which critiqued elements of nationalism while still supporting the *Freeman's* perspective on offensive British imperialism. But Spain, and particularly southern Spain, also provided her with a more sobering paradigm. As we have seen, most of the places Lynch visited presented the opportunity to discuss histories of struggle or conflict: either against a 'mighty enemy', or between different religious beliefs or ethnicities. In most cases these conflicts had taken place in the past, however recent that past might have been, and however apparent its traces still were. 'Rebel Catalonia', one of her final articles on Spain, was about a struggle that was not only ongoing, but seemed to have the potential to last indefinitely. This article, one of the few Lynch published in the London *Contemporary Review*, noted that accounts of 'revolution' in Spain tended to be exaggerated by the international media, pointing out that what made the current eruption of violence in Barcelona notable was not its effect upon the local people, but its relative lack of effect:

> ... there is nothing like dwelling permanently in an atmosphere of revolution to breed an amused indifference to its consequences. To-day I get a letter from Barcelona, a mere good-humoured comment on the state of siege ... My correspondent has been inured by a residence of a quarter of a century to the troublous and threatening atmosphere of Barcelona, where it may be that people eat, drink, dance and make love upon an ever-menacing social earthquake.[101]

Lynch evidently admired such sangfroid – it is highly likely that the 'correspondent' was Nannie; her analysis also drew attention to the darker implications of becoming 'inured' to a 'social earthquake'. It was evidence of a comprehensive political and cultural stalemate in which both sides have become so accustomed to the situation that no viable alternative is sought, and the mounting pressures are overlooked: 'I infer that it really does not matter which colour of minister governs a country. It is safe for half the nation to go to the dogs, to be misgoverned and pillaged.'[102] She observed that some Catalonian grievances seemed justified, going so far as to suggest that 'revolution' might not only be inevitable, but also necessary: 'however heartily we may deplore these revolutionary outbreaks beyond the Pyrenees ... revolutions are never nice or comfortable matters, but without revolutions we should never have progressed beyond the morals and manners of the Middle Ages'.[103] She personally endorsed a more 'moderate' path whereby Catalonia would be given the status of a 'separate and self-governing province':

> Considering the antagonistic differences of the two races, this latter arrangement is wise, sober, and essential. Races cannot agree in open hostility any more than dogs, but while civilisation makes for extended boundaries and is opposed to the formation of small States, some such concession must eventually be made to racial animosities if Spain is not to be swallowed up in one of these ever-recurring crises.[104]

Her assertion that certain longstanding ethnic and cultural conflicts could only be solved by separating the combatants as you might separate a pair of fighting dogs has implications for the conditions under which 'sympathy' between antipathetic communities might be attained. Lynch suggested that unless some sort of autonomy was granted to the Catalonians, it would be impossible for any negotiations to take place. Although she did not present the formation of independent 'small States' as the ultimate solution to 'racial animosities', she did argue for the importance of a form of devolution for nations caught in self-destructive cycles of violence and repression, and was careful not to designate 'revolution' as purely uncivilised and retrograde.

The most striking aspect of 'Rebel Catalonia' is that Lynch's analysis of the situation was rooted in an unusually direct comparison between the conflict in Spain and ongoing hostilities between the English and Irish. The article opened with the following paragraph, worth quoting at length:

> When you hear Castilian and Catalonian speak of each other, and become intimate with the character of these two so contrasted races, you no longer wonder at the unrest and ill-humour of rebel Catalonia. Imagine the practical go-ahead Anglo-Saxon governed by the dreamy and indolent Celt; and while deeming and regarding himself the superior of the two, feeling that the dominant race regards him with arrogant disdain. For Irish and English are not more unlike than Castilian and Catalonian. They clash in every respect, and not the smallest of Catalan grievances is the obligation to speak Spanish at a disadvantage. For, like the Irish, they speak it always with a pronounced accent which offends the Castilian

ear, but, unlike the Irish, they do not bring as an atonement eloquence or picturesque fervour. They have no winning qualities in speech or character – these rude Catalonians; they are harsh and discourteous, sharp in money dealings, tight-fisted, resolute in gain, like all commercial races. But they are active, thriving, practical, progressive, and the root of their incendiary disposition is a permanent dissatisfaction at having to knuckle under to a race they hold to be their inferior. Now the very qualities upon which they pride themselves ... are repugnant to the haughty Castilian, who sets no value on this thriving, active, practical national temperament, while the Catalonian's lack of breeding, his coarseness and dreadful dialect fill him with something like horror. And so the old quarrel of ill-mated races under one flag rages, and as in all quarrels, each is convinced that the wrong is on the other side.[105]

Here, Lynch presented English audiences with an image of themselves that was both familiar and unsettling. She opened on safe territory, aligning the 'practical, go-ahead' Catalan with the 'Anglo-Saxon', in opposition to the 'dreamy, indolent' Castilian 'Celt'. No sooner has she assigned these recognisable national characteristics than she represented them in a startlingly negative light. The Catalonians are not only 'practical', but rude, arrogant, hard-headed and commercially minded – in other words, very much like Lynch's least flattering depictions of the English. Having established this, Lynch pushed her comparison further. For all their sense of their own superiority, the Catalonians remain under the political control of the Castilians, and not the other way around. Lynch's audience was being asked not only to take the hint about their own image abroad, but to imagine themselves in the position of a subjugated people. In Spain, the 'Celts' are the ones running the country, and it is they who view 'commercial' Anglo-Saxon qualities as 'repugnant' and underbred – thus inverting the dominant nineteenth-century stereotype of the Irish. Political dominance was revealed here as a matter of historical contingency, rather than the outcome of inevitable natural law, as many imperialist commentators liked to suggest. More tellingly still, having aligned the Catalonian 'Anglo-Saxons' with the English by nature and the Irish by predicament, she then drove the point home, picking up on two of the most visible and criticised signifiers of Irishness and transposing them accordingly. The Catalonians, like the Irish, have been forced to speak another language, doing so with an accent both mocked and reviled. When their frustrations erupt, as they inevitably do, they are accused of 'turbulence and unprovoked aggressiveness'.[106] In this way, Lynch dragged into the foreground the Irish context that had remained in the background for many of the travel pieces written for an English readership. In doing so, she not only drew attention to an equally enduring conflict going on much closer to home, but provided exactly the sort of perspective which, she argued, had to be present in order for there to be any hope of a resolution. She encouraged readers to wander beyond the confines of their own national interest group, and to imagine themselves as 'the other side'; to actively engage with their perspective, as well as to take note of the less pleasant aspects of their own behaviour.

In 'Rebel Catalonia', Lynch deployed techniques we have seen at work throughout her travel writing, making overt references to the English–Irish situation through the prism of the differences and rifts in Spanish society. As well as offering political commentary, in this piece Lynch detailed the landscape, as well as the towns, villages and cultural practices, of the passage from southern France into southern Spain. By train, by steamer, by mule, on foot, Lynch's familiarity with the language and the terrain was made evident in this piece and in her other substantial body of writings on both Spain and France. Political and educational systems, and the lives of women in these countries, form the oblique subject of her *vagabondage*. As we have seen, the range of Lynch's travels was extensive and varied, encompassing not only the length and breadth of Spain and France, but the Canaries, Italy and Greece, too. The latitude and diversity of the travel writing recovered so far provide us with insights into not only Lynch's *oeuvre* but also publishing and marketing contexts, readership and the reception of travel writing during the late nineteenth century. They also lead us to consider her best-known work, *Autobiography of a Child*. Describing herself as a 'born traveller' with 'the vagabond's instinct of forming pleasant friendships along the highroads that are buried with the last hand-shake', the Irish narrator of *Autobiography of a Child* recalls her first encounter with the English town of 'Lysterby', noting its 'spired churches, rough, clean little streets' with an eye honed for topographical detail.[107] Here, as elsewhere, Lynch addresses both the pleasures and the perils of independence. The freedom to roam 'along the highroads', to select passing companions, and to observe as one does so, suggests parity with similarly independent male travellers. Yet her description of friendships 'buried with the last hand-shake' implies not only casual, almost fraternal intimacy, but something a little lonelier, a little more final. Rather like 'A Backward Glance at the City of the Pale', this book looked to the past in order to reflect upon the painful nexus of national and personal identity, placing the fraught relationship between Ireland and England at its heart. But in doing so, Lynch also questioned the discourses of history itself, and what might or might not be told about the lives of girls and women.

CHAPTER 6

Autobiography of a Child: Identity, memory, genre

In April 1899, Hannah Lynch sent what appears to be her first short letter to Louise-Cécile Vincens. Unusually, it was written in English. Less unusually, it described a face-off between Lynch and an antagonist:

> Dear Madame Vincens,
>
> I send you a copy of the 'Autobiography of a Child' which threatens to make a terrible scandal. Rome is at my heels, bishops [are?] barking and threatening me with actions and who [?] knows what. I hear I am to be dreadfully handled [?] in the Catholic and High Church papers. I await my doom in fear and trembling.
>
> I should like to hear what you think of the book.[1]

Lynch's account might have been colourful, but it was not entirely exaggerated. The following document, sent from the legal firm representing the then bishop of Birmingham in March 1899, is still to be found in the archive of *Blackwood's Magazine*. The bishop was of the opinion that the convent could be identified from the description that Lynch had provided, exposing the author and her publishers to the threat of a lawsuit:

> The Bishop has made a personal enquiry at the Convent into the charges made against the Superior and Sisters and the result thereof in his opinion justifies his characterizing the statements regarding the Sisters & the Medical Officer who is still living as gross libel.[2]

Autobiography of a Child was a book that people still recalled, if vaguely, when almost every other detail of Lynch's career had been forgotten.[3] It is also a book that draws together many of her central concerns – with personal and national history, with the lives of young women, and with literary inheritance – although its publication history and reception were singular. *Blackwood's* ran the piece as an anonymous serial between October 1898 and April 1899. They published it as a book, this time under Lynch's name, later in the same year alongside an American edition by the New York firm Dodd & Mead. Three years later, while Lynch was living and working in Paris, the book was translated into French, and was serialised in another notable literary periodical, *La Revue de Paris*, between February and March 1902, this time under the title 'Très Véridique Histoire d'une Petite Fille'. Once again, the work made the transition into book form, and was published by Hachette in the same year.[4] A brief outline of its subject matter gives a taste of why this, of all Lynch's provocative writings, might have made such an impact. Its powerful first-person narrative relays the story of a young Irish girl from her earliest memory to around twelve years of age, tracing the shaping of the 'Dublin Angela' into the 'English Angela' and ultimately the 'Irish rebel'.[5] This tale is told from the perspective of her older self, now a 'hopeless wanderer' with youth and optimism behind her.[6] The narrative opens with a startling sketch of her mother, 'a handsome, cold-eyed woman, who did not love me', before relating fragmented memories of an idyllic time spent in rural Kildare while 'put out to nurse' until the age of seven.[7] This 'nursery biography' is followed by reminiscences of life in a prosperous Dublin household.[8] The household is populated by this brilliant – yet intolerant and often violent – mother, a kindly but ineffectual stepfather, and a crowd of sisters and stepsisters who had been 'left to grow up without love or moral training, cuffed and scolded, allowed illimitable liberty from dawn to dark … [and] were more like boys than girls'.[9] Marked out by her paternity and her extreme sensitivity, Angela suffers an 'infancy in hell'.[10] Viewed as a troublemaker, she is sent to an English convent in the fictional town of Lysterby, where the pattern of trauma and abuse is repeated in a different institutional context. A key episode in this pattern, and the event that drew the accusation of 'gross libel', is the brutal whipping instigated by another beautiful but vindictive woman, the young nun Sister Esmerelda. The narrative of Angela's convent experience is interrupted by a reminiscence of her first return home, where she finds herself an object of curiosity because of her English accent and boarding-school tales. The setting for this home visit is Dalkey, the out-of-town residence of her well-to-do parents. It provides an occasion to describe some of her sisters, to evoke the antics of a large, unruly and unsupervised family, and to allude to her mother's 'colossal intelligence' and to exotic and glamorous visitors, some with Fenian connections.[11] Angela is an inveterate reader as well as a storyteller. Books clearly shape the formation of her rebel identity in a narrative where the condition of being Irish in England, and a girl in Ireland, is held up for scrutiny by the narrator, as she revisits the past through the innocent eyes of her younger self.

This first-person narrative, combined with the titular allusion to auto-biography, caused some confusion for Lynch's first readers, and unresolved questions of genre persist. Some were convinced that it was a true story. One reviewer in the American *Literary World* asserted: 'That this is a record of personal experience no one who reads Hannah Lynch's book can doubt.'[12] Others were less sure. In December 1899, the *Academy* issued the following 'somewhat amusing' explanation to a reader who had protested at *Autobiography*'s omission from its survey of notable books for the year: 'General literature and fiction were entrusted to different critics, one of whom omitted *Autobiography of a Child* because he thought it was fiction, the other because he thought it was not.'[13] Our research into Lynch's background, and access to family documents, has revealed that the book was indeed rooted in lived experience, at least to an extent. The extended family of sisters and stepsisters, the stepfather, the moderately wealthy background, the convent education away from Ireland and the Fenian sympathies at home were largely autobiographical. Two of the girls were sent to a convent in Coventry as well as to a convent near Paris.[14] Furthermore, although Lynch fictionalised some characters, others who were obviously part of the family social circle at the time were named. For example, the famous Fenian Jeremiah O'Donovan Rossa makes a brief appearance. The handsome and heroic 'Edmond', who thrills the sisters with his tales of adventure, is probably Edmund O'Donovan, son of the Irish historian and Gaelic scholar John O'Donovan.[15] But if some contemporary readers seized on the book as a form of testimony, for others it was better understood as a study in child psychology, a popular topic at the end of the nineteenth century. In its review, the London *Bookman* observed that 'there seems to be a fashion at present for books treating of the psychology of childhood', noting that 'among the books we have read, what strikes us most is the utter unhappiness which is generally represented as the child's lot'.[16] Later critics have analysed *Autobiography* with this signature in mind, too, paying particular attention to the relationship between Angela and her mother.[17] However, we will argue that reading *Autobiography* through a single critical lens will always limit interpretation of a text that draws freely and self-consciously upon a wide range of related discourses. These include not only autobiography and child study, but biography, memoir, fiction, *Bildungsroman*, *Künstlerroman*, rebel tale, Gothic thriller, Victorian classic and fairy tale.[18] In this chapter, we will examine this textual hybridity in detail, taking into account a variety of critical responses and placing the text in the context of selections of Lynch's short fiction as well as other writing of the period. Ala Alryyes has argued that by 'underscoring the loss and suffering prevalent in national narratives, children become the loci of vulnerable cultural memory ... determinants of the future of the race and, hence, the nation'.[19] We will explore ways in which *Autobiography* connects with this observation through its attempts to resurrect such suppressed 'cultural memory', replete with the losses and sufferings of Irish history, and of young Irish women within that history. We will draw on scholarship on Irish autobiography in our discussion of the autobiographical resonances of the text and its metanarratives, including its remodelling of Charlotte Brontë's *Jane Eyre*. In doing so, we will consider how to read the multiple layers that constitute this complex and richly suggestive book.

The fact that so much criticism omits the political dimension of *Autobiography of a Child* seems mystifying at first. The text resonates with the ways in which nationality, as a concept and as a set of conditions, impacts upon Angela from her earliest moments. Not only is the first part of the narrative set in Ireland, featuring prominent republicans and key sites in the struggle for independence, but, throughout, the book discusses anti-Irish prejudice, poverty, emigration, exile, brutality, incarceration and even execution. One explanation might be its association with the firm of Blackwood's. Although it was definitely not as jingoistic as *John Bull* – the magazine that had linked Lynch directly to the assassinations in Phoenix Park – *Blackwood's Magazine* was nonetheless a conservative publication supportive of Britain's imperial project.[20] This was not the sort of context that would encourage readers towards an anti-colonial perspective. But here it is worth noting that the initial serial publication of *Autobiography* coincided almost exactly with an equally subversive but far more famous work: Joseph Conrad's *Heart of Darkness*.[21] Conrad was delighted to be published in this respected and remunerative outlet, and the tales of adventure, romance and the exotic that characterised the preferences of the magazine's publishers made a plausible context for his tale.[22] It has been argued that this was also the perfect audience for Conrad's repeated deformation of the tropes of adventure and travel narratives, and his resulting critique of empire's absurdities and atrocities.[23] Could the same be said of Lynch's novel? If Conrad drew upon, and subverted, the masculine genre of imperial adventure, Lynch performed the same operation on an unthreatening feminine genre, the 'nursery biography'. As we will see, when pressured about the controversial content of the book, Lynch took refuge in this exact designation. Furthermore, her short fiction about children, which included pieces such as 'A Village Sovereign' and 'The Little Marquis', was marketable, and like Conrad she needed both prestige and payment. These pieces were widely reprinted, demonstrating not only the popular interest in childhood psychological and social development, but the way in which this subject matter could appeal to very different markets and publishing venues.[24] Such a position was relevant not only to Lynch's ongoing struggle to survive as a saleable yet 'literary' writer, but allowed a degree of latitude when it came to the representation of politically sensitive issues.[25]

This strategy can be examined by looking at 'A Village Sovereign' in more detail. The story had initially been published anonymously in *Macmillan's Magazine*, in August 1897.[26] According to Tynan, it was specifically selected by Lynch to appear in Tynan's revised *Cabinet of Irish Literature* in 1902–03.[27] The note that Lynch prepared as a preface reinforced the connection between the story and *Autobiography of a Child*: 'She is the author of ... 'Autobiography of a Child' which excited great interest when it ran in *Blackwood's*. It has since, in French dress, appeared in one of the principal French reviews.'[28] In 1904, 'A Village Sovereign' was republished in the sixth volume of Justin McCarthy's encyclopedic anthology *Irish Literature*.[29] Both these lavish, multi-volume collections sought to represent the quality and range of Irish literary writing, and, in the case of the volume of *Cabinet* in which Lynch appeared, the quality and range of Irish women's writing.[30] However, both collections trod carefully with respect to politics. As Margaret Kelleher has demonstrated, the initial project 'was overtly characterized by an editorial policy seeking to avoid "prejudice, political or religious" that "could wound the feelings or offend the taste of any class or creed"'.[31] But in fact the selections and omissions were often more 'politically robust than such a seemingly non-contentious policy might suggest', revealing not an absence of politics but a carefully inscribed inclusion.[32] 'A Village Sovereign' is marked with the traces of these several concerns, producing strange narrative tensions and resulting in probably the most ambivalent closing paragraph of any of Lynch's tales. Once again, as in *Autobiography of a Child*, the story was a domestic one, and the setting an Irish village very similar to that of the opening sequences of the later work. The 'sovereign' in question is 'Norry', a charming toddler who, like Angela in *Autobiography*, has the run of the community. In the course of the piece this charm, combined with Norry's total innocence of social hierarchy, allows her to approach the other 'sovereign' in the equation, the neglectful and exploitative absentee landlord, the Marquis of Grandby. Grandby has directly encountered his tenants' anger only once, when a local woman refuses to pick up some money he has thrown at her from his carriage.[33] If this one instance of female resistance makes an impression, then Norry's adoption of him, including her insistence that 'he isn't Markiss', has an even more profound effect.[34] In an unprecedented gesture, when passing through the village while preparing to 'start by the earliest train for his son's estates in a neighbouring county', Grandby hears that she is seriously ill and visits the family cottage.[35] He pays for a doctor, and holds her in his arms during the crisis, reflecting on the way in which 'the opening and closing of baby lids held all the mystery, the gravity, the import of the universe'.[36] Norry recovers, and the legitimate resentments held by the community are quickly converted to admiration. The story concludes with the following passage:

> As for the Marquis of Grandby, he was regarded in the light of a public benefactor. Had he not put down the means of restoring their sovereign to them, and was he not one of her devoted servants? Who could dare challenge his perfections now? Bother the rents! He might raise them any day if he liked, and be sure he wouldn't be shot. Bless you, there he goes along the street, the best-hearted gentleman in Ireland. Three cheers, boys, for the Marquis of Grandby.[37]

Whether or not this final paragraph enacted its own, more subversive, conversion – turning the sentimental tale into satire, and the delightful story of rural childhood into an attack upon the ongoing political condition of Ireland – would entirely depend upon the perspective and interests of the reader. It is certainly possible to read Lynch's story both as an endorsement and an indictment of the power of sympathy. As in Conrad, shifts in narrative perspective play a vital role in creating this effect. Such a concluding passage makes it difficult for the reader to conclude anything, as it slides rapidly from narrative report in the past tense, through free indirect discourse, and finally into present tense, direct speech. The power of such generic and narrative uncertainty lies in just this ability to permit deeply conventional, and all but forbidden, discourses to overlap one another, keeping multiple possibilities in play.

This sense of uncertainty, and of potentially conflicting interpretations, is a key element to bear in mind when approaching *Autobiography*. Several of these concerns coincided in one of the earliest announcements of the series, which appeared in the *Athenaeum* on 24 September 1898:

> The new serial in *Blackwood*, 'The Autobiography of a Child' ... will be on entirely new lines. It is, we believe, the faithful narrative of an actual experience, the work of a powerful writer whose identity is but thinly veiled. The story of an unhappy childhood will be told without reserve, with an intensity akin to that of the sisters Brontë, but with nothing of their gloom, the various incidents being narrated with piquancy and wit.[38]

This announcement set up several expectations. The idea that the work was 'faithful' to 'actual experience', and would be narrated 'without reserve' by an author 'but thinly veiled' clearly indicated something autobiographical. But on the other hand, this assertion was qualified – 'we believe' – and modified further by the emphasis placed upon the literary quality of the text. Even this was slightly slippery, anticipating something on 'entirely new lines' that would also be reminiscent of one of the classic texts of an earlier era, and promising a book that combined 'powerful' evocations of unhappiness with 'piquancy and wit'. After the intervention by the bishop in March 1899, Lynch published an explanatory letter, which appeared in the *Academy* on 22 April. The same letter was circulated in the American press a few months prior to the publication of the Dodd & Mead edition of *Autobiography*, via the American *Bookman*:[39]

> Sirs: My unpretentious little story, *Autobiography of a Child*, has been referred to as history. May I protest against the misapplication of a title so solemn and serious to a matter so fragile and fugitive as a tale of childhood? The story is essentially a work of imagination, an effort to interpret the vision and mind of a child and tell her story from her point of view as I imagined she would tell it. Such a task has nothing at all of the nature of history. Its concern is impression and pictures, not facts. In the drama of existence facts are of comparative insignificance. The important thing is not what is relatively true, but what we believe to be true, since this alone reveals temperament and character. Shelley and an Oxford don would hold very different opinions of Oxford as an institution, and both would be equally sincere and worthy of attention in their expression of their diverse opinions.[40]

First, Lynch reinserted the distance between her position as author and the implications of the term 'autobiography', a distance that had existed comparably, although not identically, through her initial anonymity. This permitted her and her publishers to back out of a tricky situation. The letter was initially framed by a becoming, if slightly unconvincing, feminine modesty. Without saying so explicitly, it reminded the readers – designated as male – that tales of childhood – 'unpretentious', 'fragile' and 'fugitive' – were predominantly the province of women. But this was Lynch, and it was not long before the veil dropped. Having presented the work as ephemeral, she went on to position 'imaginative' works at the very centre of an understanding of the 'drama of existence'. Lynch's point – that 'impressions and pictures' trump 'facts' when it comes to the essentially subjective nature of experience – confirms her specific technical commitment to literary impressionism. Just as Conrad had reminded readers that they would find meaning in his writing 'according to your deserts', she pointed out the way in which interpretation 'reveals temperament and character'.[41] As such, although this controversy and Lynch's public response to it provide essential insights into the various layers that constitute *Autobiography*, they do not provide a tidy answer.[42] And there was one reviewer, writing in the *Outlook*, who introduced the idea that *Autobiography*'s status as an Irish text had a role to play in its ambivalence. 'The Irish sketches are particularly good, while the introduction of more than one notorious – or should we say famous? – personage lends an air of almost historical accuracy to what we have been told by the author is "essentially a work of imagination".'[43] The fact that known, named individuals featured in the book certainly contributed to its position on the boundary of 'historical accuracy' and 'imagination'. Equally important was the reviewer's hint at the difficulty of writing unified history within a divided culture, in which those same individuals could be at once 'famous' and 'notorious'.

Therefore, the liminality and ambivalence of *Autobiography of a Child* cannot be dismissed, even if the text is understood to contain autobiographical elements. Elizabeth Grubgeld discusses *Autobiography* in the context of mainly Anglo-Irish women writers and life writing, choosing to ignore the 'Angela' persona and reading it as Lynch's account of her own life.[44] Likewise, Claudia Nelson in her *Family Ties in Victorian England* describes the work as 'a rare middle-class memoir for the time of a violent mother and unhappy childhood'.[45] J.W. Foster is more cautious, noting that 'If *Autobiography of a Child* is fiction, it reads with the unflagging honesty of autobiography'.[46] Significantly, Foster chooses not to compare *Autobiography* with a more straightforwardly autobiographical text, but with Joyce's *Portrait of the Artist as a Young Man*. Indeed, he argues that it presents 'a reverse of *Portrait of the Artist as a Young Man*: the artistic ambition has been killed not roused by adversity, for Angela is a girl and thus already labours under disability'.[47] This suggests a further comparison with George Moore, whose autobiographical *Confessions of a Young Man* (1888) and the later *Hail and Farewell* (1911–14) use *Bildungsroman* and *Künstlerroman* to recount the institutional traumas of their very young protagonists. These cruelties, which include beatings and starvation, are survived partially through reading. As Moore recalls:

And my poets were taken to school, because it pleased me to read 'Queen Mab' and 'Cain', amid the priests and ignorance of a hateful Roman Catholic college. And there my poets saved me from intellectual savagery; for I was incapable at that time of learning anything.

> In those days children were not treated mercifully, and I remained at
> Oscott till my health yielded to cold and hunger and floggings.[48]

While Moore depicts his 'hateful Roman Catholic college' as a place of
'ignorance' and 'intellectual savagery', Lynch's narrator is more ambivalent. The
same deprivations and physical punishments apply, but compensations are to
be found not from books brought from home, but from those 'liberally supplied
by the convent library':

> I learnt to read with amazing rapidity, and my favourite books were of a
> kind liberally supplied by the convent library – Tyburn, wonderful tales of
> the escapes and underground adventures of Jesuits, double walls, spring-
> doors, mysterious passages, whitened bones in long-forgotten boxes.
> Thanks to my ingenuity and vivid imagination, our days became for us
> all a wild romance. Relegated to the infirmary by prolonged illnesses, the
> result of semi-starvation naturally, I had leisure to read laboriously various
> volumes of this edifying literature.[49]

Although the older narrator's description of 'this edifying literature' sounds an
ironic note, these melodramatic tales of persecution are far from trivial to her
younger self. Her appetite for reading is enhanced by literal starvation, which
paradoxically feeds her imagination, and ultimately her rebellious spirit. Thus,
she begins her own 'stupendous fiction that was to communicate its thrill even
to some of the big girls' about 'the ghost of a beautiful Catholic persecuted in
the days of Tyburn', forging the sort of positive, female, communal identity she
fails to find within the family.[50] Indeed, rebellious girls and artistic vocations
mark another intersection between Moore and Lynch, particularly in relation to
his novel *A Drama in Muslin* (1886). *Autobiography of a Child* could be read as a
'prequel' to this earlier text, as Moore begins with the heroine, Alice Barton, on
the cusp of adulthood. Her as yet unformed desire to become a writer is hinted
at in the opening chapter of the novel with her not entirely successful end-of-
year school play, 'King Cophetua'. In addition, her mother's cruel treatment of
this plain but clever daughter, in favour of the more beautiful and thus more
marriageable Olive, might be read as a precursor of Angela's monstrous mother.

In the context of questions of genre and the treatment of the
'autobiographical mode', Moore's and Lynch's writing overlap in significant
ways, too. The blending of fact and fiction, the invented and the recollected, is
a deliberate feature of Moore's writing.[51] In fact, as Grubgeld has pointed out:
'Moore himself makes quite clear in his statements about autobiography that

he expects his own contemporaries to accept his life writings as fictions.'[52] In his 'The Autobiographical Imagination and Irish Literary Autobiographies', Michael Kenneally considers this a characteristic effect of Irish autobiographical writing, and offers a useful distinction between different forms:

> As with the memoir, the essential distinction between the autobio-
> graphical novel and the literary autobiography is one of focus. Although
> autobiographical novelists freely plunder episodes from their past, their
> concern is with wider, supra-personal goals which have more to do with
> society than individual history, with aesthetics than the self, with literature
> than biography. In turning to personal history, the autobiographical
> novelist is involved in an act of imaginative liberation of the self, of
> sanitizing experiences so that they can be enlisted in the service of a truth
> whose validity transcends the personal.[53]

In the light of this definition, Lynch's *Autobiography* can be categorised, along with works of her contemporaries Joyce and Moore, as an autobiographical novel.[54] The events and experiences of the narrative, the wrenching of a small child from her idyllic rural life with a nurse back into the fraught household of her Dublin family, the traumatic transition to boarding school in a foreign country where the most important lesson learned is resistance to cruelty and hardship, are rooted in Lynch's own past. But, unlike Moore's practice in his *Confessions* and later autobiographical writing, these details are not provided as a means to disclose the self, though aspects of the self are revealed through the narrative process. Instead, they offer a disclosure and critique of Dublin society, of relations between England and Ireland and of the doubly cruel and unjust situation for girls. This critique of social and political conditions is enabled by the immediate remodelling of generic expectations through the narrator's extraordinary and seemingly unnatural declaration of antipathy towards 'My mother ... who did not love me' in the opening pages.[55] The subversion of assumptions so close to the heart of late-Victorian society establishes another narrative of 'unnatural' conditions, specifically those that shape young women for the limited career choices open to them in Ireland.[56] In an outburst that might be described as a slippage from the fictional 'I' to the autobiographical 'I', the narrator describes Ireland as:

> ... the very wretchedest land on earth for woman, the one spot on the
> globe where no provision is made for her, and where parents consider
> themselves as exempt of all duty, of tenderness, of justice in her regard,

when her lot as daughter, wife, and old maid bears no resemblance to the ideal of civilization.[57]

This lack of provision results in a system of exploitation and double standards, where 'Irishmen go to America, marry, and make their fortunes; but the landlord and shopkeeper at home are paid by the savings of the peasant-girls, without a "thank you" from their parents ... "Tis but her duty, to be sure".[58] The flaws in the institution of marriage are only glimpsed, through the reference to a family servant who 'had fallen from petted servitude into troubled servitude', having left her role to wed an 'exacting' Englishman.[59] Lynch reserves her most pointed attack for the inadequate education of, and support for, girls destined to be governesses: 'impoverished and illiterate daughters [who] go abroad and support the family'.[60] The autobiographical 'I' apparently overwhelms her fictional persona when the narrator states that 'I have never met an Irish governess on the continent who had a sou to spend on her private pleasures for the simple reason that she sent every odd farthing home'.[61] Lynch's earlier critique extends beyond the economic deprivations and exploitations they face, to emotional and sexual vulnerability. The embedded tale of the innocent and beautiful Molly O'Connell, seduced by her employer and cast out to die of tuberculosis, resonates with numerous other earlier and contemporary texts, from Brontë to Hardy to the New Woman novels of the 1890s. Blame is firmly attributed to her flawed, even useless education from 'the nuns of Southampton': 'But to send out into the world, to earn her living among selfish and indifferent strangers, a young girl of such bewildering exquisiteness, and never once hint to her the kind of perils that would beset her, give her no knowledge of man, nor of herself, nor of nature!'[62] Lynch connects this narrative of vulnerability and exploitation to Irishness more generally, as Angela's 'everyday papa' in Kildare will also die of consumption, 'the ruthless disease of the Irish peasant' before he has 'lived half his life through'.[63]

The financial constraints that forced young Irish women into taking up such precarious positions are also touched on in *Autobiography*, providing an intriguing counter-narrative to Joyce's 'The Dead', written only a few years after Lynch's novel was published. In his one and only portrait of upper middle-class Dublin in *Dubliners*, where the spinster sisters Aunts Julia and Kate teach music and live a modest but genteel existence, Joyce celebrates 'Irish hospitality'. It is precisely this famous hospitality the narrator blames for the straitened circumstances of her own family, requiring the sacrifices of the daughters. Again, the tone of the narration at this point suggests an autobiographical origin. Recounting the illicit ball the children hold in their Dalkey home, the narrator gives a scathing account of a fickle Dublin society descending on and enjoying the hospitality of those who live in 'a pleasant seaside resort, within easy distance of the metropolis', to the eventual detriment of their generous hosts.[64]

> Irish hospitality is justly famous. There is nothing to match it on the face of the earth. But Irish abuse of hospitality is, perhaps, insufficiently recorded, and there is nothing more speedily forgotten than the unlimited favours of 'open house' ... My parents kept 'open house' with a vengeance, which is the reason to-day that none of us possess the needful sixpence to jingle on the traditional tombstone.[65]

The autobiographical 'I' largely remains concealed in the narrative. However, in this passage it almost overwhelms the narrating 'I', offering a glimpse of self-disclosure that autobiographical fiction largely avoids.

In her *Literary Autobiographies of Twentieth-century Irish Women*, Taura S. Napier argues that Irish women's autobiography is particularly notable for this avoidance. She considers the differences between male autobiographies and women's writing, suggesting that Irish women autobiographers use the trope of the other as a way of 'deflect[ing] centrality within the self-narrative from themselves onto another person or persons', or 'the "other" becomes a created double of the autobiographical self through which aspects of the life may be expressed that are born of fear and desire, and are usually sequestered in the imagination'.[66] Napier's outline is particularly suggestive for a reading of Lynch's *Autobiography*, especially in the light of her analysis of Mary Colum's autobiography *Life and the Dream*, where her childhood is represented through 'a fictional double created from her earlier writings'.[67] In Lynch's text, this fictional self or other, Angela of Lysterby, is doubly fragmented, becoming the 'English Angela' and the 'Dublin Angela', thus highlighting identity as construct and in particular a construct of narratives. Identity as a construct of course has resonances both in terms of nation and gender, and Lynch's highly wrought narrative draws attention to this, too. Given that Lynch is ostensibly not writing an autobiography but a fictional autobiography, there is a double displacement at work here, where the fictional 'Angela of Lysterby' may or may not be an autobiographical 'I'. But what becomes clear, with some knowledge of Lynch's biography, is the proximity of autobiographical and fictional self. Through creating a fictional double – the older narrating self, 'the hopeless wanderer' (the persona she deploys in her travel writing) and the child, 'Angela of Lysterby' – Lynch reveals quite explicitly the inseparability of fiction and autobiography. Napier argues that Colum, indebted to Proust and Goethe, sought 'a fusion of the autobiographical *künstlerroman* and fictional self-creation'.[68] Goethe is of particular interest when considering Lynch's work, and even her defence published soon after its serialisation.[69] For in this letter Lynch does not deny the facts are there, but what is important is how they have been imagined and, by extension, how they have been recreated. The narrator of the biography highlights this in her recognition that the memory of her monstrous mother does not cohere with her later relationship with her. Relating her strange antipathy to her mother, she notes: 'I recall this feeling, to-day quite dead, as part of my childhood's sufferings, and I wonder that the woman who inspired it should in middle life appear to me a woman of large and liberal and generous character, whose foibles and whose rough temper in perspective have acquired rather a humorous than an antipathetic aspect'.[70] This observation follows her puzzling over 'the most vivid recollection of those early years', a train journey to Cork, which does not seem rooted in reality at all.[71] The narrator's inability to distinguish fiction from reality in her memories alerts us to its inevitable blurring in any kind of memoir. Later in the narrative the older Angela describes her own vivid imagination as a young girl, and her propensity to spin yarns: 'I embroidered fact and invented fiction with the readiness of the fanciful traveller', hinting at the possibility that this same vivid imagination might still be at work.[72] The reference to fancy is also suggestive of Lynch's deployment of the fairy-tale mode throughout the narrative.[73] One of many examples is Angela recalling that her mother was 'worse than the traditional step-mother of fairy tale' as a way of invoking the child's perspective, especially the imaginative and artistic child, and also as another form of distancing and displacement, so characteristic of Irish women's autobiographical writing.[74] These self-conscious modes of narration destabilise the idea of any clear classification of the text, highlighting an artifice and craftedness that conceals and reveals.

This metanarrative is also realised through the double-narrative perspective of the text, the older, jaded narrator looking back on her childhood through the eyes of her fractured and traumatised younger self. The text draws attention not only to the nature of memory and its creative distortions, but to the question of narrative, of storytelling itself. The narrator muses on childhood and memory in the opening chapter, outlining the method for her own memoir in the following key paragraph:

> I have always marvelled at the roll of reminiscences and experiences of childhood told consecutively and with coherence. Children live more in pictures, in broken effects, in unaccountable impulses that lend an

unmeasured significance to odd trifles to the exclusion of momentous facts, than in story. This alone prevents the harmonious fluency of biography in an honest account of our childhood. Memory is a random vagabond, and plays queer tricks with proportion. It dwells on pictures of relative unimportance, and revives incidents of no practical value in the shaping of our lives. Its industry is that of the idler's, wasteful, undocumentary, and untrained. For vividness without detail, its effects may be compared with a canvas upon which a hasty dauber paints a background of every obscure tint in an inextricable confusion, and relieves it with sharply defined strokes of bright colour.[75]

Lynch sets out to reproduce this effect of 'pictures' and 'broken effects' through a series of portraits of times, places and people, beginning with the image of the narrator's mother as she recalls her: 'The picture is clear before me of the day I first walked.'[76] Her idyllic childhood in Kildare, the torments of being back in Dublin, and then England, the household in Dalkey are all fragments of memoir with vividly realised characters and events, often half glimpsed and only half understood by the child Angela. But the portraits, including the unknown lady 'in a silk gown of many shades' who rescues her from her mother's harshness, her eccentric grandfather 'with a long black cloak flung round his shoulder and a slouched felt hat that left revealed his abundant white hair', her eldest sister who was a 'bewitching beauty' and 'had large dusky blue eyes in constant communion with the heavenly spheres', all form the 'sharply defined strokes of bright colour' against the 'inextricable confusion' of the past.[77] The painterly analogy is a self-reflexive one, too. Early in the narrative Lynch hints at one of the subjects of her tale – art, writing itself – through the image of the butterfly: 'So the child, the poet tells us, is always mother of the woman, and not even the sane and sobering influence of the years has taught me that serious matters are of greater consequence than the catching of some beautiful butterfly.'[78] Revising Wordsworth so that his words might fit with her themes of female lineage, the butterfly is an allusion to her 'first subject', Mary Jane, 'my dearest friend' who 'lived in a little cottage at the top of the village'.[79] She is the first subject of the little Angela's dominion in the village she is sent out to nurse in, but it is also the first portrait she draws in the narrative of her life: 'Upon my memory she is eternally impaled.'[80] But Mary Jane is also a crucial figure in connecting the very early portions of the text, in which the narrator links the fragmentary quality of childhood memories, their 'broken effects', to the political condition of Ireland at the time. Mary Jane's conversation reveals the extent to which these fragments retain their sharp edges, demonstrating that even idyllic rural Ireland is marked by poverty, emigration and resistance. The narrating Angela recalls her friend as being possessed of 'inexhaustible gifts, including a complete knowledge of the views of New York, an enthusiasm for that mysterious being Mary Stuart, and an acquaintance with national grievances vaguely embodied in a terror of Queen Victoria's power over her Irish subjects'.[81] When her stepsisters hear that Angela is about to be sent to England, they tease her by telling her that 'I should be submitted to insult, perhaps torture, because I was Irish.'[82] Mary Jane shares this opinion. However, she counsels bravery, her tearful response foreshadowing another crucial, and devastating, separation:

> Mary Jane was weeping on the steps. She handed me a bag of gingerbread and two apples, and told me I was not to be 'down'.
>
>   'Tis yourself that's worth all the English that ever was born,' she asserted, and I dolorously assured her that whatever happened, even if the Queen came in person to hang me, I would keep 'up'.[83]

Despite these and other painful memories associated with life in Ireland, the reader is also presented with a counter-narrative of a lively, literary and artistic environment, which nurtures the aspiring artist. Its allusions are to music as well as literary and popular reading matter – the narrator's references to the Gothic, melodrama, rebel tales, legends, myths and ghost stories are indicative of this. For example, her eccentric grandfather who believes he is Hamlet takes her to the pantomime and to 'the Opera or the Opera-Bouffe with equal readiness', and her sister Pauline, who possesses 'the golden key of the chambers of fiction', tells her 'with an extraordinary vivacity of recital the stories of "East Lynne" "The Black Dwarf", "Rob Roy", and "Kenilworth".[84] Female authors such as Lady Georgiana Fullerton, Miss Braddon and George Eliot are part of Angela's literary education, but most important is her encounter with Shakespeare. The same sister opens

> the fairyland of Shakespeare to me. With a rapture I would I now could feel, I thrilled to the glamour of the moonlight scene of the 'Merchant' … I only remember one other sensation as passionate and vivid and absorbing, my first hearing of the Moonlight Sonata, also at an age when it was perfectly impossible that I should understand more than a mouse or a linnet a particle of its beauty or meaning.[85]

This is even after the 'fairyland of Shakespeare' had been initially introduced by a dizzying blow to the head from her mother.[86]

Many of the texts invoked reflect the young Angela's penchant for adventure, drama and even horror. In fact, the narrator directly connects the idea of artistic sensibility, the nature of childhood and the love of horror and terror on several occasions:

> Deep down in the heart of childhood – even bitterly suffering childhood – is this dramatic element, this love of sensation, this vanity of the artist. So much of childhood is, after all, make-believe, unconscious acting. We are ill, and we cannot help noting the effect of our illness upon others. The amount of sympathy we evoke in grown-up people is the best evidence of our success as experimental artists with life.[87]

Later she notes: 'Not to imagine oneself afraid is to miss the peculiar zest of enjoyment.'[88] These connections between the production of fear, either through reading matter or experience, childhood and artistic development, are made most strikingly in the centrally Gothic section of the novel, the prelude to, and description of, the brutal whipping of the child Angela in Chapters 14 and 15, 'The White Lady of Lysterby' and 'An Exile in Revolt'. This section is worth examining in some detail, not only since it builds up to one of the main sources of shock and horror for the reader, but because it is a meeting point for many of the central themes and preoccupations of the text.

The narrator introduces the tale of her brutal punishment instigated by Sister Esmeralda, the 'Grand Inquisitor' and 'exquisite monster', through a recollection of the 'edifying literature' cited above.[89] The Gothic setting of the convent itself, an old manor house, also offers the perfect stage for Angela's drama of cruelty through which Lynch critiques at once Catholicism and the British. Events are set in motion when Angela is accused by a particularly horrible little boy, Frank, of breaking a statue of an angel. It is her refusal to confess that results in a beating, highlighting not only injustice, but institutional brutality in a broader context, too. She remembers Frank with scorn and loathing: 'Noble youth, future pillar of the British empire, I picture you an admirable hypocrite and bully!'[90] Angela's acquired reading and storytelling at school become acts of survival and resistance, and, as a victim of Frank's tale-telling, the narrator's tale enacts another form of rebellion, and even revenge. Embedded in tales of reading and telling, might Angela be embellishing her ordeal? In a narrative so multilayered, where slippage between fact and imagination, memory and fiction is consistently highlighted, a tale of concocted accusations and unfair punishment, which may well have been based on experience, required a Gothic twist. Ironically, too, the fictions of and about Angela of Lysterby, which get her into so much trouble, anticipate Hannah Lynch's storytelling, which also gets her into trouble with the bishop, who accuses her of telling lies.

The text's interest in the power of telling, in the resistant power of girls, their habits and passions as readers, the deprivations they can endure, and even the overtones of Gothic, also connect *Autobiography* to *Jane Eyre*. The *Athenaeum* and the *Academy* were overt in their comparisons with Brontë, while the *Bookman* observed that there was 'something Brontësque' about the vicious treatment Angela receives.[91] Sally Shuttleworth uses this comparison to illustrate the overlap between literary texts and studies of child psychology, describing *Autobiography* as a 'rewriting of *Jane Eyre* under the influence of the Child Study movement'.[92] This intersection was apparent at the time, and not only to literary reviewers. In his 'Bibliography of Child Study for the Year 1899', Louis Wilson noted *Autobiography*, observing that it was 'Written in an interesting style' and might be 'of some value on several child study topics'.[93] As the range of works collected under Wilson's rubric, as well as his interest in 'style', suggest, the movement between literary interpretations of childhood and scientific narratives of early development was very much two-way.[94] Within *Autobiography*, these mutual aims would be supported by the reference to a highly regarded literary text, and one that also troubled the category of 'autobiography', had been considered shocking on its initial publication, and whose author had Irish heritage.[95] And it is this final aspect of Lynch's appropriation of *Jane Eyre* that seems most resonant. For, although *Autobiography of a Child* lacks many of the elements of Brontë's text, the most specific moments of comparison – the events leading up to her beating – connect directly to politics.

In the famous scene from Chapter 2 of the first section of *Jane Eyre*, Jane is confined in the large, abandoned 'red room' at Gateshead Hall. Her crime is having tried to defend herself against the spoiled and vindictive John Reed (clearly a template for Frank), who also makes a false accusation against her. Trapped with her rage and anxiety, forced into an awareness of her position as a 'heterogenous thing', an 'interloper', and a 'revolted slave', Jane considers whether she should protest against the injustice of her position by running away, or 'never eating or drinking more, and letting myself die'.[96] The ensuing 'mental battle' drives her to the edge of hysteria, to a 'species of fit', and finally to unconsciousness.[97] In *Autobiography of a Child*, events unfold rather differently. As she will not confess to something she did not do, Angela is confined to 'the old community room ... a big white chamber, with a good deal of heavy furniture in it and told by Sister Esmerelda to wait until she is released.[98] Driven by 'the influence of that terrible exasperation injustice always provokes in me', she takes action:[99]

> My desire was to thwart her in her design to free me when she had a mind to. My object was to die alone and forsaken in that big white chamber, and so bring remorse and shame upon my tyrants ... I dragged over to the door all the furniture I could move. In my ardour I accomplished feats I could never have aspired to in saner moments. A frail child of eight, I nevertheless wheeled arm-chairs, a sofa, a heavy writing-table, every seat except a small stool, and even a cupboard, and these I massed carefully at the door as an obstruction against the entrance of my enemy.
>
> And then I sat down on the stool in the middle of the chamber, and tore into shreds with hands and teeth a new holland overall.[100]

Although this scene does engage with psychology, it could also be read as the dramatisation of a moment of radicalisation, as the solitary prison of the earlier novel becomes a theatre of protest. Like Jane, Angela considers a hunger strike – as we have already noted, hunger is a theme that runs through Lynch's text – but in *Autobiography* this is more overtly about turning her punishment on her captors.[101] Far from begging to be released, as Jane will do, Angela constructs a barricade, turning her confinement in the room into an ownership of it. And finally, in an action that could be viewed both as the action of a violent, uncontrollable 'wild cat' and of a prisoner using the only tools at their disposal, Angela symbolically shreds her brand new overall with 'hands and teeth'. When Sister Esmerelda gloatingly extracts her, Angela picks up the stool and hurls it in her face:[102]

> My wickedness was past sermonising. I was simply led up-stairs to a brown cell, and here the red-cheeked lay-sister, a big brawny creature, stripped me naked. Naked, mind, though convent rules forbid the whipping of girls. I was eight, exceedingly frail and delicate. The superioress took my head tightly under her arm, and the brawny red-cheeked lay-sister scourged my back with a three-pointed whip till the blood gushed from the long stripes, and I fainted.[103]

This experience leaves her hospitalised and unconscious, creating a different sort of rupture in her memory, and consequently in the narrative. However, she emerges from this traumatic break with a newly shaped identity: 'I never uttered a groan, and I like to remember this infantine proof of my pride and resolute spirit.'[104] In stating this, the narrator also notes a corresponding shift in the genre of the tale: 'Little Angela of Kildare and Dublin, over whom I have invited the sympathetic reader to weep, was a pallid and pathetic figure. But Angela of Lysterby held her own – more even than her own, for she fought for others as well as for herself, and gave back (with a great deal more trouble at least) as much pain and affliction as she endured.'[105] An important element of Angela's Irish identity emerges through her experiences in England, a combative self which is forged through a different sort of conflict to that she has experienced as the internal 'exile', the 'scape-goat of the nursery' at home. Notably, this self fights as part of a collective, rather than out of purely individual interest, marking another phase in Angela's transition from child to adult, as she begins to act according to principle. This reminds the reader of Angela's earlier association with the more politically aware Mary Jane, who, the older narrator comments, 'must have grown up to be a woman of principles'.[106] When the demonic Sister Esmerelda calls Angela a 'common Irish thing' some time after her beating, Mary Jane's parting words suddenly return to her, their meaning and purpose finally understood. She retorts: 'I'm not a common Irish thing, I'm as good as Lady Adelaide – or you.'[107]

This dramatic moment also throws new light upon the text's references to political rebellion and punishment, and upon the 'notorious – or should we say famous – personages' who appear on its pages. One of these, her godfather, is recalled in another brief encounter:

> He bore himself gallantly, wore top-boots, a long coat with several little capes to it, and carried a smart riding-crop in his hand … I had never seen him before, and to my lasting regret I have never seen him since. He was out in '48, was proscribed, and had wandered about in strange lands. He died in China, having first sent my mother a pretty case of Imperial tea …[108]

Here, the exiled Fenian is depicted as the very image of courtly masculinity. The 'pretty case of Imperial tea' not only reinforces the thoughtfulness and delicacy of an individual implicated in violent rebellion, but once again links the so-called feminine, domestic sphere with the masculine sphere of political action. This overlay is made most apparent, however, in Angela's recollection of a visit to Kilmainham. The trip is made in the company of her mother, her stepfather and a beautiful, cheerful young woman who is staying with them. This young woman fascinates Angela, not only because of her looks, but because her mother is extremely attentive to her. This is uppermost in the little girl's mind as the journey begins:

Another vivid picture I have of this young girl is a gloomier and more impressive one ... She did not smile once that day, and the extreme sadness of her face riveted my attention ... A brilliant young lady in long dresses, whom my parents treated with every kindness and consideration, could be just as miserable apparently as a small neglected girl. It was truly a wonderful discovery.[109]

As the drive continues, Angela remains 'riveted' by this woman's grief, and slowly discerns the reason for it:

We drove along the Kilmainham road, I now know, and as we went farther north, the pretty girl's tears flowed more freely, only she did not cry as we children cry. She bit her lips, and every moment thrust her handkerchief angrily into her eyes. My mother seemed to scold her for having wished to come that way, and I thought wanted to divert her attention from something the girl was evidently anxious to see. We stopped near a large building, and there was my stepfather turned towards us and speaking a strange jargon. From dint of puzzling over each word, I arrived at the extraordinary conclusion that somebody this young girl loved was in prison, that it was not wicked apparently to be locked up in prison, and that the woodwork they were gazing at, my stepfather with his hat in his hand, was something bad men were getting ready for her friend's destruction. The young girl stared up at the woodwork with streaming passionate eyes, and then buried her face in her handkerchief, and rocked from side to side in a dreadful way.[110]

The defamiliarising power of this passage is acute, humanising what certain English newspapers would have simply labelled a 'Fenian conspirator'. The narrator goes out of her way to note that she did not, in fact, understand this 'mystery' until many years later, spelling out an order of events that many readers would surely have guessed. This explanation permits the execution to take its place unambiguously within the narrative – to take place twice, in fact, as does Jim's death from consumption, which is also described through the perspective of the young Angela and then explained by the older narrator. But it also allowed the narrator to continue to use the device of innocence to reframe a history of struggle. This struggle is not only related to Tyburn and its Catholic martyrs, rather ambiguously bracketed by Gothic narrative devices and historical distance; it was also connected to specific and more present memory, held just at the brink of what it is tolerable to recall. But, once again, the specificity of this memory within the text does not necessarily link *Autobiography of a Child* seamlessly into Lynch's own autobiography. While the mention of the sweetheart once again recalls Emmet, a figure who has haunted Angela's imagination from childhood, there are no records of Fenian executions taking place at Kilmainham during Lynch's own early life.[111] Instead, the wooden scaffold, and the tearful young woman, are more resonant of the 1883 trials and executions of 'the Invincibles', and in particular Joe Brady, who had been found guilty of assassinating Burke.[112] Both this scene, and Angela's imprisonment and beating, represent a sort of montage from the cycle of violence and repression that has engulfed both child and nation. This cycle turns history into reiteration, further removing the possibility of autobiography as a linear sequence, and collapsing any distinction between the personal and the political.

It is on this final point that Shuttleworth's observations on the effect of 'child study' upon the text, *Autobiography*'s political commentary, and *Jane Eyre*'s account of the problems experienced by passionate and vulnerable young women, coalesce. Angela is profoundly shaped by her upbringing, but where did the dividing line between nature and nurture fall?[113] The critic to struggle most directly with this question, and to draw national identity into it, was Mary Robinson. As a friend, Robinson's review was understandably positive.[114] She drew particular attention to the book's account of the lasting psychic damage effected by routine emotional and physical abuse: 'A cuff and a blow at home, years of neglect at school, alternated in the education of Angela, and the proud little spirit grew up hurt and thwarted, maimed by the cruelty of its initiation into life.'[115] While noting this violence, Robinson also determined that the doubled narrative perspective enabled the adult self to intervene on behalf of the mother figure:

> Yet over and over again, by an effect of that curious double vision which is the most remarkable distinction of a remarkable book, the grown-up Angela intervenes and protects the harsh mother from the arraignment of her child. The daughter of five and thirty observes in the mother she forgives qualities which necessarily escaped the observation of the bruised and battered little scapegoat of eight. She sees the fine side of the harsh and violent Scotswoman who made her, after all, so Irish, while correcting in her, too severely, but not without noble result, the natural deficiencies of the Irish temper.[116]

Robinson's interpretation clearly sought to preserve something of the ideal of motherhood – indeed it was she, rather than Lynch's narrator, who seemed more intent on protecting the mother from 'the arraignment of her child'.[117] But alongside this ran a corresponding anxiety with regard to the role Angela's national identity played in her upbringing. Robinson's response was contradictory on this point, as her account of the 'harsh' mother attempted both to criticise and to condone. She argued that Angela had both been 'made ... so Irish' and laboured under 'natural deficiencies' in need of correction, that this correction was both 'too severe' but 'not without noble result'. This contradiction reflected an ongoing unease about how to designate – not to mention how to discipline – 'Irishness' as much as it did a desire to preserve some redeeming element of Angela's mother's behaviour. Lynch's text had directly attacked the idea that all mothers were nurturing, revealing the violent hierarchies of family life in unsparing detail – she warned that readers for whom 'motherhood is sacred' would 'not like to read of it'.[118] Such a revision had implications for late-Victorian maternal ideology at a different level, also undermining the idea that the female head of a 'family' of nations would automatically understand, love and respect her 'children'. This was a theory that Mary Jane's fear of Queen Victoria had already thrown into doubt, and which had been hinted at in Kate Raymond's rule over her household in *An Odd Experiment*. But Robinson's unease was also an effect of exactly the 'curious double vision' she sought to describe. Her review seems to refer most closely to Chapter 25, 'The Shadows', in which the older narrator observes that, as 'it would appear that the Irish habit of boasting is an incorrigible weakness ... I am glad to acknowledge the priceless debt of common-sense to a Scottish mother'.[119] This is the same chapter in which the narrator reiterates her 'outsider' status within the family, and describes the depression she still experiences as a 'mark of my unblessed race'.[120] Throughout, the text had warned the reader that it would not be able to reproduce a faithful account of childhood experience due to the particular nature of children's perception, the blurring of fact and fantasy, and the persistence and resonance of cultural narratives. As a result, the adult narrator is at a loss to produce a unified interpretation of her past, and hence her present. This is reinforced in Angela's case by the layers of prejudice to which she is exposed as an Irish girl, prejudices which shape her responses to others, and theirs to her, in specific directions. Even after her rebellion in the convent as a child, the older Angela is still prone to blaming her unhappiness on her 'race', finding a crumb of comfort for her brutal upbringing in the idea that it will have suppressed what 'would appear' to be peculiarly Irish failings before they had a chance to develop. Robinson's struggle to decide whether Angela was born or made 'Irish' hits the mark, while missing the point. In order to make a decision, both the narrating Angela and the reader would need the sort of omniscient perspective that the book refuses to provide. Instead of answers, the text presents questions, requiring that, if we must make decisions about 'character and temperament', we do so with our own 'character and temperament' equally in mind. In other words, *Autobiography of a Child* not only enacts, but significantly troubles, the act of recovery Alryyes imagines.

Nature and nurture, gender and nation, childhood and memory, past and present constitute the many lenses through which the fractures of identity are explored in *Autobiography*. As this work demonstrates, Angela's experiences are not just textured by her gender, they are also determined by various readings of her nationality, and by a struggle for autonomy. Fracture and plurality are also a condition of the narrative itself and, as such, the multiple generic signatures of *Autobiography* – reworking of a classic text, political and social exposé, act of literary impressionism, autobiographical fiction and marketable work by a woman writer – exist in dialogue. This dialogue, like many other conflicts within Lynch's writing, resists easy resolution. Unlike *Jane Eyre* or *A Drama in Muslin*, or even *Portrait of the Artist*, *Autobiography of a Child* refuses an ending that promises personal happiness or artistic fulfilment. Instead, the narrator remains a 'hopeless wanderer' rather like Edmond or her godfather, haunted by the 'inexorable word "failure".'[121] Whether or not this 'failure' also refers to the condition of Ireland, or the position of women, towards the end of the nineteenth century can only be speculated upon. What is certain is that Lynch's text, unsparing though it is, constituted the most enduring success of her career.

Photographic card (family collection). Inscribed on reverse: 'This photo is of aunt Hannah – spent life writing in Paris.'

Epilogue

In a sense, this book began with a series of conclusions, presenting four contrasting tributes to Lynch written shortly after her death. Our aim was to fill in the substantial lacunae between those accounts, to bring Lynch more fully into the daylight, and along with her a series of other significant figures and contexts. It is clear that research on Lynch – and on her sisters – contributes to the ongoing historical recovery of the Ladies' Land League. It builds upon accounts of the movement focused largely on Anna Parnell, providing valuable information on the way in which the alliances formed through the league persisted well after the dissolution of the movement and Anna Parnell's retreat from the public eye. Tracking Lynch has underlined the presence of other elided Ladies' Land League figures in the early formations of the Irish Literary Revival, such as Frances Sullivan and Rose Kavanagh. It has also foregrounded the literary dimensions of this movement and its contributions to emergent revivalist culture. Lynch's own writings based on her observations of Dublin literary coterie culture of the period both provide a trenchant, feminist critique of the later Celtic Twilight, and point to a critical and creative alternative that foregrounded women's writing as exemplary of cultural-revivalist impulses.

We have argued that Lynch's early novels set in Ireland, with their naturalist leanings and open challenge to social and sexual mores, offer a counter-narrative to those discourses that came to dominate notions of the Irish Literary Revival. In Lynch's texts masculine heroism is deflated, the condition of women in Ireland is lamented rather than mythologised, and alternative templates for women are proposed. Her engagement with Land War issues is further illustrative of the 'vortex of genres' in which she and other *fin-de-siècle* writers worked, and her writing intersects in surprising and revelatory ways with prose writers from the period, including Mabel Robinson and George Moore. This Lynch, Moore and Robinson triad crossed religious, national, class and gender boundaries. They were linked through London literary networks, preoccupations with Irish nationalism and female independence, and the quest for a literary form through which these preoccupations could be explored.

These unexpected crossings are traceable throughout Lynch's career, and offer a number of possible routes for future research. Lynch's early familial, political and literary affiliations shed valuable new light on established lines of connection between Dublin, London, Paris and beyond. Figures such as Wilde, Yeats, Moore – and to a lesser extent Maud Gonne – have long been used to illuminate the connection between these three capitals. Reading about Lynch provides an insight into an equally vibrant, but far less conspicuous, literary and journalistic scene in which a range of independent women were trying to negotiate a path. Her presence at the first Literary Ladies' dinner, in a row of women writers either associated with Ireland, with the Ladies' Land League, or with both, invites further exploration of interlocking cultural and political networks of the period. Lynch's friendships with journalists and editors such as Alice Corkran and Frances Low, as well as the extent and variety of her own periodical publications, strongly suggests that some of these networks will be recoverable via the 'periodical communities' of the later nineteenth and early twentieth centuries. Although our study has focused mainly on Ireland, Britain and France, it is clear that Lynch might well have been published more extensively in magazines in the United States. Her connections to Greece and Spain, the latter of which have received recent attention in *Hannah Lynch and Spain: collected journalism of an Irish New Woman, 1892–1903* by Pere Gifra-Adroher and Jaqueline Hurtley, suggest new avenues for exploration. Within this study we have examined a couple of different paradigms for Lynch's inter- or transnational writing identity. She can clearly be designated as 'cosmopolitan' by current standards, and yet it is doubtful whether she herself would have been happy with that label. As we have seen, by the end of her life she viewed herself as markedly different from those she placed in that category, such as Renée Vivien and Henry James. In Chapter 3 we suggested that 'Mesopotamian', a more idiosyncratic alternative, might suit Lynch's variegated background better. But neither of these positions, nor Lynch's long-held anti-imperialism, can be used as evidence of a preference for narrow forms of nationalism. Even her advocacy of an interpersonal politics of sympathy, which to an extent we can see her applying to the wider world, was always complicated and ambivalent, seldom able to overcome the historical and emotional forces with which it was enmeshed. She might have used the phrase 'debatable ground' to refer to Ireland specifically, but having surveyed Lynch's writing it could be applied to almost every territory to which she addressed herself.

The phrase could certainly be applied to Lynch's life. At present her personal archive is scattered and fragmentary, marked by spaces that might always remain unfilled. Even the portions that we have reassembled contain a series of major and minor fractures. Tynan's papers, with their offers of London introductions for Lynch, give a strong indication of why she might have been so surprised, not to mention upset, when her 'good friend' satirised the Yeats circle with which Tynan was so closely associated. As we have seen, Tynan's letters to Father Matthew Russell do not record her feelings in the months immediately after the publication of the Yeats spoof. But in the years to come Tynan did reflect on her on/off relationship with Lynch, and seemed to be ultimately regretful and puzzled by what had actually separated them. This schism was not the only time when Lynch revealed a vulnerability to perceived slights and criticisms from those who might have been important allies. For instance, her conviction that she had been snubbed by Pereda, when he viewed the incident entirely otherwise, puts a different complexion on her comical outline of her first meeting with the formidable Spanish author. This also calls to mind a late letter to Louise-Cécile Vincens, in which Lynch apologised for an unspecified misunderstanding – 'je vous a donné de la peine et j'en suis harcie à cause de mon malentendu' – clearly anxious not to lose her friendship or her valuable connections.¹ Vincens' reply is untraced as yet, but as their correspondence appears to fizzle out around this point, perhaps she did distance herself. This would explain why Vincens did not know of Lynch's final decline and death, and had to write to Mary Robinson for information. Such incidents could be interpreted in so many ways. They could serve as a reminder that Lynch often found herself crossing barriers of gender, class and national culture more or less simultaneously. They could operate as evidence of the relatively tenuous nature of many of her connections. After all, *Miss Brown*, Vernon Lee's book-length satire on Mary Robinson's early circle, caused Robinson considerable upset and embarrassment. Yet theirs was a loving relationship, and Lee was forgiven, a courtesy that was not as readily available to Lynch. We could use such incidents to demonstrate Lynch's quick temper, or her bad judgement. We could read them as the expression of her sense of her own worth, or as the opposite, as a prickly and brittle self-defensiveness. And when spread out across such an active and outspoken adulthood, are a few tensions really so surprising? Tynan, the Robinsons and Vincens, like Alice Meynell, were ambitious and influential modern women who made good use of established feminine virtues of affection and hospitality to construct powerful networks. Lynch clearly valued these qualities, but she valued other things – not least her right to reply – as much, if not more. Did this begin early? We have no evidence, yet, of day-to-day interactions in the Lynch-Cantwell household when Hannah and her sisters were growing up, but if there is any truth in *Autobiography of a Child*, it was intellectually adventurous and far from genteel. Lynch might have been sceptical of the New Woman as early as the 1880s, but she could be said to have embodied the New Woman's predecessor – the 'New Girl' – in her own mentally and physically challenging childhood. How easily would this have been assimilated into the necessary public-facing persona, especially when provocations – real, imagined or something of both – abounded?

The process of studying Lynch's negotiation of this 'debateable ground', and of seeking ways to articulate it, has compelled us to question our location and terms of reference, too. This has operated in parallel with a general opening of the critical field that has taken place in the last decade and a half, itself partly a consequence of the wealth of material that has been made available by large-scale digitisation projects. As this study testifies, our work has been shaped enormously by the growth of interest in Land War fiction, the Irish New Woman, cosmopolitanism, travel literature, female networks and periodical culture. The scholarly landscape that a student of this period will encounter in 2019 looks very different indeed from that of 2009. However, the fact that Lynch consciously deviated from standard designations (even when deviation was part of the designation, as was the case for the New Woman) generates important challenges. The field it opens up shares some features of what Heidi Hansson has called the 'interspace'. This zone, neither inside nor outside but possessing powerful elements of both positions, was the liberating yet unstable area Hansson christened just over a decade ago. Hansson's theorisation was formed with Emily Lawless as its focal point, the writer whose work Lynch promoted on account of its representation of women's lives in Ireland. Certainly, Lawless' topographical description of Ireland's history – 'a long, dark road, with many blind alleys, many sudden turnings, many unaccountably crooked portions' – chimes with Lynch's experiments in narrative complexity as well as with the multiple personal and political entanglements that dominate her plotlines.[2] And, as the study of women such as Lawless and Lynch has grown, so this space has become identifiable in scholarship, too, opening routes with the capacity to reshape even recently recovered narratives. As Lynch wandered not only between, but also across, countries and categories, her 'vagabond's scrutiny' has a further parallel in the *vagabondage* of Dúnlaith Bird's 2012 study. Bird, quoting the Swiss-Russian traveller Isabelle Eberhardt, loosely defined the term thus: 'the physical mobility of the traveller and the textual mobility of the author are identified in this study as *vagabondage* … the search for identity through motion, a physical and textual elaboration "sans itineraire fixe surtout".'[3] It is hard to know exactly what Lynch would have made of a comparison between Eberhardt and herself. Like Hansson's 'interspace', Bird's '*vagabondage*' is not an absolutely perfect fit for the subject of this study. And yet, the term still speaks powerfully to Lynch as a figure: for its volatile blend of marginality and liberty, for its associations with distinctive colonial and diasporic experiences, as well as for its determination not to be defined by them. Bird quotes Eberhardt's rather cutting comment: 'Un droit que bien peu d'intellectuels se soucient de revendiquer, c'est le droit à l'errance, au vagabondage.'⁴ As Lynch can be viewed as such a wandering intellectual, so her writing encourages us towards a form of intellectual nomadism in our own turn, sceptical of the 'fixed itineraries' of settled literary history, however and whenever they appear.

Towards the very end of the project, something happened that brought this lesson home with curiously perfect timing. A photograph, described as being of Lynch, surfaced in the family archive. It was the first – and remains the only – image of her that we had ever seen, and it is reproduced above and on the cover. The label on the card shows that it was taken in one of the studios of the Napoléon photographic company, which had premises in central Barcelona. This innovative and prestigious family firm was renowned for its portraiture, winning a series of awards, including a gold medal at the Universal Exhibition in Barcelona in 1888. The location, and the Napoléon's high-ranking clientele, strongly suggest a connection to Nannie. Appropriately, then, it is at once a formal portrait – the heavy leather chair and the hangings in the background suggest patrician opulence – and an intimate one. The young woman depicted, seated at a desk with eyes fixed on one of her books, seems oblivious to her surroundings and to the presence of the viewer. Her dark dress, with its immaculate white lace cuffs and collar, adds to this sense of composure. The place and the composition of the photograph – with its emphasis on literary study – all align with what we know of her life and work. Yet somehow Lynch had surprised us once again, betraying no trace of the restless unconventionality that (without even realising it) we had expected to see. Like one of her own characters, who are often forced to confront their preconceptions, we suddenly saw her afresh. It is therefore the case that this book, which began with a series of endings, should end with a form of beginning. We wonder which new territories this study might open up, and what other new discoveries might be made about, and due to, the life and writing of Hannah Lynch.

Timeline

- **Dublin:** Hannah Lynch born 25 March **1859**.
- **Near Paris:** Convent education alluded to in John P. Gibbs, 'Tribute to Hannah Lynch: an Irishwoman of great literary ability who did hard work in the Parnell movement'; and mentioned in Lynch's own writing on education for girls.
- **Coventry, England**. It is possible she attended a convent here, the source of material for her *Autobiography of a Child*.

1880

- **London:** Lynch studies music at Lansdowne Cottell's Academy (Gibbs, 'Tribute to Hannah Lynch').

1881

- **London (February):** Report of the inaugural meeting of London branch of the Ladies' Land League, held 'yesterday afternoon' at Kenley Lodge, Macaulay Road, Clapham Common, where Hannah Lynch was elected 'hon. sec.' (*Freeman's Journal*, 22 February 1881).
- **Isle of Wight (April):** Clarendon Boarding House, Ventnor.
  (Gibbs, 'Tribute to Hannah Lynch', family records, and the 1881 census returns, taken 3 April, show a 'Hanna' [*sic*] Lynch, a twenty-two-year-old 'student of literature' born in Dublin around 1859, living in Ventnor.
- **Dublin (December):** 'Lynch was present on 15 December for the most significant DMP raid on the Abbey Street premises' of the Ladies' Land League (Myles Dungan, *Mr Parnell's Rottweiler: censorship and the United Ireland newspaper, 1881–1891*, p. 89).

1882

- **Dublin (January):** Hannah and Nannie Lynch are arrested on 14 January 1882 (Beverly E. Schneller, *Anna Parnell's Political Journalism*).

Lynch (and her sisters?) edits *United Ireland* and smuggles type out of Ireland (Katharine Tynan, *Twenty-five Years: reminiscences*; and Henry George in Kenneth C. Wenzer (ed.), *Henry George, The Transatlantic Irish, and Their Times*).

Key Publications:
'The Massingers' is serialised in the *Shamrock* (24 June–25 November 1882).

1883

- **Passage East, County Waterford:** According to the Counahan family biography, Lynch held a position as a governess in Passage East, County Waterford. Her *Shamrock* article published in March suggests she was based here early in the year and possibly late 1882.
- **Dublin (July):** Letter to Harriet Taylor, 3 July 1883 from 10 South Frederick Street (Harriet Taylor Correspondence, vol. 20 of Mill-Taylor Papers, Special Collections, London School of Economics).

Key Publications
'A Glimpse of South Ireland in Winter', published in the *Shamrock* (March 1883) and more than likely written while working as a governess in Passage East, County Waterford.
'Nature's Constancy in Variety', *Irish Monthly*, August 1883.
'Christmas on the Hills: tales', *Shamrock*, Christmas double number (December 1883–January 1884).

1884

- **London:** Lynch meets Oscar Wilde with Katharine Tynan at Lady Wilde's salon in London (Tynan, *Twenty-five Years*).

Key Publications
'A Backward Glance at the City of the Pale', *Donahoe's Magazine*, November 1884.
With several others, Lynch contributes to 'A Castle Christmas-Eve; or The Tales the Portraits Told', *United Ireland*, 20 December 1884.
'Marjory Maurice' is serialised in the *Shamrock*, starting on 27 December 1884.

1885

- **London (March):** Letter to Katharine Tynan from Ponsonby Lyons about Hannah Lynch in the Reading Room in the British Museum, dated 23 March 1885 (Katharine Tynan Letters, National Library of Ireland).
- **Dublin (July):** Letter from Tynan to Matthew Russell, 29 July 1885: 'Hannah Lynch is at home for a bit' (Irish Jesuit Archives).
- **Lutra, Tenos (now more commonly known as Tinos) (October):** Letter from Lynch to Father Thomas Dawson, 3 October 1885 (Brotherton Library, University of Leeds).
- **Lutra, Tenos (December):** Letter from Lynch to Dawson, 5 December 1885 (Brotherton Library, University of Leeds).

Key Publications
'Marjory Maurice' serialised in the *Shamrock*, from 27 December 1884–28 March 1885.
'Defeated' is published in *Beeton's Christmas Annual*, 1885.
Through Troubled Waters (London: Ward, Lock & Co., 1885).

1886

- **Lutra, Tenos (February):** Letter from Lynch to Dawson, 18 February 1886 (Brotherton Library, University of Leeds).
- **Athens (March):** Letter from Lynch (14 Maison Mélas, Rue d'Ecole, Athens) to the editor, *Century Magazine*, 20 March 1886 (Archives and Manuscripts, New York Public Library).

Key Publications
'The Ursulines of Tenos', *Irish Monthly*, May 1886.
'November in a Greek Island', *Irish Monthly*, July 1886.

1887

- **Athens (September):** Letter from Lynch to Dawson, 5 September 1887 (Brotherton Library, University of Leeds).
- **Dublin (December):** On 11 December 1887, Lynch attends Katharine Tynan's literary salon 'Whitehall' in Clondalkin, Dublin, and meets Yeats, Æ, and Douglas Hyde. Following this encounter she lampoons Yeats, Æ and Tynan's salon in the *Dublin Evening Telegraph*.

1888

- **London (March):** Letter from Lynch to Dawson, 24 March 1888. Sent from 49 Woburn Place, Russell Square: '… suffering diabolically with my arms – sort of writer's cramp' (Brotherton Library, University of Leeds).

Key Publications
'A Dublin Literary Coterie: sketched by a non-pretentious observer', *Dublin Evening Telegraph*, 14 January 1888.
'Laogaire or Wrecked on Success', serialised in the *Weekly Freeman*, 10 March–17 November 1888.

1889

- **London (May):** On 31 May 1889, Lynch attends the inaugural Literary Ladies' dinner at the Criterion Restaurant (Anon., 'Women Who Write: the Literary Ladies' dinner', *Pall Mall Gazette*, 1 June 1889).
- **Dublin (November):** Letter from Lynch to Dawson, 11 November 1889, sent from 3 Hastings Terrace, Sandycove (Brotherton Library, University of Leeds).

Key Publications
'A Story of Chios', *Macmillan's Magazine*, January 1889.
'A Girl Revolutionist', *Girl's Realm*, February 1889.
'The Last of the O'Moores', *Weekly Freeman Xmas Sketch Book*, December 1889.

1890

- **Paris (May):** Letter from Lynch to Louise-Cécile Vincens ['Arvède Barine'], sent on 21 May 1890 from 30 Avenue de Breteuil, Paris (Bibliothèque Nationale de France).

Key Publications
'The Little Marquis', *Macmillan's Magazine*, October 1890.

1891

- **Paris:** Lecture on Robert Louis Stevenson, mentioned in *Hearth and Home*, 21 May 1891.

Key Publications

'The Romantic Episode in the Life of Miss Charlotte O'Mara', *Murray's Magazine: a home and colonial periodical for the general reader*, September 1891.

The Prince of the Glades, 2 vols (London: Methuen, 1891).

George Meredith: a study (London: Methuen, 1891).

1892

- **[Paris and Spain?]**: Articles on Paris, and about a voyage on a Spanish steamer published this year (listed below).

Key Publications

Daughters of Men: a novel (London: William Heinemann, 1892).

Rosni Harvey: a novel, 3 vols (London: Chapman & Hall, 1892).

Perrens, Francois Tommy, *The History of Florence under the Domination of Cosimo, Piero, Lorenzo de' Médicis, 1434–1492*, trans. from the French by Hannah Lynch (London: Methuen, 1892).

'Paris in Midsummer', *Freeman's Journal*, 31 August 1892.

'On Board a Spanish Steamer', *Freeman's Journal*, 27 December 1892.

1893

- **London (November)**: Letter from Lynch to Dawson, sent 23 November 1893 from Kent Cottage, East Molesey, Hampton Court (Brotherton Library, University of Leeds).

1894

- **London (January)**: Letter from Lynch to Dawson, sent 4 January 1894 from Kent Cottage, East Molesey, Hampton Court (Brotherton Library, University of Leeds).
- **London (October–late December)**: Letter from Lynch to Dawson, 21 December 1894, sent from 47 York Street, Portman Square: 'I have been in town now for two months but my health has been so wretched' (Brotherton Library, University of Leeds).
- **Dublin (November? early December?)**: Letter from Lynch to Dawson, dated 21 December (see above). It makes reference to her sister Virginia's death and Lynch's return from Ireland (Brotherton Library, University of Leeds).

- **Rochefort, France:** The article 'A Day in Pierre Loti's Town' records a visit there. Lynch discusses **St Jean d'Angély**, a nearby town, in 'In the Woods of La Pellouaille'.
- **[Spain?]:** 'Along the Spanish Highways' suggests an extensive trip through Spain with a special focus on Barcelona, where Lynch's sister Nannie lived, probably during 1894.

Key Publications
'A Day in Pierre Loti's Town', *Speaker*, 13 October 1894.
'In the Woods of La Pellouaille', *Speaker*, 27 October 1894.
'Along the Spanish Highways', *Good Words*, December 1894.

1895

- **Margate (January?–February):** Letter from Lynch to Dawson, Sunday 24 February 1895, from 18 Albert Terrace, Margate: 'an invalid for six weeks' (Brotherton Library, University of Leeds).
  F. Mabel Robinson writes in support of Hannah Lynch's application to the Royal Literary Fund, 16 February 1895 (British Library, London).
- **London (March):** Letter from Lynch to the Royal Literary Fund, 15 March, from 47 York Street, Portman Square (British Library, London).
  Lynch gives a lecture to the Irish Literary Society on 'Irishmen in the Service of Spain' on Saturday 23 March. This lecture is reported in some detail in the *Freeman's Journal*, 26 March 1895.
- **Madrid (April):** Letter from Lynch to Alice Corkran (sold privately online at auction) dated April 1895, from 6 Playa del Rey, Madrid. Concerns translation of a novel from Russian to French about Sophia Kovalevsky, and notes lack of payment for an article.
- **Santander (summer):** Meets J.M. Pereda, as related in her article 'A Spanish "Master" at Home'. See also 'Pereda y Hannah Lynch', translated for us by Pere Gifra-Adroher (Castañeda, Salvador Garcia, 'Pereda y Hannah Lynch o La Pequeña Historia de un Malentendido', *Siglo Diecinueve: literatura Hispánica*, vol. 1, 1995.
- **[Santiago de Compostela?]:** Possible source of material for an article published in December.
- **[Canary Isles?]:** Lynch's articles on Tenerife published in January 1896 were presumably based on a visit during this year.
- **London (September):** Letter from Lynch to Gaston Paris, 27 September 1895, sent from 14 St Mary Abbots Terrace, Kensington (Bibliothèque Nationale de France (BNF)).

- [**Oxford?**]: Presumably her October article in the *Freeman's Journal* was based on a visit here during this year.

Key Publications

'My Friend Arcanieva', *Macmillan's Magazine*, December 1895.

Echegaray, José, *The Great Galeoto: folly or saintliness. Two Plays done from the verse of Jose Echegaray into English Prose by Hannah Lynch* (London: John Lane, 1895).

'Around Tarragona', *Speaker*, 12 January 1895.

'Oxford', *Freeman's Journal*, 28 October 1895.

'A Spanish "Master" at Home', *Speaker*, 16 November 1895.

'Santiago de Compostela', *Freeman's Journal*, 28 December 1895.

1896

- **Paris:** Letter dated simply 'Mardi 1896' to Vincens, from 15 Avenue de Breteuil (BNF).

  Lynch gives a lecture in Paris on 'The Irish Peasant: fact and fiction', reported in the *Freeman's Journal*, Saturday 13 June 1896.

Key Publications

'Impressions of the Canary Isles: I', *Good Words*, January 1896.

'The Irish Peasant: fact and fiction', *Freeman's Journal*, 13 June 1896.

Denys d'Auvrillac: a story of French life (London: J. Macqueen, 1896).

Dr Vermont's Fantasy and Other Stories (London: J.M. Dent & Co., 1896).

Lynch's 'Paris Letters' for the *Academy* (London) begin in November.

1897

- **Toledo (Late September? Early October?)** (Castañeda, 'Pereda y Hannah Lynch').
- **Santander (October):** Meets Pereda on 27 October 1897, a meeting that results in a misunderstanding (Castañeda, 'Pereda y Hannah Lynch').
- **Paris (November):** Letters from Pereda sent to Hannah Lynch in Paris dated 3, 20 and 29 November (Castañeda, 'Pereda y Hannah Lynch').

Key Publications

Jinny Blake: a tale (London: J.M. Dent & Co., 1897).

An Odd Experiment (London: Methuen, 1897).

'A Village Sovereign', *Macmillan's Magazine*, August 1897.

'An Unnoted Corner of Spain', *Blackwood's Magazine*, July 1897.
'Monserrat', *Freeman's Journal*, 31 July 1897.
Lynch's 'Paris Letters' appear in the *Academy*.

1898

- **Paris (April):** Letter from Hannah Lynch to Pereda, 17 April 1898, Paris (Castañeda, 'Pereda y Hannah Lynch').

Key Publications
Toledo: the story of an old Spanish capital (London: Dent, 1898).

1899

- **Paris (March):** Letter from Lynch to Vincens, 15 March 1899, sent from 15 Avenue de Breteuil (BNF).
- **Paris (April):** Letter from Lynch to Vincens, [20?] April, 60 Avenue de Breteuil (BNF).
- **Paris (September):** Letter from Lynch to Vincens, 22 September, 60 Avenue de Breteuil (BNF). In this month Lynch also writes to the editor of *Century Magazine* in relation to an article of hers about Venice (New York Public Library).
- **[Switzerland and Italy? (including Lucerne, Verona and Venice)]:** Several travel pieces published this year, as well as the letter to the editor of *Century Magazine*, suggest a recent trip through Italy.

Key Publications
Autobiography of a Child (Edinburgh and London: William Blackwood & Co., and New York: Dodd, Mead & Co., 1899).
'Irish and French Patriotism', *St James's Gazette*, 20 January 1899.
'From Lucerne to Verona', *Freeman's Journal*, 22 August 1899.
'In Provence', *Blackwood's Magazine*, September 1899.
'George Meredith', *Bookman* (London), November 1899.
'Venice I', *Freeman's Journal*, 29 December 1899.
'Venice II', *Freeman's Journal*, 30 December 1899.
Lynch's 'Paris Letters' continue to appear in the *Academy*.

1900

- **Paris (March–May):** Lynch publishes seven articles on the Paris Exhibition in *Hearth and Home*.

Mary Robinson's letters to her mother in May 1900 refer to her meeting with Lynch several times in Paris (http://www.le-petit-orme.com/lettres-de-mary-duclaux (accessed 4 October 2018)).

- **London (June):** An article on 'Women Writers at Dinner' appears in the *St James's Gazette* (26 June 1900). It includes Hannah Lynch in the list of attendees at the dinner that took place in the Criterion the day before.
- **Dublin (late summer?):** Letter from Lynch to Vincens, dated Monday 20 August, refers to a long stay in Ireland with her mother (BNF).

Key Publications

Clare Monro: the story of a mother and daughter (London: J. Milne, 1900).

'Two Old Italian Towns', *Freeman's Journal*, 1 January 1900.

'A Girl's Ride on an Engine', *Girl's Realm*, vol. 2, March 1900.

'"Fecondite" vs. "The Kreutzer Sonata" or "Zola vs. Tolstoi"', *Fortnightly Review*, January 1900.

'Paris and the Exhibition', *Hearth and Home*, 1 March–10 May 1900.

Lynch's 'Paris Letters' continue to appear in the *Academy*.

1901

- **Paris (January):** Letter from Lynch to Vincens, 29 January 1901 (BNF).
- **Henley-on-Thames (April?):** Letter from Lynch to Vincens, April? 15th (BNF).
- **Barcelona (May–June):** Postcard from Lynch to Vincens, 20 May 1901, sent from 17 Plaza Urquinaona. States that Lynch will be in Spain until mid-June and is going to Majorca for a fortnight (BNF).
- **Majorca (end May? June?):** See above.
- **Paris (July):** Letter from Lynch to Gaston Paris, 30 July, sent from 60 Avenue de Breteuil (BNF).
- **London (August):** Letter from Lynch to Gaston Paris, 20 August 1901, sent from 22 Handel Mansions, Handel Street (BNF).

Key Publications

French Life in Town and Country (New York and London: G.P. Putnam's Sons, 1901).

'Insanity in Literature', *Academy*, 17 August 1901.

'Sully Prudhomme', *Academy*, 28 December 1901.

Lynch's 'Paris Letters' continue to appear in the *Academy*.

1902

- **Greece (March):** Postcard from Lynch to Vincens, 31 March 1902 (BNF).
- **Athens (April):** Letter from Lynch to the editor of *Century Magazine*, 30 April 1902. From Athens, but using Avenue de Breteuil headed paper (New York Public Library).
- **[Paris?] (September):** Letter from Lynch to Vincens, sent on 16 September 1902. Lynch discusses the *Contemporary Review* (BNF).

Key Publications
'A. Mary F. Robinson', *Fortnightly Review*, 1 February 1902.
'The Young French Girl Interviewed', *Nineteenth Century*, February 1902.
'On the Acropolis', *Academy*, 14 June 1902.
'Rebel Catalonia', *Contemporary Review*, July 1902.
'Paul Bourget, Preacher', *Contemporary Review*, July 1902.
Lynch's 'Paris Letters' continue in the *Academy*.

1903

- **Paris (January):** Letter from Lynch to the editor of *Century Magazine*, 19 January 1903, from 60 Avenue de Breteuil. Discusses her novel on modern French life (never published and not currently located) (New York Public Library).
- **Paris (April):** Lynch correspondence with the Royal Literary Fund, 12 April 1903, sent from 60 Avenue de Breteuil (British Library).
- **Olmet, Vic sur Cère (August):** This is the address of Emile Duclaux and Mary Duclaux [Mary Robinson]. Letter from Lynch to Edmund Gosse and held in his papers, sent 19 August 1903. Lynch thanks him for supporting her application to the Royal Literary Fund and explains her drawn-out illness (Brotherton Library, University of Leeds). On 23 August, Lynch writes again, thanking him for his letter and the cheque from the Royal Literary Fund (Brotherton Library, University of Leeds).
- **Paris (November–December):** Further letter from Lynch to the editor of *Century Magazine* about the novel she is finishing. Sent on 7 November 1903, from 60 Avenue de Breteuil (New York Public Library).
  Letter from Lynch to Gosse, sent on 23 December 1903, from 60 Avenue de Breteuil. Lynch mentions the novel she hoped to complete and send to Mr Heinemann but has not, due to ill health (Brotherton Library, University of Leeds).

Key Publications

'The Girls of Spain', *Girl's Realm*, May 1903.

'Persecution in France Today and Fifty Years Ago', *Contemporary Review*, July 1903.

Paris, Gaston, *Mediaeval French Literature*, trans. from the French by Hannah Lynch (London: Dent, 1903).

Lynch's 'Paris Letters' conclude in July of this year.

1904

- **Paris (January):** Lynch dies on 11 January from stomach cancer (letter from Mary Robinson to Vincens: BNF).

  13 January 1904: following a service at Saint Philippe du Roule, Hannah Lynch is buried. Pere Gifra-Adroher and Jacqueline Hurtley note that Nannie Lynch purchased two burial plots in the Pierre Grenier cemetery on 12 January 1904 (p.19., n.9), and details of her death and burial are held in Boulogne-Billancourt, Archives Municipales and recorded in the file Cimetière Boulogne-sur-Seine. (Our thanks to Jacqueline Hurtley for sending us a copy of this document.) Death notices in several papers made reference to Lynch being buried in Père Lachaise.

Notes and References

INTRODUCTION

1   Anon., 'Over the Initials "K.H." in the *Pall Mall Gazette*, Mrs Hinkson Pays a Last Generous Tribute to Miss Hannah Lynch', *Tablet*, 30 January 1904, p. 178.

2   John P. Gibbs, 'Tribute to Hannah Lynch: an Irishwoman of great literary ability who did hard work in the Parnell movement', *Gaelic American*, 13 February 1904, p. 5.

3   Frances Low, 'A Woman's Causerie', *Speaker*, 15 December 1906, pp. 319–20.

4   Agnes Mary Frances Robinson (1857–1944) was married twice, and took her married name as her writing name on both occasions. Her first husband, James Darmesteter, died in 1894. She remarried in 1901, and her second husband, Emile Duclaux, director of the Pasteur Institute in Paris, died in May 1904. To avoid confusion we refer to her simply as 'Mary Robinson' throughout this study, although we retain her given name in the notes.

5   Lynch's manuscript writing in French presents numerous challenges to accurate transcription and translation (not least as her handwriting is unusually hard to read, even in English). For this reason, we have quoted all such passages without translation, and indicated where indecipherable or unclear portions occur. However, given the significance of Robinson's letter, and its relative legibility, a translation seems appropriate: 'This is such a sad story. The poor girl, ill (or so we were told) of coli-enteritis, had been suffering for months with horrible stomach pains. She came to see us that summer in Auvergne – I found her very changed. But, such was her enthusiasm, her courage, that she used to recover from an atrocious attack to laugh, to chat, or even to take long walks in the mountains. "It's nerves," she used to say – I found her even more unwell on our return to Paris in November. But my husband was gravely ill. I could leave him only rarely to look after my poor little neighbour. Fortunately, the good Madame Clere sent her an excellent sick-nurse. Towards the end of December, Dr Lereboullet [?], who was treating her devotedly, insisted on a serious examination. He was immediately alarmed, even pronounced (but not in front of the sick girl) the terrible word that we were all to dread ... It was a cancer! On 28 December, I went with her to Dr Tuffier's, who gave us real hope, and who generously offered to give her an operation which would be followed (he said) with long years of health. Dear Madame, it was a useless butchery! Surrounded by devoted friends, by her sisters, one who had come from Ireland and the other from Barcelona, that the ferocious hospital regulations allowed to wait by her bedside only a few hours every day – having everything that she required to ease [?] her final days – poor Hannah. She died at night, all alone, in the paying ward [?] of the Dubbeau Pavilion, at Beaujour. All this is so horrible that I cannot talk about it. [...] She had the most tragic end in the world.' Mary Robinson Duclaux to Louise-Cécile Vincens (Arvède Barine), n.d., Bibliothèque Nationale de France, FR Nouvelle Acquisitions, 18342: f. 226. Thanks to Marie Dumas, who worked on the translation of the letter with us.

6   'Hannah Lynch is little spoken of in her own country today. Hers is a striking instance of a clever writer passing out of public memory in the course of a generation or less, because she never had been lucky enough to hit upon a line in fiction suitable to her own peculiar powers',

Evening Herald (September 1918), cited in P. Mac Craith, 'Hannah Lynch: a Dublin novelist', *Irish Book Lover*, vol. xxi, no. 6 (Nov.–Dec. 1933), p. 134. Or, in a tribute to 'Hannah Lynch of Virginia', P. O'C writes: 'This brilliant Cavan authoress may be forgotten in her own land but her light of genius shines in that France in which she lived and wrote and in which she still lives in her writings': 'Impressions of France, Cavan Authoress Recalled, Hannah Lynch of Virginia', *Meath Chronicle*, 24 September 1921, p. 6.

7   For recent scholarly attention to these and other Irish women writers of this period, see studies by the following authors listed in the bibliography: Kelleher, Hansson, Murphy, Morris, Standlee, O'Toole, Morris, Stevenson.

8   Hannah Lynch, 'The Irish Peasant: fact and fiction', *Freeman's Journal*, 13 June 1896, p. 5.

9   Ibid.

10 Ibid.

11 Mabel Robinson's name is also subject to variation. The most common is 'F. Mabel Robinson'. As with her sister, we retain this variant in the notes, where and if it is found.

12 The full title of this famous publication was *Blackwood's Edinburgh Magazine*. We use the more familiar, slightly shortened, title throughout this study.

13 Thomas G. Connors, 'Letters of John Mitchel, 1848–1869', *Analecta Hibernica*, no. 37, 1998, p. 304, fn. 30.

14 James Cantwell, letter to John O'Mahony, 2 November 1860, Fenian Brotherhood and O'Donovan Rossa Collection, American Catholic History Research Centre and University Archives, http://cuislandora.wrlc.org/islandora/object/achc-fenian%3A545#page/1/mode/1up (accessed 4 October 2018).

15 We are grateful to Michael Counahan, great-nephew of Hannah Lynch, for generously providing us with this and other information in a detailed biography of the family. 'Notes on Counahan Family History: based on notes by Desmond R. Counahan, with additions by other family members'. Supplied to the authors in 2007.

16 Lynch's father, Michael Lynch from County Cavan, 'was a highly successful merchant and shopkeeper in Capel Street, Dublin. Prosperity enabled him to buy a landholding at Lynchpark, Blessington, Co. Wicklow, another holding in Kerry, and some other properties': 'Notes on Counahan Family History'.

17 Bernadette Whelan records the contentiousness of this appointment, initiated by Cantwell's friendship with Thomas Francis Meagher, but opposed from various quarters because of his political affiliations and what was considered an inferior social position – owner of a tavern: *American Government in Ireland, 1790–1913: a history of the US Consular Service* (Oxford: Oxford University Press, 2010), pp. 37–40.

18 In 'Marjory Maurice', the Maurice sisters, lively and attractive members of the Ladies' Land League, are scorned by some: 'Yes; they've an uncle, but much can't be expected from him, you know; he's only a Dublin trader – a rich merchant. But that is nothing': *Shamrock*, 10 January 1885, p. 231.

19 James Stephens (1825–1901) and John O'Mahony (1816–77) were central figures within the Young Ireland movement, and went on to form and to lead the Fenians (later the Irish Republican Brotherhood).

20 Rossa was named as a family friend by the narrator of *Autobiography of a Child*, and a note made by Rossa on one of Cantwell's letters identifies him as the owner of 'The Star and Garter'.

21 Barry Kennerk records that following his rejection as a candidate, 'Cantwell quickly set about making it [the Star and Garter Hotel] a kind of rendezvous for Irish-Americans': 'A Dublin Consul under Siege: American reactions to the habeas corpus suspension crisis of 1866–1868', *Dublin Historical Record*, vol. 63, no. 1, spring 2010, p. 19. One of these Irish-American

visitors must have been John Gibbs, who gives one of the most detailed accounts of Lynch's background and life in her obituary. The significance of 'The Star and Garter' as a political landmark was not missed by James Joyce, who included a brief reference to it in the Aeolus chapter of *Ulysses*.

22 Katharine Tynan, *Twenty-five Years: reminiscences* (London: Smith Elder, 1913), pp. 76–7. Tynan's portrait of the mother both differs from and resembles the figure drawn up by Lynch in *Autobiography of a Child*: 'The mother was a woman of spirit and cleverness. She was very bookish, full of personality, and a perfect mine of stories about the men of the forty-eight and fifties and sixties. She used to drop words of wisdom into my receptive ears' (p. 78).

23 For further discussion on Tynan's split allegiances, see Whitney Standlee's 'Katharine Tynan's Novels and the Politics of Ireland's "Long Gestation", 1890–1916', in Kateřina Jenčová, Michaela Marková, Radvan Markus and Hana Pavelková (eds), *The Politics of Irish Writing* (Prague: Centre for Irish Studies, Charles University, 2010), pp. 109–17; Kieron Winterson, '"Old wine in new bottles"? Katharine Tynan, Lord Edward Fitzgerald, and George Wyndham', in Anna Pilz and Whitney Standlee (eds), *Irish Women's Writing, 1878–1922* (Manchester: Manchester University Press, 2016), pp. 156–73; and Aurelia Annat, 'Class, Nation, Gender and Self: Katharine Tynan and the construction of political identities, 1880–1930', in Fintan Lane (ed.), *Politics, Society and the Middle Class in Modern Ireland* (Houndmills: Palgrave Macmillan, 2010), pp. 194–211.

24 Tynan, *Twenty-five Years*, p. 78.

25 Ibid., p. 70. The multiple references to reading matter and storytelling in Lynch's *Autobiography* reinforce Tynan's reminiscences, or perhaps influenced them.

26 Ibid., pp. 78–9, 86–7.

27 Tynan played an important role in the shaping of the early Yeats, who she first met in 1885. As Standlee points out, 'It was to Tynan's literary reputation that Yeats was drawn rather than, as might be expected, vice versa. Recognizing in Tynan "a link to the word of literary editors", Yeats actively cultivated the friendship …': '"A World of Difference": London and Ireland in the works of Katharine Tynan', in Tom Herron (ed.), *Irish Writing London: Vol. 1: Revival to the Second World War* (London: Bloomsbury, 2012), p. 71.

28 Ciaran O'Neill, *Catholics of Consequence: transnational education, social mobility and the Irish Catholic elite, 1850–1900* (Oxford: Oxford University Press, 2014).

29 Hannah Lynch, 'Correspondence: French life', *Speaker*, 6 April 1901, p. 19. Michael Counahan records in his family history that two of Lynch's stepsisters, Brigid and Teresa, were sent to schools in Dublin, Coventry and 'a French school near Paris': 'Notes on Counahan Family History'.

30 F. Mabel Robinson, letter in support of Hannah Lynch's application, 16 February 1895, Papers of the Royal Literary Fund, British Library, file no. 2452. As James Murphy has observed, these letters were clearly intended to generate sympathy for Lynch: James H. Murphy, *Irish Novelists and the Victorian Age* (Oxford: Oxford University Press, 2011), p. 252.

31 Michael Counahan alludes to other governess positions including one in Passage East, County Waterford. Lynch's 'A Glimpse of South Ireland in Winter', which traces a journey to Waterford and its environs, suggests a possible date for when she held this position (*Shamrock*, 10 March 1883, pp. 364–6).

32 We are grateful to Conor Montague for sharing information about this scandal and about Lynch's connections there, as well as for alerting us to James Greaney's *Dunmore*. Greaney notes how closely the novel was based on the Handcock/Clanrickard case: 'Indeed, so thin was the disguise that most knowledgeable readers immediately recognised the principal characters … Practically all the copies of the book *Troubled Waters* were bought up by either the Handcocks or Lord Clanrickard and destroyed': James Greaney, *Dunmore* (n.p., The

Author, 1984), pp. 57–8. See also Catherine Corless, 'The Handcocks of Carantrila Park', *Journal of the Old Tuam Society*, no. 8, 2011, pp. 27–34. 'Carrowntrayla' is a variant spelling.

33 Anon., 'A Novel of the Period', *United Ireland*, 2 May 1885, p. 6.

34 Hannah Lynch, 'To the Editor of *United Ireland*', 9 May 1885, p. 1. Our thanks to Mary Guinan-Darmody, Tipperary Studies, Thurles, for kindly checking the page number of this article.

35 Katharine Tynan, letter to Father Matthew Russell, 5 May 1885, Irish Jesuit Archive, Dublin, MSS J27/73 (1).

36 'F.Y.E.', 'Correspondence: the French correspondent', *Speaker*, April 1901, p. 633.

37 Lynch to Vincens, 15 [April?] 1901, BNF, vol. 18345. The male reviewer later added insult to injury in a second letter by referring to Oscar Wilde as English.

38 E.A. Bennett, 'Insanity in Literature', *Academy*, vol. 61, 14 September 1901, p. 227. We discuss the influence that Lynch's Parisian circle might have wielded on her 'Paris Letter' in 'A Forgotten Franco-Irish Literary Network', *Études Irlandaises*, vol. 36, no. 2, 2011, pp. 157–71.

39 Tynan's first publication was a poem in *Young Ireland Magazine* (edited by A.M. Sullivan, 1875–91) and she credited her political awakening to the political contexts of this publication. See Standlee, 'A World of Difference', p. 72.

40 Tynan, *Twenty-five Years*, p. 129.

41 While many writers within her network, including Mary and Mabel Robinson, contributed to *Woman's World*, edited by Wilde in the late 1880s, Lynch did not.

42 Hannah Lynch, 'The English Drama of To-day', *Freeman's Journal*, 7 December 1893, p. 5. It is worth noting that Lynch was inserting herself into another high-profile debate, this time involving the drama critic William Archer in the London *Pall Mall Gazette*.

43 Ibid.

44 Anon., 'Sad Finish', *Punch*, vol. 100, 13 June 1896, p. 282.

45 Hannah Lynch, *George Meredith: a study* (London: Methuen, 1891), p. 52.

46 Ibid., p. 137.

47 Ibid., p. 157.

48 Chapman only published *Rosni Harvey* (London: Chapman & Hall, 1892), a book that Meredith felt was hampered by the requirements of the triple-decker format.

49 B.W. Matz, 'George Meredith as a Publisher's Reader', *Fortnightly Review*, vol. 86, August 1909, p. 289.

50 Rev. P. Farrelly, 'French Life in Town and Country', *Catholic World*, vol. 75, 1902, p. 760. This American reviewer was not alone, as in her *Academy* 'Paris Letter' for 4 May 1901 (p. 389) Lynch remarked upon the fact that 'Lately an Irish editor, who has never been inside a convent, acquainted his readers with the supposition that I must be a fiend because I, who have been brought up in convents, disapprove of those institutions.'

51 Thomas Dawson belonged to the Oblates of Mary Immaculate based in Inchicore and is noted for being a translator and editor of religious texts: see the *Tablet*, 18 January 1913, p. 107. A.M. Sullivan (1830–84) was a former Young Irelander, editor of the *Nation* with Isaac Butt, who inaugurated the Home Rule Party, and supporter of Parnell. Henry George was an American land reformer who visited Ireland during the period of the Land Wars and who published extensively on the subject: see Henry George Jr, *The Life of Henry George III* (New York: Doubleday & McClure Company, 1900), p. 367.

52 Hannah Lynch, letter to Thomas Dawson, 3 October 1885, Father Thomas Dawson Correspondence, BC MS 19c Dawson, Brotherton Library, University of Leeds.

53 Hannah Lynch, letter to Thomas Dawson, 11 November 1889, Father Thomas Dawson Correspondence, Brotherton Library. Lynch's interest in the case may have been personal, too. For the author of the forged letters upon which the 'Parnellism and Crime' series published in *The Times* was based was none other than Richard Pigott, original owner of the papers in

which Lynch's first publications had appeared. For further details see Margaret O'Callaghan, 'Richard Pigott', *The Dictionary of Irish Biography* (Cambridge: Cambridge University Press, 2009), http://dib.cambridge.org.libraryproxy.mic.ul.ie/quicksearch.do;jsessionid=1EF2E 8B451E00C931B84315228EEF29B (accessed 4 October 2018). In 1889 the Tenants' Defence Association, launched at the Thurles Convention, was a point of serious contention between Parnell and William O'Brien.

54 Hannah Lynch, letter to Thomas Dawson, 3 October 1885, Father Thomas Dawson Correspondence, Brotherton Library. Illegible words are indicated by [?].

55 Tynan mentions in her letters another sister, Teresa Cantwell, 'a great friend of mine', who had in 1885 a governess post in Palina, Majorca: Damien Atkinson (ed.), *The Selected Letters of Katharine Tynan: poet and novelist* (Newcastle upon Tyne: Cambridge Scholars, 2016), pp. 46–7.

56 Ponsonby Lyons, letter to Katharine Tynan, 23 March 1885, Katharine Tynan Letters, MS 39, 118, National Library of Ireland.

57 Lynch had described her ill health and precarious financial condition in a letter to Dawson in 1894: '... my health has been wretched ... Worry has everything to do with it. This has been a horribly unlucky year for me. Do you know anybody in want of a secretary or literary help of any sort? But I suppose you don't', 21 December 1894, Father Thomas Dawson Correspondence, Brotherton Library.

58 An award of twenty-five pounds was made: Papers of the Royal Literary Fund, file no. 2452, British Library.

59 See Lynch's article 'The Frenchman in English Fiction' for a discussion of this sort of misrepresentation: *Academy*, 24 July 1897, p. 71.

60 Hannah Lynch, letter to the Royal Literary Fund, 11 December 1903: Papers of the Royal Literary Fund, file no. 2452, British Library.

61 A recent entry about Hannah Lynch on the website Ecrivains – Littérateurs – Romanciers, 'Amis et Passionné du Père Lachaise' records: 'Une cérémonie religieuse à eu lieu à Saint Philippe du Roule le 14 Janvier 1904 vers midi. Son inhumation au cimetière du Père Lachaise a eu lieu ce même jour', https://www.appl-lachaise.net/appl/article.php3?id_article=6036 (accessed 4 October 2018). For details contradicting this claim, see 'Timeline', p. 176.

CHAPTER 1. The Ladies' Land League, Political and Literary Networks, and Narratives of the Irish Literary Revival

1 Gregory Castle, 'Irish Revivalism: critical trends and new directions', *Literature Compass*, vol. 8, no. 5, 2011, p. 291. See also Clare Hutton, 'Joyce, the Library Episode, and the Institutions of Revivalism', in Andrew Gibson, Len Platt and Sebastian D.G. Knowles (eds), *Joyce, Ireland, Britain* (Gainesville, FL: University Press of Florida, 2006), pp. 122–39; Margaret Kelleher, guest ed., *Irish University Review*, vol. 33, no. 1, spring/summer 2003 (Special Issue: 'New Perspectives on the Irish Literary Revival'); Betsey Taylor FitzSimon and James H. Murphy (eds), *The Irish Revival Reappraised* (Dublin: Four Courts Press, 2004).

2 See, for example, Catherine Morris, 'Becoming Irish? Alice Milligan and the Revival', *Irish University Review*, vol. 33, no. 1 (Special Issue: 'New Perspectives on the Irish Literary Revival'), spring/summer 2003, p. 79.

3 'Anna Parnell was herself an archetypal New Woman figure', Tina O'Toole, *The Irish New Woman* (New York: Palgrave Macmillan, 2013), p. 69.

4 There has been considerable attention paid to the figure of the New Woman broadly and the Irish New Woman more specifically in literary and cultural scholarship over the last two decades. See Ledger, Heilmann, Ardis, for example, and for readings of the New Woman in Irish contexts, see O'Toole, Edwards, Harvey.

5   As Michael de Nie has pointed out, 'The slighting of the Ladies' League and its memory began almost immediately after the male leaders returned to power', *The Eternal Paddy: Irish identity and the British press, 1798–1882* (Madison, WI: University of Wisconsin Press, 2004), p. 242. The neglect of the Ladies' Land League has been discussed and addressed across a range of texts now. See, for example, C.L. Innes, *Woman and Nation in Irish Society, 1880–1935* (Athens, GA: University of Georgia Press, 1993); Jane McL. Côté, *Fanny and Anna Parnell: Ireland's patriot sisters* (New York: St Martin's Press, 1991); and Beverley E. Schneller, *Anna Parnell's Political Journalism* (Bethesda, MD: Academica Press, 2005).

6   Adrian N. Mulligan draws on his readings of Ward and Luddy for this observation, '"By a Thousand Ingenious Feminine Devices": the Ladies' Land League and the development of Irish nationalism', *Historical Geography*, vol. 37, 2009, p. 163. He suggests there are limitations to this approach, however, and his own 'feminist historical geographical perspective' (p. 163) offers another valuable reading of the organisation. See also Heather Laird's reappraisal of the Ladies' Land League in her 'Decentring the Irish Land War: women, politics and the private sphere', in Fergus Campbell and Tony Varley (eds), *Land Questions in Modern Ireland* (Manchester: Manchester University Press, 2013); Margaret Ward, 'Anna Parnell: challenges to male authority and the telling of national myth', in Pauric Travers and Donal McCarthy (eds), *Parnell Reconsidered* (Dublin: UCD Press, 2013); and Tina O'Toole, *The Irish New Woman* (New York: Palgrave Macmillan, 2013).

7   O'Toole, *The Irish New Woman*, p. 68.

8   Margaret Ward, 'Gendering the Union: imperial feminism and the Ladies' Land League', *Women's History Review*, vol. 10, no. 1, 2001, p. 83.

9   McL Côté, *Fanny and Anna Parnell*, p. 291, fn. 9.

10 Margaret Ward, *Unmanageable Revolutionaries: women and nationalism* (London: Pluto Press, 1995), p. 15.

11 See 'The Ladies' Land League', *Reynolds's Newspaper* (London), 27 February 1881, p. 2. This paper, issued on a Sunday, records that the first meeting took place on the previous Monday (in other words, on 21 February). Charlotte McCarthy, daughter of Justin McCarthy MP, was elected treasurer.

12 Helen Taylor's archive contains correspondence from both Anna Parnell and Nannie Lynch, although the latter is only a brief note. See Mill-Taylor Collection, 18, Special Collections, London School of Economics. For further details on A.M. Sullivan (1830–84) and his American wife Frances Sullivan, see Ríona Nic Congáil, 'Young Ireland and the Nation: nationalist children's culture in the late nineteenth century', *Éire-Ireland*, vol. 46, nos 3 & 4, fomhar/geimhreadh (fall/winter) 2011, pp. 37–62.

13 Gavan Duffy was the first editor; A.M. Sullivan became editor and sole proprietor in 1858. John Dillon was also involved and John Mitchel contributed to it for a while, before finding it not radical enough and founding the *United Irishman*. For further details see Ann Andrews, *Newspapers and Newsmakers: the Dublin nationalist press in the mid-nineteenth century* (Liverpool: Liverpool University Press, 2014).

14 In addition, the piece included important information on the nature of the Coercion Act, in particular its recourse to detention without defence or trial. Anon., *Reynolds's Newspaper*, 27 February 1881, p. 2.

15 Tynan, *Twenty-five Years*, p. 75.

16 Ward, 'Gendering the Union', p. 80.

17 'For George Eliot, sympathy lies near the heart of moral life', Elizabeth Ermarth, 'George Eliot's Conception of Sympathy', in Harold Bloom (ed.), *Silas Marner* (New York: Chelsea House, 2003), p. 27. Robinson's associations with the word are explored in more detail in Chapter 4.

18　The story was covered in dramatic style in numerous papers, once again placing one of the Lynch sisters at the heart of the action: 'The Land League paper, *United Ireland*, was seized at six o'clock this evening. Twenty detectives surrounded while Superintendent Mallon and two inspectors entered. They seized every copy of the paper they found on the premises, but they did not seize the plant ... The entire male staff of the paper, with the exception of the foreman printer and the manager, who escaped to England, are now in custody. The papers were taken out by the back way, and carted away to the Castle' ... Just as the papers had been removed, Mrs. Moloney [*sic*], Treasurer of the Ladies' Land League; Miss Lynch, and two other members of that Association entered. Mrs. Moloney demanded to see the warrant under which the seizure was made. She was informed that there was no warrant, but that the seizure was made by direction of the Chief Commissioners of Police ... Mrs. Moloney became excited, said that the seizure was simple robbery; and that the Government, though speaking against robbery, were committing robbery themselves ... A number of the Ladies' Land League then came into the office, and snatched up whatever stray copies of the paper they could lay hands upon.' Anon. (From Our Correspondent, Dublin), 'The State of Ireland: seizure of a Land League paper', *Standard*, 16 December 1881, p. 3.

19　Kenneth C. Wenzer (ed.), *Henry George, the Transatlantic Irish and Their Times* (Bingley: Emerald Group Publishing, 2009), p. 52. Rose Kavanagh, 1860–91 (Miss Cavanaugh) contributed poetry and short stories to a range of nationalist weeklies and edited the *Irish Fireside*. 'When the Ladies' Land League set about finding women substitutes for imprisoned journalists, she offered her services, and Dublin Castle did her the honour of appointing a special detective to watch her movements', M.J. MacM., 'Rose Kavanagh', *Irish Press*, 23 June 1944, p. 2.

20　William O'Brien, *Recollections* (London: Macmillan, 1905), p. 382.

21　Ward, 'Gendering the Union', p. 80.

22　See Appendix 2 in McL. Côté, *Fanny and Anna Parnell*, pp. 262–3.

23　Anna Parnell, *The Tale of a Great Sham*, ed. Dana Hearne (Dublin: Arlen House, 1986), pp. 123–4.

24　Myles Dungan, *Mr Parnell's Rottweiler: censorship and the United Ireland newspaper, 1881–1891* (Dublin: Irish Academic Press, 2014), pp. 88–9.

25　Lynch, 'A Girl Revolutionist', *Girl's Realm*, vol. 1, no. 4, February 1899, pp. 383–8. Established in 1898, the *Girl's Realm* was an English magazine for girls which was not only 'keenly interested in developing a readership that was both contemporary and modern' but also 'used current events to create an ethos of bravery and heroism for its girl readers', Kristine Moruzi, *Constructing Girlhood through the Periodical Press, 1850–1915* (London: Ashgate, 2012), p. 163. It was edited by Alice Corkran, one of Lynch's London literary friends, who will be discussed in Chapter 3.

26　There has been much debate around definitions of the Literary Revival, especially in recent scholarship in the field. Foster's distinctions between an 'Irish Literary Renaissance' and the 'Irish Literary Revival', as a starting point, are helpful here: 'By the former (which more accurately might be termed a 'naissance') I would mean the tremendous release of literary energy in Ireland around the turn of the century, whatever its direction and ideology; to this Renaissance Moore and Joyce contributed hugely. By the Irish Literary Revival I would mean the work of those who sought to employ literature in a resuscitation of elder Irish values and culture that they hoped would transform the reality of the Ireland they inhabited', *Fictions of the Irish Literary Revival: a changeling art* (Syracuse, NY: Syracuse University Press, 1987), p. xvi.

27　Marie-Louise Legg, *Newspapers, Nationalism and the Irish Provincial Press, 1850–1892* (Dublin: Four Courts Press, 1999), pp. 119–21.

28 John Pope-Hennessy, 'What Do the Irish Read?', *Nineteenth Century*, vol. 15, June 1884, p. 932. See Clare Hutton, '"The Promise of Literature in the Coming Days": the best hundred Irish books controversy of 1886', *Victorian Literature and Culture*, vol. 39, no. 2, September 2011, pp. 581–92.

29 Yug Mohit Chaudhury, *W.B. Yeats, the Irish Literary Revival and the Politics of Print* (Cork: Cork University Press, 2002), p. 95.

30 Stephanie Rains, 'Thrilling Tales and Shocking Stories: story papers in Ireland', *Irish Media History* blog, 22 October 2015, https://irishmediahistory.com/category/story-papers (accessed 4 October 2018).

31 See Laurel Brake and Marysa Demoor (eds), *Dictionary of Nineteenth-century Journalism in Great Britain and Ireland* (Gent: Academia Press, 2009), p. 569. Published on Lower Abbey Street, the paper was composed mostly of fiction, with additional features on Irish history, language and music. See also Marie-Louise Legge, *Newspapers and Nationalism: the Irish provincial press, 1850–1892* (Dublin: Four Courts Press, 1999), p. 120. Richard Pigott, its publisher from 1866–79, was later proven the author of forged letters, published in *The Times*, falsely accusing Parnell of involvement in the Phoenix Park murders.

32 This paper began as a Belfast publication, the *Ulsterman*, interested in particular in promoting Catholic rights. For a brief history see Brake and Demoor, *Dictionary of Nineteenth-century Journalism*, p. 645.

33 'New and Improved Series. Important Announcement', *Irishman*, 24 June 1882, p. 1.

34 Ibid.

35 Rains, 'Thrilling Tales and Shocking Stories'.

36 'The New Shamrock', *Shamrock*, 24 June 1882, p. 8. For further discussion of these discrepancies in the Irish story papers see Stephanie Rains, '"Nauseous Tides of Seductive Debauchery": Irish story papers and the anti-vice campaigns of the early twentieth century', *Irish University Review*, vol. 45, 2015, pp. 263–80.

37 Katharine Tynan, *Memories* (London: Everleigh, Nash & Grayson, 1924), p. 163.

38 20 December 1884. Other contributors to this collaborative effort included: T.M. Healy MP, Justin Huntley McCarthy MP, Edmund Leamy MP, William Redmond MP, John Augustus O'Shea and J.J. O'Shea. The individual pieces were not signed, making direct attribution impossible at this point.

39 Anon., 'The Magazines', *Freeman's Journal*, 8 November 1884. Her contribution to this magazine, one of several Catholic periodicals published at that time, is also noted in the *Irish Monthly*, which describes the paper as aiming at 'a large popular circulation' with a 'very full bill of fare suited to a great variety of palates'. 'We have noticed no more original papers in any of its numbers than the one to which the place of honour is assigned in November', 'Our Contemporaries', *Irish Monthly*, vol. 13, no. 139, January 1885, p. 53, http://www.jstor.org/stable/20497223 (accessed 4 October 2018).

40 From 1892, she was a more regular contributor of travel pieces, and some of her best work appeared on its pages. For a fuller discussion of Lynch's contributions to the *Freeman's Journal*, see Binckes and Laing, '"Rival Attractions of the Season": Land War fiction, Christmas annuals, and the early writing of Hannah Lynch', in Heidi Hansson and James Murphy (eds), *Fictions of the Irish Land War* (Bern: Peter Lang, 2014), pp. 57–80. And for the most detailed scholarship on this journal, see Felix Larkin's '"A Great Daily Organ": the *Freeman's Journal*, 1763–1924', *History Ireland*, vol. 14, no. 3, 2006, pp. 44–9; '"The Old Woman of Prince's Street": *Ulysses* and *The Freeman's Journal*', *Dublin James Joyce Journal*, vol. 4, 2011, pp. 14–30; and 'Keeping an Eye on Youghal: the *Freeman's Journal* and the Plan of Campaign in east Cork, 1886–92', *Irish Communications Review*, vol. 13, 2012, pp. 19–30. For discussion of the *Weekly Freeman*, see Riona Nic Congáil, '"Fiction, Amusement, Instruction": the

Irish Fireside Club and the educational ideology of the Gaelic League', *Eire-Ireland*, vol. 44, nos 1–2, spring/summer 2009, pp. 91–117.

41 Hannah Lynch, letter to Father Thomas Dawson, 24 March 1888, Father Thomas Dawson Correspondence, Brotherton Library.

42 The Freeman's Journal Ltd published the *Dublin Evening Telegraph*, Mark O'Brien, *The Fourth Estate: journalism in twentieth-century Ireland* (Manchester: Manchester University Press, 2017), p. 11. In need of literary contacts in London, especially after potentially damaging her London networks following her spoof on Tynan's literary salon (see below), Lynch would have been especially affected by the loss of Dwyer Gray's support, adding significantly to the difficulties she articulates at this juncture.

43 Felix M. Larkin, '"Green Shoots" of the New Journalism in the *Freeman's Journal*, 1877–1890', in Karen Steele and Michael de Nie (eds), *Ireland and the New Journalism* (New York: Palgrave Macmillan, 2014), p. 44.

44 Nic Congáil, '"Fiction, Amusement, Instruction"', p. 95. The 'culturally nationalist' Irish Fireside Club became 'the largest children's association in Ireland in the late 1880s', ibid., p. 91. See also Nic Congáil's 'Culture Ireland and the Nation: nationalist children's culture in the late nineteenth century'.

45 Roy Foster, *Words Alone: Yeats and his inheritances* (Oxford: Oxford University Press, 2011), p. 130.

46 In his obituary for Lynch, Gibbs lists this magazine among the several to which she contributed. Research on this magazine so far has not revealed any publications attributed to Lynch, but it is likely she contributed anonymously or under a pseudonym, and missing issues might yield further evidence. For example, an unsigned piece, 'Why We Wouldn't Be Men' by 'A Wild Irish Girl', 2 June 1888, p. 136 is tantalisingly suggestive of Lynch's authorship. Contributions came from a diverse field – Rosa Mulholland, Speranza, Ouida, Miss Braddon, Wilkie Collins and Jules Verne, to name a few. The *Irish Fireside*, the *Weekly Freeman* and the *Freeman's Journal* remain rich resources for further research on hitherto neglected or forgotten writers and developments in magazine culture of the period.

47 Nic Congáil, '"Fiction, Amusement, Instruction"', p. 103.

48 James H. Murphy, 'Publishing for Catholic Ireland', in *The Oxford History of the Irish Book, Vol. 5: The Irish Book in English* (Oxford: Oxford University Press, 2011), p. 253.

49 Tynan, whose poetry had been noted in the *Irish Monthly* as early as March 1883, established herself in the magazine from October 1885, a couple of years after Lynch, and became a regular contributor of poetry first, and later prose. See Declan O'Keeffe's discussion of the women writers who were cultivated by and published in Matthew Russell SJ's magazine: '"The Young Writer's Saint": women writers and the *Irish Monthly*, 1873–97', in Rebecca Anne Barr, Sarah-Anne Buckley and Laura Kelly (eds), *Engendering Ireland: new reflections on modern history and literature* (Newcastle upon Tyne: Cambridge Scholars, 2015), pp. 156–76.

50 Murphy, 'Publishing for Catholic Ireland', p. 253. See also, on the *Irish Monthly*, Declan O'Keeffe, 'A Man for Others and a Beacon in the Twilight: Matthew Russell SJ and the *Irish Monthly*', *Studies: an Irish quarterly review*, vol. 99, no. 394, summer 2010, pp. 169–79, and 'The Canon of Literature and the Obstinate Quill: Matthew Russell, SJ and the *Irish Monthly*', in Gabriel Doherty (ed.), *Revisiting Canon Sheehan of Doneraile, 1852–1913* (Carrigboy, SMENOS Publications, 2014), pp. 44–68.

51 Lynch's article on Tenos was also published in *Donahoe's Magazine*, vol. 15, April 1886, pp. 316–19.

52 Hannah Lynch, letter to Father Thomas Dawson, 11 November 1889, Father Thomas Dawson Correspondence, Brotherton Library.

53 Hannah Lynch, 'November in a Greek Island', *Irish Monthly*, vol. 14, July 1886, p. 381. There is, however, a fulsome tribute to Lynch following her death by Matthew Russell in the *Irish*

Monthly, noting her genius and remembering that 'Hers was another of the many prentice hands that first tried their skill in the pages of this magazine' and that 'It was in sympathy with the bent of her mind that she lived chiefly on the continent', 'M.R.' [Matthew Russell], 'William Patrick Coyne, MA, LLD, 1866–1904: In Memoriam', *Irish Monthly*, vol. 32, March 1904, p. 122.

54 Katharine Tynan also ended up being excluded from the *Irish Monthly*, not for religious differences but in relation to her support for Parnell. See Standlee, 'A World of Difference', pp. 72–3.

55 Her earliest novel, *The Way of a Maid*, was published in 1895. Tynan's work has become the focus of recent scholarship on late nineteenth-century Irish women's writing. See, for example, Whitney Standlee, 'Katharine Tynan's Novels and the Politics of Ireland's "Long Gestation", 1890–1916', in *The Politics of Irish Writing*, pp. 109–17. See also Bonnie Roos, 'Unlikely Heroes: Katharine Tynan's *Story of the Bawn*, the Irish Famine, and the sentimental tradition', *Irish University Review*, vol. 43, no. 2, pp. 327–43.

56 See Standlee, 'A World of Difference', p. 72.

57 Ibid., p. 73. Lynch's first novel, as noted, *Through Troubled Waters*, was published by Ward, Lock & Co. and Tynan's first volume of poetry, *Louise de la Vallière, and Other Poems*, was published by Kegan Paul.

58 See Tynan's *Twenty-five Years*, pp. 76–7. In her memoir Tynan suggests that it was one of Lynch's sisters who was her particular friend, rather than Lynch herself. Her letters supply further information – that it was Teresa Cantwell 'who is a great friend of mine' (letter to Mrs Pritchard, 23 April 1885, Letters, MS 39, 118, National Library of Ireland, and reprinted in Atkinson, p. 46) and that she paid regular visits to their home. On 7 April 1887, for example, she writes to Matthew Russell that she will be staying 'a couple of days with Mrs Cantwell at Kingstown next week' (Irish Jesuit Archive, J27/73).

59 Ibid., p. 76.

60 Roy Foster discusses the conflation of the literary with the political from the mid-1880s, where 'The "literary" economy was a vital agency of modernization in nineteenth- and early-twentieth century Ireland', *Vivid Faces: the revolutionary generation in Ireland, 1890–1923* (London: Penguin, 2014), p. 149.

61 See Kathryn Laing, 'Hannah Lynch and the Narratives of the Irish Literary Revival', *New Hibernia*, vol. 20, no. 1, spring 2016, pp. 42–57. The Southwark Irish Literary Society had its origins in the Southwark Junior Irish Literary Club, which was 'Founded in the autumn of 1881 by members of the Ladies' and Men's Land Leagues based in South London'. Frances Sullivan, wife of A.M. Sullivan, was president of the children's club until 1885; see Nic Congáil, 'Young Ireland and the Nation', p. 53. Frances Sullivan was also the president of the London branch of the Ladies' Land League.

62 Francis Fahy, 'The Southwark Junior Irish literary Club, To the Editor of the *Nation*', *Nation*, 12 January 1889, p. 7.

63 Clare Hutton, 'Joyce and the Institutions of Revivalism', *Irish University Review*, vol. 33, no. 1 (Special Issue: 'New Perspectives on the Irish Literary Revival'), spring/summer 2003, p. 119.

64 For further information on the salon culture that developed around Tynan, see her memoir *Twenty-five Years*; Norah Tynan O'Mahony, 'Katharine Tynan's Childhood', *Irish Monthly*, vol. 59, June 1931, pp. 358–63; James J. McFadden and Daniel Kiefer, '"Abstracted in His Dreams": Katharine Tynan's "W.B. Yeats"', *Modern Philology*, vol. 88, no. 3, February 1991, pp. 261–77, http://www.jstor.org/stable/438108 (accessed 5 October 2018). See also Standlee and Annat.

65 Standlee, 'A World of Difference', p. 72.

66 By the mid-1890s, Yeats was criticising Tynan's work for its lack of 'Gallic passion'. More broadly, Tynan's work after 1893 was seen 'to be too far removed from the literary renaissance's

communal ethos to hold merit: that it simply was not Irish enough', Standlee, 'A World of Difference', p. 76.

67 Dominic Daly, *The Young Douglas Hyde: the dawn of the Irish revolution and renaissance, 1874–1893* (Dublin: Irish University Press, 1994), p. 92. For connections with Hyde and her membership of the Irish Literary Society in London, which he, as well as Yeats, attended see David Pearce, *Yeats's Worlds: Ireland, England and the poetic imagination* (New Haven, CT: Yale University Press, 1995), p. 125.

68 The *Dublin Evening Telegraph* was the *Freeman*'s evening newspaper.

69 Anon. [Hannah Lynch], 'A Dublin Literary Coterie Sketched by a Non-pretentious Observer', *Dublin Evening Telegraph*, 14 January 1888, p.2.

70 Ibid.

71 J.W. Foster, *Fictions of the Irish Literary Revival*, p. xii.

72 Tynan's sister Nora provides some insight into the possible source of Lynch's terminology in her description of the salon at Whitehall, which was 'enjoyed by everyone who was *anyone* [italics in original] in the artistic and literary or political life of the Dublin of that day. And we others, older or younger, who quite cheerfully dubbed ourselves "the Goths and Huns" of the assembly, also played tennis, or croquet, or danced ...', O'Mahony, 'Katharine Tynan's Childhood', p. 361.

73 Lynch, 'A Dublin Literary Coterie Sketched by a Non-pretentious Observer'. To situate Lynch and her contemporaries in the context of debates about high and low art during this period, see Linda H. Peterson, *Becoming a Woman of Letters: myths of authorship and facts of the Victorian market* (Princeton, NJ: Princeton University Press, 2009).

74 Roy Foster, *W.B. Yeats: a life. Volume One: The Apprentice Mage, 1865–1914* (Oxford: Oxford University Press, 1997), p. 73.

75 See Murphy, who discusses satire and other main features of writing of the final decade of the nineteenth century: *Irish Novelists and the Victorian Age*, pp. 229–30.

76 Lynch, 'A Dublin Literary Coterie Sketched by a Non-pretentious Observer'.

77 Ibid.

78 Low, 'A Woman's Causerie', pp. 319–20.

79 Roy Foster, *W.B. Yeats*, p. 73. Æ, or George Russell (1867–1935), writer, artist, journalist, theosophist, nationalist and participant in Dublin coterie life during the *fin de siècle*. For further information on Russell's response to Lynch's satire, see Peter Kuch, *Yeats and Æ: the antagonism that unites dear friends* (Gerrards Cross: Colin Smythe, 1986), pp. 28–9; Monk Gibbon, *The Masterpiece and the Man* (London: Hart-Davis, 1959), p. 58; Henry Summerfield, *That Myriad-minded Man: a biography of George William Russell 'Æ', 1867–1935* (Gerrards Cross: Colin Smythe, 1975), p. 28.

80 Despite Lynch's critique of Yeats and his coterie, her announcement to Dawson that she intended to go and hear Yeats give a lecture 'at the Irish Society' in January 1894 suggests either a change of heart or at least an interest in a rising literary figure. Lynch to Dawson, 4 January 1894, Father Thomas Dawson Correspondence, Brotherton Library.

81 Tynan, letter to Matthew Russell, 16 October 1888, MSS J 27/73 (2), Irish Jesuit Archive, Dublin.

82 Tynan, letter to Matthew Russell, 3 November 1888, MSS J 27/73 (2), Irish Jesuit Archive, Dublin. This positive message was somewhat undercut by the fact that Tynan congratulated herself on appearing so cordial in that first encounter: 'My resentments have a way of oozing out of my finger-tips.'

83 The *Cabinet of Irish Literature: selections from the works of the chief poets, orators and prose writers of Ireland*, 4 vols. New edition by Katharine Tynan Hinkson (London: Gresham Publishing, 1902–3). Tynan's curt reply to Low's accusation titled simply 'A Correction' was

published on the letters page of the *Speaker* on 29 December. Low was mistaken. Lynch *had* appeared in the volume, the proper title of which was *The Cabinet of Irish Literature: Volume IV*. Furthermore, this could not be a simple error, as Low had already made a similar claim in the Dublin *Freeman's Journal*, and had already been corrected. Ibid., p. 377.

84 Jane Barlow, letter to Katharine Tynan, 9 April 1894, Box 1/19, Papers of Katharine Tynan and Pamela Hinkson, GB 133 KTH, Archive Collection, Library of the University of Manchester. Mrs E.M. Lynch, Irish writer, is referenced in *Ricorso* as Edward Melville Lynch, but it appears that this was her husband. E.M. Lynch, 1846?–1917 is listed as the author of *A Few Words on Women's Suffrage* (1872) in Elizabeth Crawford, *The Women's Suffrage Movement in Britain and Ireland: a regional survey* (Abingdon: Routledge, 2006), p. 204.

85 Tynan, letter to Matthew Russell, 6 February 1904, MSS J27/73 (2), Irish Jesuit Archive, Dublin. This letter also mentions that Low had written to Tynan, who was advised not to reply by the Meynells. When Tynan wrote to Dawson in 1906, infuriated by Low's repeated accusations, Dawson refused to take sides, instead gently reminding her that she was speaking ill of the dead. 'What a pity Miss Low repeats that wrong statement! But one can see she means no unfairness to you, but only sympathy for poor Hannah. I fancy she – for that reason – purposely gives a wrong title to the book', letter from Dawson to Tynan, Holyhead, 21 January 1907, Papers of Katharine Tynan and Pamela Hinkson, GB 133 KTH, Box 1/201/5a, John Rylands University Library, University of Manchester.

86 Tynan, letter to Matthew Russell, MSS letter [date illegible], Russell Papers, MSS J27/73 (1–2), Irish Jesuit Archive, Dublin.

87 Hannah Lynch [pseud. E. Enticknappe], 'My Friend Arcanieva', *Macmillan's Magazine*, vol. 73, December 1895, pp. 139–48.

88 Hester Sigerson Piatt, 'John O'Leary as a Guide of Youth', *Ireland*, vol. 7, 19 February 1916, p. 10.

89 D.J. O'Donohue, 'John O'Leary and Friends', *Sunday Independent*, 13 July 1913, p. 5.

90 Cited in ibid.

91 For a more detailed discussion of this story, see Laing, 'Hannah Lynch and Narratives of the Irish Literary Revival', *New Hibernia*, vol. 20, no. 1, spring 2016. See also Katharine Tynan's *Twenty-five Years* for her account of Lippmann frequenting literary circles and socialising with Yeats, among others (p. 245). The satirical rendering of homosocial literary coteries, male intellectual pretensions and the sacrifice of women was not restricted to Dublin society. Lynch published two more stories with Paris settings with similar critiques. See 'A Page of Philosophy' and 'Dr Vermont's Fantasy' in *Dr Vermont's Fantasy and Other Stories* (1896). These will be discussed in more detail in Chapter 4.

92 Lynch, 'My Friend Arcanieva', p. 140.

93 Ibid., p. 139.

94 Ibid., pp. 141–2.

95 Sigerson Piatt, 'John O'Leary as a Guide of Youth', p. 10.

96 In *Irish Nationalist Women, 1900–1918* (Cambridge: Cambridge University Press, 2013), Senia Pašeta offers a different perspective, suggesting that there were 'many women who flourished in the new literary and intellectual environment which grew out of the growing interest in Irish history, language and culture and which in turn encouraged the growth of newspapers, journals, debating circles and discussion groups' (p. 27). Norman Vance has also argued against a narrative of the monolithic masculinity of the Irish Revival by illustrating Katharine Tynan's involvement, specifically her inclusion in *Poems and Ballads of Young Ireland* (1888), as 'the first flowering of the Literary Revival', *Irish Literature since 1800*, p. 116.

97 Foster, *Fictions of the Irish Literary Revival*, p. xiv.

98 Morris, 'Becoming Irish?', p. 79.

99 Lynch writes a version of this theme in her short story 'Brases', in *Dr Vermont's Fantasy and Other Stories* (London: Dent, 1896).

100 Lynch, 'The Irish Peasant: fact and fiction'. See James Cahalan's discussion of Lawless' exclusion from the revivalist canon, *Double Visions: women and men in modern and contemporary Irish fiction* (Syracuse, NY: Syracuse University Press, 1999).

CHAPTER 2. A 'Vortex of the Genres': Literary connections and intersections

1 Murphy, *Irish Novelists and the Victorian Age*, p. 167.

2 Heidi Hansson and James H. Murphy note this, highlighting that: 'Although dozens of novels concerning the land war were written from the 1880s onwards, no-one at the time considered them as a group.' See *Fictions of the Irish Land War*, p. 8. There are connections between Lynch's texts and those of other better-known Land War novels by women, such as Rosa Mulholland, *Marcella Grace: an Irish novel* (London: Kegan Paul, Trench, 1886), or Emily Lawless, *Hurrish: a study* (Edinburgh: William Blackwood, 1886). See 'The Irish Land War and its Fictions', in Hansson and Murphy (2014), the chapter on Land War fiction in Murphy's *Irish Novelists and the Victorian Age*, and Margaret Kelleher's '"Factual Fictions": representations of the land agitation in nineteenth-century women's fiction', in Heidi Hansson (ed.), *New Contexts: re-framing nineteenth-century Irish women's prose* (Cork: Cork University Press, 2008), pp. 78–91.

3 Katharine Tynan, who might seem an obvious writer to include, did not start publishing fiction until the 1890s.

4 See Alison Harvey, 'Irish Aestheticism in Fin-de-Siècle Women's Writing: art, realism, and the nation', *Modernism/Modernity*, vol. 21, no. 3, September 2014, p. 807, and Simon Joyce, 'Impressionism, Naturalism, Symbolism: trajectories of Anglo-Irish fiction at the fin de siècle', *Modernism/Modernity*, vol. 21, no. 3, September 2014, pp. 787–803.

5 Kelleher, '"Factual Fictions"', p. 79.

6 By basing the heroine of the novel, Camilla Knoys, on Parnell, Lynch draws 'a New Woman type, based on the key characteristics of her friend and compatriot', O'Toole, *The Irish New Woman*, pp. 70–1.

7 Hannah Lynch, 'Marjory Maurice', *Shamrock*, 31 January 1885, p. 277.

8 Hannah Lynch, *The Prince of the Glades: a novel* (London: Methuen & Co., 1891), vol. 1, p. 223.

9 Ibid., p. 224.

10 O'Toole, *The Irish New Woman*, p. 71.

11 The novella highlights its interrogation of notions of masculinity and femininity from the outset. Sheridan begins the narrative with the assertion that 'It is not customary for a man to deliberately set himself the task of writing down in anecdotal form the details of the first serious business in which he was engaged … ', Lynch, 'Defeated', p. 1.

12 Ibid., pp. 16–17.

13 Ibid., p. 148.

14 Ibid., p. 146.

15 Joseph Valente, *The Myth of Manliness in Irish National Culture, 1880–1922* (Urbana, IL: University of Illinois Press, 2011), pp. 28–30.

16 See Valente's analysis of Parnell and the Ladies' Land League, pp. 47–51.

17 A similar disillusion is voiced in 'A Girl Revolutionist', where Moya, trying to rouse a revolutionary crowd on her uncle's estate, finds 'the eyes of the men of Ireland were lowered. Their gallant intention to defend her to the death had changed to a meaner desire. They shuffled their feet and twisted their caubeens in a disillusioned way. The Joan of Arc a moment ago now was nothing more than "a quare young woman" whom kindly relatives allowed at large. Upon a single impulse, in silence, the men of Ireland sloped', Lynch, ibid., *Girls' Realm*, February 1899, p. 386.

18 Anon., 'Notes on Novels', *The Prince of the Glades* by Hannah Lynch, *Dublin Review*, vol. 25, no. 2, April 1891, p. 436.

19 Anon., *Irish World*, 7 October 1882, p. 5. We are grateful to Margaret Ward for alerting us to this article.

20 Gibbs, 'Tribute to Hannah Lynch', p. 5. Family records, and the 1881 census returns, show a 'Hanna' [*sic*] Lynch, a twenty-two-year-old 'student of literature' born in Dublin around 1859, living in the Clarendon Boarding House in Ventnor.

21 Hannah Lynch, 'To the Editor of *United Ireland*', *United Ireland*, 9 May 1885, p. 1.

22 Lynch, 'Defeated', p. 107.

23 'The "girl's realm" of the title encompasses the feminine ideal but also includes an equally important heroic ideal, signalling a shift in thinking about girls and their "realm" as they moved into areas that were traditionally considered male', Kristine Moruzi, *Constructing Girlhood*, p. 163. Scholarship in the field of 'girls' culture', the New Girl and periodicals has expanded rapidly. For further discussion of *Girl's Realm* and also a specific focus on Irish New Girl fiction, see essays by Beth Rodgers and Susan Cahill listed in the bibliography.

24 Lynch, 'A Girl Revolutionist', p. 387.

25 Ibid., p. 388.

26 Hannah Lynch, 'Marjory Maurice', *Shamrock*, 27 December 1884, p. 196. 'Roiville' is an obvious reference to Kingstown, which later became Dún Laoghaire, where Lynch's family had a house.

27 Ibid., 3 January 1885, p. 214.

28 Ibid., p. 197.

29 Ibid.

30 Ibid., 10 January 1885, p. 231.

31 Ibid. Dalrymple is also horrified to discover Morna's family is connected with trade.

32 See Diane Urquhart, '"A Crust to Share With You": the rhetoric of the Ladies' Land League's British campaign, 1881–2', in Tina O'Toole, Gillian McIntosh and Muireann Ó Cinnéide (eds), *Women Writing War: Ireland, 1880–1922* (Dublin: University College Dublin Press, 2016), p. 16.

33 Lynch, 'Marjory Maurice', ibid., 3 January 1885, p. 214.

34 'In Bad Company', *Funny Folks: The Comic Companion to the Newspaper*, 18 June 1881, p. 185.

35 Urquhart, 'A "Crust to Share with You"', p. 16. These lampoons are simultaneously invoked and challenged from the very beginning of Lynch's novella, starting with an epigraph from Robert Brough's 'Godiva': 'Thou tiny pearl of demagogues,/Thou blue-eyed rebel – blushing traitor,/Thou sans-culotte with dimpled toes/Whose red-cap is an opening rose,/Thou trembling agitator'. 'Marjory Maurice', *Shamrock*, 27 December 1884, p. 196.

36 Intriguingly, an alternative figure of rebellion and independence, Colonel Arabi Pasha, and the Anglo-Egyptian War are introduced as inspiration and representation of the Ladies' Land League: 'Did you hear we're going to put up Arabi's flag as soon as the procession begins?'. Ibid., 28 February 1885, p. 347. Lady Augusta Gregory published 'Arabi and his household' in *The Times*, 23 October 1882. See Muireann O'Cinneide, 'Anne Blunt, "Arabi Pasha" and the Irish Land Wars, 1880–8', in O'Toole et al. (eds), *Women Writing War*, pp. 25–38.

37 Lynch, 'Marjory Maurice', *Shamrock*, 10 January 1885, p. 229.

38 Ibid., 24 January 1885, p. 261.

39 Published on 12 February 1881, the cartoon is simply titled 'The Ladies' Land League' but carries a much longer subtitle: 'Alarm has been created by the formation of a Ladies' Branch of the Land League. Thus far, however, nothing more serious has resulted than in the adoption of a charming land league costume for the members, the effect of which was tried at an "At Home" given by Mrs Rory of "The Hills", Tipperary', *Funny Folks*, p. 44.

40 Lynch, 'Marjory Maurice', *Shamrock*, 7 February 1885, p. 293.

41 'At the time when Frank Byrne, who had so much to do with the Phoenix-park murders, was Secretary of the London Land League – his wife being Secretary of the Ladies' branch – a Mr. Thomas Quinn was Treasurer. The Byrnes lived at Avondale Place, Peckham, with Tynan … Hannah Lynch, Dr Hamilton Williams, and the rest of the murder-ring who aided Carey … No-one can deny that those who planned and carried out the Phoenix-park assassinations – Carey, Tynan, and Hannah Lynch – were in close relations and intimate friendship with the Quinns', 'A Correspondent', 'The Fenian Conspiracy', *John Bull*, 10 July 1886, p. 446. Earlier in the article, 'Hannah Lynch' is described as 'Secretary of the Dublin Ladies' Land League and Anna Parnell's *alter ego*'. We know the former role belonged to Nannie.

42 Lynch, 'Marjory Maurice', *Shamrock*, 7 February 1885, p. 293.

43 Kelleher, '"Factual Fictions"', p. 84.

44 Fannie Gallaher, *Thy Name Is Truth: a social novel* (London: J&R Maxwell Publishers, 1884), vol. i, pp. 31–2. This encounter between the fictional editor, his son and the Ladies' Land League makes a striking contrast with Anna Parnell's description of the actual encounter between Gallaher, editor of the *Freeman's Journal*, and 'Miss Lynch', discussed in the previous chapter.

45 Ibid., p. 34.

46 Ibid., p. 231. There are numerous parallels to be drawn between this and George Moore's *A Drama in Muslin*, published three years later. Aileen's desire to write a novel beginning with a description of the spectacle of the ball she attends anticipates the practices of Moore himself in preparing his own novel.

47 Gallaher's portrait of a literary-minded heroine with certain restrained feminist aspirations (a counter to the figure Lynch cut at the time?) is subsumed into popular plot conventions of the day – Aileen is discovered to be the heir of a landowner whose murder is blamed on an innocent man. There are clear resonances between this plot, Lynch's 'Defeated' and several other novels published during this period. After multiple complications are worked through and resolutions achieved, Aileen accepts her suitor, the journalist 'Boy' McDonnell, just as Minna settles down and marries Sheridan.

48 Lynch, 'Marjory Maurice', *Shamrock*, 24 January 1885, p. 261.

49 Ibid., p. 262.

50 Ibid. Hypatia of Alexandria (370?–415), mathematician, astronomer, philosopher.

51 Ibid., 28 February 1885, p. 348.

52 Ibid.

53 Ibid., 21 March 1885, p. 397.

54 Ibid., p. 398. Glasnevin cemetery, where Lynch's stepfather James Cantwell was buried.

55 For fuller discussion of both the radical and limiting features of the New Woman and New Woman fiction see, for example, Showalter, Ardis, Heilmann, Miller and Ledger listed in the bibliography.

56 Robinson's other novel, *Disenchantment* (1886), which focuses on an Irish MP at Westminster, also resonates with the aftermath of defeat and disillusionment in its title.

57 Daughters of architect and editor of the *Art Monthly* George Robinson and his wife, Frances Sparrow, whose hospitality to artists and writers at their Gower Street, Bloomsbury home led to its becoming a famous and sought-after London literary salon. Mary and Mabel were educated in Brussels before returning to London, where Mary became one of the first female students accepted at University College London and Mabel studied art at the Slade.

58 Strong hints of an early connection between Robinson and the Lynch sisters are evident, as we have seen, in the letter of support Robinson submitted to the Royal Literary Fund in 1895.

59 Vernon Lee's *roman-à-clef, Miss Brown*, presented its Mabel Robinson figure (Margery Leigh) as politically motivated – she is 'only interested in school boards and depauperisation' – although it downplayed the extent of her commitment to Irish politics. Instead, Mary Leigh

(Mary Robinson) is described, rather ambiguously, as 'Mary Leigh who was the most absent-minded of Irish enthusiasts … ', Vernon Lee, *Miss Brown* (London: William Blackwood & Sons, 1884), vol. 2, pp. 31, 142.

60 Joseph Hone, 'Supporter of the Parnell Movement', *Irish Press*, 16 September 1954, p. 6. Hone also notes a long friendship in particular with the Dillon family.

61 Marysa Demoor, 'Robinson, (Frances) Mabel (1858–1956)', *Oxford Dictionary of National Biography* (Oxford: Oxford University Press, 2004), http://ezproxy-prd.bodleian.ox.ac. uk:2167/view/article/60276 (accessed 3 December 2015). Parnell's response to her attendance at the House of Commons from 1877 was a series of articles: 'How They Do in the House of Commons: notes from the ladies' cage' was published in America in the *Celtic Monthly* (May–July 1880), http://ezproxy-prd.bodleian.ox.ac.uk:2167/view/article/60276 (accessed 3 December 2015).

62 There is little information currently available about Charlotte McCarthy, and the art connection we posit is speculative.

63 Justin McCarthy records this visit in his autobiography, *An Irishman's Story* (London: Macmillan, 1905), noting that she was a friend of his daughter and that she had never been to Ireland before, so they tried to show her 'as many as possible of Ireland's most beautiful, historic scenes' (p. 270). In addition, she had 'the happy chance of seeing Dublin under conditions which peculiarly illustrated the national life in some of its most important movements', an aspect of her 'fast becoming a convert to the principles of Irish Nationalism', pp. 271–3.

64 Demoor, 'Robinson, (Frances) Mabel (1858–1956)'.

65 Mabel Robinson to her mother, Bibliothèque Nationale de France, Fonds Anglais, 258.

66 Robinson published this text under a pseudonym. Interestingly, the Ladies' Land League is alluded to but not treated in any detail. See William Stephenson Gregg, *Irish History for English Readers: from the earliest times to 1885* (London: Vizetelly & Co., 1886).

67 This was the third of Robinson's novels to be published by Vizetelly and Co., which also published George Moore's fiction during his Zola/Naturalism phase. It was in fact Moore who 'had given a helping hand to Mabel Robinson by placing the manuscript of her first novel, *Mr Butler's Ward*, in Vizetelly's line (initiated by *A Mummer's Wife*) of naturalistic one-volume novels', Adrian Frazier, *George Moore, 1852–1933* (New York and London: Yale University Press, 2000), p. 121.

68 'Following the defeat of Gladstone's first Home Rule bill in June 1886, some of Charles Stewart Parnell's lieutenants decided to raise morale and lower rents by renewing the land war that had caused so much havoc and fear since the founding of the Irish National Land League in October 1879. Although Parnell opposed this new agitation, in October 1886 Timothy Harrington, John Dillon and William O'Brien launched the "Plan of Campaign" that called for withholding rent on estates whose owners refused to reduce them by 20–40%. Tenants who joined the Plan would hand over their rent, less the reduction, to a trustee – often the parish priest – who held it in escrow until the landlord surrendered to their demands', http://www.historyireland.com/18th-19th-century-history/three-oxford-liberals-and-the-plan-of-campaign-in-donegal-1889 (accessed 8 April 2014).

69 Robinson's *Mr Butler's Ward* does have Irish land war connections although these are not foregrounded. She also published a short story, 'The Lady Land Leaguer', in *Voluntaries for an East London Hospital* (London: David Stott, 1887), pp. 149–68. The story does give a glimpse into hardships endured by a Miss Mulligan, seamstress and Land Leaguer in Donegal, but it pays more attention to romance than politics.

70 Little critical attention has been paid to this novel, although it was quite well received in contemporary reviews. James Murphy wonders whether Robinson was not 'trying to effect some degree of imagined reconciliation and understanding between England and Ireland'

through the apparent elision of cultural and national differences in this novel (Murphy, *Irish Novelists and the Victorian Age*, pp. 189–90). Another explanation, which will be considered in Chapter 4, might lie in Robinson's shared interest in notions of 'sympathy' with her sister Mary, writer Vernon Lee and indeed Hannah Lynch, too.

71 The practice of creating thinly disguised characters of well-known political and other figures was common in Land War fiction, highlighting, according to Hansson, 'the sense that the works are intended in their immediate social and political situation rather than for posterity' (Hansson and Murphy (eds), *Fictions of the Irish Land War*, p. 108). The novel is populated by often thinly disguised and not always flattering portraits of prominent figures as well as her own friends and acquaintances (the novelist Robert Gough is clearly modelled on George Moore). One of those who attends her salon in the opening pages of the novel is the dark brooding hero Richard Talbot, a Parnellite and active member in the Plan of Campaign, who is probably modelled on Parnell and, some contemporary reviews suggest, Parnell supporters such as John Dillon, while MP William O'Brien is the likely original for the journalist Titus Orr, a reporter for the *Freeman's*.

72 Mabel Robinson, *The Plan of Campaign* (London: Methuen & Co., 1890), p. 227. The first edition was published in two volumes by Vizetelly in 1888.

73 Lauren Arrington notes that 'Most women in the Ladies' Land League were not suffragists since suffrage enjoyed a close relationship to a pro-imperialist, even racist, position; nonetheless, the women in the league set a feminist precedent', *Revolutionary Lives: Constance and Casimir Markievicz* (Princeton, NJ: Princeton University Press, 2016), p. 11.

74 Robinson, *Plan of Campaign*, p. 26.

75 Ibid., p. 176.

76 Ibid., p. 92.

77 Ibid., p. 218.

78 See Murphy and Hansson, *Fictions of the Irish Land War*.

79 Frazier, *George Moore*, p. 48.

80 George Moore's brother Maurice married Evelyn Handcock of Carantrila Park in 1891. An article in the *Irish Times*, 'Rejoicing at Carantrila Park', describes the festivities, 18 December 1891, p. 3.

81 K.S. Laing, 'On Women, on Art, on Life: George Moore (1852–1933) and Hannah Lynch (1859–1904)', in Maria Elena Jamie de Pablos and Mary Pierse (eds), *George Moore and the Quirks of Human Nature* (Oxford: Peter Lang, 2014), pp. 224–5. See this article for further details about the intersections between Moore and Lynch.

82 In its dealings with both the 'Woman question' and the 'Irish question', the novel was structurally sophisticated, where 'Comparisons of class with gender and the personal with the political are implied by the form of the narrative', Frazier, *George Moore*, p. 134. The novel has also been read as an example of the 'catholic intelligentsia novel' (Murphy, *Irish Novelists and the Victorian Age*, p. 232) and a novel of 'liberal catholic dissent', Emer Nolan, *Catholic Emancipations: Irish fiction from Thomas Moore to James Joyce* (Syracuse, NY: Syracuse University Press, 2007), p. 125.

83 Since the novel was published 'at the beginning of the lead-up to the home rule crisis, it was no wonder that the novel was read by reviewers in political terms, rather than for its social implications', Murphy, *Irish Novelists and the Victorian Age*, 2011, p. 233.

84 Murphy describes Lynch's novel as an 'early example of the interclass encounter novel', ibid., p. 232.

85 George Moore, *A Drama in Muslin* (Gerrards Cross: Colin Smythe, 1981), p. 204. Moore would have regarded Lynch as his social inferior, and Mabel Robinson depicts this snobbery in her fictionalised portrait of Moore in her novel *The Plan of Campaign*: 'he hated his country as none but the Irishmen and Germans hate their father-land? And any Irish accent

set his teeth on edge. But if he hated Ireland, he detested the middle class still more cordially' (Robinson, *The Plan of Campaign*, p. 367). Lynch's wealthy middle-class status acquired through trade, educated abroad but forced by a decline in family fortunes to the position of governess before becoming a writer, placed her in a particularly awkward but also piquant position from which to observe society.

86 Lynch, *Through Troubled Waters*, p. 95.
87 Anon., 'A Novel of the Period'.
88 Ibid.
89 Frazier, *George Moore*, p. 135.
90 Moore, *A Drama in Muslin*, p. 70. See Frazier on the model for Father Shannon and the outrage his portrait of the priest and Mass caused, *George Moore*, p. 117.
91 Lynch, *Through Troubled Waters*, p. 23.
92 Ibid., p. 23 and Moore, *A Drama in Muslin*, p. 74.
93 Moore, *A Drama in Muslin*, p. 74 and Lynch, *Through Troubled Waters*, p. 23.
94 Lynch, *Through Troubled Waters*, pp. 66–7.
95 Ibid., pp. 67–8.
96 Interestingly, Moore replicates Lynch's portrait of the condemnation of a woman from the pulpit in his 1904 novel *The Lake*.
97 Moore, *A Drama in Muslin*, p. 70 and Lynch, *Through Troubled Waters*, pp. 301–2. Although Lynch rejected the documentary school of realism in her later fiction, her first novel does share a naturalist focus on the ordinary and even sordid with Moore and Mabel Robinson, whose first novels published by Vizetelly were marketed as naturalist fiction closely associated with Emile Zola. Lynch rigorously defended her attention to the 'dark side of nature' in her retort to the editor of *United Ireland*.
98 Anon., 'A Novel of the Period'. The novel is described as belonging to the 'realistic school' of writing in a review in the *Freeman's Journal*, though not 'coarsened by Zolaism'. Anon., 'Through Troubled Waters', 3 July 1885, p. 2. Like many of her contemporaries, Lynch had engaged in debate about Zola's aesthetics. See her '"Fecondité" vs. "The Kreutzer Sonata" or "Zola vs. Tolstoi"', *Fortnightly Review*, vol. 67, January 1900, pp. 69–78. She aligned herself instead more closely with Meredith's realist fiction, which she described as 'a healthy and purely philosophic realism, which differs as widely from the realism of Fielding as it does from that of Zola', Lynch, *George Meredith*, p. 51.
99 Lynch, 'To the Editor of *United Ireland*', p. 1. William O'Brien had also been involved with the *Freeman's Journal*, where an earlier version of the novel may have been submitted, but more likely it had been destined for the *Shamrock*, which had published several earlier stories, but refused. Katharine Tynan's early fiction makes a striking contrast here since 'many of her prose works acted to justify the Irish to English readers', Standlee, 'Katharine Tynan's Novels and the Politics of Ireland's "Long Gestation"', p. 112.
100 Lynch, *Through Troubled Waters*, p. 445. James Joyce, letters to Grant Richards cited in Jeri Johnson's introduction to *Dubliners* (Oxford: Oxford University Press, 2000), pp. vii–viii.
101 'The unequivocal and fixed class distinction, which served to define both master and servant, was not applicable to the relation between employer and governess. Because of her position as a middle-class woman, who was also a domestic hireling, the Victorian governess was trapped in an intermediate and undefined position. As for class, she ranked above the servants, but she was as dependent as they were', Cecilia Wadsö Lecaros, 'The Victorian Heroine Goes A-governessing', in Brenda Ayres (ed.), *Silent Voices: forgotten novels by Victorian women writers* (Westport, CT: Praeger Publishers, 2003), pp. 27–8. See also Kathryn Hughes, *The Victorian Governess* (London: Hambledon Press, 1993).
102 Lynch, *Through Troubled Waters*, p. 24.

103 Lynch, *Autobiography of a Child* (Edinburgh and London: William Blackwood & Co., and New York: Dodd, Mead & Co., 1899), pp. 196–7.

104 Ibid., p. 197. J.W. Foster notes in his discussion of this extract that while Lynch's observations tally with other governess novels of the period, she also 'implies that a different and harsher set of circumstances obtained among Irish middle-class Catholic families, and which constituted a dark crevice of Irish life she felt constrained, as a traveller and self-taught cultural observer, to expose to the light; I know no modern dedicated study of Irish Catholic middle-class life in the Victorian and Edwardian periods': see J.W. Foster, *Irish Novels, 1890–1940: new bearings in culture and fiction* (Oxford: Oxford University Press, 2008), p. 278. Heather Ingman includes Lynch in a list of Irish writers of governess fiction, identifying an area for further research: see *Irish Women's Fiction*, p. 21.

105 Lynch, *Through Troubled Waters*, p. 45. A violent grandmother and mother feature in *Autobiography of a Child*. Mrs Harvey in *Rosni Harvey* is another terrifying mother figure who inflicts emotional and physical violence on her daughter.

106 Ibid., p. 25.

107 George Moore, *A Drama in Muslin*, p. 135. Murphy notes that popular romantic comedies of the period are 'full of characters like Mrs Barton' – what makes Moore's novel different is his parody of romantic conventions and also 'that Mrs Barton, with her ruthless ambition and unsentimental pragmatism, is at least credited with being in touch with the realities of a world where glamour and gaiety mask a struggle for survival', James H. Murphy, *Catholic Fiction and Social Reality in Ireland, 1873–1922* (Westport, CT: Greenwood, 1997), p. 26.

108 Vera Kreilkamp, *The Anglo-Irish Novel and the Big House* (Syracuse, NY: Syracuse University Press, 1998), p. 23.

109 Lynch, *Through Troubled Waters*, pp. 25–6.

110 Lynch's concern with education places her alongside several of her fellow New Woman writers, including Sarah Grand, whose conservatism to some extent she shared. Grand 'became a strenuous advocate of the proper education of women and the scandalous deprivation of it became a feminist theme in her fiction, placing her alongside Hannah Lynch in this regard': Foster, *Irish Novels*, p. 285.

111 Lynch, *Through Troubled Waters*, p. 142. Lynch uses epigraphs and dedications regularly in her fiction. This practice was especially popular with women writers as it displays 'the writer's erudition and intellectual authority and creates an authorial persona that upper- and middle-class readers may accept as culturally and therefore potentially politically aligned with themselves', Hansson and Murphy (eds), *Fictions of the Irish Land War*, p. 109. See also Susan Lanser's *The Narrative Act: point of view in prose fiction* (Princeton, NJ: Princeton University Press, 1981). Lynch was an avid admirer of George Meredith at this time and her critical study of his work, *George Meredith*, grew out of a lecture she gave on the writer in Paris.

112 Lynch, *Through Troubled Waters*, p. 57.

113 Ibid., p. 158.

114 Lynch, *George Meredith*, p. 168.

115 Ibid., p. 120.

116 Moore, *Drama in Muslin*, p. 150.

117 Lynch, *Through Troubled Waters*, pp. 452–3. Moore offers a similar celebration of the Dalkey landscape, adjacent to Killiney, in his *Parnell and His Island*: 'How cuplike is the bay! Blue mountains, blue embaying mountains, rise on every side, and amorously the sea rises up to the lip of the land' (London: Swan, Sonnenschein, Lowry & Co., 1887), p. 1.

118 Aurelia Annat notes: '... it is significant that Tynan's idealised Ireland was located in domesticated county Dublin rather than the wilderness of the West. In this she failed to conform to the imagined Ireland of the Irish Revival, despite her friends' influence',

'Imaginable Nations: constructions of history and identity and the contribution of selected Irish women writers, 1891–1945', DPhil thesis, University of Oxford, MS.D.Phil.c.23537. See also Annat, 'Class, Nation, Gender and Self: Katharine Tynan and the construction of political identities, 1880–1930', in Fintan Lane (ed.), *Politics, Society and the Middle Class in Modern Ireland* (London: Palgrave Macmillan, 2010), pp. 194–211.

119 Joyce's ambivalences are also anticipated. See Frank Shovlin, *Journey Westward: Joyce, 'Dubliners' and the Literary Revival* (Liverpool: Liverpool University Press, 2012).

120 Harvey, 'Irish Aestheticism in Fin-de-Siècle Women's Writing', p. 807.

121 Ibid.

122 Lynch, 'The Irish Peasant: fact and fiction'.

123 Ibid. In her analysis of Lawless' *Hurrish*, Harvey notes a fusion of realist and aestheticist modes into a 'realist-modernist style', Harvey, 'Irish Aestheticism in Fin-de-Siècle Women's Writing', p. 816.

124 In fact, Lynch's quarrel with the Dublin literary coteries she encountered anticipates Joyce's most ambivalent figure, Gabriel Conroy in 'The Dead', whose affinity with Europe makes him resistant to an invitation from Miss Ivors to join her on a visit to the Aran Islands.

CHAPTER 3. 'A Real Mesopotamia': London coteries and Paris letters

1 Laurel Brake's chapter 'Writing Women's History: "the sex" debates of 1889' provides an excellent account of this debate around the Women's Suffrage Bill. See Margaret Beetham and Ann Heilmann (eds), *New Woman Hybridities: femininity, feminism and international consumer culture, 1880–1930* (London: Routledge, 2004), pp. 51–73. Michelle Tusan's *Women Making News: gender and journalism in modern Britain* (Urbana, IL: Illinois University Press, 2005) dates the New Woman, as a positive political icon, to 1893. See also Gillian Sutherland, *In Search of the New Woman: middle-class women and work in Britain, 1870–1914* (Cambridge: Cambridge University Press, 2015).

2 Ian Sheehy, 'Irish Journalists and Litterateurs in Late Victorian London, 1870–1910', D.Phil. thesis, University of Oxford, 2003, p. 15: 'It means that the 1880s and 1890s are critical years for London-Irish literary life, just as they are for Irish history as a whole, since the changes in London were of course connected with similar developments in Ireland as the cultural revival gathered pace and the "de-Anglicisation" project got underway. These two decades are the juncture at which two opposing forces met in the London-Irish literary world. The deep-seated trend of emigration and integration that appeared to reach its peak in the 1880s was followed by a reaction, a move in the opposite direction, first culturally and then literally.'

3 Ibid., p. 15.

4 This lecture is reported in some detail in the *Freeman's Journal*, 26 April 1895, p. 4. In his discussion of the Irish Literary Society, David Pierce reproduces a list of writers, which includes Hannah Lynch, who gave their address as the Irish Literary Society in the *Literary Yearbook, 1897*: *Yeats's Worlds: Ireland, England and the poetic imagination* (New Haven, CT: Yale University Press, 1995), p. 125. See also Peter van der Kamp, '"Whose Revival?" Yeats and the Southwark Irish Literary Club', in Peter Leibregts and Peter van de Kamp (eds), *Tumult of Images: essays on W.B. Yeats and politics* (Amsterdam: Rodopi, 1995), pp. 157–82.

5 Justin McCarthy MP (1830–1912), Irish nationalist politician, journalist and novelist, based in London from 1871.

6 'Ford Madox Brown, a founding Pre-Raphaelite, his son Oliver (a novelist), William Rossetti (art critic), Algernon Swinburne, Eliza Lynn Linton, Kegan Paul (the publisher) and McCarthy (then on the *Daily News*) were just a few of the personalities there among many', Jerry White, *London in the Nineteenth Century: 'a Human awful wonder of God'* (London: Random House, 2011), p. 245.

7   Especially through his close companionship with Australian writer Rosa Praed (1851–1935). Allusions to meetings between a variety of writers, particularly Irish writers, at his home abound in memoirs of the period.

8   Margaret Stetz, *Facing the Late Victorians: portraits of writers and artists from the Mark Samuels Lassner Collection* (Plainsboro, NJ: Associated University Presses, 2007), p. 10.

9   Richard Whiteing, *My Harvest* (New York: Dodd & Mead, 1915), p. 59.

10 Alice Corkran's father John was born in Dublin, and worked as a Paris correspondent for several newspapers in England. Her mother Louisa was a translator. Michèle Milan, 'Found in Translation: Franco-Irish relationships in nineteenth-century Ireland', PhD thesis, Dublin City University, 2013, pp. 102–3.

11 Ibid., p.102.

12 Henriette Corkran, *Celebrities and I* (London: Hutchinson, 1902), p. 342.

13 Gertrude Atherton, *The Adventures of a Novelist* (New York: Liveright, 1932), p. 248. Elizabeth O'Connor Paschal was another London *salonnière* of the period. 'About 1888 Mrs. Howard [she had been married briefly] went to Ireland, where she met and married the politician and writer T.P. O'Connor. They lived in London, where they published a newspaper, the *Star*, and socialized with political and literary circles. Among their acquaintances and friends were George Bernard Shaw, Oscar Wilde, Bret Harte, Arthur Conan Doyle, Henry James, and Ellen Terry', Fannie Ratchford, 'Elizabeth Paschal O'Connor', *Texas Historical Association*, https://tshaonline.org/handbook/online/articles/foc12 (accessed 5 October 2018).

14 Atherton, *Adventures of a Novelist*, pp. 251–2.

15 We are indebted here to the most thorough critical account of the history, and the significance, of this group provided by Linda Hughes. See 'A Club of Their Own: the "Literary Ladies", New Women writers, and *fin-de-siècle* authorship', *Victorian Literature and Culture*, vol. 35, 2007, pp. 233–60. The event was renamed the 'Literary Women's Dinner' in 1892 and came to an end in 1914. Hughes suggests that the hostile press coverage generated by the inaugural evening might have scared off figures such as Tynan and Meynell for several years. For example, a satirical review in *Punch* 'revived the old association between sexual impropriety and unaccompanied women in public spaces', ibid., p. 242. It is hard to imagine that this would have deterred Lynch, with her history of striding purposefully towards controversy.

16 Lynch is included in a list as one of those attending the Literary Ladies' dinner again in June 1900, 'Women Writers at Dinner', *St James's Gazette*, 26 June 1900, p. 15.

17 Ibid., pp. 233–6.

18 Anon. (Our Lady Representative), 'Women Who Write: the Literary Ladies' dinner', *Pall Mall Gazette*, 1 June 1889, p. 6.

19 There is a small possibility that Miss Lynch could in fact be Mrs E.M. Lynch, also an Irish writer and certainly a member of the Irish Literary Society in London, but this is unlikely given the care taken with proper titles on the menu. Interestingly, Miss Harriet Jay, seated to Lynch's left, had had considerable success with her Irish-set novels.

20 See Low's brief obituary in *The Times*, 10 April 1939, p. 13. In Corkran's two-part article 'Journalistic London' in *Atalanta* (vol. 6, December 1892 and February 1893) she mentioned 'The Writers Club', which Low had founded in 1892. For further information about Frances Low, see Sylvia Kent, *The Woman Writer: the history of the Society of Women Writers and Journalists* (Stroud: The History Press, 2009). See also the Writers' Club archives held in the Women's Library, London School of Economics.

21 Most famously, her older brother Sidney followed a scholarship-winning academic career with the editorship of the *St James's Gazette*. In her obituary of Lynch, Low mentions Lynch's publications in this paper, although we have been unable to trace any of these, apart from a stinging letter about Davitt and Dreyfus (see p. 84). Her letter, written in response to an

anti-Dreyfusard statement made by Michael Davitt in *Le Figaro*, is the only occasion we have found when Lynch confronted the position adopted by several prominent Irish nationalists vis-à-vis '*l'affaire*'. Her works are featured and reviewed regularly, however, in the paper.

22 Alexis Easley, 'Anti/Feminism: Frances Low and the issue of women's work at the fin de siècle', in F. Elizabeth Gray (ed.), *Women in Journalism at the Fin de Siècle: making a name for herself* (London: Palgrave Macmillan, 2012), pp. 218–35.

23 For example: 'Miss Hannah Lynch, who is probably the most brilliant woman writer of the day, so far as distinction of style is concerned, has written a novel entitled "An Odd Experiment", which will shortly be published by Methuen', 'Women's Doings', *Hearth and Home*, 27 May 1897, p. 111.

24 Lynch is listed in a short article in the *Morning Post*, among those attending a garden party for authors and journalists held by the institute. 'The Institute of Journalists', 24 July 1899, p. 7.

25 The success and status of O'Connor and McCarthy might have confounded earlier stereotypes of 'drunken, reckless, nomadic' Irish journalists, but they could still be characterised as masters of 'an increasingly lucrative form of blarney'. David Dwan, *The Great Community: culture and nationalism in Ireland* (Dublin: Field Day Publications, 2008), p. 173. As Laurel Brake has pointed out, journalism was often, pejoratively, associated with women.

26 The phrase is Amanda Anderson's, taken from her analysis of the role of cosmopolitanism in the cultivation of 'detachment' in Victorian writing. Lynch works both with and against this model, as her ideological and geographical distance did not, in many cases, lead her to cultivate a 'detached' or quasi-objective style. See *Powers of Distance: cosmopolitanism and the cultivation of detachment* (Princeton, NJ: Princeton University Press, 2001).

27 Marie-Élisabeth Mitsou, 'Négoce et Transfert Culturel: Dimitrios Bikélas et le réseau intellectuel Franco-Grec dans la seconde moitié du XIXe siècle', *Rives Méditerranéennes* [online], vol. 50, 2015, http://rives.revues.org/4772 (accessed 12 August 2016), DOI: 10.4000/rives.4772

28 Having said that, Lynch's very early experiences of France – via schooling in a convent she occasionally mentioned, or even by way of James Cantwell's Parisian connections – are currently obscure.

29 'H.L.', 'Paris Letter', *Academy*, 14 March 1903, p. 154.

30 Lynch's letters to Thomas Dawson record that she moved from the suburbs to the centre of town in October. Mary Robinson's letters to her mother in May 1900 refer to her meeting with Lynch several times in Paris, http://www.le-petit-orme.com/lettres-de-mary-duclaux (accessed 5 October 2018). By June of the same year she was back in London for the Literary Ladies' dinner.

31 Lynch, letter to Thomas Dawson, 21 December 1894, Father Thomas Dawson Correspondence, Brotherton Library.

32 Ibid., 24 February 1895, Father Thomas Dawson Correspondence, Brotherton Library.

33 Lynch, letter to Alice Corkran, April 1895, private collection.

34 Lynch, letter to Gaston Paris, 27 September 1895, NAF, 24447, ff. 223–8, Bibliothèque Nationale de France. See Vadillo, *Women Poets* and White, *London in the Nineteenth Century* for further details about women writers choosing to live in Kensington during this period.

35 'Miss Hannah Lynch the novelist, whose book on Mr. George Meredith is published this week, is about to give a lecture in Paris at the Rudy Institute on Robert Louis Stevenson. Miss Lynch's former lecture on George Meredith was a great success, and was given before a brilliant assemblage including M. Taine', Anon., 'People, Places, Things', *Hearth and Home*, 21 May 1891, p. 7.

36 Lynch alluded to this lecture in the preface to *George Meredith: a study*, pp. ix–x.

37 This was noted in Ellis's 1940 autobiography *My Life*. We are grateful to Professor Adrian Frazier for sharing this information with us.

38 Alain Silvera, *Daniel Halévy and His Times: a gentleman-commoner in the Third Republic* (Ithaca, NY: Cornell University Press, 1966), p. 36.

39 'H.L.' 'Paris Letter', *Academy*, 14 March 1903, p. 254. The slight frisson generated by the word 'suggestive' was deliberate. Lynch had already alluded to Paris' charm, looks and numerous conquests.

40 Darmesteter's circles included other Jewish intellectuals, some of whom came to know Lynch, too. The most significant of these *salonnières* was Geneviève Straus, whose salon would include a host of turn-of-the-century luminaries, including Henri Bergson, Gabriel Fauré and Marcel Proust. Irish connections were also present in the form of Oscar Wilde and George Moore, but there is no evidence that Lynch met either while in Paris. Emily Bilski and Emily Braun (eds), *Jewish Women and Their Salons: the power of conversation* (New Haven, CT: Yale University Press, 2005), p. 72.

41 Darmesteter's 'dissident' liberal Judaism and Monod's 'scientific' history both influenced the sociologist Emile Durkheim.

42 Lynch, 'Romanciers Anglais Contemporains: Rudyard Kipling', *Revue Bleue: revue politique et littéraire*, series 4, vol. 6, 31 Octobre 1896, pp. 554–7.

43 Lynch, 'Oxford', *Freeman's Journal*, 28 October 1895, p. 8.

44 The chatty columns in *Myra's Journal* reinforce this point: 'Miss Lynch, who resides in Paris and is a great favourite in French circles owing to her command of the French language and literature, is one of the most interesting personalities of the day, her life in England, Ireland, Spain and Greece having been full of adventures. It is hoped that Miss Lynch's Childhood [*Autobiography of a Child*] may be followed by her Girlhood', Anon., untitled news item, *Myra's Journal*, 1 February 1899, p. 6.

45 Lynch, letters to Louise-Cécile Vincens (Arvède Barine), 20 April 1900, 9 April 1901, NAF vol. 18345, ff. 314–37.

46 Katharine de Forest, 'Recent Happenings in Paris', *Harper's Bazaar*, 9 September 1902, p. 813.

47 Atherton, *Adventures of a Novelist*, p. 253.

48 Ibid.

49 Ana Parejo Vadillo, 'Cosmopolitan Aestheticism: the affective "Italian" ethics of A. Mary F. Robinson', *Comparative Critical Studies*, vol. 10, no. 2, 2013, p. 172.

50 Hannah Lynch, 'Paul Bourget, Preacher', *Contemporary Review*, vol. 82, 1 July 1902, p. 353. This number of the *Contemporary Review* contained another substantial article by Lynch, 'Rebel Catalonia', which we discuss in Chapter 6.

51 Hannah Lynch, letter to Louise-Cécile Vincens, 16 September 1902, NAF, vol. 18345, ff. 314–37, Bibliothèque Nationale de France.

52 Hannah Lynch, 'Paris and the Exhibition I: where visitors can eat and sleep', *Hearth and Home*, 1 March 1900, p. 682; 'Paris and the Exhibition II: the pleasure side of Paris', *Hearth and Home*, 8 March 1900, p. 738.

53 Hannah Lynch, 'Paris and the Exhibition IV: Paris on the eve of the exhibition', *Hearth and Home*, 5 April 1900, p. 912.

54 Ibid.

55 Ibid.

56 There was even a sly suggestion of the relationship between British and French colonies, as she noted that 'lovers of Kipling will be enraptured by the Ceylon exhibition, where there is a miniature jungle with plenty of tigers', Hannah Lynch, 'Paris and the Exhibition VII: what to see at the exhibition', *Hearth and Home*, 10 May 1900, p. 28.

57 Hannah Lynch, 'Romanciers Anglais Contemporains: Rudyard Kipling', *La Revue Bleue*, vol. 6, no. 18, 31 October 1896, p. 557.

58 Philip Waller, *Writers, Readers and Reputations: literary life in Britain, 1870–1918* (Oxford: Oxford University Press, 2008), p. 151.

59   These 'Paris Letters' are all available in the digitised *Academy*, which currently forms part of the British Periodicals Online resource. Lynch's weekly columns lasted until February 1897, after which she contributed fortnightly – slowing to monthly at some points.

60   'H.L.', 'Sully Prudhomme', *Academy*, 28 December 1901, pp. 636–8. Lynch expressed surprise that Prudhomme had been awarded the Nobel Prize in Literature over Tolstoy, praising his writing for its 'delicate and exquisite genius' but noting that his 'aim is consistently towards the ideal'.

61   'H.L.', 'Paris Letter', *Academy*, 5 March 1898, p. 265.

62   The first edition of the *Celtic Twilight* had been published in 1893.

63   'H.L.', 'Paris Letter', *Academy*, 28 August 1897, pp. 167–8.

64   'Neptunevale' is part of an imaginary travel diary, *Les Voyageuses* (1898). This particular story is set in the west of Ireland. For Bourget's meeting with Yeats and the connections between this meeting and 'Neptunevale', see Bruce Morris, '"Neptune and the Surging Waves": Paul Bourget and W.B. Yeats', in Richard Finneran (ed.), *Yeats: an annual of critical and textual studies*, vol. 13, 1995, pp. 225–36.

65   'H.L.', 'Paris Letter', *Academy*, 28 August 1897, pp. 167–8.

66   Ibid., 11 February 1899, p. 195.

67   See her earlier letter to Father Thomas Dawson on the prospect of writing for T.P. O'Connor's the *Star* on p. 31 of this study.

68   'H.L.', 'Paris Letter', *Academy*, 5 June 1897, p. 593.

69   Ibid.

70   Ibid.

71   Ibid., pp. 593–4.

72   'H.L.', 'Paris Letter', *Academy*, 19 February 1898, pp. 210–11.

73   Ibid., p. 210.

74   Ibid.

75   Ibid., italics in original.

76   Ibid.

77   Ibid., p. 211.

78   Ibid.

79   For a detailed review of coverage of the case in the Irish press see Richard Barrett, 'The Dreyfus Affair in the Irish Nationalist Press, 1898–1899', *Études Irlandaises*, vol. 32, no. 1, 2007, pp. 77–89.

80   She would have gained access to the *St James's Gazette* via Frances Low. Its position as a Tory paper complicates Lynch's reply to Davitt even further.

81   She was replying to a comment made in Davitt's piece 'Les Rapports de la France et de L'Angleterre: l'opinion d'un Anglais', *Le Figaro*, 13 January 1899, p. 1.

82   Hannah Lynch, 'Irish and French Patriotism', *St James's Gazette*, 20 January 1899, p. 13.

83   Ibid. Lynch quoted these phrases directly.

84   Lynch, letter to Louise-Cécile Vincens, 20 April 1900, NAF 18345, ff. 314–37, Bibliothèque Nationale de France.

85   Lynch, letter to Vincens, [n.d.] 'Wednesday' [1901?], NAF 18345, ff. 314–37, Bibliothèque Nationale de France.

86   Ibid.

87   'Arvède Barine' [Louise-Cécile Vincens], 'La Gauche Feministe et le Mariage' *Revue des Deux Mondes*, 1 July 1896, pp. 106–31.

88   'H.L.', 'Paris Letter', *Academy*, 17 July 1897, p. 55.

89   Hannah Lynch to Louise-Cécile Vincens, n.d. [1899?], NAF 18345, ff. 314–37, Bibliothèque Nationale de France.

90   'H.L.', 'Paris Letter', *Academy*, 26 November 1898, p. 341.

91   See Maggie Allison's chapter on Durand in Diana Holmes and Carrie Tarr (eds), *A Belle Epoque? Women in French society and culture, 1890–1914* (New York and Oxford: Berghahn Books, 2006), pp. 37–50.

92   Alison Finch, *Women's Writing in Nineteenth Century France* (Cambridge: Cambridge University Press, 2000), pp. 181–2.

93   Hannah Lynch, 'Insanity in Literature', *Academy*, 17 August 1901, p. 157. This titled article was the subject of quite protracted debate in the *Academy*, and Lynch's correspondence shows that Vincens had a role to play in its composition. We discuss it at length in *Études Irlandaises*, vol. 36, no. 2, 2011, pp. 157–71.

94   'H.L.', 'Paris Letter', *Academy*, 5 March 1898, p. 265.

95   'H.L.', 'Paris Letter', *Academy*, 21 November 1896, p. 436.

96   Ibid.

97   Ibid.

98   'H.L.', 'Paris Letter', *Academy*, 13 July 1901, p. 38.

99   'H.L.', 'Paris Letter', *Academy*, 25 July 1903, p. 88.

100 Ibid.

101 Ibid., p. 89.

102 Ibid.

CHAPTER 4. Odd New Women: Sympathy, cosmopolitan modernity and *vagabondage*

1   Regenia Gagnier, *Individualism, Decadence and Globalization: on the relationship of part to whole, 1859–1921* (London: Palgrave, 2010), p. 69.

2   Vincent Cheng, '"Terrible Queer Creatures": Joyce, cosmopolitanism and the inauthentic Irishman', in Michael Patrick Gillespie (ed.), *James Joyce and the Fabrication of an Irish Identity* (Amsterdam: Rodopi, 2001), p. 21.

3   These narratives can be read specifically in relation to Mary Robinson's cosmopolitan coterie: '… as they travelled to other nations and cultures (creating themselves in the process) their writing equally engaged with these other nations, their languages, their cultures and, importantly, with their past', Vadillo, 'Cosmopolitan Aestheticism', p. 164. Lynch was not alone in producing this kind of narrative, and scholars have identified similar practices among her contemporaries, and in particular Irish women writers such as George Egerton. As Tina O'Toole has outlined, these Irish writers are central to 'a feminist history of ideas' … 'Locating their work in the context of a wider reading of Irish, British and European culture in the early 1890s exemplifies the impact made by their radical fictions', 'Ireland: the *terra incognita* of the New Woman project', in Heidi Hansson (ed.), *New Contexts: re-framing nineteenth-century Irish women's prose* (Cork: Cork University Press, 2008), p. 126.

4   Multilingualism is a feature of *Jinny Blake, Rosni Harvey* and *Daughters of Men* where diverse internationals switch easily between French, German, English, Greek and Spanish. Lynch's inclusion of French and Greek in *Daughters of Men* provoked some complaints among her reviewers.

5   Gagnier, *Individualism, Decadence and Globalization*, p. 69; Vadillo, 'Cosmopolitan Aestheticism', p. 172.

6   A full discussion of these epigraphs is not possible here but they do offer further insight into some of Lynch's personal and professional networks and a sense of how writing and the books she published functioned as tokens of thanks, friendship and an appeal for a sympathetic reading. For example, *Rosni Harvey* is dedicated to her sister Nannie while *Denys d'Auvrillac* is dedicated to Mary Robinson. *Daughters of Men* addresses itself to Demetrius Bikélas, a significant figure in literary and business circles in Europe of the period and who

may have helped Lynch with publishing connections. He was also the first president of the
International Olympic Committee.

7   Mr Blake 'hardly knew with which he felt more wrath – his vagabonding daughter or his new
helpless wife', *Jinny Blake*, pp. 233–4.

8   'F.Y.E.', 'The Paris Correspondent Once More: *French Life in Town and Country* by Hannah
Lynch', *Speaker*, March 1901, p. 663.

9   Hannah Lynch, 'A. Mary F. Robinson', *Fortnightly Review*, vol. 71, 1 February 1902, p. 260.

10 Emily Harrington, *Second Person Singular: late Victorian women poets and the bonds of verse*
(Charlottesville, VA: Virginia University Press, 2014), p. 72.

11 Ibid., p. 68.

12 See Kathryn Laing, 'F. Mabel Robinson: the aesthetics of sympathy and texts of transition', in
Louise Kane and Deborah Mutch (eds), *Victorian into Modern: suturing the divide, 1875–1935*
(London: Routledge, 2019).

13 The relationship between 'empathy' and 'sympathy' (within a broadly literary context) has
been explored by Suzanne Keen in *Empathy and the Novel* (Oxford: Oxford University Press,
2007).

14 Robinson, *Disenchantment* (Philadelphia, PA: J.B. Lippincott, 1886), pp. 396–7.

15 Ibid., pp. 79–80.

16 Scholarly explorations of sympathy, in particular its role in nineteenth-century and twentieth-
century literature, are numerous. These include studies by Kirstie Blair, Brigid Lowe and
Sophie Ratcliffe, in addition to those cited below.

17 Larson's discussion of the ways in which emotion is represented by authors such as Schreiner
and Hardy follows Ledger and Pykett in its determination to address the instability of the
category New Woman while asserting its shared fields of innovation and exploration: *Ethics
and Narrative in the English Novel, 1880–1914* (New York: Cambridge University Press, 2001).

18 Larson argues for a 'contextual ethics of particularity' to replace this 'separate spheres' model:
Ethics and Narrative in the English Novel, p. 49.

19 Rachel Ablow, *The Marriage of Minds: reading sympathy in the Victorian marriage plot*
(Stanford: Stanford University Press, 2007), pp. 2–7.

20 Julia Wright, 'Introduction' to Sydney Owenson, *The Missionary* (Peterborough, ON:
Broadview, 2006), p. 11.

21 Katerina Bartoszynska, 'Adam Smith's Problems: sympathy in Owenson's *Wild Irish Girl* and
Edgeworth's *Ennui*', *New Hibernia Review*, vol. 17, no. 3, autumn 2013, p. 128.

22 Jinny is the daughter of a popular Irish actor tragedian, Herbert Blake; her mother has died
young. Lynch herself may have felt a certain connection with Owenson, born of Catholic and
non-Catholic parents as well as enduring the life of a governess. In the novel, the fictional
Herbert Blake is more successful than Owenson's father, who went bankrupt. Lynch's near
contemporary L.T. Meade, for example, also makes clear allusions to Owenson and the 'wild
Irish girl' in many of her novels for girls. See Beth Rogers, 'Irishness, Professional Authorship
and the "Wild Irish Girls" of L.T. Meade', *English Literature in Transition*, vol. 56, no. 22, 2013,
pp. 146–66. See also Laing, 'Intellectual Lives and Literary Perspectives: female Irish writing
at home and abroad', in Brendan Walsh (ed.), *Knowing Their Place? The intellectual life of
women in the 19th century* (Dublin: The History Press, 2014), pp. 66–84.

23 Hannah Lynch, *Jinny Blake: a tale* (London: J.M. Dent & Co., 1897), p. 13.

24 Larson, *Ethics and Narrative in the English Novel*, p. 49.

25 Lynch, *Jinny Blake*, p. 42.

26 Ibid., p. 44.

27 Hannah Lynch, 'Brases', pp. 156–7.

28 Ibid., pp. 143–4.

29 Ibid., p. 145.
30 Ibid., p. 184.
31 Ibid.
32 Ibid., p. 147.
33 Lynch, 'A Page of Philosophy', p. 191.
34 Ibid., p. 205. As already noted, Lynch had mixed feelings about Naturalism, and about its most famous proponent Emile Zola. She applauded Zola's interventions in the Dreyfus Affair, but did not appreciate the view of women's roles put forward in a novel such as *Fecondité*. See '"Fecondité" vs. "The Kreutzer Sonata" or "Zola vs. Tolstoi"', pp. 69–78.
35 Ibid., p. 187
36 Ibid., p. 192.
37 Ibid., p. 215.
38 Lynch, 'Dr Vermont's Fantasy', p. 116.
39 Ibid.
40 Ibid., pp. 43–4.
41 Ibid., p. 43.
42 David Marshall, *The Surprising Effects of Sympathy: Marivaux, Diderot, Rousseau, and Mary Shelley* (Chicago: University of Chicago Press, 1988), pp. 1, 4.
43 Lynch might well have encountered the latter idea not only through Robinson, but also through her husband James Darmesteter's interest in the theories of nations expounded by Ernest Renan.
44 'New Woman literature primarily analyses feelings in dyadic or sometimes triadic relationships', Gagnier, *Individualism, Decadence and Globalization*, p. 63.
45 Anon., 'An Odd Experiment', *Saturday Review*, 23 October 1897, p. 450.
46 Teresa Mangum, *Married, Middlebrow and Militant: Sarah Grand and the New Woman novel* (Ann Arbor, MI: University of Michigan Press, 1998), p. 42.
47 Grand's response to *Jude*, for instance, a key text for both Ablow and Larson, had been to declare that it was 'colossal in strength' but 'ethically, it is amorphous' … 'I perceive no special teaching in it', Ann Heilmann and Stephanie Forward (eds), *Sex, Social Purity, and Sarah Grand: volume 1* (London: Routledge, 2000), p. 229.
48 Hannah Lynch, *An Odd Experiment* (London: Methuen, 1897), p. 74.
49 Ibid., p. 61.
50 Ibid.
51 Ibid., p. 30.
52 Ibid., pp. 5, 7.
53 Ibid., p. 173.
54 Ibid., p. 38.
55 Ibid., pp. 2, 3, 22, 63, 278.
56 Ibid., p. 13.
57 Ibid., p. 2.
58 Ibid., p. 56.
59 Ibid., pp. 171–2.
60 Ibid., pp. 93, 94.
61 Ibid., p. 68.
62 Ibid.
63 Ibid., pp. 84, 87.
64 Ibid., p. 228.
65 Ibid., p. 235.
66 Ibid., p. 246.

67 Ibid.

68 'You have won my sympathy, and while suffering myself through you, I am sorry for you', ibid., p. 245.

69 Ibid., p. 239.

70 Ibid., p. 269.

71 Ibid., p. 263.

72 Lynch, 'Dr Vermont's Fantasy', p. 26.

73 Richard Dellamorra, *Masculine Desire: the sexual politics of Victorian aestheticism* (Chapel Hill, NC: University of North Carolina Press, 1990). See Chapter 5 in particular.

74 Lynch, *An Odd Experiment*, p. 285.

75 This latter theme is also the focus of Lynch's least successful novel of this period, *Clare Monro: the story of a mother and daughter*, set partially in Italy.

76 *Rosni Harvey*, in terms of power and pace, is much weaker than *Jinny Blake*, partly due to the triple-decker format still insisted on by some publishers of this period. A contemporary reviewer in the *Spectator* makes this observation: 'There could hardly be a better illustration of the disadvantages of the three-volume system than that provided by this novel. It is clearly the work of an able and cultivated woman; it is both a thoughtful and a well-written book; and yet it is robbed of more than half of its legitimate effectiveness by being spun out to about double its legitimate length', Anon., 'Rosni Harvey by Hannah Lynch', *Spectator*, 28 January 1893, p. 13.

77 Hannah Lynch, *Rosni Harvey*, vol. 1, p. 9.

78 Ibid., pp. 10–11.

79 Ibid. p. 10.

80 Ibid., vol. 2. pp. 29–30, 53.

81 Rosni's journey to Smyrna and Constantinople is likely to have been based on Lynch's own travels, although we have not yet uncovered any travel writing arising from her experience there. Jinny Blake also travels to Constantinople, and Rosni Harvey's letter to Ulysses sent from the Hotel de Luxembourg, Rue de Pera suggests a familiarity with the geography of the city and that self-consciously Parisian street in a distinctly cosmopolitan area. Philip Mansell, *Constantinople: city of the world's desire, 1453–1924* (London: John Murray, 1995), p. 287.

82 Lynch, *Jinny Blake*, p. 192.

83 Ibid., pp. 44, 271.

84 Ibid., p. 15.

85 Ibid., p. 220.

86 Hannah Lynch, *Denys D'Auvrillac*, p. 19. For a fuller treatment of this novel, see Laing, 'On Women, on Art, on Life', pp. 223–43.

87 Hannah Lynch, *Daughters of Men: a novel* (London: William Heinemann, 1892), p. 23. Photini, beloved of Liszt and Rubenstein for her brilliance, may have been modelled on a handful of women pianists of the period. Lynch herself had, according to Gibbs' obituary, studied the piano at a musical academy in London: 'She wrote me from London in 1880 that she was studying the piano under Lansdowne Cottell with a view to appearing at public concerts', Gibbs, 'Tribute to Hannah Lynch', p. 5.

88 The title of the novel refers directly to gender inequality thrust on young women in rural Greek society where 'the absence of shots proclaimed to the village that a little "daughter of man", instead of the desired "son of God", had come to bless the house', ibid., p. 146.

89 Vadillo, 'Cosmopolitan Aestheticism', p. 165.

90 Lynch, *Rosni Harvey*, vol. 2, pp. 97–8. Cosmopolitan Ulysses is more than likely modelled on Demetrius Bikélas (see Chapter 4, n. 6), who belonged to one of the merchant families of the nineteenth-century Greek diaspora and whose way of life was defined by 'commercial networks, communication, mobility, cosmopolitanism'. See Ariadni Moutafidou, 'Greek

merchant families perceiving the world: the case of Demetrius Vikelas, *Mediterranean Historical Review*, vol. 23, no. 2, 2008, pp. 143–64, DOI: 10.1080/09518960802528936 (accessed 29 June 2015), p. 156. Bikélas also translated the novel into Greek in 1892, as *Women of Greece* (Athens: Hestia, 1892).

91 Lynch, *Daughters of Men*, p. 184.

92 As noted there are numerous Jamesian resonances in her novels and evidence of Lynch's knowledge of his work. In a letter sent from Paris a month before she died to the editor of *Century Magazine*, Lynch writes: 'I have been working on a Parisian novel intended to be an insider view of certain phases of French life or character (nothing to do with the cosmopolitan Paris, the legitimate field of Mr Henry James)', 7 November 1903, Century Magazine Archives, Box 59, Manuscripts and Archives Division, New York Public Library, Astor, Lenox and Tilden Foundations. In one of several letters to the editor sending work for possible publication, Lynch also mentions Demetrius Bikélas, who had already published in the magazine, once again suggesting he was a potentially important publishing connection for Lynch.

93 Lynch, *Jinny Blake*, p. 316. A contemporary reviewer of the novel noticed not Jamesian links but an indebtedness to Meredith: '"Jinny Blake" is written throughout in his tone, and not only in the phraseology, but a good many of the personages of the book also have the air of having stepped out of some of Mr Meredith's novels', E.H. Lacon Watson, 'Through Pink Glasses', *Monthly Packet*, 1 July 1897, p. 97.

94 See, for example, Kate Krueger Henderson, 'Mobility and Modern Consciousness in George Egerton and Charlotte Mew's *Yellow Book* Stories', *English Literature in Transition*, vol. 54, no. 2, 2011, pp. 185–211.

95 Heather Edwards notes, in her discussion of Emily Lawless' *Grania*, 'a blind spot in discussions of the New Woman that have relied on assumed links among modernity, the New Woman figure and the imperial centre. This closes the possibility of geographically marginal New Women figures who express place specific traits but nevertheless exhibit qualities and attitudes more typical of New Women', Heather Edwards, 'The Irish New Woman and Emily Lawless's *Grania: the story of an island*: a congenial geography', *English Literature in Transition*, vol. 51, no. 4, 2008, p. 422.

96 Dúnlaith Bird, *Travelling in Different Skins: gender identity in European women's oriental travelogues, 1850–1950* (Oxford: Oxford University Press, 2012), p. 2.

97 'Vagabondage represents a diffuse women's movement, sharing common recurring traits, which coalesces during the nineteenth century in Europe', ibid., p. 31.

98 Ibid.

99 Lynch developed her 'vagabond' persona most fully in her travel writing, the focus of the next chapter.

100 'Dr Vermont's Fantasy' is a story 'Told by the traveller' who describes herself as a 'restless vagabond': 'Dr Vermont's Fantasy', pp. 3 and 10 respectively.

101 Hannah Lynch, 'A Girl's Ride on an Engine', *Girl's Realm*, no. 17, vol. 2, March 1900, p. 466.

102 Moruzi, *Constructing Girlhood*, p. 174.

103 Lynch, 'A Girl's Ride on an Engine', p. 467.

104 Ibid., pp. 467–8.

105 Ibid., p. 468. Moruzi argues that Ella's engine journey might be read as a 'carefully coded sexual experience', demonstrating 'the power of the modern to potentially liberate young women from nineteenth-century feminine ideals about sexuality', ibid., p. 175.

106 Krueger Henderson, 'Mobility and Modern Consciousness', p. 185. For further discussion of women, modern transport, travel and cosmopolitanism, see Ana Parejo Vadillo, *Women Poets and Urban Aestheticism: passengers of modernity* (Basingstoke: Palgrave Macmillan, 2005). Lynch's heroines travel less in city contexts and more across country or sea.

107 Krueger Henderson, 'Mobility and Modern Consciousness', p. 184.

108 The journeys Lynch's eponymous heroines undertake allow her to absorb some of her own travel experiences into her fiction (there are clear analogies to be made between Lynch's travels around Spain, for example, and Jinny Blake's, while her sojourns in Greece form the background to *Rosni Harvey* and *Daughters of Men*).

109 In a letter to Father Thomas Dawson, Lynch refers very briefly to her own dramatic departure for Greece, clearly the basis for Rosni's adventure: 'I literally boarded the 'Rosmelia' [sp?] and was quite drenched as well as hauled up by a rope.' The full description of the voyage, she tells Dawson, might appear in the *Freeman's* as letters from Liverpool to Greece, but she is unsure as to whether they will be accepted. These articles do not seem to have been published: Lynch to Dawson, 3 October 1885, Father Thomas Dawson Correspondence, Brotherton Library.

110 Lynch, *Rosni Harvey*, vol. 2, p. 88.

111 Ibid., p. 90. Again, there are parallels to be drawn here between the narratives of *vagabondage* Bird analyses and Lynch's novel, where the female body is placed centre stage and the invocation of personal danger is key: Bird, *Travelling in Different Skins*, p. 49.

112 Lynch, *Rosni Harvey*, vol. 2, pp. 93, 99.

113 Bird, *Travelling in Different Skins*, pp. 53–4.

114 Lynch, *Rosni Harvey*, vol. 2, p. 102.

115 Ibid., p. 130.

116 Ibid., pp. 100, 130.

117 Ibid., p. 81.

118 Ibid., p. 145.

119 Lynch, *Jinny Blake*, p. 223. Jinny's revelation anticipates Virginia Woolf's eponymous Orlando, who discovers the cultural and social meanings of femininity on board ship back to England following her extraordinary transformation from man to woman: 'And she fell to thinking what an odd pass we have come to when all a woman's beauty has to be kept covered lest a sailor may fall from a mast-head. "A pox on them!" she said, realizing for the first time ... the sacred responsibilities of womanhood', *Orlando* (London: Grafton, 1988), p. 98.

120 Lynch, *Jinny Blake*, pp. 96, 147.

121 Ibid., p. 62.

122 Ibid., p. 313.

123 Ibid., p. 314; Gagnier, *Individualism, Decadence and Globalization*, p. 9.

124 Lynch, *Jinny Blake*, p. 167.

125 Bird, *Travelling in Different Skins*, p. 31.

126 Lynch, *Jinny Blake*, p. 140.

127 Ibid., p. 142.

128 Ibid., pp. 142–4.

129 Ibid., p. 144.

CHAPTER 5. 'The Vagabond's Scrutiny': Hannah Lynch in Europe

1 See Seamus Deane, *Strange Country: modernity and nationhood in Irish writing since 1790* (Oxford: Clarendon Press, 1996), p. 49. Deane argues compellingly for travel literature as a predominantly political discourse which makes 'use of the mask of foreignness' to 'bring home' charges of 'corruption, fanaticism, irrational behaviour and practices, institutions and individuals', ibid., p. 6.

2 Hannah Lynch, 'A Tramp Through the Forest of Fontainebleau', *Good Words*, vol. 41, December 1900, p. 466.

3 Our thanks to Professor Tadhg Foley for his insights into this subject, and more generally for his generous reading of, and commentary on, this chapter.

4   Cited in Foster, *Irish Novels*, p. 295. See Anne Jamison on Somerville and Ross and Heidi Hansson in *Emily Lawless, 1845–1913: writing the interspace* (Cork: Cork University Press, 2007). For further discussion of representations and counter-representations of the west of Ireland exuding 'Irish authenticity of the educated traveller and avid tourist alike', see Barbara O'Connor and Michael Cronin (eds), *Tourism in Ireland: a critical analysis* (Cork: Cork University Press, 1993); and Glen Hooper, *The Tourist's Gaze: travellers to Ireland, 1800–2000* (Cork: Cork University Press, 2001).

5   Bird, *Travelling in Different Skins*, p. 2.

6   Hannah Lynch, 'A Backward Glance at the City of the Pale', *Donahoe's Magazine*, no. 5, November 1884, p. 385.

7   Ibid.

8   Ibid., p. 394.

9   Ibid., p. 395.

10 Ibid., pp. 394–6. Lynch had personal experience of the raising of statues as an act of cultural resistance. Her stepfather, James Cantwell, was responsible for organising public collections to fund the statues of Edmund Burke and William Smith O'Brien that currently stand on College Green and O'Connell Street. See Cantwell's letters in the *Irish Times*: for Smith O'Brien, 30 October 1869, p. 4; for Burke, 15 July 1862, p. 2.

11 Lynch, 'A Backward Glance at the City of the Pale', p. 396.

12 Hansson, *Emily Lawless*, p. 54.

13 Hannah Lynch, 'Nature's Constancy in Variety', *Irish Monthly: a magazine of general literature*, vol. 11, August 1883, pp. 439–44.

14 Ibid., p. 439.

15 Ibid., p. 440.

16 For an insight into earlier schools of travel writing about Ireland which Lynch is, to some extent, addressing, see John McAuliffe's 'Women's Travel Writing in Mid-nineteenth Century Ireland', in M. Kelleher and J.H. Murphy (eds), *Gender Perspectives in Nineteenth Century Ireland: public and private spheres* (Dublin: Irish Academic Press, 1997), pp. 140–7.

17 Ibid., p. 441.

18 Ibid.

19 For instance, the *Idler* published a long section from the text in its number for March 1898, with the original illustrations by Helen James: see Hannah Lynch, 'Toledo', *Idler*, March 1898, pp. 250–8.

20 Anon., 'Art and Letters', *Daily News*, 23 February 1899, p. 6.

21 Anon., 'News Summary', *Leeds Mercury*, 17 May 1899, p. 4.

22 Anon., 'Toledo', *New York Times*, 4 November 1899, p. 3.

23 Anon., 'Toledo', *Freeman's Journal*, 10 May 1899, p. 6.

24 Anon., 'The New Topography', *Academy*, 2 September 1899, pp. 225–6.

25 Maurice Barrès (1862–1923), French novelist, essayist and politician. Lynch wrote favourably of his work, although condemned him roundly for his position as one of the most prominent anti-Dreyfusards.

26 Anon., 'A Plea for a "Man in the Street" Topography', *Academy*, 8 June 1901, p. 495.

27 Hannah Lynch, 'Montserrat', *Freeman's Journal*, 31 July 1897, p. 9.

28 Ibid., p. 9.

29 It was advertised in a frontispiece to the Newnes edition as being 'descriptive of the Home and Social Life of Continental Peoples, by authors whose long residence on the Continent enables them to write with fullness of knowledge and with impartiality'. This series also sold very well, and in 1901 *French Life* was named as one of the best-selling 'more popular Continental Guide-Books', despite a slump in other 'general literature', 'Monthly Reports of the Bookselling Trade', *Bookman* (London), April 1901, p. 4.

30 The article opened with the following observation: 'Miss Hannah Lynch is a lady of Irish origin who may be described without offence by a word borrowed from a French novelist (no favourite of hers) as a *déracinée*. She is accustomed to make excellent copy with her experience of travel and residence abroad; and as an authority on France she combines with the prestige of a Paris correspondent to a London periodical, the advantage of having spent, since childhood, considerable intervals of time in that country and having traversed at least a wide extent of its surface', 'F.Y.E.', 'The Paris Correspondent Once More', *Speaker*, 16 March 1901, p. 663.

31 Hannah Lynch, 'French Life', *Speaker*, 6 April 1901, p. 19.

32 Margaret Beetham's *A Magazine of Her Own* contains a section on the perceived 'feminization of the press' during the era of the New Journalism in the 1880s and 1890s (Abingdon: Routledge, 1996) pp. 123–6.

33 'F.Y.E.', 'The Paris Correspondent Once More', p. 663.

34 Lynch, 'French Life', p. 19.

35 As the now numerous scholarly accounts of travel writing illustrate, the genre became extremely popular during the nineteenth century. A glance at bibliographies gives a sense not only of this popularity, but also of the diversity of publishers involved and the range of travels made – from European countries to the Caribbean, from America to West Africa and beyond. For instance, Tim Youngs' collection *Travel Writing in the Nineteenth Century: filling in the blank spaces* (London: Anthem, 2006) contains essays on Africa, Asia, America, Australasia and the Balkans. Susan Bassnett's excellent survey of the field, 'Travel Writing and Gender', summarises major areas of concern. Peter Hulme and Tim Youngs (eds), *The Cambridge Companion to Travel Writing* (Cambridge: Cambridge University Press, 2002), pp. 225–41. Bassnett cites Cheryl McEwan's emphasis on 'the diversity of women travellers and the variations in their writing styles', and warns against attempts to homogenise the field: Cheryl McEwan, *Gender, Geography and Empire: Victorian women travellers in East Africa* (Aldershot: Ashgate, 2000), p. 9.

36 Monica Anderson, *Women and the Politics of Travel, 1870–1914* (Madison, NJ: Fairleigh Dickinson University Press, 2006), p. 14.

37 Maria Frawley, *A Wider Range: travel writing by women in Victorian England* (Madison, NJ: Farleigh Dickinson University Press, 1994), p. 35.

38 Other important voices are those of Emily Jane Pfeiffer (1827–90), a Welsh poet whose travel book *Flying Leaves from East and West* contained descriptions of social and political conditions across Europe and in the United States; Edith Somerville (1858–1949) and Violet Florence Martin (Martin Ross) (1862–1915), who wrote about their travels across Ireland, Wales, France and Denmark; Emily Lawless (1845–1913), who wrote mainly about Ireland but also about her travels abroad; Beatrice Grimshaw (1871–1953), 'who travelled widely and fearlessly in the South Seas': Foster, *Irish Novels*, p. 12. Some of Somerville and Ross' best-known European travel writing includes *In the Vine Country* and the novel *French Leave*. See Anne Jamison's (Oakman) comparative commentary on their European and Irish travel writing in 'Sitting on "the Outer Skin": Somerville and Ross's *Through Connemara in a Governess Cart* as a coded stratum of linguistic/feminist 'Union' ideals', *Éire/Ireland*, vol. 39, nos 1 & 2, spring/summer 2004, pp. 110–35.

39 Frawley, *A Wider Range*, p. 31.

40 'F.Y.E.', 'Paris Correspondent', p. 663.

41 Hannah Lynch, *French Life in Town and Country* (London: George Newnes, 1901), p. 23.

42 Ibid., pp. 45–7.

43 Ibid., p. 23.

44 Ibid., p. 12.

45 Ibid., pp. 170–1. While not strictly travel writing, commentaries such as her piece on the lives and education of young French women ('The Young French Girl Interviewed', *Nineteenth*

Century, February 1902, pp. 276–83) enabled Lynch to expand on her critical assessment of the lives of French women made elsewhere, concentrating on the ways in which religion and ideals of the 'indestructible purity of girlhood' ('The Young French Girl Interviewed', p. 277) shaped their education and thus their roles and functions in society.

46 See *Hannah Lynch and Spain: collected journalism of an Irish New Woman, 1892–1903*, eds Pere Gifra-Adroher and Jacqueline Hurtley (Venice: Edizioni Ca' Foscari, 2018).

47 Lynch clearly spoke and understood Spanish well. She translated and published, with John Lane, José Echegaray's *Grand Galeoto* and *Folly or Saintliness* in 1895.

48 Hannah Lynch, 'The Senora of To-day', *Freeman's Journal*, 24 March 1894, p. 6.

49 While Lynch invokes orientalism here and its stereotypes of oriental women, she also distances herself by admitting to imagining the reactions of the oriental to the Spanish treatment of women. Writing for a specifically Irish audience in the *Freeman's Journal*, such references may well have had specific resonances as connections between Celticism and orientalism were most fully explored by Irish revivalists at the time. See Joseph Allen Lennon's *Irish Orientalism: a literary and intellectual history* (Syracuse, NY: Syracuse University Press, 2004). Our thanks to Maureen O'Connor for suggested readings here, and for her generous and insightful commentary on the chapter.

50 Hannah Lynch, 'A Spanish "Master" at Home', *Speaker*, 16 November 1895, pp. 521–2.

51 Ibid.

52 Salvador Garcia Castañeda, 'Pereda y Hannah Lynch o La Pequeña Historia de un Malentendido', *Siglo Diecinueve: literatura Hispánica*, vol. 1, 1995, pp. 139–57. We are grateful to Pere Gifra Adroher (Universitat Pompeu Fabra) for translating this article for us, including its transcription of Pereda's correspondence.

53 Hannah Lynch, 'Impressions of the Canary Isles: i', *Good Words*, January 1896, p. 739.

54 Ibid.

55 Ibid., pp. 738–9.

56 Alec Hargreaves notes the preponderance of 'powerful sense impressions' in Loti's work, and questions Loti's self-confessed ignorance of the political economy: '… it should not be thought that his impressionistic descriptions are devoid of ideological content', A. Hargreaves, *The Colonial Experience in French Fiction: a study of Pierre Loti, Ernest Psichiari and Pierre Mille* (London: Macmillan, 1981), pp. 21–3.

57 She writes: 'M. Legros [sic] is an intelligent and fair-minded traveller, and produces the views of the landlord and Mr. William O'Brien with impartial accuracy. Personally, I would have preferred a little less politics, and more of scenery, incident, and traveller's impressions', 'H.L.', 'Paris Letter', *Academy*, 11 February 1899, p. 195.

58 Between 1899 and 1900, Loti travelled across India. The resulting account *L'Inde (sans les Anglais)*, published in 1903, resolutely avoided any mention of the colonial British presence, producing what Hargreaves terms 'pointed silences'. However, it is worth noting that this was not due to Loti's specifically anti-imperial sentiments, but to the competition for colonial territory between Britain and France at this point. 'A Backward Glance at the City of the Pale' uses a similar technique to Loti's descriptions of Rangoon, when describing the intrusion of English ugliness upon the city after the Act of Union; see Hargreaves, *The Colonial Experience in French Fiction*, pp. 30–1.

59 For a detailed discussion of this piece see Faith Binckes and Kathryn Laing, 'A Vagabond's Scrutiny: Hannah Lynch in Europe', in Elke D'Hoker, Raphaël Ingelbien and Hedwig Schwall (eds), *Irish Women Writers: new critical perspectives* (Bern: Peter Lang, 2011), pp. 111–31.

60 Yves Hervouet, *The French Face of Joseph Conrad* (Cambridge: Cambridge University Press, 1990), pp. 29–31. Lynch mentions in particular Loti's renowned 1886 novel *Pêcheur d'Islande*.

61 Hannah Lynch, 'A Day in Pierre Loti's Town', *Speaker*, 13 October 1894, p. 409.

62 Ibid.

63 Ibid.

64 Ibid.

65 Ibid., p. 410.

66 Hannah Lynch, 'From Lucerne to Verona', *Freeman's Journal*, 22 August 1899, p. 5. Reprinted in the *Weekly Freeman*, 26 August 1899.

67 For Lynch's brief account of the effect Venice had on George Sand, see 'Paris Letter', *Academy*, 8 July 1899, pp. 42–3. The review mentions Lynch's recent return from Italy, and refers to a French review of Kipling's *Plain Tales from the Hills*, in which he is compared with Loti.

68 'Venice is always too much and too much so. I cannot cope with it, it submerges me', Vernon Lee's 'Out of Venice at Last' (1925), from *The Golden Keys and Other Essays on the Genius Loci* (London: John Lane, 1925), reprinted in *Hauntings and Other Fantastic Tales* (Peterborough, ON: Broadview, 2006), p. 340.

69 Hannah Lynch, 'Venice I', *Freeman's Journal*, 29 December, p. 6.

70 Hannah Lynch, 'Venice II', *Freeman's Journal*, 30 December 1899, p. 2.

71 Ibid.

72 Hannah Lynch, 'Venice I', p. 6.

73 For instance, Arthur Symons repeatedly commented on this melancholy, and the sense of unreality hanging over a city so clearly a 'superb barbaric patchwork in which the East and West have an equal share', in *Cities of Italy* (London: J.M. Dent, 1907), pp. 75–8.

74 Lynch, 'Venice II', p. 2.

75 Lynch, 'Venice I', p. 6.

76 Lynch's account of Toledo emphasised the history of the city as both a point of confluence and conflict. In the excerpt reprinted in the *Idler*, she recounted the legend that Toledo's Jewish community had been allowed to thrive because they had written to Jerusalem to advise against Christ's execution, a document that failed to arrive in time. However, tolerance came to end with the arrival of 'the fanatic San Vicente de Ferrer … brandishing the cross in one hand and a torch in the other'. The ejection of the city's Muslims was treated with equal opprobrium, described as 'the fatal unhappy day of the expulsion of this glorious race': Lynch, 'Toledo', pp. 257–8.

77 Evgenia Sifaki, 'A Gendered Vision of Greekness: Lady Morgan's "Woman: Or Ida of Athens"', in Vassiliki Kolocotroni and Efterpi Mitsi (eds), *Women Writing Greece: essays on Hellenism, orientalism, and travel* (Amsterdam: Rodopi, 2008), p. 56.

78 Hannah Lynch, 'The Ursulines of Tenos', *Irish Monthly*, May 1886, p. 272.

79 Lynch, letter to Thomas Dawson, 11 November 1889, Father Thomas Dawson Correspondence, Brotherton Library.

80 In her discussion of Yeats' early, revisionary engagements with Arnoldian ideas of the 'Celt', Marjorie Howe observes that 'Yeats insists that this Irishness coincides with the virtues of other ancient literatures, especially the Greek tradition', *Yeats's Nations: gender, class, Irishness* (Cambridge: Cambridge University Press, 1998), p. 26.

81 Hannah Lynch, 'Greece of To-day', *Westminster Review*, vol. 139, January 1893, pp. 155–63.

82 Ibid., p. 155.

83 Ibid., p. 161.

84 Ibid., p. 157.

85 Ibid., p. 161.

86 See H. Bleackley, *The Hangmen of England* (London: Chapman & Hall, 1929 [1979]), p. 229.

87 Lynch, 'Greece of To-day', p. 163.

88 Hannah Lynch, 'On the Acropolis', *Academy*, 14 June 1902, p. 610. Ernest Renan (1823–93), who had once trained for the priesthood, was an influential Celticist, as well as a philosopher and author. Although he was generally well known in France at this point, Lynch had a specific connection to his work through James Darmesteter, Mary Robinson's first husband,

who was president of the Renan Society in Paris. Renan's 'Prayer on the Acropolis', published in 1883, was embedded in another text, 'Recollections of Youth', which stated that the 'Prayer' had been written on Renan's first trip to the Acropolis in 1865.

89 Ibid., p. 610.

90 Alexandre Falguière (1831–1900), French artist and sculptor, a contemporary of Rodin.

91 Lynch, 'On the Acropolis', pp. 610–11.

92 Ibid., p. 610.

93 Ibid., p. 611.

94 Once again, as in her earlier letter to Dawson, England was compared not to civilised and courageous Greece, but to the Turkish empire the English press had consistently vilified. And, although Lynch did not mention Ireland directly, Irish support for the Afrikaners was also well known. A few days before the publication of the article, Arthur Lynch, MP for Galway, officer in the second Irish Transvaal Brigade and a fellow Paris correspondent, had been arrested for treason in Dover. Donal McCracken's account, *Forgotten Protest: Ireland and the Anglo-Boer War*, provides a useful summary of Arthur Lynch's engagement with the Transvaal Brigade: revised edition (Belfast: Ulster Historical Foundation, 2003), pp. 126–31.

95 'My dislike of large families is born of the conviction that every large family holds a victim ... The unshared gaiety of the group is a fresh provocation of repulsion on both sides', Lynch, *Autobiography of a Child*, p. 256.

96 'H.L.', 'Paris Letter', *Academy*, 9 February 1898, p. 210.

97 Lynch, 'The Senora of To-day', p. 6.

98 Hannah Lynch, 'On Board a Spanish Steamer', *Freeman's Journal*, 27 December 1892, p. 6.

99 Ibid.

100 While this mention of Scottish harshness refers back to the Scottish mother of *Autobiography of a Child*, it also connects to T.P. O'Connor's reference to the 'harsh Scotch voice' heard at government relief depots during the Famine – 'in the name of political economy he should die': T.P. O'Connor and R.M. McWade, *Gladstone–Parnell and the Great Irish Struggle* (Toronto and London: R.S. Robertson, 1886), p. 335.

101 Hannah Lynch, 'Rebel Catalonia', *Contemporary Review*, vol. 82, July 1902, p. 58.

102 Ibid., p. 57.

103 Ibid.

104 Ibid., p. 59.

105 Ibid., p. 56.

106 Ibid.

107 Lynch, *Autobiography of a Child*, p. 137.

CHAPTER 6. *Autobiography of a Child*: Identity, memory, genre

1 Hannah Lynch, letter to Louise-Cécile Vincens, 10 April 1899, MS letter, NAF, 18345, Bibliothèque Nationale de France.

2 Hannah Lynch, letter 'To William Blackwood & Sons' [?], March 1899, Papers of William Blackwood & Sons, MS 30069.77 17.18, National Library of Scotland.

3 *Autobiography* is the only work of Lynch's to have retained critical attention into the late twentieth century and beyond. See Foster, *Irish Novels*, Elizabeth Grubgeld, *Anglo-Irish Autobiography: class, gender, and the forms of narrative* (Syracuse, NY: Syracuse University Press, 2004), and Ciaran O'Neill, *Catholics of Consequence: transnational education, social mobility and the Irish Catholic elite, 1850–1900* (Oxford: Oxford University Press, 2014).

4 The story was published in the *Revue de Paris* in four parts, in the following numbers: 1 February 1902, pp. 451–93; 15 February 1902, pp. 761–92; 1 March 1902, pp. 139–68; 15 March 1902, pp. 409–37.

5 Lynch, *Autobiography of a Child*, pp. 141, 211.

6   Ibid., p. 194.

7   Ibid., p. 2.

8   Ibid., p. 4.

9   Ibid., p. 49.

10 Ibid., p. 51.

11 Ibid., p. 251.

12 Anon., 'Minor Notices: juveniles', *Literary World*, 11 November 1899, p. 376.

13 Anon., 'The Literary Week', *Academy*, 16 December 1899, p. 711.

14 We are grateful to Michael Counahan, grand-nephew of Hannah Lynch, for generously providing us with biographical information. Drawing on his father's notes about the family, he goes on to say that the school in Coventry 'provided a background to *Autobiography of a Child*', email to authors, 24 July 2008.

15 Edmund himself was well known as a war correspondent. Tynan notes in her memoir: 'Edmund O'Donovan, who had not so long before ridden to Merv, had grown up with them like a brother. They knew the whole brilliant Irish group of war-correspondents of those days', *Twenty-five Years*, p. 77. O'Donovan makes his earliest appearance in Lynch's fiction as Mr Power in 'Marjory Maurice' – journalist and inveterate storyteller; his adventures echo closely those of O'Donovan's.

16 Anon., 'Autobiography of a Child', *Bookman* (London), May 1899, p. 55.

17 Not all these readings were supportive, either of the genre or of *Autobiography* as a representative of it. In her 1901 article 'The Literary Cult of the Child', Louise Betts Edwards bemoaned the fact that there was 'no protective law, no factory inspector' to assist the 'overworked child in fiction', whom she imagined sitting up until midnight rehearsing well-worn plot lines 'in thin night-raiment'. One of these plot-lines was that of the 'infant martyr', the popularity of which was waning, but to which she felt that the 'apocryphal' *Autobiography of a Child* belonged: *Critic*, vol. 39, no. 2, August 1901, p. 167.

18 Rosemary Lloyd's study of the child in nineteenth-century French literature provides a further useful context here, particularly as it discusses works by both George Sand and Pierre Loti. Lloyd notes the many narrative problems common to the writing about childhood, concluding that 'there can be little doubt that in attempting to resolve these problems writers drew on familiar literary patterns ... Romanticism's image of the sensitive individual as outcast, the world of the fairy-tale, the paradigm of the Bildungsroman, the stories of adventurers, saints, and martyrs, the medieval accounts of heroic children performing mighty deeds, are only some of the threads ...', *The Land of Lost Content: children and childhood in nineteenth-century French literature* (Oxford: Oxford University Press, 1992), pp. 119–20.

19 Ala Alryyes, *Original Subjects: the child, the novel, and the nation* (Cambridge, MA: Harvard University Press, 2001), p. 208.

20 'A Correspondent', 'The Fenian Conspiracy', *John Bull*, 10 July 1886, p. 446. See Chapter 2, fn. 41.

21 It was published as 'The Heart of Darkness' in *Blackwood's Magazine*. This was not the only time that Lynch and Conrad shared the same numbers of *Blackwood's*; 'Youth: a narrative' appeared alongside 'The Spaniard At Home' in the number for September 1898.

22 See David Finkelstein's *The House of Blackwood: author–publisher relations in the Victorian era* (University Park, PA: Penn State Press, 2002); and *Print Culture and the Blackwood Tradition, 1805–1930* (Toronto: University of Toronto Press, 2006).

23 'But adventure served imperialism; an "adventurous spirit" precluded subversion, and like young Marlow, readers saw what they were prepared to see', Andrea White, *Joseph Conrad and the Adventure Tradition: constructing and deconstructing the imperial subject* (Cambridge: Cambridge University Press, 1993), p. 173.

24 For instance, 'The Little Marquis' was first published in *Macmillan's Magazine*. It was reprinted in the *New York Times*, 9 November 1890, p. 18; *Littell's Living Age*, 22 November 1890, pp. 484–91; *New Zealand Tablet*, vol. xix, no. 32, 8 May 1891, p. 23 and 15 May, p. 23. The *Tablet* also refers to an earlier publication in the New York *Freeman's Journal*. Patrick Moran, editor of the magazine at the time Lynch's story appeared, was the first Catholic bishop of Dunedin.

25 The apparently innocent story of childhood in an Irish setting has as its subtext a potential critique of the popularised stereotypical representations of the Irish as childlike in works such as Ernest Renan's *La Poèsie de Races Celtiques* (1854) and Matthew Arnold's *On the Study of Celtic Literature* (1867). Although Lynch mocked this stereotype in other writings, she did not wholly avoid it in *Autobiography*. While she countered the image of rural Irish life as uncouth, noting the 'pretty speech and pretty manners' of 'Irish peasants', she continued: 'Big-hearted, foolish, emotional children, upon whose sympathetic faces ... still play the smiles and frowns, the lights and shadows, of expressive and variable childhood', *Autobiography of a Child*, p. 46.

26 Hannah Lynch, 'A Village Sovereign', *Macmillan's Magazine*, vol. 76 (May–October 1897), pp. 257–67.

27 C.A. Read [T.P. O'Connor] and Katharine Tynan Hinkson (eds), *The Cabinet of Irish Literature, Volume IV* (London: Gresham Publishing Company, 1903), pp. 209–308. As noted earlier, Katharine Tynan provided this information when responding to Frances Low's critical 1906 article. Tynan corrected Low's assertion that Lynch had not appeared in the anthology she had recently edited, citing 'A Village Sovereign': 'Miss Lynch wished to be represented by this story, and she furnished me with it, and also with a brief biography which appears before the extract', Tynan, 'A Correction', *Speaker*, 29 December 1906, p. 377.

28 Lynch, 'A Village Sovereign', p. 299.

29 The project ran into ten volumes, and was published by J.D. Morris & Co., in Philadelphia, in 1904. McCarthy was assisted by Douglas Hyde and Lady Gregory, among others. The volume in which 'A Village Sovereign' (pp. 2088–2105) appeared was designed to showcase humorous writing; however, this humour was often pointed. Lynch's story was followed by contributions from Edward Lysaght (1763–1810), whose poem 'A Prospect' was described as prefiguring 'in a vein of bitter mirth, the impending ruin of Dublin by the measure of the Union', p. 2107.

30 As Kelleher notes, the number of women authors who appeared in that volume was extremely unusual. Margaret Kelleher, 'The Cabinet of Irish Literature: a historical perspective on Irish anthologies', *Éire-Ireland*, vol. 38, nos 3–4, fall/winter 2003, p. 87.

31 Ibid., pp. 81–2.

32 Ibid.

33 'Kitty did not move so much as an eyelash in the direction of the fallen coin, but as the carriage began to roll on again, my lord lying back as proud as an invader, she ran after it, shrieking at the top of her voice: "Me lord, me lord, I telled ye owe me half-a-crown ... What I want is me money paid into me own hand, as between Christian and Christian"', 'A Village Sovereign', p. 301.

34 Ibid., p. 303.

35 Ibid., p. 305.

36 Ibid., p. 307.

37 Ibid., p. 308.

38 Anon., 'Literary Gossip', *Athenaeum*, 24 September 1898, p. 422.

39 The *Living Age*, while not reprinting the letter, also made a note of her authorship: 'It is announced that Miss Hannah Lynch is the author of the unusual and somewhat painful

serial, "The Autobiography of a Child", which is just completed in Blackwood's Magazine', 'Books and Authors', *Living Age*, 13 May 1899, p. 467.

40 'The Author of "Autobiography of a Child"' [Hannah Lynch], 'Correspondence: an explanation', *Speaker*, 22 April 1899, p. 465. Reprinted in 'Chronicle and Comment', *Bookman*, June 1899, p. 97.

41 Conrad's famous statement runs: 'My task which I am trying to achieve is, by the power of the written word, to make you hear, to make you feel – it is, before all, to make you see. That – and no more, and it is everything. If I succeed, you shall find there according to your deserts: encouragement, consolation, fear, charm – all you demand; and, perhaps, also that glimpse of truth for which you have forgotten to ask', Joseph Conrad, 'Author's Note' to 'The Nigger of the Narcissus', *New Review*, December 1897, p. 630. The same number contains a long article on *Blackwood's Magazine*.

42 This issue was highlighted by the way in which the title appeared in its French translation in 1902. By the early twentieth century, 'très véridique histoire' was an unlikely formulation to choose for straight autobiography, as it carries specific overtones of fictionality, even of the tall tale.

43 Anon, 'A Bitter Childhood', *Outlook*, 27 May 1899, p. 558.

44 See Elizabeth Grubgeld, 'Class, Gender and the Forms of Narrative: the autobiographies of Anglo-Irish women', in Susan Shaw Sailer (ed.), *Representing Ireland: gender, class, nationality* (Gainesville, FL: University Press of Florida, 1997), pp. 133–55.

45 Claudia Nelson, *Family Ties in Victorian England* (Westport, CT: Praeger Publishers, 2007), p. 65. Extracts from *Autobiography* as a sample of documentary evidence and as part of a selection of memoirs have been included in Debra Teachman's *Understanding Jane Eyre: a student casebook to issues, sources and historical documents* (Westport, CT: Greenwood Press, 2001) and in Eve Claxton, *The Book of Life* (London: Random House Group, 2005).

46 Foster, *Irish Novels*, p. 277.

47 Ibid.

48 George Moore, *Hail and Farewell*, ed. Richard Allen Cave (Gerrards Cross: Colin Smythe, 1985), p. 413.

49 Lynch, *Autobiography of a Child*, pp. 146–7.

50 Ibid., p. 148.

51 Elizabeth Grubgeld, *George Moore and the Autogenous Self: the autobiography and fiction* (Syracuse, NY: Syracuse University Press, 1994), p. 23.

52 Ibid.

53 Michael Kenneally, 'The Autobiographical Imagination and Irish Literary Autobiography', in Michael Allen and Angela Wilcox (eds), *Critical Approaches to Anglo-Irish Literature* (Gerrards Cross: Colin Smythe, 1989), p. 144.

54 Richard Coe's study of writing about childhood draws attention to the way in which the 'autobiographical novel of childhood' – the 'roman de l'enfance', or 'enfance romantisée' – 'permits adjustments to that precarious balance between literal and symbolic truth that is so difficult to maintain in autobiography pure and simple', *When the Grass Was Taller: autobiography and the experience of childhood* (New Haven, CT: Yale University Press, 1984), p. 86.

55 Ibid., p. 1.

56 For Penny Brown, it is this element of *Autobiography* which genuinely 'subverts all literary stereotypes', *The Captured World: the child and childhood in nineteenth-century women's writing in England* (London: Harvester, 1993), p. 133. It certainly blasted depictions of maternity produced by Tynan, Meynell and many others, in which the bond between mother and baby united the doctrinally proper with the scientifically 'natural'. Frances Power Cobbe's 1894

autobiography celebrated the accessibility, softness and generosity of the maternal body, best
demonstrated by her mother's fulfilment of the 'sacred duty of motherhood', feeding her own
children rather than sending them out to nurse. From 'The Life of Frances of Power Cobbe'
in Valerie Sanders (ed.), *Records of Girlhood: an anthology of nineteenth-century women's
childhoods* (Aldershot: Ashgate, 2000), pp. 183–4. Lynch's narrator reverses this ideal, taking
for granted the fact that not all women will love their babies or vice-versa, and advocating
wet-nursing as an opportunity for such children to experience affection: 'My nurse loved me
devotedly, and of course spoiled me … Women who do not love their children do well to
put them out to nurse', ibid., p. 2. Once again, Grubgeld's critique seems pertinent here, as
her description of Angela's mother as both 'a victim and a frightening fixture of the parental
house' (see Grubgeld, 'Class, Gender and the Forms of Narrative', p. 143) reminds the reader
of the double meaning of 'confinement' in the period. The narrator roundly criticises 'Irish
virtue' that leads to large families of sometimes unwanted children. See *Autobiography of a
Child*, p. 218.

57 Lynch, *Autobiography of a Child*, p. 217.
58 Ibid., p. 218.
59 Ibid., p. 75.
60 Ibid., p. 218.
61 Ibid.
62 Ibid., p. 290.
63 Ibid., pp. 6–7.
64 Ibid., p. 245.
65 Ibid., pp. 245–6.
66 Taura S. Napier, *Literary Autobiographies of Twentieth-century Irish Women* (Lanham MD:
    University Press of America, 2001), p. 12.
67 Ibid., p. 13.
68 Ibid., p. 84.
69 Napier, citing Coe, asserts that 'Goethe was the first autobiographer to address the
    relationship between the "truth" of lived experience and the "truth" of that same experience
    transposed into literature', ibid.
70 Ibid., p. 15.
71 Ibid, p. 12.
72 Ibid., p. 225.
73 For further insight into preoccupations with the child and fairy tale at the *fin de siècle*, see
    Caroline Sumpter's 'Innocents and Epicures: the child, the fairy tale and avant-garde debate
    in *fin-de-siècle* Little Magazines', *Nineteenth-century Contexts*, vol. 28, no. 3, September 2006,
    pp. 225–44.
74 Ibid., p. 4.
75 Ibid., pp. 5–6.
76 Ibid., p. 1.
77 Ibid., pp. 53, 57, 237.
78 Ibid., p. 18.
79 Ibid., p. 8.
80 Ibid., p. 18.
81 Ibid., pp. 18–19.
82 Ibid., p. 113.
83 Ibid., pp. 118–19.
84 Ibid., pp. 57, 193.
85 Ibid., p. 215.

86 Ibid., pp. 206–7. This scene was singled out by the reviewer from the *Bibliothèque Universelle*: "'Nous faisions une course en voiture à travers le pays tout parfumé de roses et ma mère parla d'aller visiter le tombeau de Shakespeare. 'Qu'est-ce que Shakespeare?' demandai-je d'un ton léger, en regardant ma soeur assise à côté de ma mère. Pif! paf! un soufflet me fit voir trente-six chandelles et envoya rouler mon chapeau sur la route. C'est ainsi que j'appris le nom de Shakespeare." Shakespeare, par la suite, a dû se faire pardonner cela. La menace constante, et souvent suivie d'effet, d'une mère aussi belle que peu maternelle projette son ombre sur tout le livre. Mais cette impression est rachetée par un récit plein d'humour et un don tout particulier d'apercevoir les ridicules', Anon., 'Chronique Parisienne', *Bibliothèque Universelle et Revue Suisse*, vol. 27, no. 79, 1902, p. 389.

87 Ibid., p. 42.

88 Ibid., p. 70.

89 Ibid., p. 152.

90 Ibid., p. 196.

91 Brontë's book, which was highly regarded by the end of the nineteenth century, had first appeared under the generically ambiguous title *Jane Eyre: an autobiography, edited by Currer Bell*. See Charlotte Brontë, *Jane Eyre*, eds Jane Jack and Margaret Smith (Oxford: Clarendon Press, 1969), p. xxiii. Its publication had ignited a similar, high-profile debate on the identity of the author and the status of the text.

92 'To read it is to gain a strong sense of personal emotion which is refracted through the concerns of the child study movement and novelistic texts', Sally Shuttleworth, 'Inventing a Discipline: autobiography and the science of child study in the 1890s', *Comparative Critical Studies*, vol. 2, no. 2, June 2005, p. 157.

93 Louis N. Wilson, 'Bibliography of Child Study for the Year 1899', *Pedagogical Seminary*, vol. 7, 1900, p. 542.

94 The texts that Shuttleworth names as part of the 'invention' of the discipline include Sand's autobiography, Loti's *Roman d'un Enfant*, and James Sully's *Studies of Childhood*; Sully was also a close friend of Stevenson. As we know, Lynch admired Sand, Stevenson and Loti, and her acquaintance and predecessor at the *Academy* Gabriel Monod published the French translation of Sully's work in 1898. All these factors strongly endorse Shuttleworth's reading of the text as part of the emerging discipline of child psychology, and of the way in which this engagement addressed Lynch's literary, biographical and social concerns.

95 *Jane Eyre* also appears in George Egerton's *Wheel of God* (London: Grant Richards, 1898), a book which outlines the experiences of a young Irish girl, and which provides an interesting counterpoint to Lynch's text. On the opening pages, the narrator recalls having recently read the book, and being 'still a-quiver with the strangeness of it', ibid., p. 3.

96 Brontë, *Jane Eyre*, pp. 12–14.

97 Ibid., p. 16.

98 Lynch, *Autobiography of a Child*, pp. 153–4.

99 Ibid., p. 154.

100 Ibid., pp. 153–4.

101 Hunger-striking became a tactic of the English and Irish suffragettes between 1909 and 1914. See Maud Ellmann's study *The Hunger Artists: starving, writing, and imprisonment* (London: Virago, 1993) for further investigation interwoven with psychoanalytic, political and literary instances of hunger-striking and self-starvation, with a focus on Irish contexts.

102 Ibid., p. 155.

103 Ibid., p. 157.

104 Ibid. All the same, the adult narrator is careful to point out that this self emerges because it must, it is a product of the injustices and deprivations that Angela endures. When one

of the nuns treats her well, she returns the behaviour: 'Wickedness dropped from me as a wearisome garment, and, divested of its weight, I trotted after her heels like a little lap dog' (Lynch, *Autobiography of a Child*, p. 161). To this nun's dismay, such fully domesticated 'good behaviour' does not prevent Angela from defending herself – and her nationality – in the exchange outlined on pp. 277–8.

105 Ibid., pp. 142–3.

106 Ibid., pp. 18–19.

107 Ibid., p. 278.

108 Ibid., pp. 69–70.

109 Ibid., p. 81.

110 Ibid., pp. 81–2.

111 'I shut my eyes, and I am back in the little parlour with its spindle chairs, an old-fashioned piano with a green silk front, its pink-flowered wall-paper, and two wonderful black-and-white dogs on the mantelpiece. There were two pictures I loved to gaze upon – Robert Emmet in the dock, and Mary Stuart saying farewell to France', Lynch, *Autobiography of a Child*, p. 1. Emmet makes a similar appearance in *The Wheel of God*, as one of the pictures pinned to the 'wonderful fourfold screen' in the nursery. However, he is accompanied by a wider range of images: O'Connell, Grattan, Sir Robert Peel, Frederick the Great, Fanny Essler, and early nineteenth-century fashion plates: Egerton, *The Wheel of God*, p. 4.

112 J.B. Hall, an Irish reporter who attended the trial of 'the Invincibles' and sketched several of the accused, including Brady, recalled: '... a pathetic figure in the front of the gallery was a gentle-faced young girl, said to be his sweetheart, and whose tearful eyes were riveted upon him to the end', *Random Records of a Reporter* (London and Dublin: Simpkin Marshall & the Fodhla Printing Co., 1928), p. 181.

113 Elsie Michie argues for a similar uncertainty in *Jane Eyre, Wuthering Heights* and even Charles Kingsley's 'simianized' depictions of the Irish. Have characters such as Hindley and Heathcliff been created, as 'the Irish have been made chimpanzees by the English treatment of them? Or is Heathcliff inherently savage, as racist caricatures imply the Irish are?', *Outside the Pale: cultural exclusion, gender difference, and the Victorian woman writer* (Ithaca, NY: Cornell University Press, 1993), p. 55.

114 Mary Darmesteter (Mary Robinson), 'Autobiography of a Child', *Academy*, 13 May 1899, p. 527.

115 Ibid.

116 Ibid.

117 'It would be a bold and inhuman assertion to make, and certainly one I am far from maintaining, that harsh treatment is the proper training of children', Lynch, *Autobiography of a Child*, p. 262.

118 'Among the mysteries of my life nothing seems so strange to me as the depth of this physical antipathy to my mother. The general reader to whom motherhood is sacred will not like to read of it', Lynch, *Autobiography of a Child*, p. 14. Rather more light-heartedly, she comments towards the end of the book: 'My father, who, I am told, was a very kindly, tender-hearted man, died some months before my birth. Had I been given the choice beforehand, and known what was in store for me, I should greatly have preferred it had been my mother who died many months before my birth', ibid., p. 287.

119 Ibid., pp. 262–3.

120 Ibid., pp. 255, 258.

121 Ibid., p. 297.

EPILOGUE

1 Hannah Lynch, letter to Vincens, n.d., no address, NAF, vol. 18345, f. 339, Bibliothèque Nationale de France. This note refers to Vincens' review of Lynch's book, and asks for her to reply by the next post if possible. It is the final letter in the sequence.

2 Hansson quotes Lawless' 1887 monograph *Ireland* in 'History in/of the Borderlands: Emily Lawless and the story of Ireland', in Irene Gilsenan Nordin and Elin Holmsten (eds), *Liminal Borderlands in Irish Literature and Culture* (Bern and Oxford: Peter Lang, 2009), pp. 51–68, at p. 59.

3 Bird, *Travelling in Different Skins*, p. 3.

4 Ibid., p. 30.

Bibliography

PRIMARY TEXTS

Archives

Archdiocese of Birmingham (solicitors of), letter to William Blackwood & Sons, Papers of William Blackwood & Sons, National Library of Scotland, Edinburgh

Cantwell, James, letter to John O'Mahony, 2 November 1860, Fenian Brotherhood and O'Donovan Rossa Collection, American Catholic History Research Centre and University Archives, http://cuislandora.wrlc.org/islandora/object/achc-fenian%3A545# page/1/mode/1up (accessed 6 October 2018)

Counahan, Michael, 'Notes on Counahan Family History: based on notes by Desmond R. Counahan, with additions by other family members', private collection, Counahan family

Lynch, Hannah, applications to the Royal Literary Fund with supporting materials [file no. 2452], Papers of the Royal Literary Fund, British Library, London

—, letter to Alice Corkran, April 1895, private collection [sold at auction online]

—, correspondence with Thomas Dawson, Father Thomas Dawson Papers, Brotherton Library, University of Leeds

—, correspondence with Edmund Gosse, Edmund Gosse Collection, Brotherton Library, University of Leeds

—, correspondence with Gaston Paris, Nouvelles Acquisitions Françaises (NAF: 24447), Bibliothèque Nationale de France, Paris

—, correspondence with Louise-Cécile Vincens [Arvède Barine], Nouvelles Acquisitions Françaises (NAF: 18345, ff. 314–37), Bibliothèque Nationale de France, Paris

— and Nannie Lynch, correspondence with the editor of *Century Magazine*, 1886–1903, Century Company Records, Manuscripts and Archives Division, New York Public Library, Astor, Lenox and Tilden Foundations, New York City

Pereda, José María a Hannah Lynch, correspondence [3, 20 y 29 de noviembre de 1897 y la última de 23 de abril de 1898], MSS 22526, La Biblioteca Nacional de España, Madrid

Robinson, A. Mary F., Correspondence, Fonds Anglais 240–52, Bibliothèque Nationale de France, Paris

—, correspondence with Louise-Cécile Vincens [Arvède Barine], FR Nouvelle Acquisitions, 18342, ff. 226–7, Bibliothèque Nationale de France, Paris

— [Mary Duclaux], correspondance familiale, lettres, http://www.le-petit-orme.com/ lettres-de-mary-duclaux [accessed 6 October 2018]

Robinson, Mabel F., correspondence with her mother and sister, A. Mary F. Robinson, Fonds Anglais 240, ff. 255–62, Bibliothèque Nationale de France, Paris

Taylor, Helen, correspondence, Mill-Taylor Collection, vol. 20, Special Collections, London School of Economics

Tynan, Katharine, correspondence, MS 39, 118, Special Collections, National Library of
    Ireland, Dublin
—, correspondence with Father Matthew Russell SJ, IE IJA/J27/73 (1–2), Irish Jesuit
    Archives, Dublin
— and Pamela Hinkson, GB 133 KTH, Archive Collection, University of Manchester Library

Short Fiction, Novels and Novellas

Lynch, Hannah (et al.), 'A Castle Christmas-Eve; or The Tales the Portraits Told', *United
    Ireland*, 20 December 1884
—, 'A Girl Revolutionist', *Girl's Realm*, vol. 1, February 1899
—, 'A Girl's Ride on an Engine', *Girl's Realm*, vol. 2, March 1900
—, 'A Page of Philosophy', *Macmillan's Magazine*, vol. 72, September 1895
—, 'The Romantic Episode in the Life of Miss Charlotte O'Mara', *Murray's Magazine: a
    home and colonial periodical for the general reader*, vol. 10, September 1891
—, 'A Village Sovereign', *Macmillan's Magazine*, vol. 76, August 1897
—, 'A Village Sovereign', in C.A. Read [T.P. O'Connor] and K. Tynan Hinkson (eds), *The
    Cabinet of Irish Literature: volume 4* (London: The Gresham Publishing Company,
    1903)
—, 'A Village Sovereign', in Justin McCarthy, Maurice Francis Egan, Douglas Hyde, Lady
    Gregory, James Jeffrey Roche and Charles Welsh (eds), *Irish Literature*, vol. 6 (10 vols)
    (Philadelphia: J.D. Morris & Co., 1904)
—, *An Odd Experiment* (London: Methuen, 1897)
—, 'Armand's Mistake', *Macmillan's Magazine*, vol. 66, August 1892, reproduced in *Living Age*,
    vol. 195, 8 October 1892
—, 'Autobiography of a Child', *Blackwood's Magazine*, vols 164–5, October 1898–April 1899
—, *Autobiography of a Child* (Edinburgh and London: William Blackwood & Co., and New
    York: Dodd, Mead & Co., 1899)
—, 'Christmas on the Hills: tales', *Shamrock*, Christmas double number, December 1883–
    January 1884
—, *Clare Monro: the story of a mother and daughter* (London: J. Milne, 1900)
—, *Daughters of Men: a novel* (London: William Heinemann, 1892)
—, 'Defeated', *Beeton's Christmas Annual*, 1885
—, *Denys d'Auvrillac: a story of French life* (London: J. Macqueen, 1896)
—, *Dr Vermont's Fantasy and Other Stories* (London: J.M. Dent & Co., 1896)
—, *Jinny Blake: a tale* (London: J.M. Dent & Co., 1897)
—, 'Laogaire or Wrecked on Success', *Weekly Freeman*, 10 March–17 November 1888
—, 'The Last of the O'Moores', *Weekly Freeman Xmas Sketch Book*, December 1889
—, 'The Little Marquis', *Macmillan's Magazine*, vol. 62, October 1890, reproduced in *Living
    Age*, vol. 187, 22 November 1890
—, 'Marjory Maurice', *Shamrock*, 27 December 1884–28 March 1885
—, 'The Massingers', *Shamrock*, 24 June–25 November 1882
— [pseud. E. Enticknappe], 'My Friend Arcanieva', *Macmillan's Magazine*, vol. 73, December
    1895
—, *The Prince of the Glades*, 2 vols (London: Methuen, 1891)
—, *Rosni Harvey: a novel*, 3 vols (London: Chapman & Hall, 1892)
—, *Through Troubled Waters* (London and New York: Ward, Lock & Co., 1885)

Criticism, Travel Writing, Translations and Other Non-fiction

'The Author of "Autobiography of a Child" [Hannah Lynch]', 'Correspondence: an explanation', *Speaker*, vol. 19, 22 April 1899, reprinted in 'Chronicle and Comment', *Bookman* (New York), June 1899

Hannah Lynch, 'A. Mary F. Robinson', *Fortnightly Review*, vol. 71, 1 February 1902

—, 'A Backward Glance at the City of the Pale', *Donahoe's Magazine*, 5 November 1884

—, 'A Day in Pierre Loti's Town', *The Speaker*, vol. 10, 13 October 1894

— [Anon.], 'A Dublin Literary Coterie: sketched by a non-pretentious observer', *Dublin Evening Telegraph*, 14 January 1888

—, 'A Glimpse of South Ireland in Winter', *Shamrock*, 10 March 1883

—, 'A Spanish "Master" at Home', *Speaker*, vol. 11, 16 November 1895

—, 'A Tramp Through the Forest of Fontainebleau', *Good Words*, vol. 41, December 1900, reproduced in *Living Age*, vol. 26, 8 September 1900

—, 'Among Feudal Memories', *Speaker*, vol. 11, 16 February 1895

—, 'Around Tarragona', *Speaker*, vol. 11, 12 January 1895

—, 'A Political Waiter of France' [Maurice Barrès], *Contemporary Review*, vol. 78, September 1900

—, 'A Story of Chios', *Macmillan's Magazine*, vol. 59, January 1889, reproduced in *Living Age*, vol. 180, 26 January 1889

—, 'Along the Spanish Highways', *Good Words*, vol. 35, December 1894

—, 'Alphonso XIII', *Good Words*, vol. 41, December 1900

—, 'Alphonse Daudet', *Fortnightly Review*, vol. 63, June 1898

—, 'A Remarkable Military Writer', *Freeman's Journal*, 4 April 1896

—, 'An Irish Sculptor', *Freeman's Journal*, 1 May 1894

—, 'An Unnoted Corner of Spain', *Blackwood's Magazine*, vol. 162, July 1897, reproduced in *Living Age*, vol. 214, 4 September 1897

—, 'Correspondence: French life', *Speaker*, vol. 4 (new series), 6 April 1901

—, 'The Drama in France', *Freeman's Journal*, 13 December 1893

—, 'The English Drama of Today', *Freeman's Journal*, 7 December 1893

—, *French Life in Town and Country* (New York and London: G.P. Putnam's Sons, 1901)

—, 'Correspondence: the French nuns', *Academy*, vol. 61, no. 1541, 16 November 1901

—, 'Correspondence: the French nuns', *Academy*, vol. 61, no. 1542, 23 November 1901

—, '"Fecondite" vs. "The Kreutzer Sonata" or "Zola vs. Tolstoi"', *Fortnightly Review*, vol. 67, January 1900

—, 'From Lucerne to Verona', *Freeman's Journal*, 22 August 1899, reprinted in *Weekly Freeman*, 26 August 1899

—, *George Meredith: a study* (London: Methuen, 1891)

—, 'George Meredith', *Bookman* (London), vol. 17, November 1899

—, 'The Girls of Spain', *Girl's Realm*, vol. 5, May 1903

—, 'Greece of Today', *Westminster Review*, vol. 139, January 1893

—, 'Impressions of the Canary Isles: i', *Good Words*, vol. 37, January 1896

—, 'Impressions of the Canary Isles: concluding paper', *Good Words*, vol. 37, January 1896

—, 'In the Woods of La Pellouaille', *Speaker*, vol. 10, 27 October 1894

—, 'Irish and French Patriotism', *St James's Gazette*, 20 January 1899

—, 'In Provence', *Blackwood's Magazine*, vol. 166, September 1899

—, 'José Echeray', *Contemporary Review*, vol. 64, July 1893

—, 'Impressions of Oxford', *Freeman's Journal*, 28 November 1895

—, 'Insanity in Literature', *Academy*, no. 1528, 17 August 1901

—, 'The Insurrection in Cuba', *Freeman's Journal*, 13 April 1895

—, 'The Irish Peasant: fact and fiction', *Freeman's Journal*, 13 June 1896

—, 'To the Editor of *United Ireland*', *United Ireland*, 9 May 1885

—, 'The Love Letters of Guy de Maupassant', *Fortnightly Review*, vol. 62, October 1897, reproduced in *Living Age*, vol. 215, 4 December 1897

—, 'M. Paul Hervieu', *Fortnightly Review*, vol. 60, October 1896

—, 'Maurice Maeterlinck', *Academy*, vol. 52, 7 August 1897

—, 'Monserrat', *Freeman's Journal*, 31 July 1897

—, 'Nature's Constancy in Variety', *Irish Monthly*, vol. 11, August 1883

—, 'November in a Greek Island', *Irish Monthly*, vol. 14, July 1886

—, 'On Board a Spanish Steamer', *Freeman's Journal*, 27 December 1892

—, 'On the Acropolis', *Academy*, vol. 62, 14 June 1902, reproduced in *Living Age*, 9 August 1902

—, 'Oxford', *Freeman's Journal*, 28 October 1895

—, 'Paris and the Exhibition', *Dublin Evening Telegraph* (a series of eight articles from 22 February 1900)

—, 'Paris and the Exhibition I: where visitors can eat and sleep', *Hearth and Home*, 1 March 1900

—, 'Paris and the Exhibition II: the pleasure side of Paris', *Hearth and Home*, 8 March 1900

—, 'Paris and the Exhibition III: characteristic French scenes', *Hearth and Home*, 15 March 1900

—, 'Paris and the Exhibition IV: Paris on the eve of the exhibition', *Hearth and Home*, 5 April 1900

—, 'Paris and the Exhibition V: first glance at the exhibition', *Hearth and Home*, 26 April 1900

—, 'Paris and the Exhibition VI: excursions round Paris', *Hearth and Home*, 3 May 1900

—, 'Paris and the Exhibition VII: what to see at the exhibition', *Hearth and Home*, 10 May 1900

—, 'Paris in Midsummer', *Freeman's Journal*, 31 August 1892

— ['H.L.'], 'Paris Letter', *Academy*, 21 November 1896

— ['H.L.'], 'Paris Letter', *Academy*, 5 June 1897

— ['H.L.'], 'Paris Letter', *Academy*, 17 July 1897

— ['H.L.'], 'Paris Letter', *Academy*, 28 August 1897

— ['H.L.'], 'Paris Letter', *Academy*, 9 February 1898

— ['H.L.'], 'Paris Letter', *Academy*, 19 February 1898

— ['H.L.'], 'Paris Letter', *Academy*, 5 March 1898

— ['H.L.'], 'Paris Letter', *Academy*, 26 November 1898

— ['H.L.'], 'Paris Letter', *Academy*, 11 February 1899

— ['H.L.'], 'Paris Letter', *Academy*, 8 July 1899

— ['H.L.'], 'Paris Letter', *Academy*, 4 May 1901

— ['H.L.'], 'Paris Letter', *Academy*, 13 July 1901

— ['H.L.'], 'Paris Letter', *Academy*, 14 March 1901

— ['H.L.'], 'Paris Letter', *Academy*, 25 July 1903

—, 'Paul Bourget, Preacher', *Contemporary Review*, vol. 82, July 1902

—, 'Pereda the Spanish Novelist', *Contemporary Review*, vol. 69, February 1896, reproduced in *Living Age*, vol. 208, 14 March 1896

—, 'Persecution in France Today and Fifty Years Ago', *Contemporary Review*, vol. 84, July 1903

—, 'Rebel Catalonia', *Contemporary Review*, vol. 82, July 1902

—, 'Romanciers Anglais Contemporains: Rudyard Kipling', *Revue Bleue: revue politique et littéraire*, vol. 618, 31 Octobre 1896

—, 'Santiago de Compostela', *Freeman's Journal*, 28 December 1895

— ['H.L.'], 'Sully Prudhomme', *Academy*, 28 December 1901

—, 'The Spaniard at Home', *Blackwood's Magazine*, vol. 164, September 1898, reproduced in *Living Age*, vol. 219, 8 October 1898

—, 'The Senora of To-Day', *Freeman's Journal*, 24 March 1894

—, *Toledo: the story of an old Spanish capital* (London: Dent, 1898)

—, 'These hills …' [extract from 'Nature's Constancy in Variety'], *The Irish Birthday Book: selections from the speeches and writings of Irish men and women both Catholic and Protestant*, arranged by 'Melusine' (New York: Catholic Publication Society, 1884)

—, 'Toledo' [extract from *Toledo: the story of an old Spanish capital*], *Idler*, March 1898, https://archive.org/details/Toledo_925/page/n1 (accessed 14 May 2019)

—, 'Two Old Italian Towns', *Freeman's Journal*, 1 January 1900

—, 'Upon Dancing', *Freeman's Journal*, 27 December 1893

—, 'The Ursulines of Tenos', *Irish Monthly*, vol. 14 May 1886

—, 'Venice I', *Freeman's Journal*, 29 December 1899

—, 'Venice II', *Freeman's Journal*, 30 December 1899

—, 'The Young French Girl Interviewed', *Nineteenth Century and After*, vol. 51, February 1902, reproduced in *Living Age*, 15 March 1902

Translations by and of Hannah Lynch

Echegaray, José, *The Great Galeoto: folly or saintliness. Two plays done from the verse of Jose Echegaray into English prose by Hannah Lynch* (London: John Lane, 1895)

Paris, Gaston, *Mediaeval French literature*, trans. from the French by Hannah Lynch (London: Dent, 1903)

Perrens, Francois Tommy, *The History of Florence under the Domination of Cosimo, Piero, Lorenzo de' Médicis, 1434–1492*, trans. from the French by Hannah Lynch (London: Methuen, 1892)

Lynch, Hannah, *Très Véridique Histoire d'une Petite Fille*, trans. de l'Anglais par M. Brandon (Paris: Hachette, 1902)

Lynch, Hannah, 'Très Véridique Histoire d'une Petite Fille', *La Revue de Paris*, vol. 1, 1 February 1902

Lynch, Hannah, 'Très Véridique Histoire d'une Petite Fille', *La Revue de Paris*, vol. 1, 15 February 1902

Lynch, Hannah, 'Très Véridique Histoire d'une Petite Fille', *La Revue de Paris*, vol. 2, 1 March 1902

Lynch, Hannah, 'Très Véridique Histoire d'une Petite Fille', *La Revue de Paris*, vol. 2, 15 March 1902

Lynch, Hannah, Κόραι της Ελλάδος [*Daughters of Greece*], trans. of *Daughters of Men*, Demetrius Bikélas (Athens: Hestia, 1892)

Other Primary Texts

'A Correspondent', 'The Fenian Conspiracy', *John Bull*, 10 July 1886

Anon. [untitled news items], *Myra's Journal*, 1 February 1899

—, 'A Bitter Childhood', *Outlook*, 27 May 1899

—, 'A Novel of the Period', *United Ireland*, 2 May 1885

—, 'Art and Letters', *Daily News*, 23 February 1899

—, 'Autobiography of a Child', *Bookman* (London), May 1899

—, 'Books and Authors', *Living Age*, 13 May 1899

—, 'Chronique Parisienne', *Bibliothèque Universelle et Revue Suisse*, vol. 27, 1902

—, 'The Institute of Journalists', *Morning Post*, 24 July 1899

—, 'The Ladies' Land League', *Reynolds's Newspaper* (London), 27 February 1881

— (From Our Correspondent, Dublin), 'The State of Ireland: seizure of a Land League paper', *Standard*, 16 December 1881

—, 'Monthly Reports of the Bookselling Trade', *Bookman* (London), April 1901

—, 'News Summary', *Leeds Mercury*, 17 May 1899

—, 'People, Places, Things', *Hearth and Home*, 21 May 1891

—, 'Sad Finish', *Punch*, vol. 100, 13 June 1896

—, 'An Odd Experiment', *Saturday Review*, 23 October 1897

—, 'Literary Gossip', *Athenaeum*, 24 September 1898

—, 'The Literary Week', *Academy*, vol. 57, 16 December 1899

—, 'Minor Notices: juveniles', *Literary World*, 11 November 1899

—, 'New and Improved Series: important announcement', *Irishman*, 24 June 1882

—, 'Our Contemporaries', *Irish Monthly*, vol. 13, no. 139, January 1885

—, 'A Plea for "Man in the Street" Topography', *Academy*, vol. 60, 8 June 1901

—, '*The Prince of the Glades* by Hannah Lynch (London: Methuen & Co., 1891)', *Dublin Review*, vol. 25, April 1891

—, 'Rejoicing at Carantrila Park', *Irish Times*, 18 December 1891

—, '*Rosni Harvey* by Hannah Lynch', *Spectator*, 28 January 1893

—, 'The Magazines', *Freeman's Journal*, 8 November 1884

—, 'The New Topography', *Academy*, no. 1462, 2 September 1899

—, 'Through Troubled Waters', *Freeman's Journal*, 3 July 1885

—, 'Toledo', *Freeman's Journal*, 10 May 1899

—, 'Toledo', *New York Times*, 4 November 1899

—, 'Why We Wouldn't Be Men' by 'A Wild Irish Girl', *Irish Fireside*, 2 June 1888

—, 'Women Who Write: the Literary Ladies' dinner', *Pall Mall Gazette*, 1 June 1889

—, 'Women's Doings', *Hearth and Home*, 27 May 1897

—, 'Women Writers at Dinner', *St James's Gazette*, 26 June 1900

Armstrong, Isabel J., *Two Roving Englishwomen in Greece* (London: Samson Low, Marston & Co., 1893)

Atherton, Gertrude, *The Adventures of a Novelist* (New York: Liveright, 1932)

'Barine, Arvède' [Louise-Cécile Vincens], 'La Gauche Féministe et le Mariage', *Revue des Deux Mondes*, vol. cxxxvi, 1 July 1896

Bennett, E.A., 'Insanity in Literature', *Academy*, vol. 61, 14 September 1901

Bleackley, H., *The Hangmen of England* (London: Chapman & Hall, 1929)

Brontë, Charlotte, *Jane Eyre: an autobiography*, eds Jane Jack and Margaret Smith (Oxford: Clarendon Press, 1969)

Conrad, Joseph, 'Author's Note' to 'The Nigger of the Narcissus', *New Review*, vol. 17, December 1897

Corkran, Alice, 'Journalistic London', *Atalanta*, vol. 6, December 1892

—, 'Journalistic London', *Atalanta*, vol. 6, February 1893

Corkran, Henriette, *Celebrities and I* (London: Hutchinson, 1902)

Darmesteter, Mary James [Mary Robinson], 'Autobiography of a Child', *Academy*, vol. 56, 13 May 1899

Davitt, Michael, 'Les Rapports de la France et de L'Angleterre: l'opinion d'un Anglais', *Le Figaro*, 13 January 1899

De Forest, Katharine, 'Recent Happenings in Paris', *Harper's Bazaar*, vol. 369, September 1902

Edwards, Louise Betts, 'The Literary Cult of the Child', *Critic*, vol. 39, August 1901

Egerton, George, *The Wheel of God* (London: Grant Richards, 1898)

'F.Y.E.', 'The Paris Correspondent Once More: *French Life in Town and Country* by Hannah Lynch', *Speaker*, vol. 4 (new series), 16 March 1901

'F.Y.E.', 'Correspondence: the French correspondent', *Speaker*, vol. 4 (new series), 6 April 1901

Fahy, Francis, 'The Southwark Junior Irish Literary Club, to the Editor of *The Nation*', *Nation*, 12 January 1889

Farrelly, Rev. P., 'French Life in Town and Country', *Catholic World*, vol. 75, September 1902

Gallaher, Fannie, *Thy Name Is Truth: a social novel* (London: J&R Maxwell Publishers, 1884)

Hone, Joseph, 'Supporter of the Parnell Movement', *Irish Press*, 16 September 1954

Lawless, Emily, *Hurrish: a study* (Edinburgh: William Blackwood & Sons, 1886)

Lee, Vernon, *Miss Brown* (London: William Blackwood & Sons, 1884)

—, 'Out of Venice at Last' (1925), reprinted in *Hauntings and Other Fantastic Tales* (Peterborough, ON: Broadview, 2006)

Mac Craith, P., 'Hannah Lynch: a Dublin novelist', *Irish Book Lover*, vol. 21, no. 6, November–December 1933

McL. Côté, Jane, *Fanny and Anna Parnell: Ireland's patriot sisters* (New York: St Martin's Press, 1991)

Macken, Mary, L., 'W.B. Yeats, John O'Leary and the Contemporary Club', *Studies: an Irish quarterly review*, vol. 28, no. 109, March 1939

MacM. M.J., 'Rose Kavanagh', *Irish Press*, 23 June 1944

Moore, George, *A Drama in Muslin* (Gerrards Cross: Colin Smythe, 1981)

—, *Confessions of a Young Man*, ed. Susan Dick (Montreal and London: McGill-Queen's University Press, 1972)

—, *Hail and Farewell*, ed. Richard Allen Cave (Gerrards Cross: Colin Smythe, 1985)

—, *Parnell and His Island* (London: Swan, Sonnenschein, Lowry & Co., 1887)

Mulholland, Rosa, *Marcella Grace: an Irish novel* (London: Kegan Paul, Trench, 1886)

O'Brien, William, *Recollections* (London: Macmillan, 1905)

O'C., P., 'Impressions of France, Cavan Authoress Recalled, Hannah Lynch of Virginia', *Meath Chronicle*, 24 September 1921

O'Connor, T.P. and McWade, R.M., *Gladstone–Parnell and the Great Irish Struggle* (Toronto and London: R.S. Robertson, 1886)

O'Donohue, D.J., 'John O'Leary and His Friends', *Sunday Independent* (Dublin), 13 June 1913

Owenson, Sydney [Lady Morgan], *The Missionary*, ed. Julia Wright (Peterborough, ON: Broadview, 2002)

Pfeiffer, Emily Jane, *Flying Leaves from East and West* (London: Field & Tuer, 1885)

Parnell, Anna, *Tale of a Great Sham*, ed. Dana Hearne (Dublin: Arlen House, 1986)

—, 'How They Do in the House of Commons: notes from the ladies' cage', *Celtic Monthly*, vol. 3, May 1880

Pope-Hennessy, John, 'What Do the Irish Read?' *Nineteenth Century*, vol. 15, June 1884

Robinson, F. Mabel, *The Plan of Campaign: a story of the fortune of war*, 3rd edn (London: Methuen & Co., 1890)

—, *Disenchantment: an everyday story* (Philadelphia: J.B. Lippincott Company, 1886)

— [pseud. William Stephenson Gregg], *Irish History for English Readers: from the earliest times to the close of the year* (London: Vizetelly & Co., 1886)

—, *Mr Butler's Ward* (London: Vizetelly & Co., 1885)

—, 'The Lady Land Leaguer', in *Voluntaries for an East London Hospital* (London: David Stott, 1887)

Sigerson Piatt, Hester, 'John O'Leary as a Guide of Youth', *Ireland*, vol. 17, 19 February 1916

Somerville, Edith and Martin Ross, *In the Vine Country* (London: Vintage, 2001)

Symons, Arthur, *Cities of Italy* (London: J.M. Dent, 1907)

Tynan, Katharine, 'A Correction', *Speaker*, vol. 13 (new series), 29 December 1906

—, *Twenty-five Years: reminiscences* (London: Smith Elder, 1913)

—, *Memories* (London: Everleigh, Nash & Grayson, 1924)

Tynan Hinkson, Katharine (ed.), *The Cabinet of Irish Literature: selections from the works of the chief poets, orators and prose writers of Ireland*, 4 vols (London: Gresham Publishing, 1902–03)

Tynan O'Mahony, Norah, 'Katharine Tynan's Childhood', *Irish Monthly*, vol. 59, June 1931

Lacon Watson, E.H., 'Through Pink Glasses', *Monthly Packet*, 1 July 1897

Whiteing, Richard, *My Harvest* (New York: Dodd & Mead, 1915)

Wilson, Louis N., 'Bibliography of Child Study for the Year 1899', *Pedagogical Seminary*, vol. 7, 1900

Obituaries

Anon., 'Hannah Lynch, Ecrivains – Littérateurs – Romanciers, Amis et Passionné du Père Lachaise', https://www.appl-lachaise.net/appl/article.php3?id_article=6036 (accessed 7 October 2018)

—, 'Over the Initials 'K.H.' in the *Pall Mall Gazette*, Mrs Hinkson Pays a Last Generous Tribute to Miss Hannah Lynch', *Tablet*, 30 January 1904

Gibbs, John P., 'Tribute to Hannah Lynch: an Irishwoman of great literary ability who did hard work in the Parnell movement', *Gaelic American*, 13 February 1904

Low, Frances, 'A Woman's Causerie', *Speaker*, 15 December 1906

'M.R.' [Father Matthew Russell, SJ], 'William Patrick Coyne, MA, LLD, 1866–1904: in memoriam', *Irish Monthly*, vol. 32, no. 369, March 1904, http://www.jstor.org.libraryproxy.mic.ul.ie/stable/20500574 (accessed 7 October 2018)

Secondary Texts

Ablow, Rachel, *The Marriage of Minds: reading sympathy in the Victorian marriage plot* (Stanford, CA: Stanford University Press, 2007)

Agathocleous, Tanya and Jason R. Rudy, 'Victorian Cosmopolitanisms: introduction', *Victorian Literature and Culture*, vol. 382, 2010

Allison, Maggie, 'Marguerite Durand and *La Fronde*: voicing women of the belle époque', in Diana Holmes and Carrie Tarr (eds), *A Belle Époque? Women in French society and culture, 1890–1914* (New York and Oxford: Berghahn Books, 2006)

Alryyes, Ala, *Original Subjects: the child, the novel and the nation* (Cambridge, MA: Harvard University Press, 2001)

Anderson, Amanda, *Powers of Distance: cosmopolitanism and the cultivation of detachment* (Princeton, NJ: Princeton University Press, 2001)

Anderson, Monica, *Women and the Politics of Travel, 1870–1914* (Madison, WI: Fairleigh Dickinson University Press, 2006)

Andrews, Ann, *Newspapers and Newsmakers: the Dublin nationalist press in the mid-nineteenth century* (Liverpool: Liverpool University Press, 2014)

Annat, Aurelia, 'Class, Nation, Gender and Self: Katharine Tynan and the construction of political identities, 1880–1930', in Fintan Lane (ed.), *Politics, Society and the Middle Class in Modern Ireland* (Houndmills: Palgrave Macmillan, 2010)

—, 'Imaginable Nations: constructions of history and identity and the contribution of selected Irish women writers, 1891–1945', DPhil thesis, University of Oxford, 2009

Ardis, Anne, *New Women, New Novels: feminism and early modernism* (New Brunswick, NJ: Rutgers University Press, 1990)

Arrington, Lauren, *Revolutionary Lives: Constance and Casimir Markievicz* (Princeton, NJ: Princeton University Press, 2016)

Ashley, Mike, *The Age of the Storytellers: British popular fiction magazines, 1880–1950* (London: British Library and Oak Knoll Press, 2006)

Atkinson, Damien (ed.), *The Selected Letters of Katharine Tynan: poet and novelist* (Newcastle upon Tyne: Cambridge Scholars, 2016)

Barrett, Richard, 'The Dreyfus Affair in the Irish Nationalist Press, 1898–1899', *Études Irlandaises*, vol. 321, 2007

Bartoszynska, Katerina, 'Adam Smith's Problems: sympathy in Owenson's *Wild Irish Girl* and Edgeworth's *Ennui*', *New Hibernia Review*, vol. 173, autumn 2013

Bassnett, Susan, 'Travel Writing and Gender', in Peter Hulme and Tim Youngs (eds), *The Cambridge Companion to Travel Writing* (Cambridge: Cambridge University Press, 2002)

Beetham, Margaret, *A Magazine of Her Own: domesticity and desire in the women's magazine, 1800–1914* (Abingdon: Routledge, 1996)

— and Heilmann, Ann (eds), *New Woman Hybridities: femininity, feminism and international consumer culture, 1880–1930* (London: Routledge, 2004)

Bilski, Emily and Braun, Emily (eds), *Jewish Women and Their Salons: the power of conversation* (New Haven, CT: Yale University Press, 2005)

Binckes, Faith, 'Hannah Lynch (1859–1904)', *Oxford Dictionary of National Biography* (Oxford: Oxford University Press, 2004)

Binckes, Faith and Laing, Kathryn, '"Rival Attractions of the Season": Land War fiction, Christmas annuals, and the early writing of Hannah Lynch', in Heidi Hansson and James H. Murphy (eds), *Fictions of the Irish Land War* (Bern: Peter Lang, 2014)

—, 'Irish Autobiographical Fiction and Hannah Lynch's Autobiography of a Child', *English Literature in Transition*, vol. 552, 2012

—, 'A Vagabond's Scrutiny: Hannah Lynch in Europe', in E. D'Hoker, R. Ingelbien and H. Schwall (eds), *Irish Women Writers: new critical perspectives* (Bern: Peter Lang, 2011)

—, 'A Forgotten Franco-Irish Literary Network: Hannah Lynch, Arvède Barine and Salon Culture in fin-de-siècle Paris', *Études Irlandaises*, vol. 362, 2011

—, 'From "Wild Irish Girl" to "Parisianised Foreigner": Hannah Lynch and France', in Eamon Maher and Eugene O'Brien (eds), *War of the Words: literary rebellion in France and Ireland* (Rennes: Publication du CRBC Rennes-2, TIR, 2010)

Bird, Dúnlaith, *Travelling in Different Skins: gender identity in European women's oriental travelogues, 1850–1950* (Oxford: Oxford University Press, 2012)

Blair, Kirstie, *Victorian Poetry and the Culture of the Heart* (Oxford: Oxford University Press, 2006)

Brake, Laurel, *Subjugated Knowledges: journalism, gender and literature in the nineteenth century* (London: Palgrave, 1994)

—, 'Writing Women's History: "the sex" debates of 1889', in Margaret Beetham and Ann Heilmann (eds), *New Woman Hybridities: femininity, feminism, and international consumer culture, 1880–1930* (London and New York: Routledge, 2004)

— and Marysa Demoor (eds), *Dictionary of Nineteenth-century Journalism in Great Britain and Ireland* (Ghent: Academia Press, 2009)

Brown, Penny, *The Captured World: the child and childhood in nineteenth-century women's writing in England* (London: Harvester, 1993)

Buzard, James, *The Beaten Track: European tourism, literature, and the ways to culture, 1800–1918* (Oxford: Oxford University Press, 1993)

Cahalan, James M., *Double Visions: women and men in modern and contemporary Irish fiction* (Syracuse, NY: Syracuse University Press, 1999)

Cahill, Susan, 'Making Spaces for the Irish Girl: Rosa Mulholland and Irish girls in fiction at the turn of the century', in K. Moruzi and M. Smith (eds), *Colonial Girlhood in Literature, Culture and History, 1840–1950* (London: Palgrave Macmillan, 2014)

—, 'Where Are the Irish Girls? Girlhood, Irishness, and L.T. Meade', in Claudia Mitchell and Carrie Rentschler (eds), *Girlhood and the Politics of Place* (New York: Berghahn Books, 2016)

Cappock, Margarita, 'Aloysius O'Kelly and the *Illustrated London News*', *Irish Arts Review Yearbook*, vol. 12, 1996

Carey, Richard, 'Vernon Lee's Vignettes of Literary Acquaintances', *Colby Quarterly*, vol. 93, September 1970

Castañeda, Salvador Garcia, 'Pereda y Hannah Lynch o La Pequeña Historia De Un Malentendido', *Siglo Diecinueve: literatura Hispánica*, vol. 1, 1995

Castle, Gregory, 'Irish Revivalism: critical trends and new directions', *Literature Compass*, vol. 85, 2011

Chaudhury, Yug Mohit, *W.B. Yeats, the Irish Literary Revival and the Politics of Print* (Cork: Cork University Press, 2002)

Cheng, Vincent, '"Terrible Queer Creatures": Joyce, cosmopolitanism and the inauthentic Irishman', in Michael Patrick Gillespie (ed.), *James Joyce and the Fabrication of an Irish Identity* (Amsterdam: Rodopi, 2001)

Clarke, Frances, 'Hannah Lynch (1862–1904)', in *The Dictionary of Irish Biography: volume 5* (Cambridge: Cambridge University Press, 2009)

Claxton, Eve, *The Book of Life* (London: Random House Group, 2005)

Clear, Catríona, 'The Ladies' Land League', in S.J. Connolly (ed.), *The Oxford Companion to Irish History* (Oxford: Oxford University Press, 2002)

Coe, Richard, *When the Grass Was Taller: autobiography and the experience of childhood* (New Haven, CT: Yale University Press, 1984)

Cohen, Margaret and Dever, Carolyn, *The Literary Channel: the inter-national invention of the novel* (Princeton, NJ: Princeton University Press, 2001)

Colby, Vineta, *Vernon Lee: a literary biography* (Charlottesville, VA: University of Virginia Press, 2003)

Coleman, Ann, 'Far from Silent: nineteenth-century Irish women writers', in Margaret Kelleher and James H. Murphy (eds), *Public and Private Spheres: gender perspectives in nineteenth-century Ireland* (Dublin: Irish Academic Press, 1997)

Connors, Thomas G., 'Letters of John Mitchel, 1848–1869', *Analecta Hibernica*, no. 37, 1998

Corless, Catherine, 'The Handcocks of Carantrila Park', *Journal of the Old Tuam Society*, no. 8, 2011

Crawford, Elizabeth, *The Women's Suffrage Movement in Britain and Ireland: a regional survey* (Abingdon: Routledge, 2006)

Crimmins, Sonia, 'Hannah Lynch, 1862–1904', MA in Women's Studies, University College Cork, 2006

Daly, Dominic, *The Young Douglas Hyde: the dawn of the Irish revolution and renaissance, 1874–1893* (Dublin: Irish University Press, 1994)

De Côté, Jane, *Fanny and Anna Parnell: Ireland's patriot sisters* (New York: St Martin's Press, 1991)

De Nie, Michael, *The Eternal Paddy: Irish identity and the British press, 1798–1882* (Madison, WI: University of Wisconsin Press, 2004)

Deane, Seamus, *Strange Country: modernity and nationhood in Irish writing since 1790* (Oxford: Clarendon Press, 1996)

Delap, Lucy, *The Feminist Avant-garde: transatlantic encounters of the early twentieth century* (Cambridge: Cambridge University Press, 2007)

Dellamorra, Richard, *Masculine Desire: the sexual politics of Victorian aestheticism* (Chapel Hill, NC: University of North Carolina Press, 1990)

Demoor, Marysa, 'Robinson (Frances) Mabel (1858–1956)', *Oxford Dictionary of National Biography* (Oxford: Oxford University Press, 2004), http://ezproxy-prd.bodleian. ox.ac.uk:2167/view/article/60276 (accessed 3 December 2015)

Dungan, Myles, *Mr Parnell's Rottweiler: censorship and the United Ireland newspaper, 1881–1891* (Dublin: Irish Academic Press, 2014)

Dwan, David, *The Great Community: culture and nationalism in Ireland* (Dublin: Field Day Publications, 2008)

Easley, Alexis, 'Anti/Feminism: Frances Low and the issue of women's work at the *fin de siècle*', in F. Elizabeth Gray (ed.), *Women in Journalism at the Fin de Siècle: making a name for herself* (London: Palgrave Macmillan, 2012)

Edwards, Heather, 'The Irish New Woman and Emily Lawless's *Grania: The Story of an Island*: a congenial geography', *English Literature in Transition, 1880–1920*, vol. 514, 2008

Ellmann, Maud, *The Hunger Artists: starving, writing, and imprisonment* (London: Virago, 1993)

Ermarth, Elizabeth, 'George Eliot's Conception of Sympathy', in Harold Bloom (ed.), *Silas Marner* (New York: Chelsea House, 2003)

Fauset, Eileen, *The Politics of Writing: Julia Kavanagh, 1824–77* (Manchester: Manchester University Press, 2009)

Ferguson, Frank, 'The Industrialization of Irish Book Production, 1790–1900', in James H. Murphy (ed.), *The Oxford History of the Irish Book in English, 1800–1891* (Oxford: Oxford University Press, 2011)

Finch, Alison, *Women's Writing in Nineteenth Century France* (Cambridge: Cambridge University Press, 2000)

Finkelstein, David, *The House of Blackwood: author-publisher relations in the Victorian era* (University Park, PA: Penn State Press, 2002)

—, *Print Culture and the Blackwood Tradition, 1805–1930* (Toronto: University of Toronto Press, 2006)

Foster, John Wilson (ed.), *The Cambridge Companion to the Irish Novel* (Cambridge: Cambridge University Press, 2006)

—, *Irish Novels, 1890–1940: new bearings in culture and fiction* (Oxford: Oxford University Press, 2008)

—, *Fictions of the Irish Literary Revival: a changeling art* (Syracuse, NY: Syracuse University Press, 1987)

Foster, Roy, *W.B. Yeats: a life. Volume One: the apprentice mage, 1865–1914* (Oxford: Oxford University Press, 1997)

—, *Words Alone: Yeats and his inheritances* (Oxford: Oxford University Press, 2011)

—, *Vivid Faces: the revolutionary generation in Ireland, 1890–1923* (London: Penguin, 2014)

Frawley, Maria H., *A Wider Range: travel writing by women in Victorian England* (Madison, WI: Farleigh Dickinson University Press, 1994)

Frazier, Adrian, *George Moore, 1852–1933* (New York and London: Yale University Press, 2000)

Gagnier, Regina, *Individualism, Decadence and Globalization: on the relationship of part to whole, 1859–1920* (Basingstoke: Palgrave Macmillan, 2010)

George Jr, Henry, *The Life of Henry George* (New York: Doubleday & McClure Company, 1900)

Gibbon, Monk, *The Masterpiece and the Man* (London: Hart-Davis, 1959)

Gifra-Adroher, Pere and Hurtley, Jacqueline (eds), *Hannah Lynch and Spain: collected journalism of an Irish New Woman, 1892–1903* (Venice: Edizioni Ca' Foscari, 2018)

Gomez, Teresa and Gifford, Terry, *Women in Transit Through Literary Liminal Spaces* (London: Macmillan, 2013)

Greaney, James, *Dunmore* (n.p., The Author, 1984)

Groves, P., *Petticoat Rebellion: the Anna Parnell story* (Cork: Mercier Press, 2009)

Grubgeld, Elizabeth, *Anglo-Irish Autobiography: class, gender, and the forms of narrative* (Syracuse, NY: Syracuse University Press, 2004)

—, 'Class, Gender and the Forms of Narrative: the autobiographies of Anglo-Irish women', in Susan Shaw Sailer (ed.), *Representing Ireland: gender, class, nationality* (Gainesville, FL: Florida University Press, 1997)

—, *George Moore and the Autogenous Self: the autobiography and fiction* (Syracuse, NY: Syracuse University Press, 1994)

Hall, J.B., *Random Records of a Reporter* (London and Dublin: Simpkin Marshall & the Fodhla Printing Co., 1928)

Hansson, Heidi, *Emily Lawless, 1845–1913: writing the interspace* (Cork: Cork University Press, 2007)

— (ed.), *New Contexts: re-framing nineteenth-century Irish women's prose* (Cork: Cork University Press, 2008)

— and Murphy, James H. (eds), *Fictions of the Irish Land War* (Bern: Peter Lang, 2014)

—, 'History in/of the Borderlands: Emily Lawless and the story of Ireland', in Irene Gilsenan Nordin and Elin Holmsten (eds), *Liminal Borderlands in Irish Literature and Culture* (Bern and Oxford: Peter Lang, 2009)

Hargreaves, Alec, *The Colonial Experience in French Fiction: a study of Pierre Loti, Ernest Psichiari and Pierre Mille* (London: Macmillan, 1981)

Harrington, Emily, *Second Person Singular: late Victorian women poets and the bonds of verse* (Charlottesville, VA: Virginia University Press, 2014)

Harvey, Alison, 'Irish Aestheticism in Fin-de-Siècle Women's Writing: art, realism, and the nation', *Modernism/Modernity*, vol. 21, no. 3, 2014

Heilmann, Anne and Stephanie Forward (eds), *Sex, Social Purity, and Sarah Grand: volume 1* (London: Routledge, 2000)

Heilmann, Anne, *New Woman Strategies: Sarah Grand, Olive Schreiner, Mona Caird* (Manchester: Manchester University Press, 2004)

— (ed.), *Feminist Forerunners: New Womanism and feminism in the early twentieth century* (London: Pandora, 2003)

—, *New Woman Fiction: women writing first-wave feminism* (Basingstoke: Palgrave Macmillan, 2000)

Hervouet, Yves, *The French Face of Joseph Conrad* (Cambridge: Cambridge University Press, 1990)

Hooper, Glen, *The Tourist's Gaze: travellers to Ireland, 1800–2000* (Cork: Cork University Press, 2001)

Howe, Marjorie, *Colonial Crossings: figures in Irish literary history* (Dublin: Field Day, 2006)

—, *Yeats's Nations: gender, class, Irishness* (Cambridge: Cambridge University Press, 1998)

Hughes, Kathryn, *The Victorian Governess* (London: Hambledon Press, 1993)

Hughes, Linda, 'A Club of Their Own: the "Literary Ladies", New Women writers, and *fin-de-siècle* authorship', *Victorian Literature and Culture*, vol. 351, 2007

Hutton, Clare, 'Joyce, the Library Episode, and the Institutions of Revivalism', in Andrew Gibson, Len Platt and S.D.G. Knowles (eds), *Joyce, Ireland, Britain* (Gainesville, FL: University Press of Florida, 2006)

—, '"The Promise of Literature in the Coming Days": the best hundred Irish books controversy of 1886', *Victorian Literature and Culture*, vol. 392, 2011

—, 'Joyce and the Institutions of Revivalism', *Irish University Review*, vol. 331, Special Issue: 'New Perspectives on the Irish Literary Revival', spring–summer 2003

Ingman, Heather, *Irish Women's Fiction: from Edgeworth to Enright* (Dublin: Irish Academic Press, 2013)

Innes, C.L., *Woman and Nation in Irish Society, 1880–1935* (Athens, GA: University of Georgia Press, 1993)

Jamison (Oakman), Anne, '"Sitting on the Outer Skin": Somerville and Ross's *Through Connemara in a Governess Cart* as a coded stratum of linguistic/feminist "Union" ideals', *Éire-Ireland*, vol. 39, 2004

—, *E. Œ. Somerville and Martin Ross: female authorship and literary collaboration* (Cork: Cork University Press, 2016)

Janis, Ely M., *The Land League and Transatlantic Nationalism in Gilded Age America* (Madison, WI: University of Wisconsin Press, 2015)

Jordan, Shirley, 'New Women's Writing and the Feminist Heritage in France', in Adalgisa Giorgio and Julia Walters (eds), *Women's Writing in Western Europe: gender, generation and legacy* (Newcastle upon Tyne: Cambridge Scholars, 2007)

Joyce, James, *Dubliners*, ed. Jeri Johnson (Oxford: Oxford University Press, 2000)

Joyce, Simon, 'Impressionism, Naturalism, Symbolism: trajectories of Anglo-Irish fiction at the fin de siècle', *Modernism/Modernity*, vol. 211, September 2014

Keen, Suzanne, *Empathy and the Novel* (Oxford: Oxford University Press, 2007)

Kelleher, Margaret and O'Leary, Philip (eds), *The Cambridge History of Irish Literature, Volume 2* (Cambridge: Cambridge University Press, 2006)

Kelleher, Margaret, 'The Cabinet of Irish Literature: a historical perspective on Irish anthologies', *Éire-Ireland*, vols 383–4, fall/winter 2003

— (guest ed.), Special Issue: 'New Perspectives on the Irish Literary Revival', *Irish University Review*, vol. 331, spring/summer 2003

—, '"Factual Fictions": representations of the land agitation in nineteenth-century women's fiction', in Heidi Hansson (ed.), *New Contexts: re-framing nineteenth-century Irish women's prose* (Cork: Cork University Press, 2008)

—, 'Prose Writing and Drama in English, 1830–1890: from Catholic emancipation to the fall of Parnell', in Margaret Kelleher and Philip O'Leary (eds), *The Cambridge History of Irish Literature, Volume 1* (Cambridge: Cambridge University Press, 2006)

—, 'Writing Irish Women's Literary History', *Irish Studies Review*, vol. 91, 2001

Kelleher Kahn, Helena, *Late Nineteenth-century Ireland's Political and Religious Controversies in the Fiction of May Laffan Hartley* (Greensboro, NC: ELT Press, 2006)

Kenneally, Michael. 'The Autobiographical Imagination and Irish Literary Autobiography', in Michael Allen and Angela Wilcox (eds), *Critical Approaches to Anglo-Irish Literature* (Gerrards Cross: Colin Smythe, 1989)

Kennerk, Barry, 'A Dublin Consul under Siege: American reactions to the habeas corpus suspension crisis of 1866–1868', *Dublin Historical Record*, vol. 631, spring 2010

Kent, Sylvia, *The Woman Writer: the history of the Society of Women Writers and Journalists* (Stroud: The History Press, 2009)

Kooistra, Lorraine Janzen, *Poetry, Pictures and Popular Publishing: the illustrated book and Victorian visual culture, 1855–1875* (Athens, OH: Ohio University Press, 2011)

Kreilkamp, Vera, *The Anglo-Irish Novel and the Big House* (Syracuse, NY: Syracuse University Press, 1998)

Krueger Henderson, Kate, 'Mobility and Modern Consciousness in George Egerton and Charlotte Mew's *Yellow Book* Stories', *English Literature in Transition*, vol. 542, 2011

Kuch, Peter, *Yeats and AE: the antagonism that unites dear friends* (Gerrards Cross: Colin Smythe, 1986)

Laing, K.S., 'Intellectual Lives and Literary Perspectives: female Irish writing at home and abroad', in Brendan Walsh (ed.), *Knowing Their Place: the intellectual life of women in the 19th century* (Dublin: The History Press, 2015)

—, 'Hannah Lynch and Narratives of the Irish Literary Revival', *New Hibernia Review*, vol. 201, 2016

—, 'George Moore and F. Mabel Robinson: Paris and the woman artist', in Michel Brunet, Fabienne Gaspari and Mary Pierse (eds), *George Moore and His French Ongoing Connections* (Bern: Peter Lang, 2015)

—, 'On Women, on Art, on Life: George Moore (1852–1933) and Hannah Lynch (1859–1904)', in Maria Elena Jaime de Pablos and Mary Pierse (eds), *George Moore and the Quirks of Human Nature* (Bern: Peter Lang, 2014)

—, 'F. Mabel Robinson: the aesthetics of sympathy and texts of transition', in Louise Kane and Deborah Mutch (eds), *Victorian into Modern: suturing the divide, 1875–1935* (London: Routledge, 2019)

Laird, Heather, 'Decentring the Irish Land War: women, politics and the private sphere', in Fergus Campbell and Tony Varley (eds), *Land Questions in Modern Ireland* (Manchester: Manchester University Press, 2013)

Lanser, Susan, *The Narrative Act: point of view in prose fiction* (Princeton, NJ: Princeton University Press, 1981)

Larkin, Felix, '"A Great Daily Organ": the *Freeman's Journal, 1763–1924*', *History Ireland*, vol. 143, 2006

—, '"The Old Woman of Prince's Street": *Ulysses* and *The Freeman's Journal*', *James Joyce Journal*, no. 4, 2011

—, 'Keeping an Eye on Youghal: *The Freeman's Journal* and the Plan of Campaign in east Cork, 1886–92', *Irish Communications Review*, vol. 131, 2012

—, '"Green Shoots" of the New Journalism in the *Freeman's Journal, 1877–1890*', in Karen Steele and Michael de Nie (eds), *Ireland and the New Journalism* (New York: Palgrave Macmillan, 2014)

Larson, Jill, *Ethics and Narrative in the English Novel, 1880–1914* (Cambridge: Cambridge University Press, 2001)

Ledger, Sally, *The New Woman: fiction and feminism at the* fin de siècle (Manchester: Manchester University Press, 1997)

Legg, Marie-Louise, *Newspapers and Nationalism: the Irish provincial press, 1850–1892* (Dublin: Four Courts Press, 1999)

Lennon, Joseph Allen, *Irish Orientalism: a literary and intellectual history* (Syracuse, NY: Syracuse University Press, 2004)

Loeber, Rolf and Loeber, Magda, *A Guide to Irish Fiction, 1650–1900* (Dublin: Four Courts Press, 2006)

—, 'Literary Absentees: Irish women authors in nineteenth-century England', in Jaqueline Belanger (ed.), *The Irish Novel in the Nineteenth Century: facts and fictions* (Dublin: Four Courts Press, 2005)

Lloyd, Rosemary, *The Land of Lost Content: children and childhood in nineteenth-century French literature* (Oxford: Oxford University Press, 1992)

Lowe, Brigid, *Victorian Fiction and the Insights of Sympathy: an alternative to the hermeneutics of suspicion* (London: Anthem Press, 2007)

Macleod, Jock, *Literature, Journalism and the Vocabularies of Liberalism: politics and letters, 1886–1916* (London: Palgrave Macmillan, 2013)

Madden-Simpson, Jane, *Women's Part: an anthology of short fiction by and about Irish women, 1890–1920* (Dublin: Arlen House, 1984)

Mangum, Teresa, *Married, Middlebrow and Militant: Sarah Grand and the New Woman novel* (Ann Arbor, MI: University of Michigan Press, 1998)

—, 'Style Wars of the 1890s: the New Woman and the Decadent', in Nikki Lee Manos and Maeri-Jane Rochelson (eds), *Transforming Genres: new approaches to British fiction of the 1890s* (New York: St Martin's Press, 1994)

Mansell, Philip, *Constantinople: city of the world's desire, 1453–1924* (London: John Murray, 1995)

Marshall, David, *The Surprising Effects of Sympathy: Marivaux, Diderot, Rousseau, and Mary Shelley* (Chicago: University of Chicago Press, 1988)

Matz, B.W., 'George Meredith as a Publisher's Reader', *Fortnightly Review*, vol. 86, August 1909

McAuliffe, John, 'Women's Travel Writing in Mid-nineteenth Century Ireland', in Margaret Kelleher and James H. Murphy (eds), *Gender Perspectives in Nineteenth Century Ireland: public and private spheres* (Dublin: Irish Academic Press, 1997)

McBride, Lawrence, W. (ed.), *Images, Icons and the Irish Nationalist Imagination, 1870–1925* (Dublin: Four Courts Press, 1999)

McCracken, Donal, *Forgotten Protest: Ireland and the Anglo-Boer War* (Belfast: Ulster Historical Foundation, 2003)

McEwan, Cheryl, *Gender, Geography and Empire: Victorian women travellers in East Africa* (Aldershot: Ashgate, 2000)

McFadden, James J. and Kiefer, Daniel, '"Abstracted in His Dreams": Katharine Tynan's "W.B. Yeats"', *Modern Philology*, vol. 883, February 1991

McL. Côté, Jane, *Fanny and Anna Parnell: Ireland's patriot sisters* (New York: St Martin's Press, 1991)

Meaney, Gerardine, 'Decadence, Degeneration and Revolting Aesthetics: the fiction of Emily Lawless and Katherine Cecil Thurston', *Colby Quarterly: Irish women novelists, 1800–1940*, vol. xxxiv, no. 2, 2000

Michie, Elsie, *Outside the Pale: cultural exclusion, gender difference, and the Victorian woman writer* (Ithaca, NY: Cornell University Press, 1993)

Milan, Michèle, 'Found in Translation: Franco-Irish relationships in nineteenth-century Ireland', PhD thesis, Dublin City University, 2013

—, 'Found in Translation: Franco-Irish translation relationships in nineteenth-century Ireland', *New Voices in Translation Studies*, vol. 8, 2012

Miller, Jane Eldridge, *Rebel Women: feminism, modernism and the Edwardian novel* (London: Virago, 1994)

Mills, Sara, *Discourses of Difference: an analysis of women's travel writing and colonialism* (London and New York: Routledge, 1991)

Mitsou, Marie-Élisabeth, 'Négoce et Transfert Culturel: Dimitrios Bikélas et le réseau intellectuel franco-grec dans la seconde moitié du xixe siècle', *Rives Méditerranéennes*, vol. 50, 2015, http://rives.revues.org/4772 (accessed 12 August 2016), DOI: 104000/rives.4772

Morris, Bruce, '"Neptune and the Surging Waves": Paul Bourget and W.B. Yeats', in Richard Finneran (ed.), *Yeats: an annual of critical and textual studies*, vol. xiii, 1995

Morris, Catherine, 'Becoming Irish? Alice Milligan and the Revival', *Irish University Review*, vol. 331, Special Issue: 'New Perspectives on the Irish Literary Revival', spring/summer 2003

—, *Alice Milligan and the Irish Cultural Revival* (Dublin: Four Courts Press, 2012)

Moruzi, Kristine, *Constructing Girlhood through the Periodical Press, 1850–1915* (Aldershot: Ashgate, 2012)

__, and Michelle J. Smith (eds), *Colonial Girlhood in Literature, Culture and History, 1840–1950* (London: Palgrave Macmillan, 2014)

Moutafidou, Ariadni, 'Greek Merchant Families Perceiving the World: the case of Demetrius Vikelas', *Mediterranean Historical Review*, vol. 232, 2008

Mulligan, Adrian N., '"By a Thousand Ingenious Feminine Devices": the Ladies' Land League and the development of Irish nationalism', *Historical Geography*, vol. 37, 2009

Murphy, James H., *Irish Novelists and the Victorian Age* (Oxford: Oxford University Press, 2011)

—, 'Novelists, Publishers and Readers, 1830–90', in James Murphy (ed.), *The Oxford History of the Irish Book in English, 1800–1891* (Oxford: Oxford University Press, 2011)

—, 'Publishing for Catholic Ireland', *The Oxford History of the Irish Book. Vol. 5: the Irish book in English* (Oxford: Oxford University Press, 2011)

—, 'Between the Drawing Room and the Barricades: autobiographies and nationalist fictions of Justin McCarthy', in Bruce Stewart (ed.), *Hearts and Minds: Irish culture and society under the Act of Union* (Monaco: Princess Grace Library, 2002)

—, '"Things Which Seem to You Unfeminine": gender and nationalism in the fiction of some upper middle class Catholic women novelists, 1880–1910', in Kathryn Kirkpatrick (ed.), *Border Crossings: Irish women writers and national identities* (Tuscaloosa, AL: University of Alabama Press, 2000)

—, 'Canonicity: the literature of nineteenth-century Ireland', *New Hibernia Review*, vol. 72, 2003

Nally, Claire and Strachan, John R., *Advertising, Literature and Print Culture in Ireland, 1891–1922* (Basingstoke: Palgrave Macmillan, 2012)

Napier, Taura, S., *Literary Autobiographies of Twentieth-century Irish Women* (Lanham, MD: University Press of America, 2001)

Nelson, Claudia, *Family Ties in Victorian England* (Westport, CT: Praeger Publishers, 2007)

Nic Congáil, Riona, '"Fiction, Amusement, Instruction": the Irish Fireside Club and the educational ideology of the Gaelic League', *Éire-Ireland*, vol. 44, nos 1–2, spring/summer 2009

—, 'Young Ireland and the Nation: nationalist children's culture in the late nineteenth century', *Éire-Ireland*, vols 463–4, winter 2011

Nolan, Emer, *Catholic Emancipations: Irish fiction from Thomas Moore to James Joyce* (Syracuse, NY: Syracuse University Press, 2007)

O'Brien, Mark, *The Fourth Estate: journalism in twentieth-century Ireland* (Manchester: Manchester University Press, 2017)

O'Callaghan, Margaret, 'Richard Pigott', *The Dictionary of Irish Biography*, 9 vols (Cambridge: Cambridge University Press, 2009), http://dib.cambridge.org.libraryproxy.mic.ul.ie/quicksearch.do;jsessionid=1EF2E8B451E00C931B84315228EEF29B (accessed 7 October 2018)

Ó Cinnéide, Muireann, 'Anne Blunt, "Arabi Pasha" and the Irish Land Wars, 1880–8', in Tina O'Toole, Gillian McIntosh and Muireann Ó Cinnéide (eds), *Women Writing War: Ireland, 1880–1922* (Dublin: UCD Press, 2016)

O'Connor, Barbara and Cronin, Michael (eds), *Tourism in Ireland: a critical analysis* (Cork: Cork University Press, 1993)

O'Keeffe, Declan, 'A Man for Others and a Beacon in the Twilight: Matthew Russell SJ and the *Irish Monthly*', *Studies: an Irish quarterly review*, vol. 99, no. 394, summer 2010

—, '"The Young Writer's Saint": women writers and the *Irish Monthly*, 1873–97', in Rebecca Anne Barr, Sarah-Anne Buckley and Laura Kelly (eds), *Engendering Ireland: new reflections on modern history and literature* (Newcastle upon Tyne: Cambridge Scholars, 2015)

—, 'The Canon of Literature and the Obstinate Quill: Matthew Russell, SJ and the *Irish Monthly*', in Gabriel Doherty (ed.), *Revisiting Canon Sheehan of Doneraile, 1852–1913* (Wells: Smenos Publications, 2014)

O'Neill, Ciaran, *Catholics of Consequence: transnational education, social mobility and the Irish Catholic elite, 1850–1900* (Oxford: Oxford University Press, 2014)

O'Neill, M., 'The Ladies' Land League', *Dublin Historical Record*, vol. 354, September 1982

O'Sullivan, Niamh, *Aloysius O'Kelly: art, nation, empire* (Dublin: Field Day Publications; Notre Dame: Notre Dame University Press, 2010)

—, 'The Iron Cage of Femininity: visual representation of women in the 1880s land agitation', in Tadhg Foley and Seán Ryder (eds), *Ideology and Ireland in the Nineteenth Century* (Dublin: Four Courts Press, 1998)

—, *Every Dark Hour: a history of Kilmainham Jail* (Dublin: Liberties Press, 2007)

O'Toole, Tina, 'Ireland: the *terra incognita* of the New Woman project', in Heidi Hansson (ed.), *New Contexts: re-framing nineteenth-century Irish women's prose* (Cork: Cork University Press, 2008)

—, *The Irish New Woman* (New York: Palgrave Macmillan, 2013)

—, 'The (Irish) New Woman: political, literary and sexual experiments', in Holly Laird (ed.), *The History of British Women's Writing, 1880–1920* (Basingstoke: Palgrave Macmillan, 2016)

—, 'The New Woman and the Boy in *Fin de Siècle* Irish Fiction', in Ruth Connolly and Ann Coughlan (eds), *New Voices in Irish Criticism 5* (Dublin: Four Courts Press, 2004)

Pašeta, Senia, *Irish Nationalist Women, 1900–1918* (Cambridge: Cambridge University Press, 2013)

Peterson, Linda H., *Becoming a Woman of Letters: myths of authorship and facts of the Victorian market* (Princeton, NJ: Princeton University Press, 2009)

Pierce, David, *Yeats's Worlds: Ireland, England and the poetic imagination* (New Haven, CT: Yale University Press, 1995)

Pilz, Anna and Standlee, Whitney (eds), *Irish Women's Writing, 1878–1922* (Manchester: Manchester University Press, 2016)

Rains, Stephanie, *Commodity Culture and Social Class in Dublin, 1850–1916* (Dublin: Irish Academic Press, 2010)

—, '"Nauseous Tides of Seductive Debauchery": Irish story papers and the anti-vice campaigns of the early twentieth century', *Irish University Review*, vol. 45, 2015

—, 'Thrilling Tales and Shocking Stories: story papers in Ireland', *Irish Media History* blog, 22 October 2015, https://irishmediahistory.com/category/story-papers (accessed 4 October 2018)

Randall, Bryony, 'Everything Depend[s] on the Fashion of Narration': women writing women writers in short stories of the fin-de-siècle', in R. Kim and C. Westall (eds), *Cross-gendered Literary Voices* (New York: Palgrave Macmillan, 2012)

Ratchford, Fannie, 'Elizabeth Paschal O'Connor', *Texas Historical Association*, https://tshaonline.org/handbook/online/articles/foc12 (accessed 7 October 2018)

Ratcliffe, Sophie, *On Sympathy* (Oxford: Oxford University Press, 2008)

Rodgers, Beth, 'Competing Girlhoods: competition, community, and reader contribution in the *Girl's Own Paper* and *The Girl's Realm*', *Victorian Periodicals Review*, vol. 453, 2012

—, 'Irishness, Professional Authorship, and the "Wild Irish Girls" of L.T. Meade', *English Literature in Transition, 1880–1920*, vol. 562, 2013

—, '"I am glad I am Irish through and through and through": Irish girlhood and identity in L.T. Meade's *Light o' the Morning; or, The Story of an Irish Girl*', in K. Moruzi and M. Smith (eds), *Colonial Girlhood in Literature, Culture and History, 1840–1950* (London: Palgrave Macmillan, 2014)

Roos, Bonnie, 'Unlikely Heroes: Katharine Tynan's *Story of the Bawn*, the Irish Famine, and the sentimental tradition', *Irish University Review*, vol. 432, 2013

Sanders, Valerie (ed.), *Records of Girlhood: an anthology of nineteenth-century women's childhoods* (Aldershot: Ashgate, 2000)

Schaffer, Talia, *The Forgotten Female Aesthetes: literary culture in late Victorian England* (Charlottesville, VA: University of Virginia Press, 2000)

Schneller, Beverley E., *Anna Parnell's Political Journalism* (Bethesda, MD: Academica Press, 2005)

Shaw, Marion and Randolph, Lyssa, *New Women Writers of the Late Nineteenth Century* (London: Northcote House, 2007)

Sheehy, Ian, 'Irish Journalists and Litterateurs in Late Victorian London, 1870–1910', DPhil thesis, University of Oxford, 2003

Shovlin, Frank, *Journey Westward: Joyce, 'Dubliners' and the Literary Revival* (Liverpool: Liverpool University Press, 2012)

Showalter, Elaine, *A Literature of Their Own: British women novelists from Brontë to Lessing* (Princeton, NJ: Princeton University Press, 1977)

Shuttleworth, Sally, 'Inventing a Discipline: autobiography and the science of child study in the 1890s', *Comparative Critical Studies*, vol. 52, 2005

Sifaki, Evgenia, 'A Gendered Vision of Greekness: Lady Morgan's "Woman: Or Ida of Athens"', in Vassiliki Kolocotroni and Efterpi Mitsi (eds), *Women Writing Greece: essays on Hellenism, orientalism, and travel* (Amsterdam: Rodopi, 2008)

Silvera, Alain, *Daniel Halévy and His Times: a gentleman-commoner in the Third Republic* (Ithaca, NY: Cornell University Press, 1966)

Smith, Brian, 'Josephine Cantwell: Kingstown's First Lady', *Dun Laoghaire Journal*, vol. 11, 2002

Smith, Janet, 'Helen Taylor's Anti-imperial Feminism: Ireland and the Land League question', *Women's History Network Journal*, vol 24, spring 2016

Standlee, Whitney, *Power to Observe: Irish women novelists in Britain, 1890–1916* (Bern: Peter Lang, 2015)

—, '"A World of Difference": London and Ireland in the works of Katharine Tynan', in Tom Herron (ed.), *Irish Writing London. Vol. 1: Revival to the Second World War* (London: Bloomsbury, 2012)

—, 'Katharine Tynan's Novels and the Politics of Ireland's "Long Gestation", 1890–1916', in Kateřina Jenčová, Michaela Marková, Radvan Markus and Hana Pavelková (eds), *The Politics of Irish Writing* (Prague: Centre for Irish Studies, Charles University, 2010)

Stetz, Margaret, *Facing the Late Victorians: portraits of writers and artists from the Mark Samuels Lassner Collection* (Plainsboro, NJ: Associated University Presses, 2007)

Stevens, Julie Ann, *The Irish Scene in Somerville and Ross* (Dublin: Irish Academic Press, 2007)

Summerfield, Henry, *That Myriad-minded Man: a biography of George William Russell 'Æ', 1867–1935* (Gerrards Cross: Colin Smythe, 1975)

Sumpter, Caroline, 'Innocents and Epicures: the child, the fairy tale and avant-garde debate in *fin de siècle* little magazines', *Nineteenth-century Contexts*, vol. 283, September 2006

Sutherland, Gillian, *In Search of the New Woman: middle-class women and work in Britain, 1870–1914* (Cambridge: Cambridge University Press, 2015)

Taylor Fitzsimon, Betsey and Murphy, James H. (eds), *The Irish Revival Reappraised* (Dublin: Four Courts Press, 2004)

Teachman, Debra, *Understanding Jane Eyre: a student casebook to issues, sources and historical documents* (Westport, CT: Greenwood Press, 2001)

Travers, Pauric, '"No Turning Back": Anna Parnell, identity, memory and gender', in Donal McCarthy and Pauric Travers (eds), *The Ivy Leaf: the Parnells remembered* (Dublin: UCD Press, 2006)

Urquhart, Diane, '"The Ladies' Land League Have [*sic*] a Crust to Share with You": the rhetoric of the Ladies' Land League's British campaign, 1881–1882', in Tina O'Toole, Gillian McIntosh and Muireann Ó Cinnéide (eds), *Women Writing War: Ireland, 1880–1922* (Dublin: UCD Press, 2016)

Vadillo, Ana Parejo, 'New Women Poets and the Culture of the *Salon* at the *Fin de Siècle*', *Women: a cultural review*, vol. 101, 1999

—, *Women Poets and Urban Aestheticism: passengers of modernity* (London: Palgrave, 2005)

—, 'Cosmopolitan Aestheticism: the affective 'Italian' ethics of A. Mary F. Robinson', *Comparative Critical Studies*, vol. 102, 2013

Valente, Joseph, *The Myth of Manliness in Irish National Culture, 1880–1922* (Urbana, IL: University of Illinois Press, 2011)

Vance, Norman, *Irish Literature Since 1800* (London: Longman, 2002)

Van der Kamp, Peter, 'Whose Revival? Yeats and the Southwark Irish Literary Club', in Peter Leibregts and Peter van der Kamp (eds), *Tumult of Images: essays on W.B. Yeats and politics* (Amsterdam: Rodopi, 1995)

Wadsö Lecaros, Cecilia, 'The Victorian Heroine Goes A-governessing', in Brenda Ayres (ed.), *Silent Voices: forgotten novels by Victorian women writers* (Westport, CT: Praeger Publishers, 2003)

Ward, Margaret, 'Anna Parnell: challenges to male authority and the telling of national myth', in Pauric Travers and Donal McCarthy (eds), *Parnell Reconsidered* (Dublin: UCD Press, 2013)

—, 'A Terrible Beauty? Women, modernity and Irish nationalism before the Easter Rising', in Brendan Walsh (ed.), *Knowing Their Place: the intellectual life of women in the 19th century* (Dublin: The History Press, 2015)

—, *Unmanageable Revolutionaries: women and nationalism* (London: Pluto Press, 1995)

—, 'Gendering the Union: imperial feminism and the Ladies' Land League', *Women's History Review*, vol. 101, 2001

—, 'The Ladies' Land League and the Irish Land War, 1881/2: defining the relationship between women and nation', in Ida Blom, Karen Hagemann and Catherine Hall (eds), *Gendered Nations: Europe and beyond* (Oxford and New York: Berg Publishers, 2000)

Weiman, Lisa, 'National Treasures and Nationalist Gardens: unlocking the archival mysteries of Bean na h-Éireann', *Tulsa Studies for Women's Literature*, vol. 272, fall 2008

Wenzer, Kenneth C. (ed.), *Henry George, the Transatlantic Irish, and Their Times* (Bingley: Emerald Group Publishing, 2009)

Whelan, Bernadette, *American Government in Ireland, 1790–1913: a history of the US Consular Service* (Oxford: Oxford University Press, 2010)

White, Andrea, *Joseph Conrad and the Adventure Tradition: constructing and deconstructing the imperial subject* (Cambridge: Cambridge University Press, 1993)

White, Jerry, *London in the Nineteenth Century: 'a Human awful wonder of God'* (London: Random House, 2011)

Index